First World War
and Army of Occupation
War Diary
France, Belgium and Germany

3 DIVISION
Divisional Troops
529 (East Riding) Field Company Royal Engineers,
231 Field Company Royal Engineers
and Divisional Signal Company
13 September 1914 - 31 October 1919

WO95/1404

The Naval & Military Press Ltd
www.nmarchive.com
Published in association with The National Archives

Published by

The Naval & Military Press Ltd

Unit 10 Ridgewood Industrial Park,

Uckfield, East Sussex,

TN22 5QE England

Tel: +44 (0) 1825 749494

www.naval-military-press.com

www.nmarchive.com

This diary has been reprinted in facsimile from the original. Any imperfections are inevitably reproduced and the quality may fall short of modern type and cartographic standards.

© **Crown Copyright**
Images reproduced by permission of The National Archives, London, England, 2015.

Contents

Document type	Place/Title	Date From	Date To
Heading	France 3rd Division Troops Divisional Signal Company 1914 Aug-1919 May Missing 1915-Feb. Mar. Apr. 1916 Jan. Feb. Mar.		
War Diary	Capt. A.C. Johnston, Promoted to Command 3rd signals Coy., 3rd Division. 7th February 1915	07/03/1915	17/04/1915
Heading	11/4104 3rd Division 3rd Signal Coy. R.E. Vol I 5.8-31.12.15		
War Diary	Bulford	05/08/1915	10/08/1915
War Diary	Amesbury	16/08/1915	16/08/1915
War Diary	Rouen	17/08/1915	19/08/1915
War Diary	Aulnoy	20/08/1915	22/08/1915
War Diary	Noirchain	23/08/1915	25/08/1915
War Diary	Bertry	26/08/1915	12/09/1915
War Diary	Braine	13/09/1914	31/12/1914
Miscellaneous	3rd Signal Coy. R.E.		
Heading	11/4256 3rd Division 3rd Signal Coy. R.E. Vol II 1-31.1.15		
War Diary	Mont Noir	01/01/1915	31/01/1915
Heading	121/6344 3rd ivision 3rd Signal Coy. R.E. Vol IV May-June July		
War Diary		00/05/1915	00/07/1915
Heading	121/7466 3rd Division 3rd Signal Co. R.E. Aug-Oct. 15 Vol V		
War Diary		00/08/1915	28/10/1915
Heading	3rd Signal Co. R.E. Nov-Dec. VI & VII		
War Diary	Steenvoorde	01/11/1915	31/12/1915
Heading	3rd Divisional Engineers.3rd Signal Company R.E. April-1916 (part) Missing 1916 Jan. Mar.		
War Diary	Westoutre	25/04/1916	30/04/1916
Heading	3rd Divisional Engineers. 3rd Signal Company R.E. May 1916		
War Diary	Westoutre	01/05/1916	27/05/1916
War Diary	Fletre	28/05/1916	31/05/1916
Heading	3rd Divisional Engineers. 3rd Signal Company R.E. June 1916		
War Diary	Fletre	01/06/1916	17/06/1916
War Diary	Tilques	18/06/1916	30/06/1916
Heading	3rd Divisional Engineers. 3rd Signal Company R.E. July 1916		
War Diary	Tilques	01/07/1916	01/07/1916
War Diary	Le Meillard	02/07/1916	02/07/1916
War Diary	Flesselles	03/07/1916	04/07/1916
War Diary	Corbie	04/07/1916	08/07/1916
War Diary	Bray	08/07/1916	26/07/1916
War Diary	Treux	27/07/1916	31/07/1916
Heading	3rd Divisional Engineers 3rd Divisional Signal Company R.E. August 1916		
Heading	Capt. R.E. Commanding 3rd Signals Company R.E.		
War Diary	Treux	01/08/1916	11/08/1916
War Diary	Bray	12/08/1916	20/08/1916

War Diary	Treux	21/08/1916	22/08/1916
War Diary	Bernaville	23/08/1916	24/08/1916
War Diary	Frohen-Le-Grand	25/08/1916	25/08/1916
War Diary	Flers	26/08/1916	26/08/1916
War Diary	Monchy-Cayeux	27/08/1916	27/08/1916
War Diary	Noeux-Les-Mines	28/08/1916	31/08/1916
Heading	3rd Divisional Engineers. 3rd Signal Company R.E. September 1916		
War Diary	Noeux-Les-Mines	01/09/1916	21/09/1916
War Diary	Bomy	22/09/1916	30/09/1916
Heading	3rd Divisional Engineers. 3rd Signal Company R.E. October 1916		
War Diary	Bomy	01/10/1916	04/10/1916
War Diary	Monchy Cayeux	05/10/1916	06/10/1916
War Diary	Bertrancourt	07/10/1916	17/10/1916
War Diary	Bus-Les-Artois	18/10/1916	31/10/1916
Heading	3rd Divisional Engineers. 3rd Signal Company R.E. November 1916		
War Diary	Bus-Les-Artois	01/11/1916	30/11/1916
Heading	3rd Divisional Engineers. 3rd Signal Company R.E. December 1916		
War Diary	Bus Les Artois	01/12/1916	09/01/1917
War Diary	Canaples	10/01/1917	28/01/1917
War Diary	Flers	29/01/1917	30/01/1917
War Diary	Villers Chatel	31/01/1917	07/02/1917
War Diary	Lingereuil	08/02/1917	10/02/1917
War Diary	Walus	11/02/1917	24/02/1917
War Diary	Cole "D" Arras	24/02/1917	28/02/1917
War Diary	Warlus	01/03/1917	05/03/1917
War Diary	Warlus Code "D" Arras	06/03/1917	09/04/1917
War Diary	Bois De Boeufs E. Arras	10/04/1917	13/04/1917
War Diary	Warlus	14/04/1917	23/04/1917
War Diary	Arras	24/04/1917	30/04/1917
Diagram etc	Y.C. Exchange		
Map	Maps		
War Diary	Arras	01/05/1917	15/05/1917
War Diary	Warlus	16/05/1917	22/05/1917
War Diary	Lignereuil	22/05/1917	03/06/1917
War Diary	Arras	03/06/1917	22/06/1917
War Diary	Le Cauroy	23/06/1917	05/07/1917
War Diary	Benqury?	06/07/1917	31/07/1917
War Diary	Haplincourt	01/08/1917	01/08/1917
War Diary	1 28 C 1.5	01/08/1917	31/08/1917
Diagram etc	8th Infantry Brigade Communications		
Heading	Signal 3rd Div. Vol 26		
Map	76 Bde Signals Diagram 11.8.1917		
War Diary	Haplincourt	01/09/1917	17/09/1917
War Diary	Proven	18/09/1917	01/10/1917
War Diary	Ypres	01/10/1917	01/10/1917
War Diary	Winnizeele	02/10/1917	04/10/1917
War Diary	Renescure	05/10/1917	06/10/1917
War Diary	Bapaume	06/10/1917	06/10/1917
War Diary	Haplincourt	07/10/1917	10/10/1917
War Diary	Monument	12/10/1917	31/10/1917
War Diary		28/00/1917	28/00/1917
War Diary		01/00/1917	31/00/1917

War Diary	Monument Commemoratif	01/11/1917	30/11/1917
War Diary	(Sheet 57 C) H. 15 C "The Monument"	01/12/1917	10/12/1917
War Diary	H. C/s at The Monument H. 15 C (Sheet 57 C)	11/12/1917	13/12/1917
War Diary	The Monument	14/12/1917	14/12/1917
War Diary	Behagnies	14/12/1917	31/12/1917
Heading	3rd Division Signal Coy. 1918 Jan.-1919 May		
War Diary	Behagnies	01/01/1918	06/01/1918
War Diary	Behagnies & Gomiecourt	07/01/1918	07/01/1918
War Diary	Gomiecourt	08/01/1918	29/01/1918
War Diary	Boisleux-Au-Mont	30/01/1918	28/02/1918
Heading	3rd Divisional Engineers. 3rd Divisional Signal Company R.E. March 1918		
Miscellaneous	The D.A.G. 3rd Echelon		
War Diary	Boisleux Au Mont	01/03/1918	22/03/1918
War Diary	Bretencourt	23/03/1918	29/03/1918
War Diary	Lucheux	30/03/1918	31/03/1918
Heading	3rd Divisional Engineers. War Diary 3rd Divisional Signal Company R.E. April 1918		
War Diary	Bruay	01/04/1918	01/04/1918
War Diary	Labeuvriere	02/04/1918	04/04/1918
War Diary	Fouquieres	05/04/1918	07/04/1918
War Diary	Labeuvriere	08/04/1918	10/04/1918
War Diary	Oblinghem	11/04/1918	12/04/1918
War Diary	Labeuvriere	13/04/1918	30/04/1918
Diagram etc	3rd Div. Sigs Circuit Diagram		
Diagram etc	Circuit Diagram 3rd Div. Sigs		
Diagram etc	Circuit Diagram		
Diagram etc	Diagram of Visual Communications as at 8 pm 15.4.18 Sigs Y.C.		
Diagram etc	Diagram of Visual Communications as at 8 pm 16.4.18 Sigs Y.C.		
Diagram etc	Diagram of Visual Communications as at 8 pm 17.4.18		
Diagram etc	Diagram of Visual Communications as at 8 pm 18.4.18		
Diagram etc	System of Visual Communications as at 8 pm 19.4.18		
War Diary	Labeuvriere	01/05/1918	31/05/1918
Diagram etc	System of Visual Communications		
Diagram etc	System of Visual Communication		
Diagram etc	3rd Division Signals System of Visual Communication		
Diagram etc	3rd Division Signals Visual Communication		
Diagram etc	Wireless, P B-A & Visual Communication 3rd Division Signals		
Diagram etc	R.E. Signals Division 18.5.18 Wireless & Visual Communication		
Diagram etc	System of Wireless & P.B.-A Communication		
War Diary	Wireless Stations-in-Communication 9-5-1918		
Diagram etc	Circuit Diagram 8 pm 1.5.18		
Diagram etc	Circuit Diagram 8 pm 3.5.18		
Diagram etc	Circuit Diagram 8 pm 7.5.18		
Diagram etc	Circuit Diagram 8 pm 8.5.18		
Diagram etc	Circuit Diagram 8 pm 9.5.18		
Diagram etc	Circuit Diagram 8 pm 11.5.18		
Diagram etc	Wireless Diagram 3rd Division Signals		
Diagram etc	Circuit Diagram 3rd Division Signals 8 pm 18.5.18		
War Diary	Labeuvriere	01/06/1918	31/07/1918
War Diary	Labeuvriere sheet 36B Dllc. 5.4	01/08/1918	06/08/1918
War Diary	Auchel sheet 36B C28a. 1.7	07/08/1918	12/08/1918

War Diary	Bavincourt sheet 51C P 35a 2.4	13/08/1918	14/08/1918
War Diary	Bavincourt P 35a 2.4 sheet 51 C	15/08/1918	19/08/1918
War Diary	Pommiers W25C 4.8 sheet 51 C.	20/08/1918	24/08/1918
War Diary	Vicinity of Bienvillers E. 4 C 2.4 sheet 51 C.	25/08/1918	27/08/1918
War Diary	Boiry St. Martin S20a 8.6 sheet 51C.	28/08/1918	28/08/1918
War Diary	Hamelincourt A 11b. 7.8 sheet 51C	29/08/1918	02/09/1918
War Diary	Vicinity Ransart X13a. 6.5 sheet 51C.	03/09/1918	05/09/1918
War Diary	Humbercamps V29a. 3.0	06/09/1918	10/09/1918
War Diary	Gomiecourt & A 30 a. 6.9 sheet 57C.	11/09/1918	14/09/1918
War Diary	Beugny I 17a. 6.9 Sheet 57C N.W.	15/09/1918	28/09/1918
War Diary	Hermies J24a 7.4	29/09/1918	30/09/1918
War Diary	Flesquieres L19a. 5.6 sheet 57C	01/10/1918	08/10/1918
War Diary	Hermies J24a. 7.4 sheet 57C.	09/10/1918	12/10/1918
War Diary	Flesquieres L19a. 5.6 sheet 57C.	13/10/1918	19/10/1918
War Diary	Cattinieres H12c. 8.9 sheet 57B.	20/10/1918	21/10/1918
War Diary	Quievy D 13 c 7.0 57 b	22/10/1918	22/10/1918
War Diary	Solesmes E 1 C 6.8 57 B	23/10/1918	28/10/1918
War Diary	Solesmes E 1 C 6.8	29/10/1918	30/10/1918
War Diary	Quievy D 13 C 7.0 57 B	30/10/1918	30/10/1918
War Diary	Quievy D 19. a. 1.6. 57 B.	01/11/1918	31/01/1919
War Diary	Duren	01/02/1919	28/02/1919
War Diary	(Lindenthal) Cologne	01/03/1919	09/04/1919
War Diary	Cologne	10/04/1919	30/04/1919
War Diary	Nippes Cologne	01/05/1919	20/05/1919
War Diary	Dunkirk	21/05/1919	24/05/1919
Heading	3rd Division War Diaries 1/1st East Riding Field Coy. R.E. August to December 1916		
Heading	3rd Divisional Engineers. 1/1st East Riding Field Company R.E. August to December 1916		
War Diary	Mericourt	01/08/1916	05/08/1916
War Diary	The Citadel	06/08/1916	15/08/1916
War Diary	Minden Post	16/08/1916	20/08/1916
War Diary	Happy Valley	21/08/1916	21/08/1916
War Diary	Morlancourt	22/08/1916	23/08/1916
War Diary	Monplaisir	24/08/1916	25/08/1916
War Diary	Ligny Sur Canche	26/08/1916	26/08/1916
War Diary	Grand Riez	27/08/1916	27/08/1916
War Diary		28/08/1916	28/08/1916
War Diary	Fontaine Lez Boulans	28/08/1916	28/08/1916
War Diary	Tangry	29/08/1916	29/08/1916
War Diary	Hesdigneul	30/08/1916	30/08/1916
War Diary	Philosophe	31/08/1916	31/08/1916
Heading	3rd Division Engineers. 1/1st East Riding Field Company R.E. September 1916		
War Diary	Philosophe	01/09/1916	22/09/1916
War Diary	Noeux-Les-Mines	23/09/1916	23/09/1916
War Diary	Auchel	24/09/1916	24/09/1916
War Diary	Ligny-Lez-Aire	25/09/1916	30/09/1916
War Diary	3rd Divisional Engineers. L/1st East Riding Field Company R.E. October 1916		
War Diary	Ligny-Lez-Aire	01/10/1916	05/10/1916
War Diary	Bergueneuse	06/10/1916	07/10/1916
War Diary	St. Pol	08/10/1916	08/10/1916
War Diary	Mailly-Maillet	09/10/1916	18/10/1916
War Diary	Courcelles Au-Bois	19/10/1916	31/10/1916

Heading	3rd Divisional Engineers. 1/1st East Riding Field Company R.E. November 1916		
War Diary	Courcelles Au 0 Bois	01/11/1916	30/11/1916
Heading	3rd Divisional Engineers. 1/1st East Riding Field Company R.E. December 1916		
War Diary	Courcelles Au Bois	01/12/1916	31/12/1916
Heading	3rd Division War Diaries 529th East Riding Field Coy. from 1st January to 31st December 1917		
War Diary	Courcelles-Au-Bois	01/01/1917	09/01/1917
War Diary	Puchevillers	10/01/1917	10/01/1917
War Diary	Pernois	11/01/1917	28/01/1917
War Diary	Amplier	29/01/1917	29/01/1917
War Diary	Barly	30/01/1917	30/01/1917
War Diary	Sericourt	31/01/1917	31/01/1917
War Diary	Caucourt	01/02/1917	01/02/1917
War Diary	Ambrines	02/02/1917	03/02/1917
War Diary	Warlus	04/02/1917	17/02/1917
War Diary	Arras	18/02/1917	28/02/1917
Heading	Vol 8 War Diary for month ending 31st March 1917 529th (E. Riding) Field Company R.E.		
War Diary	Arras	01/03/1917	31/03/1917
Heading	Vol 9 War Diary for month ending April 30th 1917 Unit. 529th (E. Riding) Field Company R.E. (T) Vol 9		
War Diary	Arras	01/04/1917	30/04/1917
Heading	Vol 10 War Diary for month ending 31st May 1917 529th (E. Riding) Field Co R.E. Vol 10		
War Diary	Arras	01/05/1917	09/05/1917
War Diary	Tilloy	10/05/1917	14/05/1917
War Diary	Duisans	15/05/1917	17/05/1917
War Diary	Noyellette	18/05/1917	18/05/1917
War Diary	Wanquetin	19/05/1917	31/05/1917
Heading	Vol XI War Diary for month ending 30th June 1917 Unit. 529th (E. Riding) Field Company R.E. Vol XI		
War Diary	Wanquetin	01/06/1917	02/06/1917
War Diary	Houlette Work	03/06/1917	09/06/1917
War Diary	Tilloy	10/06/1917	19/06/1917
War Diary	Arras	20/06/1917	20/06/1917
War Diary	Caumnesnil	21/06/1917	30/06/1917
Heading	Vol 12 War Diary for month ending 31st July 1917 Unit. 529th (E. Riding) Field Company R.E. (T) Vol 12		
War Diary	Achiet-Les Petit	01/07/1917	01/07/1917
War Diary	Lebucquiere	02/07/1917	31/07/1917
Heading	Vol 13 War Diary for month ending 31st August 1917 Unit 529 (E. Riding) Field Company R.E.G.		
War Diary	Lebucquiere	01/08/1917	31/08/1917
Heading	Vol 14 War Diary For Month Ending 30th September 1917 Unit. 529th (E.Riding) Field Company R.E.		
War Diary	Lebocquiere	01/09/1917	05/09/1917
War Diary	Barastre	06/09/1917	18/09/1917
War Diary	Vlamertinghe	19/09/1917	21/09/1917
War Diary	Ypres	22/09/1917	28/09/1917
War Diary	Brandhoek	29/09/1917	29/09/1917
War Diary	Winnezeele	30/09/1917	04/10/1917
War Diary	Mal Hove	05/10/1917	05/10/1917
War Diary	Wizernes	06/10/1917	06/10/1917
War Diary	Bapaume	06/10/1917	06/10/1917

War Diary	Barastre	07/10/1917	10/10/1917
War Diary	Favreuil	10/10/1917	11/10/1917
War Diary	Ecoust	12/10/1917	31/10/1917
Heading	Vol 16 War Diary for month ending 30th November 1917 Vol 16		
War Diary	Ecoust	01/11/1917	30/11/1917
Heading	Vol 17 War Diary for month ending 31st December 1917 Vol 17		
War Diary	Ecoust	01/12/1917	26/12/1917
War Diary	Hamlincourt	27/12/1917	31/12/1917
Heading	3rd Divisional War Diaries 529th East Riding Field Coy. 1918 Jan-1919 Sep.		
Heading	Vol 18 War Diary for month ending 31st January 1918 Vol 18		
War Diary	Hamelincourt	01/01/1918	28/01/1918
War Diary	Boiry-Becquerelle & Wancourt	29/01/1918	31/01/1918
War Diary	Vol 19 War Diary for month ending 28th February 1918 Vol 19		
War Diary	Wancourt	01/02/1918	28/02/1918
Heading	3rd Divisional Engineers 529th (East Riding) Field Company R.E. March 1918		
Heading	War Diary for month ending 31st March 1918 Vol 19		
War Diary	Nancourt	01/03/1918	23/03/1918
War Diary	Wailly	23/03/1918	27/03/1918
War Diary	Grosville	28/03/1918	28/03/1918
War Diary	Gouy-En-Artois	29/03/1918	29/03/1918
War Diary	Oppy	30/03/1918	31/03/1918
Heading	3rd Divisional Engineers War Diary 529th (East Riding) Field Company R.E. April 1918		
Heading	Vol 21 War Diary for month ending 30th April 918 Vol 21		
War Diary	Dieval	01/04/1918	03/04/1918
War Diary	Hersin	04/04/1918	06/04/1918
War Diary	Aix-Noulette	07/04/1918	10/04/1918
War Diary	Chocques Area	11/04/1918	11/04/1918
War Diary	Chocques	12/04/1918	13/04/1918
War Diary	Lenglet	14/04/1918	17/04/1918
War Diary	Band Pits at D. 24, b, 3, 7, 5	18/04/1918	21/04/1918
War Diary	Sand Pits D. 24 b. 30.75.	22/04/1918	30/04/1918
Heading	Vol 22 War Diary for month ending 31st May 1918 Vol 22		
War Diary	Sand Pits D 24 a 8.6	01/05/1918	31/05/1918
War Diary	Vol 23 War Diary for month ending 30th June 1918 Vol 23		
War Diary	Sand Pits D 24 a 8.6	01/06/1918	30/06/1918
Heading	Vol 24 War Diary for month ending 31st July 1918 Vol 24		
War Diary	Bois des Dame D 22 b 3.5.	01/07/1918	31/07/1918
Heading	Vol 25 War Diary for month ending 31st August 1918 Vol 25		
War Diary	Hd Qrs & Waggen Line	01/08/1918	01/08/1918
War Diary	Bois De Dames Sheet 44 B D. 22 b 30.40	01/08/1918	01/08/1918
War Diary	Forward Billets	01/08/1918	01/08/1918
War Diary	Vendin Les Bethune	02/08/1918	02/08/1918
War Diary	Bethune Combined 36A SE 36	03/08/1918	03/08/1918
War Diary	36 B N E 36 C	04/08/1918	04/08/1918

War Diary	E 3. a 50.90.	04/08/1918	07/08/1918
War Diary	Amettes sheet 44 B B. 3. d.	09/08/1918	20/08/1918
War Diary	Berles au Bois Lens II	21/08/1918	21/08/1918
War Diary	Map Ry.	22/08/1918	22/08/1918
War Diary	Ayette Pits 51 C S E. 51 b. S W 57 d. N E 57C N W	23/08/1918	31/08/1918
War Diary	51 C S E	23/08/1918	23/08/1918
War Diary	51 b. S.W.	23/08/1918	23/08/1918
War Diary	57 d. N.E.	24/08/1918	24/08/1918
War Diary	57 C N. W.	24/08/1918	31/08/1918
War Diary	Map. Ry.	01/09/1918	01/09/1918
War Diary	Ervillers	01/09/1918	01/09/1918
War Diary	Pte 51C. S.E.	01/09/1918	01/09/1918
War Diary	Pte 51F. J. W.	01/09/1918	01/09/1918
War Diary	Pte 51D NE	01/09/1918	01/09/1918
War Diary	Pte 51C NW	01/09/1918	06/09/1918
War Diary	Map Ry. France 51C 1/40000	07/09/1918	10/09/1918
War Diary	Map Ry.	07/09/1918	10/09/1918
War Diary	Ayette (Sheet)	11/09/1918	16/09/1918
War Diary	Map. Ry. 57 C. N.E.	16/09/1918	18/09/1918
War Diary	E dt. 7 b. J. 26 b. 0.0	19/09/1918	30/09/1918
War Diary	Map. Ry. 57 C N.E.	01/10/1918	01/10/1918
War Diary	L. 19 a. 7.4.	02/10/1918	12/10/1918
War Diary	Map. Ry. 5.7. C. N.E.	13/10/1918	13/10/1918
War Diary	L. 19. a. 7.4	13/10/1918	18/10/1918
War Diary	Map Ry. 57 B. N.W.	19/10/1918	19/10/1918
War Diary	H. 12 a 4.5.	20/10/1918	20/10/1918
War Diary	Map. Ry. 57 B 1/40000 C.19.a.	21/10/1918	21/10/1918
War Diary	Quievy	22/10/1918	22/10/1918
War Diary	Map Ry. 57 B. N.E. D. 13 d. 91	22/10/1918	28/10/1918
War Diary	Solesmes	29/10/1918	29/10/1918
War Diary	Map Ry. France 57 B. N.E. 1/20000	29/10/1918	29/10/1918
War Diary	D. 6 d. 5.6.	30/10/1918	31/10/1918
War Diary	Map Ry. 57 B. N.E. 1/20000 D.6 d. 65 Solesmes	01/11/1918	04/11/1918
War Diary	Map Ry. 51 S.E.	05/11/1918	05/11/1918
War Diary	La Sablonniere	06/11/1918	10/11/1918
War Diary	La Longueville sheet 51 N.W. 36 A. 6.8	11/11/1918	19/11/1918
War Diary	Namur sheet 8	20/11/1918	21/11/1918
War Diary	Namur sheet 8 Bersillies	22/11/1918	22/11/1918
War Diary	L'Abbaye (Bilgrum)	22/11/1918	30/11/1918
War Diary	Marche sheet 8 Scy.	01/12/1918	04/12/1918
War Diary	Maressee	05/12/1918	05/12/1918
War Diary	Soy.	06/12/1918	06/12/1918
War Diary	Franczel	07/12/1918	10/12/1918
War Diary	Marche & Cierqeux	11/12/1918	11/12/1918
War Diary	Germany sheet I.M. 1/100000	12/12/1918	12/12/1918
War Diary	Nevndore Andler	13/12/1918	13/12/1918
War Diary	Frauenrnon	14/12/1918	14/12/1918
War Diary	Blankenheim Map I.L.	15/12/1918	15/12/1918
War Diary	Holzmulheim	16/12/1918	16/12/1918
War Diary	Munstereifel	17/12/1918	17/12/1918
War Diary	Kessnick	18/12/1918	18/12/1918
War Diary	Froitzheim	19/12/1918	19/12/1918
War Diary	Duren	20/12/1918	22/12/1918
War Diary	Germany sheet I L Duren	23/12/1918	31/12/1918
War Diary	Duren sheet I.L. Germany	01/01/1919	28/02/1919

Heading	Vol 32 3 Div War Diary for month ending 31st March 529th Field Coy. R.E. Vol 32		
War Diary	Cologne	01/03/1919	30/04/1919
Miscellaneous	M 2		
War Diary	Cologne	01/05/1919	30/09/1919
Heading	Northern Division (Late 3 Div) 231 Field Coy R.E. 1919 April-1919 Oct. form 40 Div.		
Heading	War Diary 231 Field Coy R.E. April 1919		
War Diary	Cologne (Braling Field)	01/04/1919	30/04/1919
War Diary	Braunsfeld (Cologne)	01/05/1919	31/05/1919
Heading	231st Field Coy. R.E. War Diary July 1919		
War Diary	Braunsfeld	01/07/1918	02/07/1918
War Diary	Braunsfeld & Deutz	03/07/1919	17/07/1919
War Diary	Braunsfeld & Deutz	18/07/1919	31/07/1919
War Diary	Braunsfeld Cologne	01/08/1919	31/08/1919
Heading	War Diary 231 Field Coy. R.E. September 1919		
War Diary	Braunsfeld (Cologne)	01/09/1919	21/09/1919
War Diary	Braunsfeld	22/09/1919	30/09/1919
War Diary	Braunsfeld (Cologne)	01/10/1919	31/10/1919

FRANCE

3 DIVISION TROOPS

DIVISIONAL SIGNAL COMPANY

1914 AUG — 1919 MAY

MISSING: 1915 - FEB. MAR. APR.
1916 JAN. FEB. MAR.

1404

Capt. A.C. Johnston, Promoted to Command
3rd Signal Coy., 3rd Division. 7th February 1915.

1915.

7th March.   Rode over to the Scherpenberg in the early morning. There must have been a good deal of rain lately as the going was very heavy.

During the morning people began to arrive to see "Granny" our huge 15" howitzer shoot off its first round, and by noon Sir John French, Smith-Dorrien and numerous other Generals arrived on the scenes. Wytschaete tower was to be the mark for "Granny". The first shot fell 200 yards short in the wood in front of the tower, the explosion was simply terrific and shot up an enormous column of smoke like the bursting of a great land mine which almost hid Wytschaete completely from view. They say that the explosion affects anyone within 700 yards of the burst so that the shell must do a fearful amount of damage if it falls anywhere near a body of troops. The second shell fell a bit nearer the tower and must have done a lot of damage as there was a cloud of brick dust etc., over Wytschaete for some time after. The next two rounds were fired at Hill 74 where the Germans have a lot of reserve trenches. Both shells dropped exactly right which shows also that "Granny" is an accurate gun; one does not know of course whether there were many Germans there but one could actually see through one's glasses the crater formed by the shell and this at a distance of over 6,000 yards. The gun undoubtedly seems to be a great success and I expect it will make the Germans a bit nervous to say the least of it.

I hear now that we are going to start showing activity all along the front with bombardments of special places, and feints so as to pin the Germans to this front while the Russians are hammering them in the East. One gathers that these new German levies have not been a great success; they were all right chasing the Russians while they were retreating, but now that the latter have turned on them, it is another story. The Germans may want to send some troops from this side to stiffen them up, and we want to prevent this for the present, and later on as the weather improves start an advance. If the Germans choose to have a go at us, so much the better, as I am sure we can knock them about badly and they would be wasting their strength. In the meantime we shall try and engage their attention as much as possible.

About 4 p.m. I rode off and had tea with Sunny Gabb and saw some of the regiment who were all very cheery. Went on and saw the Headquarters 7th Brigade for a few minutes and thence rode back to Mont Noir.

1915.

8th March.
Rather a busy day back at Mont Noir till late in the afternoon when I went out for a longish walk with Gillingham going along one of my lines as far as Locre, and then back along a couple more to the chateau.

A lot of firing going on today mostly on our part in pursuance of our plan to worry the Germans as much as possible. "Granny" had another shoot and knocked Messines tower down !

1915.

12th March. Got up very early and went up to the Scherpenberg about 6 a.m. As there was a thick mist rendering it impossible for the gunners to see, the attack was postponed and we all just had to wait about for it to clear; there were staff officers also up from the 5th Division, II Corps and Second Army.

During last night the 3/Worcesters and the 1/Wilts moved up to the newly dug assembly trenches opposite Spanbroek Hill, and which were situated a little behind our 'E' and 'F' trenches and were supposed to be hidden from view from the Germans. Here the two regiments were to lie while the bombardment was taking place, and then at a given moment to get up and rush forward to the assault.

As our fire trenches which have been occupied all the winter are now much too broad to jump across, and as it would have checked the impetus of the assault very much if the men had had to get in and then climb out of our trenches, little wooden bridges were brought up during the night. These were to be put up just as the moment for the assault arrived by the battalions of the 85th Infantry Brigade who were holding the trenches.

Any wire entanglements also in front of our trenches were also removed during the night and everything done to enable the assaulting columns to get a clear rush from the assembly trenches to the German position which was about 200 yards in front of our front trenches.

The men of the 85th Infantry Brigade were to stay in their position while the 3/Worcesters and 1/Wilts went through them, and to be ready to hold on should the attack fail and the Germans develop a strong counter-attack.

The artillery of this Division and also of the 5th Division were to prepare for the assault. First of all they were to carefully register all their guns on to their several objectives i.e., the 18½pdrs on to various portions of the wire entanglements in front of the German trenches, the 4.5" hows. likewise on to the trenches themselves, the 6" hows. likewise and also on to Spanbroekmolen and the ruins of Spanbroek Cabinet which the Germans have put into a state of defence and made into a supporting point, and "Granny" our 15" how. on to the redoubt which the Germans have built on the rear slopes of Spanbroek Hill [point 76] and which has been located and photographed by our aviators.

After all the guns had thus carefully ranged on to these various targets, there was to be a bombardment for half an hour, every gun firing as many rounds as it could. It was hoped by this means to prepare the way for the assault by inflicting a certain amount of loss on the Germans and shaking their moral. The 18-pdr. fire would tear away and make gaps in the German wire entanglements, the howitzers would knock the trenches and supporting points about, and "Granny" would demolish the redoubt. Everything of course depended on accurate shooting by the guns.

When the moment for assault came, the artillery were to lengthen their range and form a zone of fire in rear of the German position, so as to prevent any reinforcements from coming up to support the garrison on the hill.

In the assault the 1/Wilts were on the left and the regiment on the right. The reserve companies of each were to be ready with sandbags, tools etc, with which to strengthen and put into a state of defence any ground gained, also to commence digging a communicating trench forward from our original line to the newly gained position.

There was a third battalion in reserve to the whole attack, also two flanking parties on each flank who consisted chiefly of R.E. and whose role was to block the trenches to the right and left down which the Germans might attempt to re-gain lost ground or harass our attack.

The 5th Division on our right were co-operating by fire, but were not to make any real attack until we had gained a footing on Spanbroek Hill, while there were also diversions at other parts of the line.

The mist was what caused us all the trouble as in the first place the whole show had to be postponed; this meant that the assaulting troops had to lie about getting colder and stiffer every minute; besides the waiting about before doing an attack is always unpleasant-if one has a nasty job to do, one always likes to get it over quickly.

As the mist cleared it was possible to see 500 yards or more, and unfortunately it appears that our assembly trenches, which were meant to be hidden from the Germans, could be seen by them; consequently the show was given away and we lost a certain number of men before even the attack had started. Later it cleared a bit more and enabled the guns to begin registering, but the light was still not good, and after results proved that the ranging had not been good.

I think there was still some doubt whether the assault would take place, when a message arrived to say that the First Army was making excellent progress down south, that there were indications of the Germans withdrawing troops from these parts and rushing them down to help against our First Army, and that therefore our attack should not be delayed a moment longer than possible.

We therefore commenced the bombardment at 3.30 p.m. unfortunately I suppose largely owing to the haze our fire was not accurate, consequently the 18-pdrs. failed to properly cut the wire, and the howitzers to damage the trenches etc.

At 4.10 p.m. the assault was launched, the 1/Wilts on the left had no luck, were unable to get through the wire, and coming under a very heavy cross fire from machine guns etc., were unable to get on. The regiment fared better, the right company got into some of the German trenches and the flank party blocked the trenches to the right. These fellows held on gallantly till dark. The left company got three quarters of the way and carried some houses which the Germans use as an advanced post; they had another 40 yards or so to do, and were preparing to try and do it with another rush; though there was a very heavy fire, they might have succeeded, but then happened the worst thing that can possibly happen to any troops - they were shelled by their own artillery. Six of our heavy howitzer shells dropped right into them, they killed a lot of our men and naturally knocked the heart out of their attack.

Even taking the mist into consideration, I cannot help feeling that this was real bad gunnery on the part of the 5th Divisional Artillery who it appears were the culprits, though at that period of the proceedings they should have been shelling well behind the German line.

The attack therefore failed, and the troops were withdrawn after dark, though at one time it was being considered whether we should not try a night attack or not. It is a great disappointment of course but I think one wants to look at it all from a wider point of view, and if the attack succeeded in pinning some troops to this section of the line and preventing the Germans sending any more down south, it will not altogether have failed.

The losses, as was I fear inevitable, have been heavy, the 1/Wilts losing 5 officers killed and 3 wounded, and the regiment no less than 8 officers killed and one severely wounded, the 2/E.Surrey's also who were in that section of the trenches lost from shell fire 5 officers. The losses in the rank and file came to about 300 all told.

I am glad to say the communications worked excellently, and we were getting messages back from the front trenches inside of 5 minutes to the Scherpenberg.

There were a great many people up here, too many, and they rather got in the way; particularly staff officers of the Corps and Army who sent back enormous long messages about the operations, which anyway would have been sent back by us in due course, even if these officers had not been there.

Got back to the Chateau eventually about 9 pm. Heard that all my particular friends have got through this show today all right.

1915.

14th March.

Again misty, so that our artillery is not having a chance.

A quiet and uneventful day up at the Scherpenberg. After we had closed down there about 4.30 p.m. I went into Locre and paid a short visit to the regiment, then began to walk back to the Chateau.

When I was on Mont Rouge suddenly all at once a tremendous bombardment started mostly against the 27th Division on our left. One gets a fine view from Mont Rouge and it was really a wonderful sight. Right along the line there was a succession of flashes which showed up unusually brilliantly in the fading light, and made it all look as if the whole place was on fire, particularly as soon the whole line was wreathed in smoke.

All our guns were answering as hard as they could so that there was a fearful din.

It was obvious that something big was happening though not actually against our Division for the moment, except that our left Brigade was getting shelled a bit. I hurried on to get back to Mont Noir however I knew that Forsyth was there to watch the office so there was nothing to worry about. When I got back I found the office working at high pressure and messages flying in every direction. It appears that the Germans had blown up the Mound, had rushed about 8 of our trenches, and had penetrated into St.Eloi and some of the support trenches.

The 2/D.C.L.I. were holding on to their trenches all right but obviously a nasty hole had been made in our line. St.Eloi is a bad part of our line for us to lose ground as it means the Germans are all the more behind the flank of our troops covering Ypres whose position might become critical if the Germans really made progress here. However the 2/Irish Fusiliers and 1/Leinsters were being rallied between St.Eloi and Vormezeele and the reserve brigade of the 27th Division was moving up while the artillery of both divisions were shelling the Germans for all they were worth.

They are great soldiers these Huns, they have certainly sprung a surprise on the 27th Division and on all of us for that matter, since none of us ever dreamt that they have got the number of guns up here that they have suddenly produced. They choose just the right place to attack at the right moment and cover their assault with a really heavy ans accurate bombardment. There are no half measures about them, and they go for the assault in earnest and in sufficient strength to force their way through in spite of heavy losses for the moment which is probably real economy in the long run.

Rather different by comparison to our half-hearted show of 3 days ago. The tremendous bombardment went on right into the night, it was so dark that one could not see one's hand in front of one's face, so our fellows must have been having a pretty rotten time of it. There must have been an awful mix-up, no one knowing where anyone else is, nor what the situation was, bullets flying in every direction, units all intermingled, the possibility or probability of bumping into bodies of Germans at any moment and anywhere, and the whole time such a din going on that one could not hear oneself speak.

During the night two counter-attacks were made, and the Germans were driven out of St.Eloi and some of the trenches, but they were still holding on to the Mound which unfortunately commands a lot of our trenches from the rear, and on which they had firmly planted themselves with some maxims.

The Germans could not have chosen a better time to attack as a big relief, in which the 27th Division, ourselves and other Divisions on our right were concerned, was taking

place this evening, and in fact had actually begun. The 27th
Division were taking over a few of our left hand trenches,
while we were taking over a good many more trenches on our
right from the 5th Division who were doing likewise, there
being a general shift along the British front down south-
wards, to help the First Army I presume, who are doing so
well. This had all to be stopped, some of our battalions
had already moved to Dranoutre and had to be recalled.

The 7th Infantry Brigade at Locre were detailed as Army
Reserve and ordered to be ready to move off at short notice
to the assistance of the 27th Division if required, however
they were not wanted.

The German attack besides inflicting a fairly heavy
loss on us, and seizing some trenches at an awkward corner
for us, was probably chiefly intended to keep us busy up
here and to prevent oursending any troops to the assistance
of the First Army, and in this they most carefully succeeded.

I only hope we get the Mound and the other trenches
back all right as that is rather an important corner.

Except for a short burst of shelling and some rapid
fire on to some of our trenches in the evening to make us
think we were going to be attacked also, very little
happened on our front.

1915.

15th March.	Stayed back at Mont Noir and signed a few papers down at the Company.

Heard some more about the German attack on St.Eloi. They seem to have bombarded our trenches very heavily for about 5 minutes only, and then lengthened their range at once. At the same time they sprang no less than 6 mines under the Mound and our trenches, and then rushed at our trenches in great numbers. Apparently the 2/Irish Fusiliers held on well for a bit and got rather knocked about, but I fancy the 2/D.C.L.I. on the right did not do very well and went back rather quickly.

The counter-attack got back St.Eloi and the support trenches and was well carried out by the [3rd or 4th] 60th Rifles. But the Germans held on to the Mound, therefore rendering the front trenches still untenable for us as it commands them from the rear.

Today our artillery is bombarding the Mound, and a night attack on it will probably follow.

Walked via Mont Rouge to the Scherpenberg in the afternoon. Had tea with Ralph and some other fellows in the regiment at a farm just underneath the hill and then walked home with Forsyth.

Had an interesting talk with a fellow in the regiment who had got into the German trench the other day. It was apparently very deep and narrow, quite dry and well revetted with hurdles. They were 'traversed' frequently and the back of the trench was very high. This made it impossible for our fellows to shoot into the next trench which was about 40 yards further on. It must be a great protection from anything in the shape of reverse fire, also from splinters of shell which may have burst just behind. None of their loopholes of course pointed to the front but always diagonally so as to bring a cross fire on to the ground in front. They seem to be very neat loopholes made of iron plates with a very small aperture. The German rifle allows of only the muzzle having to be put through it, and when it is not in use they pull a little lever and a shutter closes the aperture. There were numerous dugouts which had apparently had been made quite comfortable, some of them having pictures in them and in one there was actually a bed !

Our 5th Divisional Artillery seem to have been terribly bad and simply bombarded 'E.1' our own trench. Though the German wire on this bit had been well cut, it seems that their trench had not been damaged in the least. There were only a few men in this trench who our fellows killed, it was really a snipers trench connected by a winding communicating trench to their main trench about 40 yards further on. Our fellows as mentioned above could not shoot at this main trench, the Germans bombed them with hand-grenades, and as our bombing party had been unable to get up, our fellows could not reply in anyway so had a bad time, but held on till dark when they were told to retire. I believe if they had shoved in more troops at once, that we might have got a firm footing there.

1915.

11th April.

Chief event of the day was that the Germans shelled quite close to our day headquarters, which came as rather a surprise to us. I rather doubt that they were actually aiming at us in particular, unless one of their aeroplanes has located our position; they may possibly have done this owing to the wooden pathway the General has had built from the wood to his hut which probably shows up a good deal from above; they were all "pip squeaks" [small shrapnel] which don't do much harm unless they are burst exactly right. One as a matter of fact went right through a hut in which 5 officers were sitting and not one of them was touched !

Late in the afternoon the Huns put a couple of "crumps" [large howitzer shell] right into a fxxm farm about 600 yards away, this time to our right.

In the afternoon rode along one of my lines to the 9th Infantry Brigade where I had an interesting talk with Wavell, the brigade major, who told me something of their experiences when they were sent off to the 28th Division in front of Ypres to take the place of the 85th Infantry Brigade who came to us temporarily.

Things certainly had become to a pretty serious pass there. They found the men cowering in the bottom of the trenches, not daring to show themselves for a moment, the Germans had completely got the ascendancy and did what they liked, the first night they were there a German officer and a dozen men walked round and into them from behind so as to capture the trench, a sort of thing they have been doing fairly often I fancy; certainly once we seem to have lost a trench to a German fatigue party bringing up rations, who really got into the trench by mistake. Also the Germans used to coolly walk about behind their lines in the dark with lanterns, and next day in broad daylight they calmly came out of their trenches and began mending the wire in front of them, as if it was the most ordinary sort of thing to do. However this was soon stopped by the 9th Infantry Brigade and they have now got the Germans well in hand there.

As a matter of fact I don't think the 28th Division had a fair chance. They took over from a bad French Corps who seem to have been losing trenches a good deal without saying anything about it, and who handed over only a support line of trenches which in places were waist deep in mud, half full of dead bodies, not continuous, commanded by the German trenches, and most of them actually had communicating trenches running forward from them into the German lines. The Germans therefore were absolutely 'on top' from the very beginning, while the 28th Division was inexperienced and compôsed of men just home from warm climates such as Hong Kong, India etc., who were soon knocked up by the cold and damp.

The staff of this Division was also composed of various officers just collected together mostly from G.H.Q and Army Staffs who therefore really knew nothing about Divisional work or the actual handling of troops, supply arrangements and staff work generally were therefore bad, and consequently caused unnecessary trouble and discomforts for the troops.

The Signal Company was an inexperienced territorial one joining the Division at the last moment, and communications were therefore very indifferent, and units were frequently out of touch. A great pity as that Division had fine material to work with, being composed entirely of regular troops of long service. Certainly their Brigade, which has been with us and has now learnt a bit, could not be better, and has put in a lot of excellent work the last few weeks.

After seeing Wavell rode back and saw the 7th Infantry Brigade people for a bit; then walked back to Reninghelst along a couple of my lines, most of which I know by now,

1915.

15th April.

A quiet day. Walked along one of our artillery telephone lines to the 5th Division with Castier, my new subaltern for looking after artillery communications, very young and inexperienced but no doubt he will learn.

In the afternoon we were warned that there was a possibility of a German attack this evening. It appears that a reliable agent has come in to say that the Germans have been making preparations for a big attack on the Ypres salient for tonight, that they have been quietly reinforcing their line, that they have been building bridges etc, over their reserve trenches to enable them to bring up their guns to close range quickly, and that they are going to have batteries of 20 tubes every 40 metres which are to spray our lines with an asphyxiating gas !! Hindenburg is also said to have arrived in these parts.

A prisoner was caught this morning who pretty well corroborated the above. All the same the night passed without incident. But I cannot help feeling that these Germans are up to something or other, and that these prisoners and people, who come in with much to say, are really men sent over on purpose to give us false information.

The prisoner who we collared a few days ago, and who said there was no mining going on in front of us was obviously lying; and this latest story does not seem to be coming true.

They are undoubtedly clearing civilians out of the towns behind their line, and their Army Headquarters have moved back a bit; one wonders whether perhaps they are not making arrangements for a possible retrograde movement to say the Scheldt line, and are spreading these false reports to cover their arrangements.

However we are not ready yet to start trying to advance, and I expect lack of ammunition and equipment for the new armies is the reason.

It is very annoying to go on sitting still here when one feels one ought to start going at these fellows and so help the French to relieve the pressure on the Russians.

1915.

17th April.   Heard more details about the show on the night of the 14th. Apparently what happened was this :- A little after 11 p.m. the Germans started a heavy rifle fire on to our trenches about St.Eloi, a few minutes later they blew up Mine House which is on the road just to the left of Q.1, the house was completely demolished of course, and just the very left hand end of Q.1. badly shaken up; then a very heavy bombardment was made on our support and reserve lines for some time, but no attack was pushed in; our artillery answered at once and for some time there was a fearful din, but things eventually quieted down.

Our communications were quite successful on the whole, and word came through at once. Although some of the battalion lines were cut by the shelling, we were able to get messages back from Q.3. by means of lamp signalling, which was very satisfactory as we had arranged this expressly for such an emergency.

We also had started a mine going towards the German trench from underneath Mine House. More than likely when the Germans got there, possibly the night before, they heard our fellows working, and saw that they would not be able to get on any further, or to bring their mine underneath our trench. They therefore decided to do as much damage as possible and anyway to stop our mining here.

They consequently started the rifle fire to make us man our trenches thickly, then sprung their mine to bury our miners and to damage Q.1. as much as possible, and also to make us think an attack was about to begin. They then shelled the ground heavily behind our line in the hopes that they would inflict losses on troops being sent up to reinforce. As a matter of fact about 20 men were hurt by the mine and another 20 only by the shelling, so that as it turned out the whole thing was very fortunate for us.

Our mine prevented their bringing their mine under our trench which they would then have blown up with heavy loss to us compared to the little damage that was actually done. They were also unable to push in an attack, and I don't suppose our gunners fired without some effect.

Walked out to see the Headquarters of the regiment in the farm behind the wood in front of Dickebusch Pond, had tea there and then came back to the huts about 6 p.m. so as to be handy in case things should begin to hum when the 5th Division show started.

At 7 p.m. the show began by 3 mines being sprung underneath the German trenches on Hill 60; they were most successful as they wrecked the German line and blew up or buried about 150 Germans. The assault of the hill was then carried out by the 1/West Kents and 2/K.O.S.B. who took the Hill without any difficulty and with little loss. Very heavy shelling was opened on both sides. The Germans for one thing had not got their guns registered on to what had been their own Hill, and anyway shelled behind the line chiefly with a view to catching our reserves and preventing reinforcements coming up.

Our people therefore had a short respite in which to start digging themselves in, and consolidating their position, the supporting battalions were busy in bringing up sandbags etc, and digging communication trenches up from our old line to the new. Though there was a lot of heavy firing all through the night, they were able to make good headway both with the front line and with the communication trenches, so that they were better able to resist the very heavy counter-attack which the Germans launched at 5.30 a.m. and which lasted till 7 a.m.   There was very severe fighting much of it hand-to-hand and, though we lost pretty heavily, we held on to all the ground gained and inflicted very severe losses on the Germans, a machine gun of ours in particular doing great execution.

Hill 60 is an important point as, with it in our

possession, a large area of country behind our line is shut out from view of the Germans, who formerly could watch the whole of this tract and got a fine view of many of our trenches.

3rd Division

121/4104

3rd Signal Coy: R.E.

Vol I. 5.8 — 31.12.14

ARMY FORM C 2118

INSTRUCTIONS REGARDING WAR DIARIES AND WAR DIARY
INTELLIGENCE SUMMARIES ARE CONTAINED IN
F.S. REGS. PART II. AND THE STAFF MANUAL INTELLIGENCE SUMMARY
RESPECTIVELY TITLE PAGES WILL BE PREPARED (ERASE HEADING NOT REQUIRED)
IN MANUSCRIPT

3rd Sig Coy R.E.

Hour Date Place	Summary of Events and Information	Remarks & References to Appendices
1914		
5th Aug BULFORD	Mobilisation ordered	
10th Aug BULFORD	Mobilisation completed. All went smoothly	
16th Aug AMESBURY	Entrained 4.58 a.m. Reached SOUTHAMPTON 6.40 a.m. Embarked on S.S. ITALIAN PRINCE and started 12.30 p.m.	
17th Aug ROUEN	Arrived Rouen 2.0 p.m. disembarked and marched to rest camp	
18th Aug ROUEN	At rest camp	
19th Aug "	Marched to Gare du Nord, entrained started 2.55 p.m.	
20th Aug AULNOY	Arrived 2.2 a.m. marched to bivouac	
21st Aug	Marched to GOEGNIES	
22nd Aug	Marched to NOIRCHAIN	

ARMY FORM C.2118

WAR DIARY
or
INTELLIGENCE SUMMARY

Instructions regarding War Diaries and Intelligence Summaries are contained in F.S. Regs. Part II. and the Staff Manual respectively. Title pages will be prepared (erase heading not required) in manuscript.

Hour	Date	Place	Summary of Events and Information	Remarks & References to Appendices
	23rd Aug	NOIRCHAIN	Battle of MONS. Call to 7th, 8th & 9th Bdes.	
	24th Aug		Marched to BARMERIES	
	25th Aug		Marched to BERTRY	
	26th Aug	BERTRY	Battle of LE CATEAU. Call to all 3 Bdes.	
	27th Aug		Marched to BEAUREVOIR	
			Marched to HAM	
	28th Aug		Marched to CRISSOLLES	
	29th Aug		Marched to CUTS	
	30th Aug		Marched to MONTIGNY	
	31st Aug		Marched to VAUMOISE	
	1st Sept		Marched to VILLERS St GENEST	
	2nd Sept		Marched to MONTHYON	
	3rd Sept		Marched to LA HAUTE MAISON	
	4th Sept		Marched to CRECY	

ARMY FORM C2118

WAR DIARY
or
INTELLIGENCE SUMMARY

Instructions regarding War Diaries and Intelligence Summaries are contained in F.S. Regs Part II. and the Staff Manual respectively. Title pages will be prepared (erase heading not required) in manuscript.

Hour. Date.	Place	Summary of Events and Information	Remarks & References to Appendices
5th Sept		Marched to CHATRES	Shortage in motor cyclists owing to sickness, losses due to over work.
6th Sept		Marched to HAUTEFEUILLES	
7th Sept		Marched to LA BRETONNERE	
8th Sept		Marched to BOSSIERES	
9th Sept		Marched to BETU	
10th Sept		Marched to DANNARD	
11th Sept		Marched to GRAND ROZOY	
12th Sept		Marched to BRAINE	
13th Sept	BRAINE	Fell to CHASSIMY, VAILLY and BRENELLE.	
to			
2nd Oct		Later to R.G. observy station near railway bridge.	
2nd Oct. 6.0pm		Marched to ARCY St RESTITUE	
3rd Oct 6.0pm		Marched to LA FERTE MILON	

Instructions Regarding War Diaries and WAR DIARY
Intelligence Summaries are contained in   or
F.S. Regs Part II. and the Staff manual   INTELLIGENCE SUMMARY
respectively. Title pages will be prepared (erase heading not required)
in manuscript.

ARMY FORM C. 2118

Hour Date Place	Summary of Events and Information	Remarks & References to Appendices
4th Oct 5.30pm	Marched to CREPY EN VALOIS	
5th Oct 10.0 am	Marched to PONT ST MAXENCE arriving 4.0pm Entrained 8.0pm	
6th Oct	Arrived RUE 6.0am detrained 12 noon Marched to ABBEVILLE	
7th Oct	Remained at ABBEVILLE	
8th Oct	Marched to LE BOISLE	
9th Oct	Marched to HUBY	
10th Oct	Marched to PERNES	
11th Oct	Marched to HINGES	

ARMY FORM C.2118
WAR DIARY
or
INTELLIGENCE SUMMARY

Instructions regarding War Diaries and Intelligence Summaries are contained in F.S. Regs Part II. and the Staff Manual respectively. Title pages will be prepared (erase heading not required) in manuscript

Hour. Date	Place	Summary of Events and Information	Remarks & References to Appendices
12th Oct		Marched to Zelobes (relieved 7th & 8th Bdes)	
13th Oct		HdQrs moved to Lacouture (relieved as above)	
13th to 16th Oct		At Lacouture	
17th Oct		HdQrs moved to Neuve Chapelle	
18th, 19th, 20th & 21st Oct		At Neuve Chapelle	
22nd Oct		HdQrs returned to Lacouture	
23rd to 30th Oct		At Lacouture	
31st Oct		Marched to Meteren	
1st to 5th Nov		Rest at Meteren	

ARMY FORM C2118

INSTRUCTIONS REGARDING WAR DIARIES AND WAR DIARY
INTELLIGENCE SUMMARIES ARE CONTAINED IN OR
F.S. REGS PART II. AND THE STAFF MANUAL INTELLIGENCE SUMMARY
RESPECTIVELY TITLE PAGES WILL BE PREPARED (ERASE HEADING NOT REQUIRED)
IN MANUSCRIPT

HOUR DATE PLACE	SUMMARY OF EVENTS AND INFORMATION	REMARKS & REFERENCES to APPENDICES
6th Nov.	Marched with two cable wagons to YPRES called to 7th & 9th Bdes.	
7th to 19th Nov.	At YPRES	
20th Nov.	Marched to MONT NOIR	
25th Nov.	Called to 7th, 8th & 9th Bdes. PHQ & SCHERPENBERG (obg HQ of Divn)	
26th Nov to 31st Dec.	At MONT NOIR	

Critchett
Capt.

44

Date	3rd Signal Coy. R.E.					
	Killed		Wounded		Other Ranks	
	Officers		Officers	Missing	Killed	Wounded Missing
18.10.14						1
27.10.14					1	1

3rd Division

3rd Signal Coy: RE.

Vol iii. 1 – 31.1.15

121/4256

agg
27W

Instructions regarding War Diaries and Intelligence Summaries are contained in F.S. Regs Part II. and the Staff Manual respectively. Title Pages will be prepared in manuscript.

ARMY FORM 2118
WAR DIARY or INTELLIGENCE SUMMARY
(Erase heading not required) 3rd Signal by R.E.

Hour. Date. Place	Summary of Events and Information	Remarks & References to Appendices
1st Jan 1915 to 31st Jan 1915. MONT NOIR	No change in situation. 27th Divn embused here on our left — communication established with them.	

Marchant
Cap RE

121/6344

3rd Burwood

3rd Signal Coy RE

Vol IV May - June - July.

ARMY FORM C 2118

WAR DIARY
or
INTELLIGENCE SUMMARY

(Erase heading not required)

Instructions regarding War Diaries and Intelligent Summaries are contained in F.S. Regs Part II. and the Staff manual respectively. Title pages will be prepared in manuscript.

Hour. Date. Place	Summary of Events and Information	Remarks & References to Appendices
May 1915	HQ and No 1 Section with 3rd Div HQ at WESTOUTRE No 2 Section — 7th Brigade at DICKEBUSCH No 3 Section — 8th Brigade at LA CLYTTE No 4 Section — 9th Brigade at VOORMEZEELE Communication maintained between these points by cable supplemented by dispatch riders	
June 1915	HQ & No 1 Section with 3rd Div in rear POPERINGHE No 2 Section — 7th Brigade YPRES No 3 Section — 8th Brigade ECOLE YPRES No 4 Section — 9th Brigade VLAMERTINGHE Communication between these points maintained by cable D R and visual	

A. C. Johnston Capt
OC 3rd Sig Coy RE

ARMY FORM C.2118

INSTRUCTIONS REGARDING WAR DIARIES AND INTELLIGENCE SUMMARIES ARE CONTAINED IN F.S. REGS PART II. AND THE STAFF MANUAL RESPECTIVELY TITLE PAGES WILL BE PREPARED (ERASE HEADING NOT REQUIRED) IN MANUSCRIPT

WAR DIARY
OR
INTELLIGENCE SUMMARY

Hour. Date. Place	Summary of Events and Information	Remarks & References to Appendices
July 1915	HQ at POPERINGHE No 2 Section with 7th Brigade YPRES Remainder of Company with 8th & 9th Brigades near VLAMERTINGHE Communication maintained by cable and D.R.	

A. C. Johnston Capt
OC 3rd Sig Coy R.E.

12/7466

3/10 Knudsen

3: Shipment Co. R.E.

Aug–Dec '15

II vols

ARMY FORM C.2118

WAR DIARY
or
INTELLIGENCE SUMMARY

Instructions regarding War Diaries and Intelligence Summaries are contained in F.S. Regs Part II. and the Staff Manual respectively. Title pages will be prepared (erase heading not required) in manuscript.

3rd Signal Coy RE

Hour. Date	Place	Summary of Events and Information	Remarks & References to Appendices
August 1915 September October		HQ & No1 Section with 3rd Dn is HQ at RENINGHELST maintained communication with 7th 8th & 9th Brigades whose headquarters were in Ypres and at Zillebeke. Communication also maintained with the rest billets of the above brigades near ONDERDOM, with the R.E Park near DICKEBUSCH and with certain other units about BASSEBOOM	Communication chiefly cable supplemented by motor despatch riders and visual
Oct 25th		Moved to rest billets at STEENVOORDE	

3rd Signal Co. R.E.

Nov - Dec.

VI + VII

ARMY FORM C.2118

Instructions regarding War Diaries and Intelligence Summaries are contained in F.S. Regs Part II. and the Staff Manual respectively. Title pages will be prepared in manuscript.

WAR DIARY for Nov and Dec 1915
~~or INTELLIGENCE SUMMARY~~ (Erase heading not required)

3rd Signal Coy RE

Hour. Date	Place	Summary of Events and Information	Remarks & References to Appendices
November 1 – 22nd 1915	STEENVOORDE	3rd Division resting in the STEENVOORDE – WINNEZEELE area	
Nov 23rd – Dec 31st		On 22nd 3rd Signal Coy marched from STEENVOORDE via BOESCHEPE to RENINGHELST and took over Communications of 24th Division	
		Communication maintained from 3rd Div HQ in Reninghelst to :- 76th Inf Brigade on VERBRANDEN MOLEN – YPRES CANAL front 9th or 8th Inf Brigade on ST ELOI front 8th or 9th Inf Brigade in reserve at ZEVECOTEN 5th Corps Flank Divisions (2nd Canadian and 9th Divs) Divisional Troops	Cable supplemented by visual and motor despatch riders

A C Johnston Capt
O C 3rd Sig Coy RE
31/12/15

3rd Divisional Engineers.

3RD SIGNAL COMPANY R.E.

APRIL 1916.

(part)

MISSING
1916 JAN - MAR

Army Form C. 2118

3rd Signal Company *?E*
3rd Division

WAR DIARY
or
INTELLIGENCE SUMMARY
(Erase heading not required.)

Place	Date	Hour	Summary of Events and Information	Remarks and references to Appendices
WESTOUTRE	April 1916 25th		Unit marched from "Rest area" at FLETRE and marched WESTOUTRE without midday, advanced parties (Signal Officer, staff & linemen) having been sent on previously to take over from 50th Division signals. Capt. Kaye-Long temporarily in command after Capt. Tyzack had left for Motor Division. Capt. Petch arrived about midday from 6th Div. Signals to take over command the unit. At this date 8th Inf. Bde. was already in the line & 9th Inf. Bde. in process of going in. The 150th Inf. Bde. remain in right sector for the present, also 50th Div. Artillery not yet relieved. Command of sector handed over to 3rd Div. (Hqrs. the HILDEN (S.E. 20) from 10 p.m. Handing over of signals good on the whole, with exception of an Battalion in left (8th Inf. Bde.) sector.	
	26th		Day spent in trying to make the best of very bad field (and patch) which had been occupied by previous Signal units. No decent standings for horses + whole billet unfit for either men or horses. Great difficulty in getting new billets owing to strict orders against moving of tents. Camp found at foot of SCHERPENBERG hill for accommodation of 5th Corps Cable (SV) Section (under 2/Lt Edmonds),	

Army Form C. 2118

WAR DIARY
or
INTELLIGENCE SUMMARY
(Erase heading not required.)

Instructions regarding War Diaries and Intelligence Summaries are contained in F. S. Regs., Part II. and the Staff Manual respectively. Title Pages will be prepared in manuscript.

Place	Date	Hour	Summary of Events and Information	Remarks and references to Appendices
WESTOUTRE	April 26th (cont'd)		attached to this division for purposes of carrying lines in this area. At this new camp they will be nearer their work & closer to front.	
	27th		Spent artillery activity during night on station on SCHERPENBERG HILL Canadian front (on our left front), also false "gas alarm". 3V Cable station moved to new camp and 3rd Sec. bayonets manned 3 detachments, most of the wagons & dismounted divisions into accented camp & proceeded to improve it. Weather fortunately very good. 2/Lt. Ramage (9th Inf. Bde Signal Section) engaged in connecting buried cable from Batt'n HQ (+ Advanced Brigade HQ) to fleeting buried guard cable from Batt'n HQ in neighbourhood of KEMMEL (E. of VIERSTRAAT - Luppert Company HQ in LINDENHOEK road), with working party of 300 men from Entrenching Battalion. Unfortunately 1 Officer + 4 men wounded by "spans" during the night.	
	28th		Unit employed in extending and improving new camp. Some work of burying cables proceeding in 9th Inf. Bde sector.	
	29th		Work in camp as before. Some work in N.M.T. Bde sector.	
	30th		Bde. H.Q. shelled during morning & H.Q. would temporarily to LOCRE Front 1 a.m. Germans made gas attack on our right Brigade & attached 75th Inf.	

Army Form C. 2118

WAR DIARY
or
INTELLIGENCE SUMMARY
(Erase heading not required.)

Instructions regarding War Diaries and Intelligence Summaries are contained in F.S. Regs., Part II. and the Staff Manual respectively. Title Pages will be prepared in manuscript.

Place	Date	Hour	Summary of Events and Information	Remarks and references to Appendices
WESTOUTRE	April 30th (cont)		on small front, getting into a portion of trench-line between my Right Brigade & Left Brigade of 24th Division. Enemy was driven out of this soon afterwards & our artillery kept up a heavy bombardment for an hour. Lines held well during this time. Men working in court during morning 2/Lt. Phillips Service at Div. H.Q. (fun-in service) at 6 p.m. Signal went on Informing Officer from 3rd Canadian Division (8th Inf. Bde.) expecting nothing particular. St. Eloi being Entrenching Batt. at work on tunnel line near VIERSTRAAT. Very little work done owing to gas alarm (false).	

H.W.T.Wilk

COMMANDING 2ND SIGNAL COMPANY R.E.

3rd Divisional Engineers.

3RD SIGNAL COMPANY R.E.

MAY 1916.

Army Form C. 2118

3rd Signal Company R.E.
3rd Division

WAR DIARY
or
INTELLIGENCE SUMMARY
(Erase heading not required.)

Place	Date	Hour	Summary of Events and Information	Remarks and references to Appendices
WESTOUTRE	1916 May 1st		Work continued in putting up huts etc. in new camp at WESTOUTRE. 3rd Div. Artillery took over from 50th Div. Artillery. Lt. Poulsany supervising working party of 300 men of Entrenching Battn. working on buried line near VIERSTRAAT.	
	2nd		Maintenance party going through 6 line route (4 poles) to Brigades. Party of 300 men working on buried line under Lt. Ramage (9th Inf. Bde.).	
	3rd		Capt. Hays-Sorg went on leave to Ireland. Party of 220 men working on same line as on 1st May (under Lt. Pulliny - 8th Inf. Bde.), also party of 80 on buried line from test station to new Brigade H.Q. in Right Brigade Sector (76th Inf. Bde.) under Lt. Hill.	
	4th		Line put through from R.A. Headquarters in WESTOUTRE to Lt. Bellon. Section south of LOCRE. Party of 250 men working under Lt. Ramage in 9th Inf. Bde. sector.	
	5th		Same party working under Lt. Ramage in 9th Inf. Bde. sector.	

Army Form C. 2118

WAR DIARY
or
INTELLIGENCE SUMMARY
(Erase heading not required.)

Instructions regarding War Diaries and Intelligence Summaries are contained in F. S. Regs., Part II. and the Staff Manual respectively. Title Pages will be prepared in manuscript.

Place	Date	Hour	Summary of Events and Information	Remarks and references to Appendices
WESTOUTRE	1916 May 6th		Small maintenance party on "H pole" route East of LOCRE — RENINGHELST road (near SCHERPENBERG Hill). Party of 200 men of Entrenching Battn. working under Lt. Ramage in 9th Inf. Bde. sector and party of 50 men under Lt. Hill in 76th Inf. Bde. sector (burying through Battn. cables back to new Brigade H.Q. to North of KEMMEL HILL).	
	7th		Sunday. Men employed in camp during morning; continuing erection of huts, etc.; dinner cleaning harness. Church Parade divine in behalf. Service at 6 p.m. Party of 250 men under 2/Lt. Edwards ("SV" Cable Section) working in 2nd Inf. Bde. sector on neighbourhood of YORK HOUSE (Left Batt" H.Q.).	
	8th		Party of 230 men under Lt. Ramage continuing work on line near YORK HOUSE. Party of 50 men (from Brigade) working under 2/Lt. Hill (75th Inf. Bde.) on buried lines on KEMMEL HILL — two extra "pair" cables being buried in the same trench for purposes of KEMMEL defence scheme. (new Hqn 5th Corps)	

1875 Wt. W593/826 1,000,000 4/15 J.B.C. & A. A.D.S.S./Forms/C. 2118.

Army Form C. 2118

WAR DIARY
or
INTELLIGENCE SUMMARY

(Erase heading not required.)

Place	Date	Hour	Summary of Events and Information	Remarks and references to Appendices
WESTOUTRE	1916 May 9		Party of 250 men under 2/Lt. Edwards working on burial line between YORK HOUSE and ROSSIGNOL.	
		10"	2/Lt.C.H. Martin arrived from 24" Division Signals to take over No 3 Section (8th Inf. Bde.) from Lt. Tulliving who is posted to 6th Div. Signals. Party of 250 men under Lt. Ramage finished line between YORK HOUSE and ROSSIGNOL.	
		11"	Lt. Tulliving left for 6th Div Signals. Party of 90 men of Intenburg Batt? working during afternoon on burial line on KEMMEL HILL under 2/Lt. Hill (7/8th Inf Bde.) and party of 260 working at night under 2/Lt. Edwards (line from 9th Inf Bde. 'A' Fermal Road finished) under 2/Lt. Edwards. Party of 24 Gunners and 12 Infantry (1 man per regiment in Division) went by motor bus to CASSEL for a course of 2nd Army Signal School.	
		12"	2/Lt. Bailey went on leave to England. Inman working each day on lines to Brigades, renewing stays, putting up "marking bands" + pale + also making new bits of wire in + about Divisional Office. Remainder of men left busy erecting cookhouses + attending to general sanitation of two camps at WESTOUTRE. Party of 350 men	

Army Form C. 2118

WAR DIARY or INTELLIGENCE SUMMARY
(Erase heading not required.)

Instructions regarding War Diaries and Intelligence Summaries are contained in F.S. Regs., Part II. and the Staff Manual respectively. Title Pages will be prepared in manuscript.

Place	Date	Hour	Summary of Events and Information	Remarks and references to Appendices
NESTOUTRE	1916 May 12th (cont'd)		working under Lt. Ramage on same kind of line in 9th Inf. Bde. sector.	
	13th		Party of 210 men working under Lt. Edwards in 9th Inf. Bde. sector.	
	14th		Party of 250 men of Entrenching Batt. working under 2/Lt. Hill on burial line near KEMMEL (on new 76th Inf. Bde. H.Q.) Capt. Ramage returned from leave (late night).	
	15th		Sunday. Owing to wet state of ground no working party was asked for for this night, as it is extremely difficult to dig to depth when there is much water in the trench. Return to Battalion signed by Officers & then by Capt. Vigers (5th Corps Signals) in Cinema at LOCRE — special mention being made of Listening Apparatus (both our & enemy's).	
	16th		Party of 240 men working under Lt. Ramage in neighbourhood of HARINGHEBEEK (E. of ROSSIGNOL WOOD). Unfortunately about 6 men of party were hit — none seriously — and one hastily buried, owing to trench collapsing. Party from No.1 Sect. travel about ½ mile by airline for 76th Inf. Bde. on KEMMEL HILL (from new Brigade H.Q.)	

WAR DIARY
or
INTELLIGENCE SUMMARY
(Erase heading not required.)

Army Form C. 2118

Instructions regarding War Diaries and Intelligence Summaries are contained in F.S. Regs., Part II. and the Staff Manual respectively. Title Pages will be prepared in manuscript.

Place	Date	Hour	Summary of Events and Information	Remarks and references to Appendices
WESTOUTRE	1916 May 17th		2/Lt. Hobby, 66th (East Lancs) Territorial Regiment, arrived from England to be attached to the unit for instruction — for one week. He was sent out to No. 2 Section (76th Inf. Bde.). Party of 250 men working under Lt. Ramage on new buried line in 1st Inf. Bde. sector. "Gas Alert" signalled by 24th Divn. (on our right) about 9 p.m.	
	18th		2/Lt. Hobby, 2/Lt. Woodman, 20th Hussars and Lt. Muncey R.F.A. arrived for attachment to 1st Inf. Bde. and 3rd Divn. R.A. (Signals) respectively. Party of 200 men working under 2/Lt. Hill (76th Inf. Bde.) on buried line on KEMMEL HILL during afternoon + thirty + fifty men working on repaired part of same line at night time.	
	19th		Party of 250 men working under Lt. Ramage on buried line in 1st Inf. Bde. sector.	
	20th		Same work as on previous day. 2/Lt. Barclay returned from leave.	
	21st		Sunday. Party of 300 men working on buried lines on KEMMEL HILL under 2/Lt. Hill (76th Inf. Bde.)	

Army Form C. 2118

WAR DIARY
or
INTELLIGENCE SUMMARY
(Erase heading not required.)

Place	Date	Hour	Summary of Events and Information	Remarks and references to Appendices
NESTOUTRE	1916 May 22nd		Party of 200 men working under Lt. Ramage on burial line in 9th Inf. Bde. sector.	
	23rd		Party of 100 men working under Lt. Ramage & Lt. Vigne (5th Corps Signals), completing line to "K1A" from 9th Bde. Battle H.Q. Cables brought night of to work (K1A) but not brought in owing to length of tying required for purpose not having arrived. Party of 60 men and working under Lt. Hill on KEMMEL HILL line. Party of 40 men and 6 Linemen (from Div. H.Q.) working under Lt. Bradley on "O.P." line near VIERSTRAAT.	
	24th		Party of 200 men working on buried route to KEMMEL HILL under 2nd Lt. Spice (5th Bty) this progress made in spite of very wet weather last night. Lt. Bradley completing O.P. line near VIERSTRAAT. Capt. Webb Reports from POPERINGHE on leave.	

WAR DIARY or INTELLIGENCE SUMMARY

Army Form C. 2118

Place	Date	Hour	Summary of Events and Information	Remarks and references to Appendices
WESTOUTRE	25th May		Lt. Ramage & 2nd Lt. Phelps left 4.45 a.m. for HAZEBROUCK en route for leave. A party of 200 men under 2nd Lt. Burfee continued work on buried routes back to Hazebrouck Rly. Stn.	
	26th		The Company packing up & preparing to move. Horse inspection by A.D.V.S. at 9.20 a.m. result in a clean bill of health reported. A working party of 200 men under 2.Lt. operated 2 p.m. in continuation of burial route across KEMMEL & N/44. Other stores from 50th Div. arrived.	
	27th		Company unexpected 9 a.m. marched from FLETRE via MONT NOIR, SCHAEPKEN + METEREN, arrived at FLETRE 12 n.n. Camp pitched, wagons parked, horses lines at 9.30 a.m.	
FLETRE	28th		Sunday – parade at 6 training formation Church Parade. Remainder of day for purpose of work in general. 5.45 p.m.	

Army Form C. 2118

WAR DIARY
or
INTELLIGENCE SUMMARY
(Erase heading not required.)

Instructions regarding War Diaries and Intelligence Summaries are contained in F. S. Regs., Part II. and the Staff Manual respectively. Title Pages will be prepared in manuscript.

Place	Date	Hour	Summary of Events and Information	Remarks and references to Appendices
FLETRE	29th		1st parade 6.30 am – 7.15 am. Cable drill with Nos. 1 & 3 Detachments. Exercise & fatigue for remainder from 8.30 am – 11. Stables 11.30 – 11. Battalion Signal Officers Class 10-12. Lecture on horse management to operators 2.30–3.15. Fatigues and harness cleaning in afternoon. Stables 5-6 pm.	
	30th		No cable drill on account of wet weather. Exercise for all horses 8.30–11. Stables 11.30–1. Lecture on shoeing etc by the Farrier Sergt to all operators. Harness and waggon cleaning in afternoon.	
	31st		6.30 am – 7.15 Morning Stables. 8.30–11 Cable drill with Nos 2 & 4 Detachments. Exercise and grazing for remainder. Midday Stables. 2 pm. Clean arms and smoke helmet inspection. Lecture on fitting harness by Sergt Purkess to the operators. 5–6 Evening Stables. Lt. MARTYN – 8th I. Bde on leave.	

E. Kaye Parry
CAPT. R.E.
COMMANDING 32ND SIGNAL COMPANY R.E.

3rd Divisional Engineers.

3RD SIGNAL COMPANY R.E.

JUNE 1916.

Army Form C. 2118

3rd Signal Company
R.E.

Vol 12

WAR DIARY
or
INTELLIGENCE SUMMARY
(Erase heading not required.)

Instructions regarding War Diaries and Intelligence Summaries are contained in F.S. Regs., Part II. and the Staff Manual respectively. Title Pages will be prepared in manuscript.

Place	Date	Hour	Summary of Events and Information	Remarks and references to Appendices
FLETRE	June 1		Parades as usual. Cable drill with Nos 1 & 3 detachments. Jumping for riders F.G. Court Martial on Driver Daly.	
	2nd		Parades as usual. Cable Drill Nos 2 & 4 Detachments. Jumping & Exercise Wagons cleaned in afternoon.	
	3rd.		King's Birthday & a holiday. Sunday hours. Exercise party 9-10-15. Jumping 10.15 am – 11am. Lecture by A.D.A.S. 5th Corps on the Fullerphone given to Battalion Signal Officers and N.C.O's. No.1 Cable Detachment ordered to proceed to RENINGHELST to connect up C.R.A. with all his Bdes. 3rd Div: Arty ordered up to assist Canadians. No.2 detachment standing by. 2/Lt PHILLIPS returned from leave.	
	4th		Sunday hours. No exercise party. Stables and jumping. 9th Bde. ordered up in Reserve. 2/Lt PHILLIPS sent to join them in Lt. RAMAGES absence. Church Parade 5.45 pm.	
	5th.		Lt. RAMAGE returned from leave and joined 9th.I. Bde in RENINGHELST this morning. 2/Lt. PHILLIPS returned to Div. H.Qrs. Cable drill with Nos 3 & 4 Detachments as usual. Some Jumping 11 – 11.30 am. Two days rations sent up to No.1. Detachment in RENINGHELST. Lecture to operators on horse management 2 – 3 pm. Harness and other work in afternoon.	

1875 Wt. W593/826 1,000,000 4/15 J.B.C. & A. A.D.S.S./Forms/C. 2118.

Army Form C. 2118

WAR DIARY
or
INTELLIGENCE SUMMARY
(Erase heading not required.)

Instructions regarding War Diaries and Intelligence Summaries are contained in F.S. Regs., Part II. and the Staff Manual respectively. Title Pages will be prepared in manuscript.

Place	Date	Hour	Summary of Events and Information	Remarks and references to Appendices
FLÊTRE	June 6th		Capt. Wilk returned from leave during afternoon. 8th Inf. Bde. ordered to "stand by" ready to move at short notice, as the Huns are still on leave. 2/Lt. Phillips and went out to look after Signal Section.	
	7th		Wet day. Service for horses.	
	8th		2 detachments on cable drill.	
	9th		Same as previous day.	
	10th		One cable detachment & one detachment of horses Convoy cable drill. detachment went to RENINGHELST to relieve Sergt. Perkins' detachment who were maintaining our Artillery Lines there; letter detachment returned to FLÊTRE. 8th Inf. Bde. moved from their H.Q. near MT. DES CATS in the evening (7.30 P.M.) to RENINGHELST.	
	11th		Sunday. Church parade service in Canteen at 6 A.M. 8th Inf. Bde. took over lines (near ST. ELOI) from 9th Inf. Bde. at night.	
	12th		3 cable detachments (1 for drivers) out on drill.	

Army Form C. 2118

WAR DIARY
or
INTELLIGENCE SUMMARY
(Erase heading not required.)

Instructions regarding War Diaries and Intelligence Summaries are contained in F. S. Regs., Part II. and the Staff Manual respectively. Title Pages will be prepared in manuscript.

Place	Date	Hour	Summary of Events and Information	Remarks and references to Appendices
FLETRE	June 13th		Foggy wet morning. Three cable detachments (1 of stations) out again. Bn. arrived at EPERLECQUES after a 3 days march.	70th Rgt
	14th		Three cable detachments out. Riding Class for Officers & men Pioneers started under Sergt. Gardiner.	
	15th		Six cable detachments (one for stations) and Riding Class again out.	
	16th		Same work as previous day. Baths for as many as possible of Company at METEREN in afternoon. Capt. Hay-Parry & C.S.M. Edwards went to TILQUES in afternoon to arrange billets for Company whose divisions had to training area there.	
	17th		Riding Class & Exercise Party out as usual. Advanced party with stores & small Signal Office staff out on to TILQUES.	
	18th (Sunday)		Reveille 4 a.m. Moved off from FLETRE with horse transport (under Capt. Hays-Parry + 2/Lt Phillips) at 7.30 a.m. Halted at EBBLINGHEM (2 water & feed) & arrived TILQUES at 4 p.m. Only one horse slightly troubled.	
TILQUES	19th		Settling down into new billets. Riding class out during morning.	

1875 Wt. W593/826 1,000,000 4/15 J.B.C. & A. A.D.S.S./Forms/C. 2118.

WAR DIARY
or
INTELLIGENCE SUMMARY
(Erase heading not required.)

Army Form C. 2118

Instructions regarding War Diaries and Intelligence Summaries are contained in F. S. Regs., Part II. and the Staff Manual respectively. Title Pages will be prepared in manuscript.

Place	Date	Hour	Summary of Events and Information	Remarks and references to Appendices
TILQUES	June 20th		3 Cable detachments (1 for drivers) and Riding Class out during morning. "M" Cable Section, underfull. Blakers joined from 2nd Corps Signals.	
	21st		Fine wet during morning as a personal day. Signal drill for 3 hours in afternoon.	
	22nd		Two cable detachments out laying lines between NORTLEULINGHEM (9th Bde H.Q.) and GANSPETTE (4 "Royal Fusiliers"), detachments starting work from either end & meeting. Drivers and detachments also out (last day). Officers Riding Class on report. "M" Cable Section doing riding drill etc. Divisional Signal Captain in afternoon — in 2 group West of MOULLE. 8th A.L. Bde. at SALPERWICK was counted to telephone from morning to 3 Div: Sigs at ST MARTIN-AU-LAERT.	
	23rd		Two cable detachments and Riding Class out. "M" Cable Section had no detachment out. Signal drill in afternoon.	

1875 Wt. W593/826 1,000,000 4/15 J.B.C. & A. A.D.S.S./Forms/C. 2118.

Army Form C. 2118

WAR DIARY
or
INTELLIGENCE SUMMARY
(Erase heading not required.)

Instructions regarding War Diaries and Intelligence Summaries are contained in F.S. Regs., Part II. and the Staff Manual respectively. Title Pages will be prepared in manuscript.

Place	Date	Hour	Summary of Events and Information	Remarks and references to Appendices
TILQUES	June 24th		Rifle and musketry gas helmet inspection & issue of steel helmets to majority of men, followed by Infantry drill (5½ hours) from reveille. Signalling & signal classes (Infantry & R. Sappers) afternoon.	
	25th		Sunday. No Church service available. Cricket match in afternoon against Artillery School – won 38-29 against us.	
	26th		Fiends to meet in morning rode with wagons packed in order to give men an idea of what they are allowed to take with them on trek & what they would throw away. Exercise in Riding Class (operations) afternoon. To have a Infantry drill in afternoon.	
	27th		Two cable detachments and Riding Class turn out. ("M" Cable Station and one cable detachment out each morning.) 2 hours Infantry drill in afternoon.	
	28th		Wet morning. Exercises Party & Riding Class out when weather cleared. Games.	

1875 Wt. W593/826 1,000,000 4/15 J.B.C. & A. A.D.S.S./Forms/C. 2118.

WAR DIARY
or
INTELLIGENCE SUMMARY
(Erase heading not required.)

Army Form C. 2118

Place	Date	Hour	Summary of Events and Information	Remarks and references to Appendices
TILQUES	from 28th (cont'd)		N.C.Os - not working under Capt. Hayes Long, 2/Lt. Phillips going lectus on the Fullerphone to men of No. 4 Sect: (1st Inf Bde) and Battalion Signal Officers of that Brigade.	
	29th		Two cable detachments and Riding Class out in morning. Infantry still in cantonments followed by 2/Lt Hastings Buggins etc. to Tilques in afternoon. 2/Lt Phillips taking class of officers + N.C.Os in instruments and morning.	
	30th		Two cable detachments and Riding Class out in morning. Infantry still in cantonments and in afternoon class in Fullerphone. Capt Hayes Long took party of 1 N.C.O. + 2 men to Recruit Depot near CAESTRE the evening, into try back 6 horses the following morning. Division under 6 hours notice to move (by train) from midday this day.	

[signature] Capt. R.E.
COMMANDING 2nd SIGNAL COMPANY R.E.

3rd Divisional Engineers.

3RD SIGNAL COMPANY R.E.

JULY 1916.

WAR DIARY or INTELLIGENCE SUMMARY

Army Form C. 2118
Vol 13
3rd Signal Company, R.E.

Place	Date	Hour	Summary of Events and Information	Remarks and references to Appendices
TILQUES	1916 July 1st		Orders received (about 2 a.m.) for Division to move by rail to join 2nd Corps. Heads of Divisions entraining at ST OMER, WIZERNES & AUDRUICQ. H.Q. & No.1 Section 3rd Signal Coy & M/Cyclists Section entraining at ST OMER at 8 p.m. — train due to leave at 11 p.m. Infantry schools, Transport & Riding Class Signalling class for Sappers during morning. Lorries started 4.30 p.m. 5.30 p.m. Cookhouse & Baggage packed & loaded on at 6.50 p.m. Entrainment started at 8 p.m. Train left at 11 p.m. Capt. Kay, Major Lt. Bruton & 2/Lt. Phillips accompanied Troops on train. Capt. McKK going down to 2nd Corps H.Q. at VILLERS BOCAGE in advance during afternoon.	
LE MEILLARD	2nd		Train reached Regulating Station (CANDAS) about 7 a.m. & was sent on to DOULLENS where Company detrained, detraining being complete by 9 a.m. Company not together then till after 2 p.m. C.C. detachment moved on to MEZEROLLES (6 miles W. of DOULLENS) about noon & arranged to lay four cables from their to their H.Q. at LE MEILLARD. Company Office (telephone & engineered wires) established in an estaminet in MEZEROLLES working to 2nd Corps through General Hays & Civil Post Office. There is- DOULLENS (Somme)	

Army Form C. 2118

WAR DIARY
or
INTELLIGENCE SUMMARY
(Erase heading not required.)

Instructions regarding War Diaries and Intelligence Summaries are contained in F.S. Regs., Part II. and the Staff Manual respectively. Title Pages will be prepared in manuscript.

Place	Date	Hour	Summary of Events and Information	Remarks and references to Appendices
VILLERS BOCAGE	July 2 (cont.)	4 p.m.	Company did not reach LE MEILLARD till about 4 p.m. having encountered a bad bit of road, rising to Brigade Map. One detachment of "M" Coy. per lorries at one arrival to map, then 4 others from LE MEILLARD to meet other detachment. App from 4 others from LE MEILLARD to 2nd Corps about 6 p.m. Line through from LE MEILLARD to 2nd Corps about 6 p.m. Communication to Brigade about under 2 hours notice to move. 8" at BERNEUIL, 9" at BERNAVILLE, 7" at GEZAINCOURT by D.R. Brigade billeted as follows — 8" at BERNEUIL, 9" at BERNAVILLE, 7" at GEZAINCOURT	
FLESSELLES	3rd		Orders issued by Division at 5.30 a.m. for march to VIGNACOURT area (W of VILLERS BOCAGE). Brigade marched at 8.30 a.m. & Div. H.Q. at 2 p.m. Billets as follows — Div. H.Q. 4 A of Bde at FLESSELLES, R. of Bde at VIGNACOURT, 8th Inf. Bde. at NAOURS, H.Q. Div. R.A. at MONTONVILLERS and 76th Inf. Bde. at NAOURS, H.Q. Div. R.A. at MONTONVILLERS and Artillery Brigades in same BETHENCOURT — HALLOY (where there are making facilities under being very scarce in this neighbourhood unfit for stream.) Faulty turn off lines from FLESSELLES to VILLERS BOCAGE caused some trouble, there was got night about 5 p.m. empty to train to march with Divisional Band, who Rays Bangl, & empty to train to march with Divisional Band, who were very slow. Footsloggers did not reach FLESSELLES till 8 p.m.	

1875 Wt. W593/826 1,000,000 4/15 J.B.C. & A. A.D.S.S./Forms/C. 2118.

WAR DIARY or INTELLIGENCE SUMMARY

Army Form C. 2118

Place	Date	Hour	Summary of Events and Information	Remarks and references to Appendices
	July 3rd (Cont.)		Div H.Q. in Chateau at PLESSIELLES. Communication to 2nd Corps & 76th Inf. Bde. by telephone & mounted orderly/orderlies.	
PLESSIELLES	4th		Morning spent in "cleaning up" in camp. Orders received to move late in afternoon. Divisional H.Q. moved to CORBIE, with Brigades in following villages 8th at ALLONVILLE & 9th at POULAINVILLE & 76th at COISY, Artillery at DAOURS. Communication to Brigades by D.R. Division now under 13th Corps. Established subsidiary Signal Office in 13th Corps Office at CORBIE.	
CORBIE	5th		Brigades moved Eastward at night to following positions. 8th Bde. Group (A Group) to CORBIE & VAUX, 9th Bde. Group (B Group) to LAHOUSSOYE, 76th Bde. Group (C Group) to FRANVILLERS. Div H.Q. remained at CORBIE.	
	6th		Brigades continued to march Eastward – A Group & C Group to BOIS LES CELESTINS & B Group to MORLANCOURT – marching by night. Div H.Q. still at CORBIE	
	7th		8th Inf. Bde. marched up to BRAY and relieved the 53rd Inf. Bde. of 18th Division that night. Other Brigades & Div. H.Q. remained in same position	

WAR DIARY or INTELLIGENCE SUMMARY

Army Form C. 2118

Place	Date	Hour	Summary of Events and Information	Remarks and references to Appendices
CORBIE BRAY	July 8th		Division H.Q. moved to 18th Div. dngnts N. of BRAY during morning & 9th & 76th Bdes. took over remainder of 18th Div. line, positions of Brigades being 9th on Left, 8th in Centre & 76th on Right. Brigade H.Q. as follows – 9th in CORBIE, 8th in Battle H.Q. in dngnts (German) North of CORBIE & 76th in BILLON WOOD. Work commenced at once on pushing cable forward. 2/Lt. Phillips with party of Royal Scots (1 Company) dug trench & buried 2 pairs D5 cable from 8th Bde. Battle H.Q. back to No. 1 Report Centre (most forward point of existing buried lines).	
	9th		Work continued on lines to new Brigade Battle H.Q's & lines forward from there to trenches. 2/Lt. Phillips with 2 Companies Infantry recommenced dug trench & laid & buried D5 cable forward from 8th Bde. Battle H.Q. to top of ridge near MONTAUBAN. Lt. Ramsay (9th Bde.) buried cables forward from his Bde. Battle H.Q. He (9th Bde.) buried cables forward from Battalion Battle H.Q. (during night). Three Brigades laid cables from CATERPILLAR WOOD, Capt. Page-Roy to forward line in BILLON WOOD, in former place of with cable detachment laid lines from old 54th Bde. H.Q. and BRONFAY FARM) to join lines in BILLON WOOD, in another line for Gunners proposed as Divisional Battle H.Q. – was another line for Gunners was BRONFAY FARM. 2/Lt. Barclay very busy with German Communications as all the Artillery of 18th Div. as well as our own is working over mm cations as well as all the Artillery of 18th Div. as well as our own is working over (some 96 guns). C.R.A.	

Army Form C. 2118

WAR DIARY
or
INTELLIGENCE SUMMARY

(Erase heading not required.)

Instructions regarding War Diaries and Intelligence Summaries are contained in F.S. Regs., Part II. and the Staff Manual respectively. Title Pages will be prepared in manuscript.

Place	Date	Hour	Summary of Events and Information	Remarks and references to Appendices
BRAY	July 10 to 11th to 13th		Work continued on laying out and digging in cables (mostly 3 ft. trenches & not filled in) connecting up new Brigade H.Q's to each other & to supporting artillery groups. Old 54th Inf. Bde. H.Q. just North of BRONFAY FARM selected as Battle H.Q. for the division. Telephone Exchange installed there and airlines (3 twin + 1 single) run from present Div. H.Q. (near BRAY) to there by 13 Corps Signals.

Work continued on same lines. 2/Lt. Phillips superintending a working party of about 2 Companies (for digging trenches) each day. Sites chosen for Visual Stations (receiving) on MONTAUBAN Ridge, to work with Battalions when they advance to the BAZENTIN-LE-GRAND ridge. Divisional Visual Station also established on ALBERT - PERONNE road, North of Sig.l Report Centre at BRONFAY FARM. At the last moment (afternoon of 13th) the 76th Inf. Bde. were withdrawn from our right & held in reserve (H.Q. near CARNOY), so that a lot of our work on cables in the Western part of the 27th Inf. Bde. (9th Division) on our right (however as a present to the same cause!) 40 trigger were sent to 9 Inf. Bde. - were it is all in the same cause!) 16 to 8 Inf. Bde., 16 to 9 Inf. Bde. morning of 13th & distributed thus 16 to 8 Inf. Bde., & 4 to 76th Inf. Bde. "PL" Wireless Station at 9th Inf. Bde. H.Q. & "PK" Station held in reserve at Div. Battle H.Q. Office at latter place (for R. Staff) being left at H.Q. near BRAY | |

Army Form C. 2118

WAR DIARY
or
INTELLIGENCE SUMMARY
(Erase heading not required.)

Instructions regarding War Diaries and Intelligence Summaries are contained in F.S. Regs., Part II. and the Staff Manual respectively. Title Pages will be prepared in manuscript.

Place	Date	Hour	Summary of Events and Information	Remarks and references to Appendices
BRAY	July 14th		After preliminary bombardment attack was launched at 3.25 a.m. with great success. The 8th Inf. Bde. were held up by wire on the right & suffered fairly heavily, but the 9th Inf. Bde. captured BAZENTIN-LE-GRAND with comparatively small losses. Good visual signalling in 8th Bde. (first message from E. Yorks, stating they were held up by wire, came through by lamp about 3.40). Zones had to be by air, were held well during day & formed lines to CATERPILLAR SMASH. WOOD VALLEY & those were sent out by Battalions as they advanced also held quite well. In the afternoon 8th Inf. Bde. established H.Q. at Quarry North of MONTAUBAN (in the valley) & "Pt." Wireless Station was erected there. In the evening 9th Inf. Bde. H.Q. moved from their H.Q. in "the LOOP" (in the old German trenches North of CARNOY) to a new position in the valley N.W. of MONTAUBAN.	
	15th		Work commenced in extending lines (in trenches) formerly laid forward from 8th Inf. Bde. H.Q. on the MONTAUBAN RIDGE to CATERPILLAR WOOD Valley. 2/Lt. Phillips with party of 2 Companies digging trenches for these lines & a train of D6 cable lines laid to new 9th Inf. Bde. H.Q. Lt. Hett (XX Cable section) went up to re-cover at BRAY with this section to commence the cable runs of the Corps already out & not going to forward movement.	

WAR DIARY or INTELLIGENCE SUMMARY

Army Form C. 2118

Place	Date	Hour	Summary of Events and Information	Remarks and references to Appendices
BRAY	July 16th to 18th		Very busy days laying cable (some in trenches & some across country). Positions of Infantry & Artillery Brigades continually varying, & Lt. of German artillery and other new cable had to be put out. Infantry causing a lot of trouble in maintenance of lines, especially in the neighbourhood of CATERPILLAR WOOD VALLEY and at MONTAUBAN.	
	19th		Lt. Hill, commanding No. 2 Section (76th Inf. Bde.) was killed by shell near the Dummy in CATERPILLAR WOOD VALLEY, & his wiring party Officer & the next felt his loss keenly. Divisional Cable H.Q. moved in the evening to COPSE 5 & took over from the 9th Div. 2/Lt. Phillips went to 76th Inf. Bde. to take on command of No. 2 Section.	
	20th to 24		Very busy days, trying to "sort out" and tidy up lines in Offices & learn the rather complicated network out of doors. There were difficulties experienced in keeping lines through, owing to increased activity of enemy's artillery. Every opportunity taken of salving cable & collecting empty drums & other regtl. stores. Brigades lost heavily in attacks on DELVILLE WOOD and LONGUEVAL. (both G.R. and Brigade sections) was very busy during this time as regards casualties as the shelling — especially in MONTAUBAN & LONGUEVAL was very heavy at times.	

WAR DIARY
or
INTELLIGENCE SUMMARY

Army Form C. 2118

Place	Date	Hour	Summary of Events and Information	Remarks and references to Appendices
BRAY	July 24th		2/Lt. P.D. Cassott-Sutherland R.E. joined the unit as Supernumerary Officer (from 13th Corps Signals) vice 2/Lt. Phillips, now commanding No. 2 Section.	
	25th		Division relieved by 2nd Division, the "handing over" of lines, wireless + wireless stations etc. working very smoothly. G. Staff returned from Battle H.Q. at B COPSE to dugouts at BRAY while Brigades bivouacked at HAPPY VALLEY (8th), SAND PITS (9th) and BOIS DE TAILLES. Communication by wire via 2nd Div. Rear H.Q. at the CITADEL. Command of Divisional area handed over 6.30 p.m. 8th Inf.	
	26th		Day spent in "cleaning up" after a strenuous fortnight of warfare. Bde. moved to MEAULTE in the evening.	
TREUX	27th		Divisional H.Q. moved to TREUX, handing over the dugouts at BRAY to the French (a cable section from 13th Corps Signals being left in the dugouts through there). H.Q. at TREUX taken on from 55th Division, who were moving up nearer the front (in Corps Reserve). 9th Inf. Bde. moved to VILLE-SUR-ANCRE. Communication to them by ████████. No line available at present to 8th Inf. Bde. at	

Army Form C. 2118.

WAR DIARY
or
INTELLIGENCE SUMMARY.
(Erase heading not required.)

Hour, Date, Place	Summary of Events and Information	Remarks and references to Appendices
July 27th (cont.)	MEAULTE, as this area had only just been handed over from 15th to 13th Corps. 76th Inf. Bde. still at BOIS DE TAILLES in communication to them by men through 55th Division at the CITADEL.	
28th	Morning spent in settling down in camp and gaining of original offices & various lines running therefrom in various directions (not used in the way of signals — to identify lines, no linesman sent out to repair). Wireless detachments being instructed in "section of winds" to "procedure" by Cpl. McNair. 13th Corps still unable to produce any line to MEAULTE. Day & still having heard & took from TREUX to DERNANCOURT, there were put through & two with attempts to find a pair of cables in the evening for the 16th place to MEAULTE, also being through, about 9 pm. 76th Inf. Bde. moved in to MÉRICOURT taking th[e] place of the 16th Inf. Bde., communication by rotating horse of lines. Signal Clerks (44 men) from Battalion accepted.	
29th	Clean arms and clothing inspection followed by Ride (for Operators & a few D.Rs.) & Exercise Wireless station	

Army Form C. 2118.

WAR DIARY
or
INTELLIGENCE SUMMARY.
(Erase heading not required.)

Instructions regarding War Diaries and Intelligence Summaries are contained in F.S. Regs., Part II. and the Staff Manual respectively. Title pages will be prepared in manuscript.

Hour, Date, Place	Summary of Events and Information	Remarks and references to Appendices
TREUX July 29th (cont.)	Another one station going out about a mile or nothing for the other, which stayed in camp. Signal Class worked onto three signals & evening practice, flag whistle.	
" 30th	Sunday. Work for Signal Class and Wireless detachments during morning. Afternoon free. Church parade service on grass in front of Chateau at 6 p.m.	
" 31st	Unity of linesmen staying the ring-lead lines, some of which were in a bad state of repair. Work for Signal Class, Wireless detachments, Operators R & G's on 29th inst. Ring out weather such as one we came to TREUX still continues, making attempts at stream for bathing, making attempts.	

M. H. T. Webb
CAPT. R.E.
COMMANDING 3rd SIGNAL COMPANY R.E.

3rd Divisional Engineers

3rd DIVISIONAL SIGNAL COMPANY R. E.

AUGUST 1 9 1 6

A.A. & Q.M.G.
3rd Div.

Herewith War Diary for
this unit for August, 1916

[signature]
CAPT. R.E.
COMMANDING 3rd SIGNAL COMPANY R.E.

1.9.16

Army Form C. 2118.

WAR DIARY
or
INTELLIGENCE SUMMARY.
(Erase heading not required.)

3rd Signal Company R.E.
3rd Division

Instructions regarding War Diaries and Intelligence Summaries are contained in F.S. Regs., Part II. and the Staff Manual respectively. Title pages will be prepared in manuscript.

Hour, Date, Place	Summary of Events and Information	Remarks and references to Appendices
TREUX 1916 August 1st	Party of linesmen under Sergt. Hatter building airline (fair) from railway at DERNANCOURT to MÉAULTE to replace cable put out on 28th ult. Work for Wireless detachments, Rooting Class, & Despatch Riding Class as before. General Foster paid short visit in the evening.	Vol 14
" 2nd	Party of linesmen noting up cable between DERNANCOURT and MÉAULTE. Work for remainder as before.	
" 3rd	Cable detachment under Sergt. Wooler out practising. Work for remainder as usual.	
" 4th	Work as on previous day (no cable detachment out). Party of N.C.O.s & men granted leave to visit AMIENS, travelling by train from MÉRICOURT. 3rd Div. Train Horse Show. Capt. NEOR & 2nd Lieut. PHILLIPS on The Bay & Roan respectively, won 1st & 2nd prizes in jumping. Lieut. Smith won 1st & 2nd prizes in the company open event. Lieut. Pirkhan & 2nd Lieut. W.O. Lloyd. Lieut. Stratton won prizes in light work.	
" 5th	Cable detachment practising work: Signal Class as before ditto.	

(73989) W4141—463. 400,000. 9/14. H.&J.Ltd. Forms/C. 2118/10.

WAR DIARY
or
INTELLIGENCE SUMMARY.
(Erase heading not required.)

Army Form C. 2118.

Instructions regarding War Diaries and Intelligence Summaries are contained in F.S. Regs., Part II. and the Staff Manual respectively. Title pages will be prepared in manuscript.

Hour, Date, Place	Summary of Events and Information	Remarks and references to Appendices
TREUX. Aug 6th	Advance party left for SUTTON AND FELIX. 4th SAMUEL MARTIN. 4 days camp before starting for the front. Eventually moving to CORBIE, 5 days later on to CHAMPS CAMP.	
Aug. 7th	One cable detachment out as usual. Signal Class went to Divisional Staff. Went for manoeuvres in afternoon – chiefly to get Capt. Hebb & 2/Lt.	
VILLE-SOUS-CORBIE	in the change of weather. Phillips returned from PARIS. Briggs, Leonard & Roy on command of others in general. Hallam going to 5 Corps.	
8th	W.K. for signal class. Riding class as before. Weather funeral. Waiting on orders as if nothing were going to 4 Army having expected the Signal station - ours to	
9th	an arrivals journey tomorrow morning. One cable detachment out. Work by manuals as usual. Inspection of arms 2 pm Officers.	
10th	High as a furnace day. Rain fell today – first time for some three weeks.	

Army Form C. 2118.

WAR DIARY
or
INTELLIGENCE SUMMARY.
(Erase heading not required.)

Instructions regarding War Diaries and Intelligence Summaries are contained in F. S. Regs., Part II. and the Staff Manual respectively. Title pages will be prepared in manuscript.

Hour, Date, Place	Summary of Events and Information	Remarks and references to Appendices
TREUX August 11th	Work as previous day. Half an hour's Infantry drill at 8.30 a.m. handed over to command of Division, 9th and 76th Inf. Bde. moved to SANDPITS during the day. Divis: Ramage & Martyn & 2/Lt C- Sutherland returned from 4 days course in Special Buzzer at Cavalry Reserve Bngade at DAOURS	
BRAY 12th	Divisional H.Q. moved to FORKED TREE (on BRAY – ALBERT road). 8th Inf. Bde. moved to HAPPY VALLEY. Communication to Corps by 2 telephone lines (London superimposed on one) and to each Bde. by a telephone pair with double superposed	
" 13th	Sunday. Preparations made for improving existing communication from our future Battle H.Q. (at present occupied by 55th Divn) at BILLON COPSE to the front — i.e. Eastwards.	

(73989) W4141—463. 400,000. 9/14. H.&J.Ltd. Forms/C. 2118/10.

WAR DIARY
or
INTELLIGENCE SUMMARY.
(Erase heading not required.)

Army Form C. 2118.

Instructions regarding War Diaries and Intelligence Summaries are contained in F.S. Regs., Part II. and the Staff Manual respectively. Title pages will be prepared in manuscript.

Hour, Date, Place	Summary of Events and Information	Remarks and references to Appendices
BRAY August 14th	Party of 400 men from 8th Inf. Bde. working under 2/Lt. Cruett-Sutherland, digging trench (3 ft) from MACHINE GUN WOOD (N. of MARICOURT) to near Bde. H.Q. (they began construction about North of FAVIÈRE WOOD. Party trying to join up from D5 without not much Staff sent up to give Battn H.Q. to compass taking over. Unfortunately two men of no 1 or no 2 Wireless detachments were killed while on their way up to Wireless Station N. of FAVIÈRE WOOD. 9th & 28th Inf. Bde. moved to dugouts in CARNOY VALLEY & 8 Inf. Bde. 2 GREAT BEAR COPSE	
" 15th	Trench completed and cables put through from MACHINE GUN WOOD to new Bde. H.Q. French left flank no Corps Artillery wished it; now it too heavy ammo of their rifles & machine Cable detachment laid line for R.A. Division Officer at BILLON COPSE taken over from 55th Div.	
" 16	New Brigade H.Q. more or less completed. Lines brought into dugouts & stores sent up there during morning. The Brigade (9th & 76th) attached nothing worthy of mention, from stores being by the time. 8th Inf. Bde. moved up to office in CARNOY 5.30 p.m. VALLEY vacated by 76th Inf. Bde.	

Army Form C. 2118.

WAR DIARY
or
INTELLIGENCE SUMMARY
(Erase heading not required.)

Instructions regarding War Diaries and Intelligence Summaries are contained in F. S. Regs., Part II. and the Staff Manual respectively. Title Pages will be prepared in manuscript.

Place	Date	Hour	Summary of Events and Information	Remarks and references to Appendices
BRAY	1916 August 17		Line to 9th & 7th Bde HQs being improved and another 2 pairs between Divnl. and "CARNOY CUTTING" Office (8th Inf. Bde.) being put through.	
	18th		Line from BRIQUETERIE found to Bde. HQs was totally cut by shell fire taken back from BRIQUETERIE due in bad condition and somewhat south, maintaining Linesmen were withdrawn from there. Communication by air route (via MACHINE GUN WOOD and FAVIÈRE WOOD) was satisfactory.	
	19th		35 Division asked to relieve us. Linesmen came out, attempt made by us to move taken along lines by an Linesmen Officer, staff arrived in afternoon. Handing over went very smoothly. 75th Inf. Bde. when relieved moved detachment rested up to HAPPY VALLEY & 7th Inf. Bde. to CITADEL several miles cable in neighbourhood of BILLON COPSE.	
	20th		Sunday. 8th Inf. Bde. moved from CARNOY CUTTING to SANDPITS, 14 Corps H.Q. moved from ETINEHEM at 4 p.m. & opened at new camp near MÉAULTE; this change was made on account of unhealthy condition of ETINEHEM.	

Army Form C. 2118.

WAR DIARY
or
INTELLIGENCE SUMMARY

(Erase heading not required.)

Instructions regarding War Diaries and Intelligence Summaries are contained in F. S. Regs., Part II and the Staff Manual respectively. Title Pages will be prepared in manuscript.

Place	Date	Hour	Summary of Events and Information	Remarks and references to Appendices
TREUX	1916 August 21st		20th Division moved from TREUX during morning and took up places at FORMED TREE Camp as Corps Reserve. Divisional H.Q. opened at TREUX with 8th Inf. Bde. at MEAULTE, 7th at VILLE-SOUS-CORBIE and 76th at MORLANCOURT.	
	22nd		Horse transport of Division marched to FLESSELLES. Unit marched with Div. H.Q. (mounted portion) under Capt. Hope Carey. Small office staff stayed at TREUX till following day.	
BERNAVILLE	23rd		Dismounted units of Division entrained at MERICOURT. Division moving to BERNAVILLE area. Div. H.Q. established at that village with 8th Inf. Bde. at RIBEAUCOURT, 7th at FIENVILLERS and 76th at LE MEILLARD. Communication by telegraph & telephone to 13th Corps H.Q. at DOMART-EN-PONTHIEU.	
	24th		"Clean arms" inspection and than men then employed cleaning wagons & harness.	
FROHEN-LE-GRAND	25th		Div. H.Q. moved to FROHEN-LE-GRAND with 8th Inf. Bde. at VACANS, 9th at REMAISNIL and 76th at BOUBERS-SUR-CANCHE. Communication to 3rd Army (ST POL) by telephone (with another superimposed () & to Brigades by D.R.	

WAR DIARY
or
INTELLIGENCE SUMMARY
(Erase heading not required.)

Army Form C. 2118.

Place	Date	Hour	Summary of Events and Information	Remarks and references to Appendices
FLERS	26th		Div. H.Q. moved to FLERS with 8th Inf. Bde. at BLANGERMONT, 9th at BUNEVILLE and 76th at CROIX. Communication to 3rd Army by telephone (with small exchange) & to Brigades by D.R.	
MONCHY-CAYEUX	27th		Div. H.Q. moved to MONCHY-CAYEUX, with 8th Inf. Bde. at TANGRY, 9th at COMTÉVILLE and 76th at EQUIRRE. Division was under orders for 1st Corps at midday. Army lines extended for a telephone pair (with supple instruments) to MONCHY-CAYEUX. Division is in a telephone pair (with supple instruments) to 1st Corps (at LABUISSIÈRE). Communication to Brigades by D.R.	
NOEUX-LES-MINES	28th		Div. H.Q. moved to NOEUX-LES-MINES, 8th Inf. Bde. to RUITZ, 75th to TANGRY, the 9th remaining at CONTEVILLE. Communication to 1st Corps by 2 telephone pairs to 1 wonder line, with telephones at 8th & 9th divisions. Small office left behind at MONCHY-CAYEUX to act as staff office, & D.R. with 9th & 76th Inf. Bdes., to telephone & hear communication from there to our new Div. H.Q.	
	29th		Day spent in settling down into new office & camp at NOEUX-LES-MINES and in endeavouring to trace out lines left in rested "DA" office in MAZINGARBE with a view to arranging communication between the H.Q.	

Army Form C. 2118.

WAR DIARY
or
INTELLIGENCE SUMMARY

(Erase heading not required.)

Instructions regarding War Diaries and Intelligence Summaries are contained in F. S. Regs., Part II and the Staff Manual respectively. Title Pages will be prepared in manuscript.

Place	Date	Hour	Summary of Events and Information	Remarks and references to Appendices
NOEUX- -LES-MINES	1916 August 29th (cont)		To the "Corporate Artillery 3rd Group" in NOEUX-LES-MINES and the two groups of Artillery ("HULLUCH" and "14 Bis") in MAZINGARBE. Rather a violent thunderstorm in the afternoon, with very heavy fall of rain, the streets of NOEUX-LES-MINES being turned into rivers & many of the houses flooded out.	
	30th		Party of linesmen and gun-operators sent off in lorry to MAZINGARBE Exchange to connect up H.Q. there and first rear 2/Lt. Walters land performing duties of Signal Officer to the Corporate Divisional Artillery, as 2/Lt. Barclay was still with our Division left behind on the SOMME. 9th M. Bde moved to MAREE-LES-MINES & relieve 11th Corps things & C4.	
	31st		Work continued on Artillery communications. Small party available to lay lines from PHILOSOPHE CHATEAU to connect to buried cable at MAZINGARBE CHATEAU (proposed H.Q. for 76th Inf. Bde.), the 112th Inf. Bde. H.Q being in the former place & their personal lines running from there. The 8th Inf. Bde. took on from the 111th Inf. Bde. during the day; Bde. H.Q. at PHILOSOPHE (very next signal Offices there) 76th Inf. Bde. moved into NOEUX-LES-MINES & were absorbing lines to MAZIN-GARBE Exchange in the evening; we still holding (Inc) lines between there and MAZINGARBE CHATEAU.	

H.M. ??
CAPT., R.E.
COMMANDING 3rd SIGNAL COMPANY R.E.

3rd Divisional Engineers.

3RD SIGNAL COMPANY R.E.

SEPTEMBER 1916.

Army Form C. 2118.

3rd Signal Company R.E.
3rd Division

WAR DIARY
or
INTELLIGENCE SUMMARY

(Erase heading not required.)

Instructions regarding War Diaries and Intelligence Summaries are contained in F. S. Regs., Part II. and the Staff Manual respectively. Title Pages will be prepared in manuscript.

Place	Date	Hour	Summary of Events and Information	Remarks and references to Appendices
NOEUX-LES-MINES	1916 September 1st		Work continued at MAZINGARBE, clearing up neighbourhood of "Exchange" this and making necessary preparations for 76 Inf. Bde. H.Q. being into MAZINGARBE CHATEAU. During the day the Brigadier changing his mind at the last moment the Brigade moved into PHILO-SOPHE CHATEAU.	
	2nd		Work in camp at NOEUX-LES-MINES preparing to build huts also improving surface of ground (filling in holes &c.) 1 B Inf. Bde. moved into NOEUX-LES-MINES.	
	3rd		Sunday. Service in Cinema Hall, NOEUX-LES-MINES at 7.30 a.m & 6 p.m.	
	4th		Small detachment working in area East of VERMELLES – PHILOSOPHE road, clearing cable. Work in camp continued. Subaltern & signals replacing some bad lines in our right sector (76th Inf. Bde.) just North of LOOS.	
	5th		Work continued clearing cable. Col. Moore (1st Army Signals) found a visit during the morning.	

Army Form C. 2118.

WAR DIARY
or
INTELLIGENCE SUMMARY
(Erase heading not required.)

Instructions regarding War Diaries and Intelligence Summaries are contained in F. S. Regs., Part II. and the Staff Manual respectively. Title Pages will be prepared in manuscript.

Place	Date	Hour	Summary of Events and Information	Remarks and references to Appendices
NOEUX-LES-MINES	1916 Septmbr 6th		Extensive work in camp – building huts, forge, stores etc., improving drains, filling hollows in ground with slag, etc.	
	7th		Work in camp continued.	
	8th		As in previous day.	
	9th		Party laid pair of D5 cables between FOSSE 3 (R.A. Exchange – "Hennes") to Got Box near PHILOSOPHE to give direct communication from LA HAIE O.P. Exchange to the Heavy Artillery. Work in and continued to West of Company in NOEUX-LES-MINES in the afternoon.	
	10th		Sunday. Service in the last laundry; seven denied (Communion) in YMCA Hut at Parade of Company (inch No 3 Section from 8th Jfr Bde) in camp at 11 a.m. Inspection of Military Medal by G.O.C. Division to Sapper Bullot & Kerry for good work as linesmen.	
	11th		Party clearing lines in area East of PHILOSOPHE-VERMELLES road.	
	12th		Party laying short pohel-cable line near FOSSE 3 for Gunners. Ind party came to see Gunner communications out (3rd Div.) Gunners having come up from the SOMME & being in MARLES-LES-MINES for a few days.	

Army Form C. 2118.

WAR DIARY
or
INTELLIGENCE SUMMARY

(Erase heading not required.)

Instructions regarding War Diaries and Intelligence Summaries are contained in F. S. Regs., Part II. and the Staff Manual respectively. Title Pages will be prepared in manuscript.

Place	Date	Hour	Summary of Events and Information	Remarks and references to Appendices
NOEUX-LES-MINES	1916 September 13th		Work in camp continued. 8th Inf. Batt. tendency small parties of men each day to Zest LAZZELL (1st Corps Signals) for work on buried cables in our Northern sector.	
	14th		Work as in previous day.	
	15th		Work as in previous day. Col. Moore (1st Army Signals) paid a visit during the morning.	
	16th		Party laying cable pair (D5 wire) along trenches from "FOUNTAIN" O.P. Exchange to Zest Box on LE RUTOIRE burial route, to connect with pair (on this route) from Zest Box (in PONT STREET) to "LA HAIE" O.P. Exchange (in HAY ALLEY). This was necessitated by Corps orders to the effect that O.P. Exchanges must be connected laterally.	
	17th		Sunday. Church services as for last Sunday.	
	18th		Very wet day.	
	19th		Party erecting airline from Divn. Signal Office to 8th Inf. Batt. transport lines (about ½ mile). Orders received for Capt. Grey-Parry to go to the	

WAR DIARY or INTELLIGENCE SUMMARY

Army Form C. 2118.

Place	Date	Hour	Summary of Events and Information	Remarks and references to Appendices
NOEUX-LES-MINES	1916 September 19		Signal Service Training Centre at BLETCHLEY to act as Instructor.	
	20th		Orders issued for the Sectors to move to Training Area south of AIRE, with a view to "more active operations", the Divisions on our Right and Left (40th & 18th respectively) taking over the two sectors of the line held by us (known as "14 BIS" and "HULLUCH"), our Artillery also being retained by the Artillery of these two Divisions.	
	21st		Capt. Hope Barry & left for England (Training Centre, BLETCHLEY) and Lieut. C. Wright, from 11th Corps Signals came in his place. 8th Inf. Bde. moved from NOEUX-LES-MINES to ALLOUAGNE & 9th Inf. Bde. was relieved by Bde. of 8th Divn in HULLUCH sector from NOEUX-LES-MINES to ALLOUAGNE.	
BOMY	22nd		Company mounted under Lieut. Wright (at 8.15 a.m.) for BOMY. On arrival Battalion Signallers (some 40 men) arrived on lorries borrowed from Corps Signals. 8th Inf. Bde. moved to Training Area (H.Q. at THEROUANNE), 9th Inf. Bde. moved from NOEUX-LES-MINES to ALLOUAGNE & 76th Inf. Bde. was relieved by a Brigade of 40th Divn in the 14 BIS Section. Communication from BOMY to Divnl H.Q. (at LILLERS) by telephone with numerous interruptions.	
	23rd		8th Inf. Bde. moved then H.Q. to UPEN D'AVAL (West of THEROUANNE), 9th Inf. Bde. moved to Training Area with H.Q. at ERNY-ST-JULIEN and 76th Inf. Bde.	

Army Form C. 2118.

WAR DIARY
or
INTELLIGENCE SUMMARY
(Erase heading not required.)

Instructions regarding War Diaries and Intelligence Summaries are contained in F. S. Regs., Part II. and the Staff Manual respectively. Title Pages will be prepared in manuscript.

Place	Date	Hour	Summary of Events and Information	Remarks and references to Appendices
BOMY	1916 September		moved from NOEUX-LES-MINES to ALLOUAGNE, proceeding	
	24th		Work at BOMY — settling down — new camps, fitting up Signal Office, Electric Light, etc. "Clam arm" experiments to rifle circuits in afternoon. Signalling class working at buzzer, helio, etc. Recet of six stove. Fitting huts, laying down new cables across in BOMY.	
			Sunday. Services in BOMY at 8 a.m & 6 p.m. Cavity land hair cables cuns connected to "ERNY - ST-JULIEN", to 2nd Inf. Bde. H.Q. and to VIEUX DAVAL, 8" detachment laid pair of cable from DELETTE to BOMY, with party permanent lines (pair) from former place to BOMY. 2nd Inf. Bde. moved its drawing then with H.Q. at ESTRÉE BLANCHE. 76th Inf. Bde. moved to their Brigade Hq. permanent-pair from BOMY. Communication to their Brigade by telephone made operates airframes. All these Brigades are in telephone with permanter-sympostum. 32nd Artillery moved from NOEUX-LES-MINES to LABEUVRIÈRE (W of BETHUNE)	
	25th		Some cable detachments clearing up after work. Arms stuck to anything treatments in afternoon. Artillery moved to from south of ST QUENTIN (east of AIRE).	
	26th		Same work as previous day. 1st Army Signals built line to our Artillery H.Q. connecting to same Park as that being used by 7th half Coln.	

WAR DIARY
or
INTELLIGENCE SUMMARY

Army Form C. 2118.

Place	Date	Hour	Summary of Events and Information	Remarks and references to Appendices
BONNY	1916 September 27th		Two cable detachments out during morning. Party fitting cable from ST-JULIEN (9" H. Bde. H.A.) in files. 50 mm. to Company cart in wagon to FLÉCHINELLE to bathe at Divisional Baths.	
	28th		Same programme as previous day. Another 50 men went to Divisional Baths. Divisional Routine Orders contained notice of removal of the Military Cross to 2/Lt. Ramage (No.3 Section) for work on the SOMME during July & August.	
	29th		Wet morning. Lectures (in village school) to Company on Musketry & Horsemaster -ship. Short exercise for horses later in when fine. Commenced Musketry Course in the afternoon on 30 yards range near ploughing village of PETIGNY. "Grouping" practice first.	
	30th		Two Cable detachments out during morning. Musketry Course continued in afternoon — same practice as previous day. Aeroplane from No.2 Squadron R.F.C. practiced communication with Infantry of 5th Bde. from near COYECQUE. aeroplane signalling with Klaxon in the afternoon. Brigade & Battalion H.Qs. with ground sheets & "panels" & Klaxons using flares. Aeroplane dropped map at Divisional H.Q.	

N.W.T.Hill
CAPT. R.E.
COMMANDING 5th SIGNAL COMPANY R.E.

3rd Divisional Engineers.

3RD SIGNAL COMPANY R.E.

OCTOBER 1916.

Army Form C. 2118.

Vol /6
3rd Signal Company R.E.

WAR DIARY
or
INTELLIGENCE SUMMARY
(Erase heading not required.)

Instructions regarding War Diaries and Intelligence Summaries are contained in F.S. Regs., Part II. and the Staff Manual respectively. Title Pages will be prepared in manuscript.

Place	Date	Hour	Summary of Events and Information	Remarks and references to Appendices
BOMY	1916 October 1st		Sunday. Attention to "Winter Time" effected at 1 a.m. - watches & clocks being put back one hour. Church Services in village at 7.30 a.m. & 6 p.m. Presentation of 1 D.C.M. and 2 Military Medals to members of the Company by the G.O.C. Division in the morning, Nos. 3 & 4 Sections of the Company being also present on parade. Conference of Brigade & Battalion Commanders, Staff, etc. (under G.O.C. Division) in the afternoon preparatory to "Attack Scheme" which it is proposed to carry out at end of training period.	
	2nd		Half the Company went to rifle range in the morning to continue Musketry Course (1 deliberate + 1 Rapid practice). Wet afternoon.	
	3rd		Wet morning. Practice attack by Division which was to have taken place on this day was cancelled. Exercise for horses during morning. Musketry in the afternoon, the weather having cleared up by then.	
	4th		"Attack" scheme took place in the morning on Plateau N. of ERNY-ST-JULIEN, followed by a demonstration of rapid fire by Trench Mortars & Stokes guns.	

Army Form C. 2118.

WAR DIARY
or
INTELLIGENCE SUMMARY

(Erase heading not required.)

Instructions regarding War Diaries and Intelligence Summaries are contained in F.S. Regs., Part II. and the Staff Manual respectively. Title Pages will be prepared in manuscript.

Place	Date	Hour	Summary of Events and Information	Remarks and references to Appendices
BOMY	1916 October 5th		Musketry practice for M.C.Os in afternoon. Company getting ready for move on following day.	
MONCHY- CAYEUX	5th		Divisional H.Q. moved to MONCHY-CAYEUX, with 8th Inf. Bde. at ERUIRRE, 9th at HERNICOURT + 76th at BOYAVAL and R.A. at WAVRANS. Communication by telephone, with sounder superimposed, to 1st Army.	
	6th		Div. H.Q. remained at MONCHY-CAYEUX with Infantry of Brigades in the neighbourhood. All transport and mounted troops of the Division marched under the C.R.A. to ETREE-WAMIN.	
BERTRANCOURT	7th		Div. H.Q. moved to camp at BERTRANCOURT (just vacated by 2nd Div. H.Q.) Infantry and dismounted troops of Division came by train from ST POL to neighbourhood of ACHEUX, transport & mounted troops marching by road and joining them. 8th Inf. Bde. Q.S. as follows — 8th at LEALVILLERS, 9th at BERTRANCOURT + 76th at ARQUEVES. R.A. H.Q. was at ARQUEVES. until night when they moved to Div. H.Q. at BERTRANCOURT. Communication from latter place to 5th Corps, at ACHEUX, by telephone, with sounder superimposed. Telephone to 9th Inf. Bde. H.Q. in camp close by.	

2449 Wt. W14957/M90 750,000 1/16 J.B.C. & A. Forms/C.2118/12.

Army Form C. 2118.

WAR DIARY
or
INTELLIGENCE SUMMARY
(Erase heading not required.)

Place	Date	Hour	Summary of Events and Information	Remarks and references to Appendices
BERTRANCOURT	1916 October 8th		Sunday. Party of 6 linesmen sent to 5th Corps Signals for jointing lead covered cable on new trunk route in tunnel. Very wet day & camp got very muddy. 9th Inf. Bde. took over northern half of sector being held by 5th Inf. Bde. (opposite SERRE village); Bde. H.Q. at BEAUSSART. 8th Inf. Bde. H.Q. also established in BEAUSSART. In the evening Communication to each of these Bdes by telephone with route superimposed (on trunk route) —————— also telephone to 76th Lgt. Bde.M.G. camp at BERTRANCOURT. Church service in one of the huts in Signal Camp (with Divisional Band) at 6 P.M. — on late Chaplain (now Senior Chaplain, 5th Corps) taking the service.	
	9th		Same Party of men sent to 5th Corps Signals to continue jointing work. Another party laying 2 cable pairs (trunk (D3)) along CENTRAL AVENUE C.T. from present Gunners Exchange North of COLINCAMPS to join to trunk route to proposed advanced Divisional H.Q. from cable in neighbourhood of our camp at BERTRANCOURT laddess the moist higher to allow passage of some Tanks, which propose to walk through in a night or two.	
	10th		Party continued jointing work on trunk cable. Party also continued work	

Army Form C. 2118.

WAR DIARY
or
INTELLIGENCE SUMMARY

(Erase heading not required.)

Instructions regarding War Diaries and Intelligence Summaries are contained in F. S. Regs., Part II. and the Staff Manual respectively. Title Pages will be prepared in manuscript.

Place	Date	Hour	Summary of Events and Information	Remarks and references to Appendices
BERTRANCOURT	1916 October			
	11th		on lines of CENTRAL AVENUE. Obtained Bomb Store at COLINCAMPS connected to Corps Exchange in "M" dugout, near by.	
	12th		Party continued work on lines of CENTRAL AVENUE, taking them as far on that, as the new Corps burial route (32 prs), as forward front of that C.T. Inspection of gas-helmets, respirators & steel helmets. Two linemen sent to Corps Signals for testing out lines.	
	13th		Work commenced on R.A. Advanced H.Q. (in TAUPIN TRENCH), cables being taken from R.A. Signal dugout (known as "M" dugout) to the sub Advanced Sig. H.Q. to pairs of 10 line buried route trunking between Advanced Sig. H.Q. (known as O.P. dugout) to "P" dugout, whence several of the Corps buried routes radiate.	
	14th		Lines between "OP" & "P" dugouts tested out. Party could not proceed with wiring of Advanced Sig. H.Q. Offices ("OP") owing to change of plans in construction of these headquarters. Some of the Company had to move out of huts to inside billets in the village of BERTRANCOURT	

Army Form C. 2118.

WAR DIARY
or
INTELLIGENCE SUMMARY
(Erase heading not required.)

Instructions regarding War Diaries and Intelligence Summaries are contained in F. S. Regs., Part II. and the Staff Manual respectively. Title Pages will be prepared in manuscript.

Place	Date	Hour	Summary of Events and Information	Remarks and references to Appendices
BERTRANCOURT	1916 October 15th		Sunday. Church service at 7.30 a.m. (in camp) and 6 p.m. (in Church Army Hut in the village).	
	16th		Party under 2/Lt. Sutherland detailed for a short period of attachment d'Artois (58th Signal Company) arrived for a short period of attachment to this unit, having come out from England to learn the latest signal work.	
	17th		Party laying trench line (fair D5 cable) from Advanced divn Sigml. ("OP") to that by a new buried route (PBB) going to LEGEND TRENCH, also connecting Divisional O.P. to a neighbouring Heavy Artillery O.P. 9th J.H. Eld. H.Q. moved to COURCELLES + 76th to LOUVENCOURT.	
BUS-LES-ARTOIS	18th		Divisional H.Q. moved in the afternoon to the Chateau at BUS-LES-ARTOIS, vacated the same morning by 51st Division, moving further south. Our old H.Q. at BERTRANCOURT taken over by 2 Lieuman. 8th Inf.Bde. moved to BUS-LES-ARTOIS, other Brigades as in previous day. LeCheme, with similar superimposed to each Brigade + to Sd Corps.	

Army Form C. 2118.

WAR DIARY
or
INTELLIGENCE SUMMARY

(Erase heading not required.)

Instructions regarding War Diaries and Intelligence Summaries are contained in F. S. Regs., Part II. and the Staff Manual respectively. Title Pages will be prepared in manuscript.

Place	Date	Hour	Summary of Events and Information	Remarks and references to Appendices
BUS-LES-ARTOIS	1916 October 19th		Settling new Office at this H.Q. 76th Inf. Bde. relieved the 9th Inf. Bde. in the line, Brigade H.Q. of former moving to COURCELLES.	
	20th		Party laying lines from 1" Howitzer Batteries at COLINCAMPS & COURCELLES to "M" Regt. for connection to Advanced Infantry Brigade H.Q. Party laying 6 pairs of cable (D3) from Advanced 9th Inf. Bde. H.Q. to "PBB" tunnel mouth. Party working on lines between "IM" & "P" dugouts, trying to get cables through where shell had cut them.	
	21st			
	22nd		Sunday. Church Services at 8 a.m. (in Chateau) & 6.0 p.m. (in Cinema in BUS Village). Work commenced on fitting up of Advanced Stn. "AS" Cable Office ("OP"). Work commenced on fitting up of attachment to this unit. Section, under Lt. Thomas, arrived for attachment to this unit.	
	23rd		Lt. Thomas, with party from his section, laying lateral lines between Advanced Brigade H.Q. of Centre & Right Brigades to make direct again safer. This was chiefly on account of having 3 R.A. Brigade H.Qs. up at the Advanced Inf. Bde. H.Q., making it very important to have alternative means of communication. Work continued on fitting up "OP" Office in connecting up lines at different Bat Boxes on arrived routes.	
	24th		Lt. Thomas & party continued work on lateral lines. Work continued at "OP" Office.	

2449 Wt. W14957/Mqo 750,000 1/16 J.B.C. & A. Forms/C.2118/12.

WAR DIARY or INTELLIGENCE SUMMARY

Army Form C. 2118.

Place	Date	Hour	Summary of Events and Information	Remarks and references to Appendices
BUS-LES-ARTOIS	1916 Oct 25th		Party laying lateral line (D5 pair) from Left Brigade H.Q. (Ashmead) to met line being laid from Right Brigade H.Q. to 31st Division (on our Left). Party from "A5" Cable Section completing lines (6 pairs) between Centre & Right Brigade H.Q. & from O.P. office being tested out.	
	26th		Party repairing route formed from O.P. office which had been taken by shell fire. Lt. Thomas with party laid 3 pairs (D5 twisted cable) from O.P. back to P dugout. It withdrawn took parts of Suffolks (70 odd) from COURCELLES dug trench from P dugout to RAILWAY AVENUE & also to act as a "C.T." from P dugout.	
	27th		Two parties (one from "A5" Section) clearing cables and tidying up in SOUTHERN and NORTHERN AVENUES. Two from O.P. back to Division being party constructing of cutting proof visual station near tested out. Lt Henry joined as 2nd Supernumerary "1M" (Ashmead R.A. H.Q.) Officer, to complete establishment of unit.	

Army Form C. 2118.

WAR DIARY
or
INTELLIGENCE SUMMARY

(Erase heading not required.)

Instructions regarding War Diaries and Intelligence Summaries are contained in F. S. Regs., Part II. and the Staff Manual respectively. Title Pages will be prepared in manuscript.

Place	Date	Hour	Summary of Events and Information	Remarks and references to Appendices
BUS-LES-ARTOIS	1916 October 28th		Parties clearing up lines in RAILWAY and NORTHERN AVENUES. Work continued on Divisional station — also in testing out lines from O.P. The "PAA" route was broken on two sections; Coyle Linesmen working on the route.	
	29th		Sunday. Church Service as for last Sunday. Day of rest after a busy week.	
	30th		Two parties (one from "AS" Cable Section) continued work in clearing up cable in trenches. New Lines of cables laid between "OP" & "IM" dugouts. A "Signals" Mess was inaugurated at Divisional H.Q.	
	31st		Two parties on same work as previous day. Electrician of Electric Light Lorry examined engine of wrecked aeroplane near our Balloon Div. H.Q. ("OP") but came to the conclusion that it was not worth re-moving.	

M.W.T. Fitt CAPT. R.E.
COMMANDING 2ND SIGNAL COMPANY R.E.

3rd Divisional Engineers.

3RD SIGNAL COMPANY R.E.

NOVEMBER 1916.

Army Form C. 2118.

3rd Signal Company R.E.

Vol 17

WAR DIARY
or
INTELLIGENCE SUMMARY
(Erase heading not required.)

Instructions regarding War Diaries and Intelligence Summaries are contained in F.S. Regs., Part II. and the Staff Manual respectively. Title Pages will be prepared in manuscript.

Place	Date	Hour	Summary of Events and Information	Remarks and references to Appendices
BUS-LES-ARTOIS	1916 November 1st		Two parties (one from "AS" Cable Section) clearing cable in trenches. Linesmen at OP putting lines through to Skin H.Q. at BUS-LES-ARTOIS. One working party clearing along the day on top of trench lines in RAILWAY AVENUE which had fallen down owing to sides of trench crumbling away; a lot of trouble is caused at this time owing to this falling-in of trenches.	
	2nd		Working parties continuing work of previous day. 5th Corps dignals running telephone pair from our suggest Office exchange to Mobile Brigade left just west of SAILLY-AU-BOIS. Line through in the evening.	
	3rd		Two working parties again working on lines in trenches. Several lines damaged by shell-fire & parties worked at putting these through.	
	4th		Two working parties continued work of previous day.	
	5th		Sunday. Church service as for last Sunday. Parade of H.Q. & Nos. 1 & 2 Sections of the Company for presentation of Military Medals by the G.O.C. Division. (to Sergt. Pankurs & Sapper Clarke).	

2449 Wt. W14957/M90 750,000 1/16 J.B.C. & A. Forms/C.2118/12.

Army Form C. 2118.

WAR DIARY
or
INTELLIGENCE SUMMARY
(Erase heading not required.)

Instructions regarding War Diaries and Intelligence Summaries are contained in F. S. Regs., Part II. and the Staff Manual respectively. Title Pages will be prepared in manuscript.

Place	Date	Hour	Summary of Events and Information	Remarks and references to Appendices
BUS-LES-ARTOIS	1916 November 6th		Party working on lines from COURCELLES to Mill (N. of COLINCAMPS) + from Mill toward an (trench line at CENTRAL AVENUE). Party from "A5" Cable Section clearing lines in trenches.	
	7th		Preparations made for digging party of 2 Battalions of 76th Inf. Bde. to lay cable trench from "1M" dugout (formed Sig. R.A. H.Q.) towards the Windmill N. of COLINCAMPS. Line of trench taped out on ground and disclosed into "Company tasks". Battalion and Company Commanders shewn over line during afternoon but digging (which was to have been done at night) cancelled owing to bad weather. Party laying two more short pairs of lines between "1M" dugout and "OP" dugout. Lines being laid from Windmill to new Artillery Brigade positions.	
	8th		Scheme for new buried route temporarily abandoned. Work continued on lines from Windmill to Artillery Brigade H.Q.s	
	9th		Work continued on distilling lines from Windmill to Brigade H.Q.	

Army Form C. 2118.

WAR DIARY
or
INTELLIGENCE SUMMARY
(Erase heading not required.)

31st Signal Co. R.E.

Place	Date	Hour	Summary of Events and Information	Remarks and references to Appendices
BUS-LES-ARTOIS	Nov. 1916. 10th		Men of Company & A.S. Section employed in camp.	
	11th		Party of A.S. Cable Section lent to Div. Arty. for poled line construction from Forward Sig. Sta Hill (of 1M") to new Arty. Bde HQs which had suddenly changed their HQs. Sgt. Woods with small party laid and DS pair from O.P. down SOUTHERN AV. to the DRESSING STA. near EUSTON DUMP for use of the A.D.M.S. and put another pair from 1M down the same route leaving a coiled end at the road end of the C.T. for use of the Arty. Did cross country line back end of the afternoon. Turned very misty and damp.	
	12th	7.30 A.M.	Party of A.S. again lent to Arty. to complete their change of communications. The line terminated yesterday at the road end of SOUTHERN AVENUE was prolonged on poles back towards COLINCAMPS to the 40th Bde R.F.A.	
		8.30 A.M.	Details to forward H.Q. Rennysine & O.P. left with rations and stores. A.S. Section reported 1 OR wounded at work by premature from 18 pdrs.	

2449 Wt. W14957/Mgo 750,000 1/16 J.B.C. & A. Forms/C.2118/12.

WAR DIARY or INTELLIGENCE SUMMARY

Army Form C. 2118.

3rd Div. Signal Co. R.E.

Place	Date	Hour	Summary of Events and Information	Remarks and references to Appendices
BUS-les-ARTOIS.	Nov. 1916. 12th		Lieut. HARVEY sent to WINDMILL Ex. to Relf Lieut. BARCLAY. Capt. WEBB went up to O.P. to establish forward Battle Stn. for 3.0.pm. Day clear. Lines O.P. to BUS giving much trouble as usual. Indirminable conducts bad earth leakage on the buried system and much induction. At 10.pm 3 lines and 5 were in working order between O.P. and BUS. Lines working through from O.P. to Advanced Brigade HQ. Lines from Brigade HQ's to Battalions also by 3 h.m. At 7 h.m. 9th Inf. Bde. H.Q. closed at COURCELLES working, and opened at Advanced Bde. H.Q. in LEGEND TRENCH. Arrangements made for Wireless Communication between attacking troops & 8" Inf. Bde. and station at OBSERVATION WOOD (close to Brigade H.Q.) also for "Power Buzzer" communication from attacking troops of 76th Inf. Bde. and Receiving Station at TOUVENT FARM. & supply of 16 pigeons sent to each Brigade, 3 4 pigeons also at Sig. H.Q. (O.P.) in case of emergency. All preparations complete for the attack following morning. Receiving station "Emerge from Contact Point and Plane established at WINDMILL (Artillery Exchange).	

Army Form C. 2118.

WAR DIARY
or
INTELLIGENCE SUMMARY
(Erase heading not required.)

Instructions regarding War Diaries and Intelligence Summaries are contained in F.S. Regs., Part II. and the Staff Manual respectively. Title Pages will be prepared in manuscript.

Place	Date	Hour	Summary of Events and Information	Remarks and references to Appendices
Bus-les-Artois	Nov. 13. 1916.	6 a.m.	Thick mist. Line from Mary Gue to Div Dump reported blown away. Small party dispatched to fix it up during more calm. O.P lines good.	
		2.0 pm	O.P. lines all reported o.k. by shell fire near Adv. Div. H.Q. Communication by D.R. and priority messages sent via R.A. lines restored possibly about	
		3.0 pm.	Evening slight drizzle set in. Sgt. HATTON and 4 O.R. sent up to help out O.P. Owing to failure of attack, Battalion lines were not extended as projected. Considerable difficulty was experienced by 76th Inf. Bde. in keeping its lines to Battalion in working order. 8th Inf. Bde. had little or no trouble. Shell fire cut communication of "O.P." on both sides (as related above). Lines to Brigades put through quickly, but "trunk" lines took longer owing to number of lines in the route (necessitating joining up pairs & stripping out if snarls). Sgt. Hatton's party denied two more pairs (stained through) between O.P & P. Artillery communication kept through well. No work done by Wireless or "Power Buzzer". The day was too misty for much work with Contact Patrol aeroplanes.	

WAR DIARY
or
INTELLIGENCE SUMMARY

(Erase heading not required.)

Army Form C. 2118.

Place	Date	Hour	Summary of Events and Information	Remarks and references to Appendices
BUS-les-ARTOIS.	Nov. 14 1916.		Staff still in residence at Forward H.Q. Day clear and cool. O.P. line going 2 of 5. Small party of this co. and from A.S. section sent up to keep old O.P. Div. Dump line linesman send out. Troops on lines normal. 2/Lt. R.M. CLARK. R.E. arrived from depot. Sent here by 5th Sigs. Army Signals. To arrange for new dispositions.	
		8.30 am		
		11.0 am		
		3.0 pm	warned Head O.P. and div H.Q. O.P. now to be closed down, and Aveen over by 76 BDE. holding from 8th INF. BDE to BUS and 9th INF. Bde. to LOUVENCOURT. Own H.Q. re-parcel at BUS about 6 p.m. Signal office at "OP" handed over to 70th Inf. Bde. Signals about 10 p.m. lines from "IM" to 3 Artillery Brigades being first thought to "OP" for use of Artillery Liaison Officer with the Infantry Bde. H.Q.	
	15th		8th Inf. Bde. relieved to take over part of the line held by 2nd Siberian Brigade H.Q. moved up to detached 2nd Div. H.Q. at "R. 24 Central" (N. of MAILLY MAILLET) in the evening; communication from BUS by cable pair, civil	

WAR DIARY or INTELLIGENCE SUMMARY

Army Form C. 2118.

Place: BUS-LES-ARTOIS

Date	Hour	Summary of Events and Information	Remarks
1916 Nov 16th		out that afternoon, to BERTRANCOURT (2 shs. Rear H.A.) - thence by a first armed system to "Q 2 to Central."	
		8th Hy. Bde. H.Q. moved to "OP" with 2 Batts. H.Q. at "SALT" (9th Inf. Bde.) Batt H.Q. 75th Inf. Bde. H.Q. moved back to COURCELLES with Battalion H.Qs. at Col. 8 & 176 y Batt. H.Q. lines through between "P" & "OP".	
17th		Party from "A5" Cable section completing lines (which they had begun before the attack on 13th) between "B" Dugout & 23rd Bde. R.F.A. Party building line between 76th Inf. Bde. H.Q. at COURCELLES and R.A. Exchange at Windmill N. of COLINCAMPS. Had front overnight and ground frozen hard.	
18th		Party relaying a line that was dug previously from "OP" to tramway station near EUSTON DUMP.	
19th		Sunday. 8 a.m. Church Service - Communion Service in Chateau & 8 p.m. Evening service in Cinema Hall BUS. 9th Inf. Bde. H.Q. moved to "OP" with 2 Battalions on line. 8th Inf. Bde. H.Q. moved back to COURCELLES joining 76th Inf. Bde. H.Q. at BUS, with 2 Battalions there & one Battalion in line.	

Army Form C. 2118.

WAR DIARY
or
INTELLIGENCE SUMMARY
(Erase heading not required.)

Instructions regarding War Diaries and Intelligence Summaries are contained in F. S. Regs., Part II. and the Staff Manual respectively. Title Pages will be prepared in manuscript.

Place	Date	Hour	Summary of Events and Information	Remarks and references to Appendices
BUS- LES- ARTOIS	1916 Nov.			
	20th		Two at VAUCHELLES.	
			Party reeling up cable line (Fanic) laid in RAILWAY AVENUE and SABYLON trench, line being no longer in use. Party of "AS" Cable Section working with linemen on burial route East of tent rows at COLINCAMPS.	
	21st		Party laying short trunk line from "Mustard" Battln H.Q. (now used as Battalion H.Q.) to Test Box on "PM" Route; when extending to "Pint" through some of the broken lines ("PAXD") between "Pepper" & "Salt". It being not party of 1st Inf. Bde. Signals which good work in clearing several test Boxes on "BEX" route (from B "dugout" forward to "Eureme" office - nr "Mustard" Battle H.Q.) B "dugout" forward to 1st Bde.	
	22nd		Party returned work on "PAXD" route. Party of "AS" Section assisting 1st Bde. Section in testing lines on "BEX" route.	
	23rd		Similar jobs as on previous day. A.D. Signals, 13th Corps (Major Boult R.E.) paid a visit to Brigade and Battalion Offices, etc. in the trenches.	
	24th		Battn. for HQ. section of 5th Corps Conference at Corps at BUS. Inspection party to performance of "the Pythos" (at SOUASTRE in evening (49th Div.) COUIN) in the afternoon.	

2449 Wt. W14957/Mg0 750,000 1/16 J.B.C. & A. Forms/C.2118/12.

WAR DIARY or INTELLIGENCE SUMMARY

Army Form C. 2118.

Place	Date	Hour	Summary of Events and Information	Remarks and references to Appendices
BUS-LES-ARTOIS	1916 Nov. 25th		Party continued work on lateral lines between PEPPER and SALT Battle H.Qs. Lines joined up, but only one pair working through satisfactorily by the evening. Linemen also trying to get terminal board through "B" dugout. Very wet day. Lecture on Heliophone by men. Lt. Whittaker (13th Corps Signals) in the Cinema Hall at BUS.	
	26th		Sunday. Church Service at 8 a.m. (in Chateau) & at 10 a.m. - 6 p.m. in Cinema Hall, BUS.	
	27th		Party working on "BEX" note now "B" dugout. Just now of their party reunited by a "firestone" from a lathing wire. Party "AS" Section closing cable in telephone SOUTHERN AVENUE. 76th Lt. Bde. relieved 1st Inf. Bde. in the line. Batt. H.Q. of former moved up to "OP" and of latter took to BUS.	
	28th		Party of men laying line for R.A. from Windmill at COLINCAMPS to Battle H.Q. of 42nd Bde. Party working on BUCK route (between BUS & COURCELLES). "AS" C.T.R. Section left for ACHEUX.	

WAR DIARY
or
INTELLIGENCE SUMMARY

(Erase heading not required.)

Army Form C. 2118.

Place	Date	Hour	Summary of Events and Information	Remarks and references to Appendices
BUS-LES-ARTOIS	1916 Nov. 29th		Party of men erecting poles and putting up cables from COLINCAMPS to new Brigade and Battery positions, also at on "BUCC" route.	
	30th		Corps established at ACHEUX. 13th Corps R.E. moving to ACHEUX. Small party lined to R.A. for poling Cable round WINDMILL Ex. St John cable gasping in trenches POSTS were placed at points to warn all moving cables to have them labelled. 2/2a DEAN (to North STAFFS Regt) a/a/h Signals arrived on depot on orders Supernumery temporarily	

N.A.T.W...
CAPT. R.E.
COMMANDING 5th SIGNAL COMPANY R.E.

3rd Divisional Engineers.

3RD SIGNAL COMPANY R.E.

DECEMBER 1916.

WAR DIARY
or
INTELLIGENCE SUMMARY

Army Form C. 2118.

Signal Coy

Vol 18

3rd Signal Company R.E.
3rd Division

Place	Date	Hour	Summary of Events and Information	Remarks and references to Appendices
BUS-LES-ARTOIS	1916 Dec. 1.		Small party lent to R.A. for further fixing their pole lines around the MILL EXCH.	
	Dec. 2.		Sgt. RAMSAY and 9 Pole Sect. went up to "B" dugouts with 3 men to test out and further look to the BEX lines between "B" and HITTITE TRENCH. More label posts were placed in the trenches and units were duly notified by Corps that this line found as these posts unlabelled were to be renamed. All available personnel were employed in making the huts more habitable and commenced to put in standings for the horses.	
		4.30 pm.	76 INF. Bde. moved down from O.P. and went into huts where the 8 Riding R.E. Co. were to be in sunken road at COURCELLES. Communication forward a bench grnd.	

Army Form C.2118.

WAR DIARY
or
INTELLIGENCE SUMMARY
(Erase heading not required.)

Instructions regarding War Diaries and Intelligence Summaries are contained in F.S. Regs., Part II and the Staff Manual respectively. Title Pages will be prepared in manuscript.

Place	Date	Hour	Summary of Events and Information	Remarks and references to Appendices.
BUS-LES-ARTOIS	1916 Dec 3rd		Sunday. Church service 8 a.m. in Chateau + 10 + 11 a.m. + 6 p.m. in Cinema, BUS.	
	4th		Party laid cable pair from Corps Signal depot at COURCELLES to 152 Company R.E. about 3/4 mile North.	
	5th		Party helping R.A. to put cables up on poles East of Montbill west of INCAMPS. Reinforcements being arrived in dribbles at BUS (officers being made into parties, etc.)	

Army Form C.2118.

WAR DIARY
or
INTELLIGENCE SUMMARY

(Erase heading not required.)

Instructions regarding War Diaries and Intelligence Summaries are contained in F.S. Regs., Part II. and the Staff Manual respectively. Title Pages will be prepared in manuscript.

Place	Date	Hour	Summary of Events and Information	Remarks and references to Appendices
Bus-lès-ARTOIS	Dec 1916. 6.		2/Lt. DEAN appointed to XX Cable Section and left to take over his new duties.	
			All spare men were on hut improvement and standing as this month we were told to get on with these outstanding affairs	
	7.		Standing for No.1 and 2 Sections were completed. Up to date, H.Q. and are on wooden floors. In the WOOD, No.1 section stableroom a dilapidated barn, No.2 wooden beams completed. No.3 completed, leaving No 4. to do.	
	8.		Lt. MARTYN from 8 Bde Section left for 2 weeks wireless course as CAMPAGNE, 2/Lt THOMAS of "A5" Cable Section temporarily taking over the Bde Section. 17. Remounts arrived today.	

2449 Wt. W14957/Mg0 750,000 1/16 J.B.C. & A. Forms/C.2118/12.

Army Form C. 2118.

WAR DIARY
or
INTELLIGENCE SUMMARY

(Erase heading not required.)

Instructions regarding War Diaries and Intelligence Summaries are contained in F. S. Regs., Part II. and the Staff Manual respectively. Title Pages will be prepared in manuscript.

3rd SIGNAL COMPANY
3RD DIVISION

Place	Date	Hour	Summary of Events and Information	Remarks and references to Appendices
BUS-LES ARTOIS	Dec. 10/16.	9th	Trench slide slip arout today, one both H.Q. moves. Communications in the Bde consequently adjusted and working satisfactorily. Small party cleared up cable obstructing NORTHERN AVENUE Road.	
		10th	2/Li. F.H. PRATT 13th Royal WARWICKS ex Signal Depot joined today as extra Supernumary. Send in from NCO. WOVR for today described, improvements to stationings, and small arms inspection ad 10 a.m. 6.0 p.m. Church Service in the Cinema Hall.	
		11th	Party laying cable from Int by near MILL (COLINCAMPS) to "M" depot to connect two portions of armd. route; some pretty strong throwing line from 8th J.f. Bde. H.Q. to 152nd Field Company. Capt Wright went to same.	
		12th	Heavy fall of snow during night, several fires on nest the "BUCL" route (at COURCELLES via "the DELL") broken by weight of snow. Parties of infantry clearing cables in trenches.	

Army Form C. 2118.

WAR DIARY
or
INTELLIGENCE SUMMARY

(Erase heading not required.)

Instructions regarding War Diaries and Intelligence Summaries are contained in F. S. Regs., Part II. and the Staff Manual respectively. Title Pages will be prepared in manuscript.

Place	Date	Hour	Summary of Events and Information	Remarks and references to Appendices
BUS-LES-ARTOIS	Dec. 1916 13th		Party erecting 3 new poles where poles were broken in previous days. 76th Inf. Bde. relieved 1st Inf. Bde. in Left Sector.	
	14th		Party erecting 2 more poles on "BUCL" route and putting up cable line between COURCELLES + tents just manned by 152nd Field Cy., R.E. Party of infantry under Lt. Chalmers (2nd Suffolk Regt.) commenced systematic cleaning of cables in trenches in Left Sector (present 76th Inf. Bde area)	
	15th		Party under 2/Lt. Brett laying trunk line (pair D5 cable) between "OP" and No. 3 Lost Box on "PBB" route, also a line from No. 4 Lost box on same route to Batt HQ. in LEGEND Trench, this line for the use of supporting Battery of Artillery. Lt. Clark Bde. an command of 8th Inf. Bde. Signals twenty six classes, thing still wing on Wheelers Carest.	
	16th		Party laying trunk line (pair D5 cable) between No. 2 Lost box on "PAA" route and RED COTTAGE — to connect Divisional O.P. at latter place to Brigade HQ. at COURCELLES. Sergt. Ramsay (9th Inf. Bde. signals) and party putting in test boxes on "BEX" route (between "B" Segment and Battalion H.Q. near OBSERVATION WOOD.)	

2449 Wt. W14957/Mgo 750,000 1/16 J.B.C. & A. Forms/C.2118/12.

Army Form C. 2118.

WAR DIARY
or
INTELLIGENCE SUMMARY
(Erase heading not required.)

Instructions regarding War Diaries and Intelligence Summaries are contained in F. S. Regs., Part II. and the Staff Manual respectively. Title Pages will be prepared in manuscript.

[Stamp: SIGNAL COMPANY 3RD DIVISION]

Place	Date	Hour	Summary of Events and Information	Remarks and references to Appendices
BUS-LES-ARTOIS	Sep 17/18		Sunday. Church service in Chateau (8 a.m. Communion service) and Cinema (9 a.m. Communion — 10 a.m. Parade service — 6 p.m. Evening service and Communion). Small party had to work on R.A. lines near COLINCAMPS windmill owing to front-gauge railway being extended across the route.	
	18"		Party laying line (twisted D5 pair) from COURCELLES Exchange to "M" dugout for connecting Brigade H.Q. to the divisional D.P. at RED COTTAGE. Party also working on "BUCQUOY" route BUS, where several lengths of one pair of wires had been brought down by transport.	
	19"		Party laid short line from "M" dugout to dressing station at COLINCAMPS and also line from "B" dugout to Advanced Dressing station near EUSTON dump; same party then laid two armoured "gimel" cables from "OP" towards Battalion H.Q. in LEGEND bund, being cable to traverse country; not sufficient cable to reach Battalion H.Q.	
	20"		Party laid gimel cable to LEGEND bund, terminal of armoured cable being extended by D5 cable previously.	

Army Form C. 2118.

WAR DIARY
or
INTELLIGENCE SUMMARY

(Erase heading not required.)

Instructions regarding War Diaries and Intelligence Summaries are contained in F.S. Regs., Part II. and the Staff Manual respectively. Title Pages will be prepared in manuscript.

Place	Date	Hour	Summary of Events and Information	Remarks and references to Appendices
AVS-LES-ARTOIS	Oct. 1916			
	21st		Improved cable. Party showing of 10 in camp preparing to join "Come" route.	
	22nd		Two parties of 50 men each working near P dugout at digging trench for buried cable. Party endeavoured to put through channel buried lines between M + N dugouts.	
	23.		Party laid field cable line (D.5 twin) from dressing station near EUSTON junction to dressing station at COINCAMPS. Similar working parties now busily digging cable trench near P dugout. Capt. WRIGHT redurned o/l leave.	

Army Form C. 2118.

WAR DIARY
or
INTELLIGENCE SUMMARY

(Erase heading not required.)

Place	Date	Hour	Summary of Events and Information	Remarks and references to Appendices
BUS-les-	1916			
ARTOIS	24th		Continuation of burying trench digging by 50 men of R.E. and men "P" and TAUPIN for contemplated 8" buy scheme. Work ceased midday. Church Service in Cinema at 6.0 pm	
	XMAS DAY 25th		Stable parades as on a Sunday.	
	26th		Work on cable trench resumed. Two shifts of 150 men. Work done more two satisfactory. Rain in afternoon. Capt WEBB R.E. went on leave.	
	27.		250 men in two shifts on trench digging. Trench filled with water overnight and much fallen in. Loss of much time and energy in clearing this. 150 yds cable put in before night. Consider trench digging in heavy weather waste of time. Infantry working party is just from the trenches march 10 miles through mud, to hold and water and do 4 hours digging. Result does not justify use of large labour parties.	

Instructions regarding War Diaries and Intelligence Summaries are contained in F.S. Regs., Part II. and the Staff Manual respectively. Title Pages will be prepared in manuscript.

Army Form C. 2118.

WAR DIARY
or
INTELLIGENCE SUMMARY
(Erase heading not required.)

Instructions regarding War Diaries and Intelligence Summaries are contained in F.S. Regs., Part II. and the Staff Manual respectively. Title Pages will be prepared in manuscript.

Place	Date 1916	Hour	Summary of Events and Information	Remarks and references to Appendices
BUS-les-ARTOIS	DEC. 28.		100 men working on trench. 300 yds road yet finished. 2/Lt. PRATT. Evacuated to LOUVENCOURT owing to stomoged leg by his horse falling on him.	
	29.		Interesting lecture at Cinema on Aeroplane photographs by Capt. Lejeune. R.F.C. Lt. MARTYN returned from leave. No more of importance. Signals 32 Divn. came over to look around preparatory to intended relief.	
	30.		76 Inf. Bde relieved 9th in Hawthorn Sector by the king 2/Lt MARTYN takes over 'B' Bde Signals 2/Lt CLARKE returns to HQ for work on buried scheme. Lt. PHILLIPS goes on 5th ARMY SIGNAL SCHOOL as an instructor. Trench digging postponed owing to night of 2-3rd.	
	31.		Smalls party sent up to cable trench over R. with pumps to clean trench and shall take of water for the purpose digging through one	

2449 Wt. W14957/M90 750,000 1/16 J.B.C. & A. Forms/C.2118/12.

Army Form C. 2118.

WAR DIARY
or
INTELLIGENCE SUMMARY
(Erase heading not required.)

3 D Signal Vol 19

Place	Date	Hour	Summary of Events and Information	Remarks and references to Appendices
BUS-les ARTOIS	Jan 1917 1st		All work suspended today except one small party who were detailed off for pumping on the cable trench and fixing up the cable drums to the dump in an old gun pit for use on the 2/3rd inst.	
	night 2nd/3		Working parties of 300 men, 100 in 3 shifts are taken up to dig, in lorries, under Lts CLARKE, WHITAKER and THOMAS (latter two 6 hrs) by Corps S.op.) Fair good digging done, 8½ being trenched in the morning. 2/Lt SUTERLAND and 15 men of the Co proceeded to lay cable in, standing ad an O.P. in TAUPIN near WATERLOO BRIDGE. Cable was 40 pairs, dun cable lead covered Paris cab.	
	night 3/4		300 men again employed on night work. Man driggle and quied night. Heavy going over wagon tracks and trench railways.	
	4		This party followed by 200 men in daylight assisted by H. SUTHERLAND and 15 men of this Co.	

2449 Wt. W14957/M90 750,000 1/16 J.B.C. & A. Forms/C.2118/12.

Army Form C. 2118.

WAR DIARY
or
INTELLIGENCE SUMMARY

(Erase heading not required.)

Place	Date	Hour	Summary of Events and Information	Remarks and references to Appendices
BUS-les- ARTOIS	Jan 1917 5		Work resumed on cable trench. Party of 13 men from the Co. put in some cable but weather forced owing to hardness of ground.	
	6			
	7		9. Bde. show down at 9 am and march out. One Officer 10. O.R. arrived from 32 Div. to carry out and so action reliefs.	
	8		76 Bde and 8th are relieved by 96 and 14 Bdes respectively and are out to the back area. 15 men go up to "P" dugouts, finish joining the "Mary and Ivy" and finish filling up.	

WAR DIARY
or
INTELLIGENCE SUMMARY

Army Form C. 2118.

Place	Date	Hour	Summary of Events and Information	Remarks and references to Appendices
BUS-lu ARTOIS	1917 Jan 9		32 Div. Signals took over existing communications in the line, and 3 Div. Signal Col: under 2/Lt SUTHERLAND marched on to CANAPLES where [g. office was already established. Bales disposed in the evening as under 8th Bde RIBEAUCOURT (permanent given over by EAR sounder superimposed) 9th Bde as PIEFFS (communications already there, working sounder superimposed) 76 Bde as PERNOIS. Took over a permanent line already existing	
CANAPLES	10		General clean up of horses, waggons limb, waggons etc. ordered for this day. Small parties out pushing in short local lines to CRE, DADOS, TRAIN etc. and installing electric lights, etc. to CHÂTEAU.	

Army Form C. 2118.

WAR DIARY
or
INTELLIGENCE SUMMARY
(Erase heading not required.)

Instructions regarding War Diaries and Intelligence Summaries are contained in F. S. Regs., Part II. and the Staff Manual respectively. Title Pages will be prepared in manuscript.

Place	Date 1917.	Hour	Summary of Events and Information	Remarks and references to Appendices
CANAPLES	Jan 11th		Mowers here send to LAVICOGNE to shoed and bury an officer's horse of this unit, light three in passing through the roads of an accident. Electric lights were run to the CRE, Mess Coy Office. Horses were exercised.	
	12.		Exercise parties and clean up.	
	13th		Capt. WEBB left for short wireless course at G.H.Q. and Lt. SUTHERLAND left for leave. Lt. CHALMERS withdrawn from No. 2. Section and brought into HQ. for temporary duties.	
	14th		Improvements to billets, soundings and marking out billets etc. for the proposed Div. Signal School announced for the 16th inst.	
	15th		4 o.r.'s from each Bn. report for the school standing tomorrow. Rifle inspection and an issue of new gas bags.	

Army Form C. 2118.

WAR DIARY
or
INTELLIGENCE SUMMARY
(Erase heading not required.)

Instructions regarding War Diaries and Intelligence Summaries are contained in F. S. Regs., Part II. and the Staff Manual respectively. Title Pages will be prepared in manuscript.

Place	Date	Hour	Summary of Events and Information	Remarks and references to Appendices
CAVAPLES	1917 Jan			
	16			
	17.			
	18		Capt WEBB resumed from the WIRELESS COURSE	
	19.			
	20.		Exercise parade. Improvements to sounding. Gradually moved against 13 King's Liverpool Regt. Sig. man 12-4-1.	

2449 Wt. W14957/M90 750,000 1/16 J.B.C. & A. Forms/C.2118/12.

Army Form C. 2118.

WAR DIARY
or
INTELLIGENCE SUMMARY
(Erase heading not required.)

Instructions regarding War Diaries and Intelligence Summaries are contained in F. S. Regs., Part II and the Staff Manual respectively. Title Pages will be prepared in manuscript.

Place	Date Nov 1917	Hour	Summary of Events and Information	Remarks and references to Appendices
CANAPLES	21.		Rifle inspection. Church. 30 rifles.	
	22.		Bde sections came in to H.Q. for combined training.	
	23.		Lectures R.A.M.C. Squad drill, improvements to billets.	
	24.		Riding schools. Signal schools. Exercises, football etc.	
	25.		Squad drill.	
	26.		2/Lt. SUTHERLAND returned off leave.	
	27.		Signal school broken up, and Bde sections returned to their Bdes.	
	28.		Buses arrive and move Inf. Bdy. and Div. H.Q.	
	29.		Div H.Q. closed at CANAPLES 11.30 a.m. and opened same hour at FLERS (Pas-de-Calais) B Co. moved by rail & marched at 9.30 arr[?] at FLERS	
FLERS			arr[?] at 8.30 p.m. R.Q.M.S. and party remained behind.	

Army Form C. 2118.

WAR DIARY
or
INTELLIGENCE SUMMARY
(Erase heading not required.)

Place	Date	Hour	Summary of Events and Information	Remarks and references to Appendices
FLERS	30		Div. H.Q. closed here at 10.30 am and opened same hour at VILLERS CHATEL. (No 2 Caval Co. moved off 10.30 ams proceeded up as far as Gouy-en-Artois until arriving ST POHL – ARRAS Road was diverted towards [illegible]. Find diverse hires. Very wet day and slight snow fall.	
VILLERS-CHATEL	31st		Quiet day. No news.	

R. Albright
Capt. R.E.
3rd Signal Co.

WAR DIARY
or
INTELLIGENCE SUMMARY

Army Form C. 2118.

3D Signal Coy

Vol 20

Place	Date	Hour	Summary of Events and Information	Remarks and references to Appendices
VILLERS CHATEL	1917 Feb	1.	Local lines put out to CRE and TRAMWAY MINGOVAL	
		2.	Communication established with 76 Bde at PENIN, party comic storm. Railway helped by a sub from 'B' laying cables from X at TINQUES to Bde	
		3.	Arty ad pd recce DIEVAL new lines out to 8 Bde at FREVILLERS and to 9 Bde at DIEVAL. Supplementary to this 'A' sent a detachment to put in a field line from 8 Bde to 9 Bde	
		4.	Communication with 8 Bde established by means of Pinnruires into BETHENCOURT - HERMIN - FREVILLERS.	
		5.		
		6.	New gas helmet parade and instruction in its use	

Army Form C. 2118.

WAR DIARY
or
INTELLIGENCE SUMMARY

(Erase heading not required.)

Place	Date 2/17	Hour	Summary of Events and Information	Remarks and references to Appendices
VILLERS CHATEL.	FEB. 7		Demonstration at AMBRINES in TT and Trench Wireless Sets. Very cold.	
LINGEREUIL	8		Div. H.Q. moved at 10.30 am. Owing to scarcity of billets "B" Sec. with 2/Lt. CLARK and 2/Lt. CHALMERS stayed behind. Very cold.	
	9			
	10			
WALUS	11		Div. H.Q. closed at noon and opened at WALUS. Billets more scarce than before, 150 men and 70 horses had to billet at WANQUETIN. Lt. RAMAGE proceeded to THIRD ARMY WIRELESS Co. for duty, the vacant section having filled by 2/Lt SUTHERLAND.	

Army Form C. 2118.

WAR DIARY
or
INTELLIGENCE SUMMARY

(Erase heading not required.)

Instructions regarding War Diaries and Intelligence Summaries are contained in F. S. Regs., Part II. and the Staff Manual respectively. Title Pages will be prepared in manuscript.

Place	Date	Hour	Summary of Events and Information	Remarks and references to Appendices
WARLUS	Feb 1917 12.		Coy. dispositions, B Bde sect. ad LIENCOURT, 9 Bde sect at HOUVAN-HOUVIGNEUL, 96 Bde in line ad ARRAS, remainder of Co. billeted ad WANQUETIN with office known as QM. and	
	13			
	14			
	15		Coy office and Sigs ad Div.HQ WARLUS.	
	16		Sankies Employed on local lines.	
	17		Two linemen sent to ARRAS to work under Corps. Sigs.	
	21			
	22			
	23		Rest of Coy. moved up to WARLUS from billets in WANQUETIN.	

Army Form C. 2118.

WAR DIARY
or
INTELLIGENCE SUMMARY
(Erase heading not required.)

Place	Date FEB.	Hour	Summary of Events and Information	Remarks and references to Appendices
WARLUS COL d'ARRAS	24	10/17	Lt. BARCLAY. Returned off leave.	
	25		Sunday. Church Parade for Company at WARLUS and for German dugout school at WANQUETIN. Infantry Enemy service.	
	26		Party completed permanent route (12 lines) through WARLUS village. Another party dismantled an old "comic" airline route over the village. "Road restrictions" (in consequence of thaw) withdrawn at last.	
	27		"Road restrictions" again on but III Corps were able to send out cable (O.P. twin) for us to commence work on communication for formed Brigade + Batt⁵ H.Q⁵. Party of 1 N.C.O. + 9 men sent to ARRAS to billet there + carry on their work (Wireless Comd (G.H.Q.)). Capt. Knight went to CAMPAGNE to attend Wireless Comd (G.H.Q.).	
	28		Work commenced on formed lines by party in ARRAS. 76th Inf. Bde. relieved by 8th Inf. Bde. in line. H.Q. + future moved from ARRAS to WANQUETIN.	

W. H. T. [signature]
CAPT. R.E.
COMMANDING 216 SIGNAL COMPANY R.E.

Vol 21
3rd Signal Company R.E.

WAR DIARY
or
INTELLIGENCE SUMMARY
(Erase heading not required.)

Army Form C. 2118.

Place	Date	Hour	Summary of Events and Information	Remarks and references to Appendices
WARLUS	March 1st		Party in ARRAS continued work on Signal Lay-out of the Company by the IDVS, 3rd Army.	
	2nd		Some work as previous day. 2/Lt. Clarke went to AVESNES to attend a short course of "Contact Patrol" work with aeroplanes of No. 12 Squadron R.F.C. There were of 76th Div. Signals and of Battalion Signal Officers & 3 Battalion Signallers also attending — the latter two doing a shorter course.	
	3rd		Some work as previous day. Lt. Phillips (76th Inf. Bde.) left for England to deliver a lecture at the Senior Officers' School, Aldershot.	
	4th		Sunday. Church Parade service for Company at WARLUS and for Groves Signal School at WANQUETIN. Voluntary evening service.	
	5th		Capt. WRIGHT returned from Wireless Course and 2/Lt CLARK from Combined aeroplane course.	

Army Form C. 2118.

WAR DIARY
or
INTELLIGENCE SUMMARY

(Erase heading not required.)

Instructions regarding War Diaries and Intelligence Summaries are contained in F. S. Regs., Part II. and the Staff Manual respectively. Title Pages will be prepared in manuscript.

Place	Date	Hour	Summary of Events and Information	Remarks and references to Appendices
WARLUS côté d' ARRAS	March 6			
	7		10 Sappers sent down to ARRAS to help Sgt. HATTON with armoured goods in tunnel.	
	8		Party of Sappers rode down to ARRAS for work with Sgt. HATTON.	
	9		Party also sent to help R.A. in work under consideration in the RUE CAPUCINES	

2449 Wt. W14957/M90 750,000 1/16 J.B.C. & A. Forms/C.2118/12.

Army Form C. 2118.

WAR DIARY
or
INTELLIGENCE SUMMARY
(Erase heading not required.)

Place	Date	Hour	Summary of Events and Information	Remarks and references to Appendices
WARLUS	MARCH			
Côte d'ARRAS	10.		Church Parade morning. Limbermen lent to 14th Div. Siege for painting. Party sent to ~~ARRAS~~ DAINVILLE on perm. line maintenance.	
	11		Jadwin Herd dis. on line to ARRAS, giving much trouble. Sgt Hatton working forward with lines. Party lent to R.A.	
	12.		Party to R.A. Party to Sgt Hatton in Arras. Both lines giving trouble. Sapper SYKES wounded as JL 88.	
	13.		Ran thro' a new line to Arras Bde.	

Army Form C.2118.

WAR DIARY
or
INTELLIGENCE SUMMARY.
(Erase heading not required.)

Place	Date	Hour	Summary of Events and Information	Remarks and references to Appendices
WARLUS côté D'ARRAS.	MARCH 14		Going up St. SAVEUR pulling out remainder forward wires and keeping ones.	
	15		Partly on usual patching in forward protections for Armrd cables	
	16			
	17		Work on Armrd protection towards and from blocks	
			Cable dumped at RUSSEL	

Army Form C. 2118.

WAR DIARY
or
INTELLIGENCE SUMMARY.
(Erase heading not required.)

Instructions regarding War Diaries and Intelligence Summaries are contained in F. S. Regs., Part II. and the Staff Manual respectively. Title pages will be prepared in manuscript.

Place	Date	Hour	Summary of Events and Information	Remarks and references to Appendices
MARLUS (side 'D') ARRAS	March 17 18		Church Parade. Inspection of Battalion rifles. Renewing gas bag &c.	
	19		Horse died of Anthrax. 2/Lt CLARK took over 9 Bde Section from 2/Lt. SUTHERLAND.	
	20		Parties daily for preparations in Arras. Arty. Inf. digging in	
	21		cables and parties for tunnel cable laying. Much cable found ones	
	22			
	23			
	24		are protected by masked boarding in tunnels. Work continues	
	25			
	26		fitting up Bdes and Divn. DIV. Signal offices	
	27			
	28			
	29			
	30			
	31			

April 1917   3rd Signal Company R.E.   Vol 22

Army Form C 2118.

WAR DIARY
or
INTELLIGENCE SUMMARY.
(Erase heading not required.)

Place	Date APRIL 1917	Hour	Summary of Events and Information	Remarks and references to Appendices
WARLUS	1.			
COL "D"	2.			
ARRAS.	3.			
	4.		9 Bde Sec moved to Battle H.Q. 76th to WANQUETIN	
	5.			
	6.			
	7.		76 Bde moved to NEW TUNNELS.	
	8.		Div HQ moved to RUSSEL CAVE ADIT HY	
	9.			

Army Form C. 2118.

WAR DIARY
or
INTELLIGENCE SUMMARY.
(Erase heading not required.)

Instructions regarding War Diaries and Intelligence Summaries are contained in F. S. Regs., Part II. and the Staff Manual respectively. Title pages will be prepared in manuscript.

Place	Date	Hour	Summary of Events and Information	Remarks and references to Appendices
Bois de Boeufs E. ARRAS.	10.		Div. Hq. moved forward to Bois du BOEUFS.	
	11			
	12		Caps Mule went sick and evacuated.	
	13			
WARLUS	14		Div. returned to WARLUS with 3 Bde in ARRAS.	
	15			
	16.			

A 5834 Wt. W4973/M687 750,000 8/16 D. D. & L. Ltd. Forms/C.2118/13.

Army Form C. 2118.

WAR DIARY
or
INTELLIGENCE SUMMARY.

(Erase heading not required.)

Instructions regarding War Diaries and Intelligence Summaries are contained in F. S. Regs., Part II. and the Staff Manual respectively. Title pages will be prepared in manuscript.

Place	Date April	Hour	Summary of Events and Information	Remarks and references to Appendices
Lahej	17.			
	18		Capt Stevenson took over the Coy. vice Capt Mill evacuated.	
	19.		Staff conference held at 4 p.m. at which GOC explained further [illegible] Instructions received to be in readiness to move on & [illegible] Lahej on a [illegible] by [illegible] & role [illegible] of supporting & relieving other of the three divisions in line.	
	20		Visited Arab posts & Capt Cornish's Coy in reserve & arrangements during the [illegible] of [illegible]. No enemy activity [illegible] & no hostile was [illegible]. Enemy was strong in strength - thought to be [illegible] & strong position from [illegible] in Lahej to [illegible] with outposts towards [illegible] in [illegible].	

Instructions regarding War Diaries and Intelligence Summaries are contained in F. S. Regs., Part II. and the Staff Manual respectively. Title pages will be prepared in manuscript.

WAR DIARY
or
INTELLIGENCE SUMMARY.
(*Erase heading not required.*)

Army Form C. 2118.

Place	Date	Hour	Summary of Events and Information	Remarks and references to Appendices
			Telephone [illegible] [illegible]	
			Suggested [illegible] that [illegible] for [illegible] guarding Ammunition dumps should be joined direct to A.A. headquarters [illegible] 7th Corps [illegible] and asked him to arrange with 7th Corps to give spare pair. He considered the present arrangement whereby the [illegible] from [illegible] [illegible] A.A. section through Divisional & Corps exchanges sufficient	
			Visited 3rd Bde & Arty [illegible] Offices	
Warlus	21		Visited Divs in Car got information as to their communications	
"	22		Company stores are checked and loaded up prepared to move at short notice	
"	23		Company standing to ready to move.	
			Supplied [illegible] to Corps Aeroplane [illegible]	
			2 orderlies to Pigeon Loft at [illegible] to receive & transmit messages to [illegible]	

A5834 Wt. W4973/M687 750,000 8/16 D. D. & L. Ltd. Forms/C.2118/13.

WAR DIARY
or
INTELLIGENCE SUMMARY.
(Erase heading not required.)

Army Form C. 2118.

Place	Date	Hour	Summary of Events and Information	Remarks and references to Appendices
Karslen	23 (contd)	12.30	Intimation received that Divisional Headquarters would leave Karoo today	
		1pm	Instructors return and to Arras to meet officer and staff informed that they would be ready by 6 pm. Intimation received that Headquarters would be moving	
		4.30	76 "a" Bln and District known as passing a state and that men would move at 9 pm. Signal officer returned from field known at	
Arras	24th	2.0 pm	Intimation received that 87 then would reach 39 then tanks in at 3.30 am tomorrow and the signals would take on 26 T. Limmer sent out to let points in 39 then forward units to know same.	
		9.30 pm	Reconnaissance through say 20 t. then t. take our communication was arranged with 39 t. then but entirely contact probably about 5 pm tomorrow when entry through there hesters line to Hap at Pons.	

WAR DIARY
or
INTELLIGENCE SUMMARY
(Erase heading not required.)

Army Form C. 2118.

Place	Date	Hour	Summary of Events and Information	Remarks and references to Appendices
Area	28		this transaction can be made to 29th then headquarters D Establishment party sent to the new N.H. proposed section. No detachment sent to Selly to maintain line forward from there.	
		12 noon	Information received that S.O.S would open at N.2.b central tomorrow of communication could be established there. Arranged to have line there by 12 noon. One detachment OB cable section placed at disposal of 3rd Bam by Corps. The mounted orderlies attached to Signal Coy during the day had considerable trouble in maintaining communication with forward Bdes. supported. Staff that line when he turned over his Hq near Brown Line to Mt. Archange S.O.C considered that forward school hut covenant to had battalion at disposal of Div. Sig. fines skel offrs.	

A6945 Wt. W1421/M160 350,000 12/16 D. D. & L. Forms/C/2118/14.

WAR DIARY
or
INTELLIGENCE SUMMARY.
(Erase heading not required.)

Army Form C. 2118.

Place	Date	Hour	Summary of Events and Information	Remarks and references to Appendices
Ava	26		Ситуация неясна should route from Arras to S.E. rockery near Tilloy.	
	27.		Advanced on Wifyre moved to dig outs in old German fire entrenchment at S.d. of Brand. But two Bns of line than from this R.E. rockery. This enabled communication to be formed and the line taken forward from Tilloy. There was heard 3 lines of trench formed from R.E. rockery to N.W. Infantry party of about 3" deep 20 about 40 yards some the brown line the trench lift 400 construction lasts antance work on forward time as	
	28			
	29			
	30		New route back of towards of Rev Bis thence the work tibis as far as Brown line and thence lies forward by armoured cable &m is rockery on line led out to R. at a forward rockery.	
			Rent [sustained] shrapnel on attacked James Thompson ?	

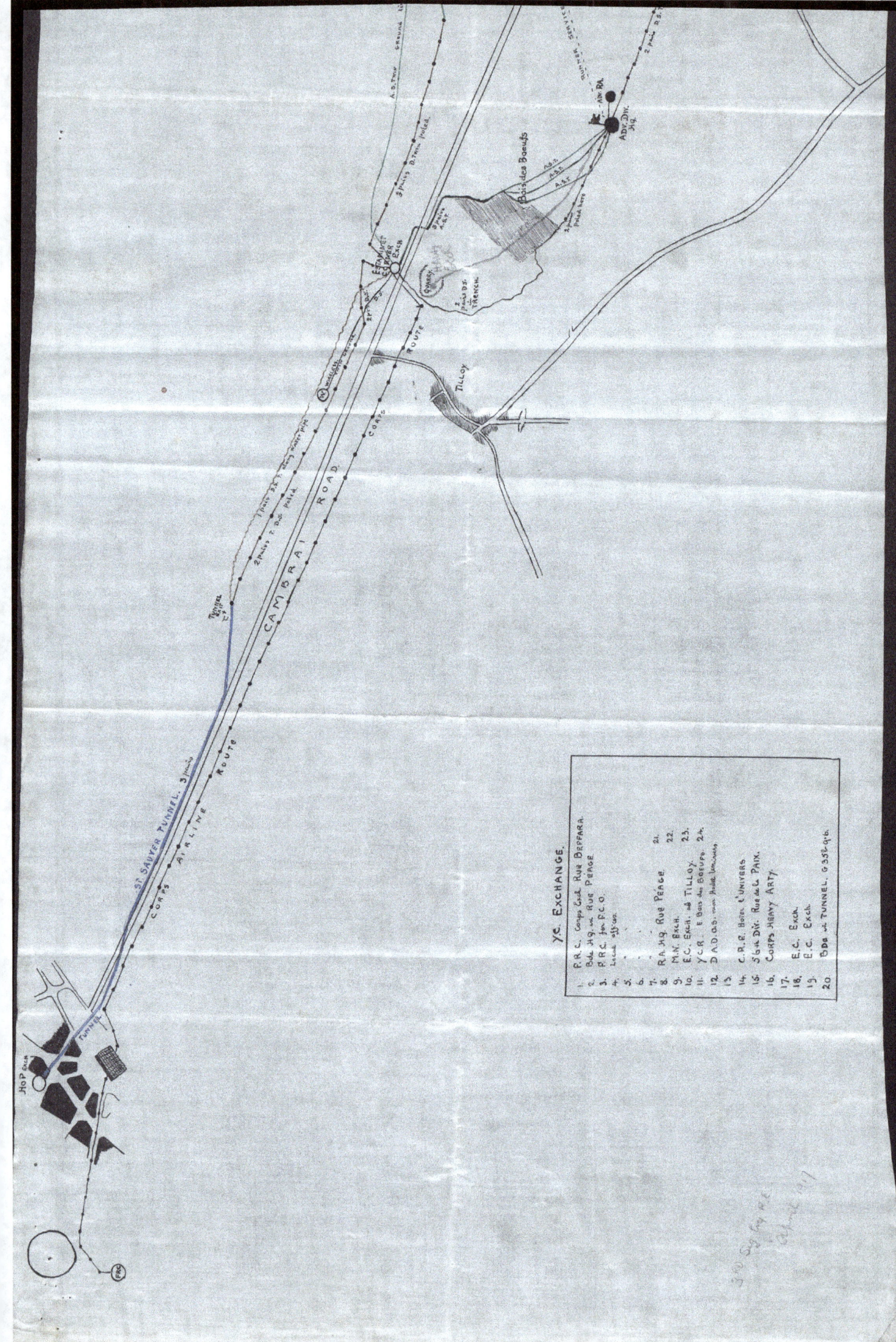

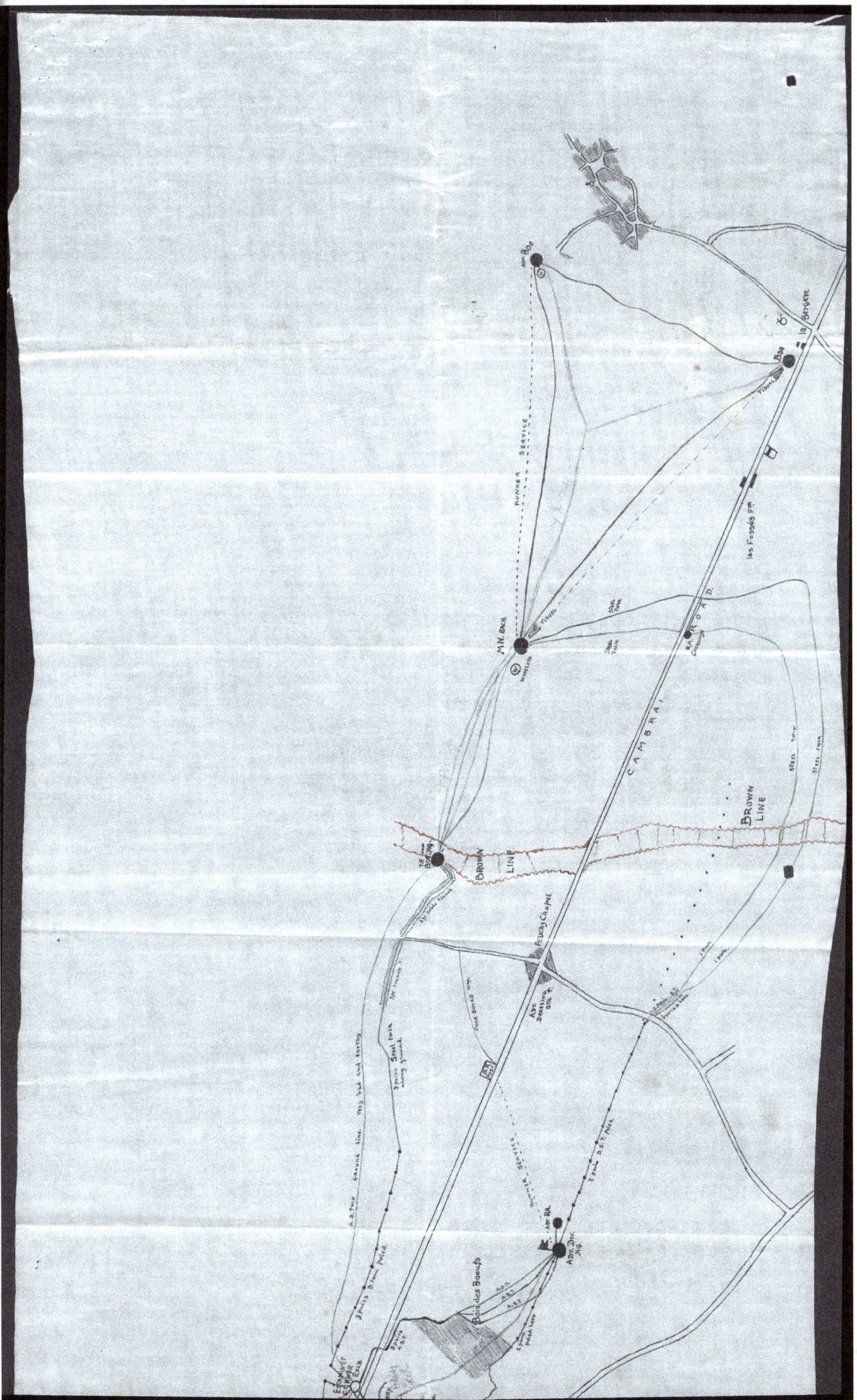

WAR DIARY
or
INTELLIGENCE SUMMARY.
(Erase heading not required.)

Army Form C. 2118.

3 D Signal Coy

J11 23

Place	Date	Hour	Summary of Events and Information	Remarks and references to Appendices
Corps	Aug 1917 1st		Completed outside jointed change over forward lines	
			Lines from E.C. exchange N by W elimenated owing to Batteries	
			having been fired with 20 yards of lines	
			Returned working when blown to pieces the	
			renewed. 76th Bn. taken last parts of Lithuani	
			were moving to rear out bring in awful state	
			brought from C.p.s and 13th Bn Rey Coy	
	2nd		Company established as follows H.Q.	
			Sharing dayts 1 off. 10 G.O. & 12 men at M.N. 3 lines at T.P.	
			in Chau bay. 2 detachments stationed at relay	
			& stations at Arg from N.S.C. and at lugoui at Rd.	
			4½ Helges	
			Visual stations established at 2 Res the Ridge and	
			150 yds in rear of M.N. lamp signals employed	
			several messages sent this line.	

Army Form C. 2118.

WAR DIARY
or
INTELLIGENCE SUMMARY.
(Erase heading not required.)

Instructions regarding War Diaries and Intelligence Summaries are contained in F. S. Regs., Part II. and the Staff Manual respectively. Title pages will be prepared in manuscript.

Place	Date	Hour	Summary of Events and Information	Remarks and references to Appendices
Ram.	3	2.30	All forward lines cut by shell fire	
		3.30	All lines through Skating Rink adrift for... Our lines to Brigade kept working all day. There are no operators on the lines	
			Copy of instructions to local communications	
			... of other causes	
			Report on communications	
			Lines to Col. Cols. Whole Cmte. have down by afternoon	
	4		Offered a area	
			Personnel hold at instructions for officers returned our factory returned	
	5		Lines locally installed	
	6			
	7			
	9			
	10		Bdy section took over lines of 3 Div from 39-10" Div. away on approaching of 37th Sig Coy. & relieving detachment of the Coy at the head & Camp & 58 Div here a party consisting of 2 Coy...	

A6945 Wt. W14922/M1160 350,000 12/16 D. D. & L. Forms/C./2118/14.

Army Form C. 2118.

WAR DIARY
or
INTELLIGENCE SUMMARY.
(Erase heading not required.)

Instructions regarding War Diaries and Intelligence Summaries are contained in F. S. Regs., Part II. and the Staff Manual respectively. Title pages will be prepared in manuscript.

Place	Date	Hour	Summary of Events and Information	Remarks and references to Appendices
Arras	11		Cpl Lineham L/P and 36 t/a & hunters their lines	
			Lt Sutherland and party of hunters out RVW to tile	
			Charge forward lines in rear of futures small operations	
-do-	12/6/15		Stores removed from 134th returned	
	15		Maintaining and extending lines	
			Lieu handed over to 29th Divison. Divisional Headquarters	
			moved to Warlus	
Warlus	16		Relieved stores checked	
	19.		Company paraded & Lyceum Officers taken over for 37th Divn	
	20		Signal Company return made of Company training begun	
			Signal Office lines extended to ground where farm at E end	
			of village was billeted in sheds of Nissen farm in lofts also	
			stables in chateau	
	22nd		One cable attachment car drivers cable wagon and 1 expert	
			& O.C. 37th Divn Arty.	

Army Form C. 2118.

WAR DIARY
or
INTELLIGENCE SUMMARY.
(Erase heading not required.)

Place	Date	Hour	Summary of Events and Information	Remarks and references to Appendices
Lynwood	22nd		Battalion Signal Officer not at Divisional H.Q. asking for list. Lil began.	
	28.		Signal Officer list continued. Arrival four officers returned at Divisional headquarters for instruction	
	24		Signal Officer class began – Company training continued	
	23 + 31		– do –	
	30		Training classes shortened	from Division H.Q. of 3rd Signallers

Army Form C. 2118.

WAR DIARY
or
INTELLIGENCE SUMMARY.
(Erase heading not required.)

WB 24

Place	Date	Hour	Summary of Events and Information	Remarks and references to Appendices
Lynwood	1st		Company proform to move to arras. All stores turned in & others not required to forward offices and forward. Also working party to help fix office	
	2		Office closes Lynmarnie 12 noon & opens at Arras same hour. The following officers changed the position which were also arrived at arras A. R.A. "76" Bde. Lt Brookwood and to report to Lsgn 61st Div only Lieuts Fraser Grenier and to Gt. that he would therefore be unable to attend the conic following day. All lines taken over 29th Div Arty and extra run to sup. Exchange to enable all line to be switch'd over at 10.0am following day. The am there were the ailines intact close to sup her proved.	
	3	6.0am		
		8.0am	All lines cut in several places via Flergns stood offices by shell fire. Lieut Reed and 6 29th Div Relving personnel and to an instrument Thro Broving repair + lines	

A6945 Wt. W14422/M1160 350,000 12/16 D. D. & L. Forms/C./2118/14.

Army Form C. 2118.

WAR DIARY
or
INTELLIGENCE SUMMARY.
(Erase heading not required.)

Instructions regarding War Diaries and Intelligence Summaries are contained in F. S. Regs., Part II. and the Staff Manual respectively. Title pages will be prepared in manuscript.

Place	Date	Hour	Summary of Events and Information	Remarks and references to Appendices
Arras	3rd (contd)		Information received that Lt. Nelson would move to offices occupied by 99th Bn at 4.30pm. Forward lines carefully patrolled with a view to moving this to Left Bn bomb service. His route laid out from BY crossings forward. Information received that approved font not recently drawn to front area. Eg. Bn sent out to Bn headquarters and P.P. he will move to Hq into L.G. Pos on Regt. formerly occupied by Y.C.P.	
	4			
		10.30am	Company two lines on Rt side of Armour Road about 1000 yds U.P. Arr looked by German aeroplane. Four horses were very slightly wounded. On upper had orders attacking horses shd abandoned. Company has been moved further from losses developed by Italian Road.	
	5			
	7		Information received that Left Bn were now there headquarters k valley W. of hamlet, the arrangement held for one	

Army Form C. 2118.

WAR DIARY
or
INTELLIGENCE SUMMARY.
(Erase heading not required.)

Place	Date	Hour	Summary of Events and Information	Remarks and references to Appendices
Arras	8		Company from Corps cyclist Battalion to try narrow trench to fill sub across twenty yards though from pontoon between stations and the Brown line.	
"	9		Construction party cut new field route above trench took entrance on slow trench, empties magneto calls and to trench cut. There may prevent these Lt.Cm. Lanceton as left the talked have last between we hangout an eyes to brigade	
"	10		Have cars party in lines have WK to the 402 offices – three forward KMV. Lt Wardle sent to 3rd Army signal school to act as monitor.	
"	11		Maintenance work continued	
"	12	10.30 am	All line out in Arras army to everything	
"	12	12 noon	All line again the north an cables had been destroyed by horse following fresh heavy cable brought down	

Army Form C. 2118.

WAR DIARY
or
INTELLIGENCE SUMMARY.
(Erase heading not required.)

Instructions regarding War Diaries and Intelligence Summaries are contained in F. S. Regs., Part II. and the Staff Manual respectively. Title pages will be prepared in manuscript.

Place	Date	Hour	Summary of Events and Information	Remarks and references to Appendices
Arras	13		Nothing to report	
	14		2nd Bn. hour to has Inauguration line OK	
	15		Line OK. Sutherland Coy Company for 1st Army Regd Company for stockroom & Ostgen exploratory fire line OK	
	16 to 21		Nothing to report	
	22		Company drawn Arra Are for Le Carroy. Arrangements had been arranged to be in Adance this div and a move to forming further back when not for days	
Le Carroy	23		After spent Le Carroy. Line thing to 8th Bn. Short other Brigade by B.R. Instruction will move and Lake attachment have and motorbus to Cole hopes and being moved to new form army for Brigade active and known to Cole area	

WAR DIARY
or
INTELLIGENCE SUMMARY.
(Erase heading not required.)

Army Form C. 2118.

Place	Date	Hour	Summary of Events and Information	Remarks and references to Appendices
L Canray	24		Company training continued. Views drawn by our Lt Croy from 3rd Post Yoke brought out Liaison & a form of instruction to Battalion against rest.	
	25. 26 28		Continuation of new section continued. Artillery Brigade observation reconnoitred + two skilled men sent from Company to cant. Rolin	
	25		Advance body sent to Adrul le Pret & travelled to open as from village and take over lines from 25" Bn in his area	
	29		Additional class and kms area	
	30		Kappers landed with one to Company running early Kms morning	

James Stammers Capt
regt Northumberland

3rd Signal Company

Army Form C. 2118.

3 Div Signal Co
July 1917
Vol 26

WAR DIARY
or
INTELLIGENCE SUMMARY.
(Erase heading not required.)

Instructions regarding War Diaries and Intelligence Summaries are contained in F. S. Regs., Part II. and the Staff Manual respectively. Title pages will be prepared in manuscript.

Place	Date	Hour	Summary of Events and Information	Remarks and references to Appendices
July	1	2.30 am	Company leave La Cauroy for Rebreuve le Petit.	
		12 noon	Officers chase to Cauroy where Advs. H.Q. Petit came here.	
	2		Advanced body with 15th Division increased by 5 cyclists, but 4th Cyl. Officer party and 15 Div for report on circuits to Infantry.	
	3		Officer party and 1st K.O.S. Divn to arrange no instruments with men.	
	4		L.L. of Taking over Offrs following day. Company know to have headquarters in area taken no for 15th. Company themselves situated in valley running N & S of 9s hundred	
			yards W. of N. Vela. Officer personnel accommodated in tents whilst on road half way between Bugny & Hellewent. Maintenance party attached to Posted Line only. Airline Section formed from Any situation present for continuous instruction in airline. Four cables attached for men drawn from Brigades signers formed for course in Cable and airline riding. Visual class formed at La Cauroy continues instruction.	

WAR DIARY
or
INTELLIGENCE SUMMARY.
(Erase heading not required.)

Army Form C. 2118.

Place	Date	Hour	Summary of Events and Information	Remarks and references to Appendices
Bray	6		Instructional classes continued.	
	7	8"	Lieut A Boyton sent to Hospital	
	9		Mobile Pigeon lofts installed at Divisional Headquarters & report as considerable saving in time of transmitting Pigeon	
			messages when left in rear of BN. HdQrs.	
	11		Capt Robertson 2nd Royal Scots & Chaplin 1st R.S. Fus & Porter 7th R.S. joined. Signal Company to serve as Battalion beyond took	
	12 13 14		Instructional classes continued.	
	15		Intimation received that this Brigade, and Corps would be attached and Rly lets to I 34b. Instructional classes heads became frequent not longer from Vetu evidence & orders that Corps HdQrs then arranged with & be lent to Battalion transitters aerial for this role class in afficial	
	#		work	

Army Form C. 2118.

WAR DIARY
or
INTELLIGENCE SUMMARY.
(Erase heading not required.)

Place	Date	Hour	Summary of Events and Information	Remarks and references to Appendices
Dupny	16.		2/Lt Prideaux leaves Company to join 3rd Army School	
	17th		Nil of note	
	21		Training of Divisional Company Continued. L/cpl ?? R.E. attached to Signal Company for duty all with Bde R.F.A.	
	22nd		8 pigeons sent to 5 & 9" Bdes. & 76 to 2 Bde.	
	23rd		Company training class continued	
	26th		Capt Rolleston returned to his Battalion for duty in trenches	
	26th		Letter sent to all Signals asking for a revised establishment of operators on headquarters of Signal Companys, Infantry and that signalers on headquarters when they are connected by Visual Signalling can will be provided	
	27.		2/Lt Charlton returned to his Battalion for duty in line. 2/Lt Boynton returned to Company from hospital - Case returned six officers who attend at Divisional headquarters for duty instruction in pigeon duties (three days Course)	
	to 29th		Ten men from R.W.F. attend class in Telephone working -	
	29th		2/Lt Cummings R.W.F. joins Company for instruction as Battalion	

Army Form C. 2118.

WAR DIARY
or
INTELLIGENCE SUMMARY.
(Erase heading not required.)

Place	Date	Hour	Summary of Events and Information	Remarks and references to Appendices
	30		Signalling Officer to Brookwood 3rd Signal Company Recruits & Trades Course SYQ.	
	31		Company training relicon continues Capt. Wilson joins Company to take command.	
			James Stevenson Major RE OC 3rd Signal Company	

Army Form C 2118.

WAR DIARY
or
INTELLIGENCE SUMMARY.
(Erase heading not required.)

Instructions regarding War Diaries and Intelligence Summaries are contained in F. S. Regs., Part II. and the Staff Manual respectively. Title pages will be prepared in manuscript.

Place	Date	Hour	Summary of Events and Information	Remarks and references to Appendices
HAPLINCOURT J28 c 1.5	1/8/17		Major J. STEVENSON Reported to command 51st (HIGHLAND) DIV" Major G.W. WILLIAMS M.C. R.E. took over command - from H.Q. VI Corps Signals.	SHEETS 57c NW 57c NE 1/20,000
	2nd		General Reconnaissance	
	3rd		New Construction - 2 pairs DX-MO route. Picks up cable between L.B-MO route.	
			diverted & relaid to new H.Q. of 9th Bde (then vacated by 188-193) C 29 a w.2	
	4th		Aprouts at new P.L. & relaid from MO forward.	
			New Construction - 2 pair DX-MO complete. R&D from LA to C29 a.2 complete.	
			2 spans put on MO-LA route young tree complete.	
	5th		Batt" Signalling course dispersed	
	6th		Main courses.	
	7th		" "	
	8th		" "	
	9th		Courses carried on as usual standing.	
	10th		" " carried on as usual standing.	
	11th		" R.E. personnel reported T.R.R.	
	12th		"VO" extemp duty - "B" reduc" "A" section	
			Corps Yacht Vaux - frequent characters.	

Army Form C. 2118.

WAR DIARY
or
INTELLIGENCE SUMMARY.
(Erase heading not required.)

Instructions regarding War Diaries and Intelligence Summaries are contained in F. S. Regs., Part II. and the Staff Manual respectively. Title pages will be prepared in manuscript.

Place	Date	Hour	Summary of Events and Information	Remarks and references to Appendices
128C.I.S.	13th	*	Gun Instruction 2 pair went Fremicourt Church to M.O. Manoeuvres	
	14th		Dismounted H finer came from RAHQ to N.W. HAPLINCOURT	
	15th		Wolf on FR-MO route. Wired up new Sig HQ office	
	16th		'B' Action moved to FREMICOURT - Erection of Nissen Huts (in new camp)	
	17th		Work on FR-MO Hutting (continued)	
	18th		Manoeuvres & Hutting	
	19th		'A' Action moved to FREMICOURT	
	20th		Manoeuvres & Hutting	
	21st		Dismounted VU-BT units H.Q. transferred from FREMICOURT	
	22nd		Carried by 25-pair (in-came) cable line RAHQ, FREMICOURT to new HQ. FREMICOURT	
	23rd		Re-stocking Wet 1 FR-MO route	
	24th		" " Mending & Hutting	
	25th		" " - carried on with 25-pair cable	
	13th		Signal School for B offers 3 50 O.R. one useful. H. men for batt'y and 2 for m.s. corps	
	*		All candidates required to Read & Read H Words for minute	

A6945. Wt. W14432/M1160 350,000 12/16 D. D. & L. Forms/C./2118/14.

WAR DIARY
or
INTELLIGENCE SUMMARY.
(Erase heading not required.)

Army Form C. 2118.

Instructions regarding War Diaries and Intelligence Summaries are contained in F. S. Regs., Part II. and the Staff Manual respectively. Title pages will be prepared in manuscript.

Place	Date	Hour	Summary of Events and Information	Remarks and references to Appendices
LEGNIS	26th		Commenced Section Training	
	27th		do	
	28th		do Maintenance	
	29th		do do	
	30th		do do	
	31st		Mounts patrols on manoeuvres	
			APPENDIX "A" — Route marches & movements of Bns & Bde. †	
			GENERAL	
	7th		MOVES OF BRIGADES. On the night 4th/5th the 9th Indian Brig moved from the HERMIES sector to HUTS at I.26.d, being relieved by 27th Bde, 9th div. On night 7/8th the 9th Bde (minus) into the LAGNICOURT area the order of battle being — 9th, 76th, 8th & 1st Bns. left to rest.	

WAR DIARY
or
INTELLIGENCE SUMMARY.
(Erase heading not required.)

Army Form C. 2118.

Place	Date	Hour	Summary of Events and Information	Remarks and references to Appendices
			S.O.S.	
			OP 3rd Bns GOC say arrival that every component is in use stood	
			Ross desert S.O.S. Now to it correct battery	
			Steps were taken to carry this out Codes being issued	
			The Bde & Artillery Sub-stations being considerable quantities	
			All Obs Lines were completed from school cells	
			To Aerial Dons Selwil — 8 wires all — 80 miles	
			O.P. Exchanges	
			Stores were established in each Compy graph front	
			in order that the SOS line from three who the exchange	
			appeared is 'B' slow systems in use on Brade	
			or to Centre for the telegraph did not find itself with	
			arrangement S.N. system was there is them in	
			Appendix 'C'	
			The Left Bdt experiment in a combination of X	
			Motto slow is 'B' & 'C'	
			The result was too. "Practice" SOS calls being received	

Army Form C. 2118.

WAR DIARY
or
INTELLIGENCE SUMMARY.
(Erase heading not required.)

Instructions regarding War Diaries and Intelligence Summaries are contained in F. S. Regs., Part II. and the Staff Manual respectively. Title pages will be prepared in manuscript.

Place	Date	Hour	Summary of Events and Information	Remarks and references to Appendices
			WIRELESS "RB"	
			The Rear Trench Sta. was installed at C.29.a.6.0 and J.4.c.5.3	
			The Loop Sta. and Amplifier between R.att.9 and B.de. HQ let the Div.	
			B.de. back the Amplifier at R.att. HQ. BPR's at Corps H.Q.	
			VISUAL	
			No much use when ours forward - too as heavy Tst. line bent very	
			nearly damaged - the sector being very quiet	
			POSITION LAMPS	
			Tent and clutter to all units. Divisional Refr. Visit "Q"	
			Aerofeile about 350 numbers were issued, user being such	
			to W. Corps	

G. Williams Major R.S.
O.C. 3RD DIV. SIG. COY.

8th Infantry Brigade Communications
Showing Especially Artillery Connections

REFERENCE
- - - - - R.G.A. Artillery Lines
———— Infantry Lines

Signed ? Das
Pd Sp '26

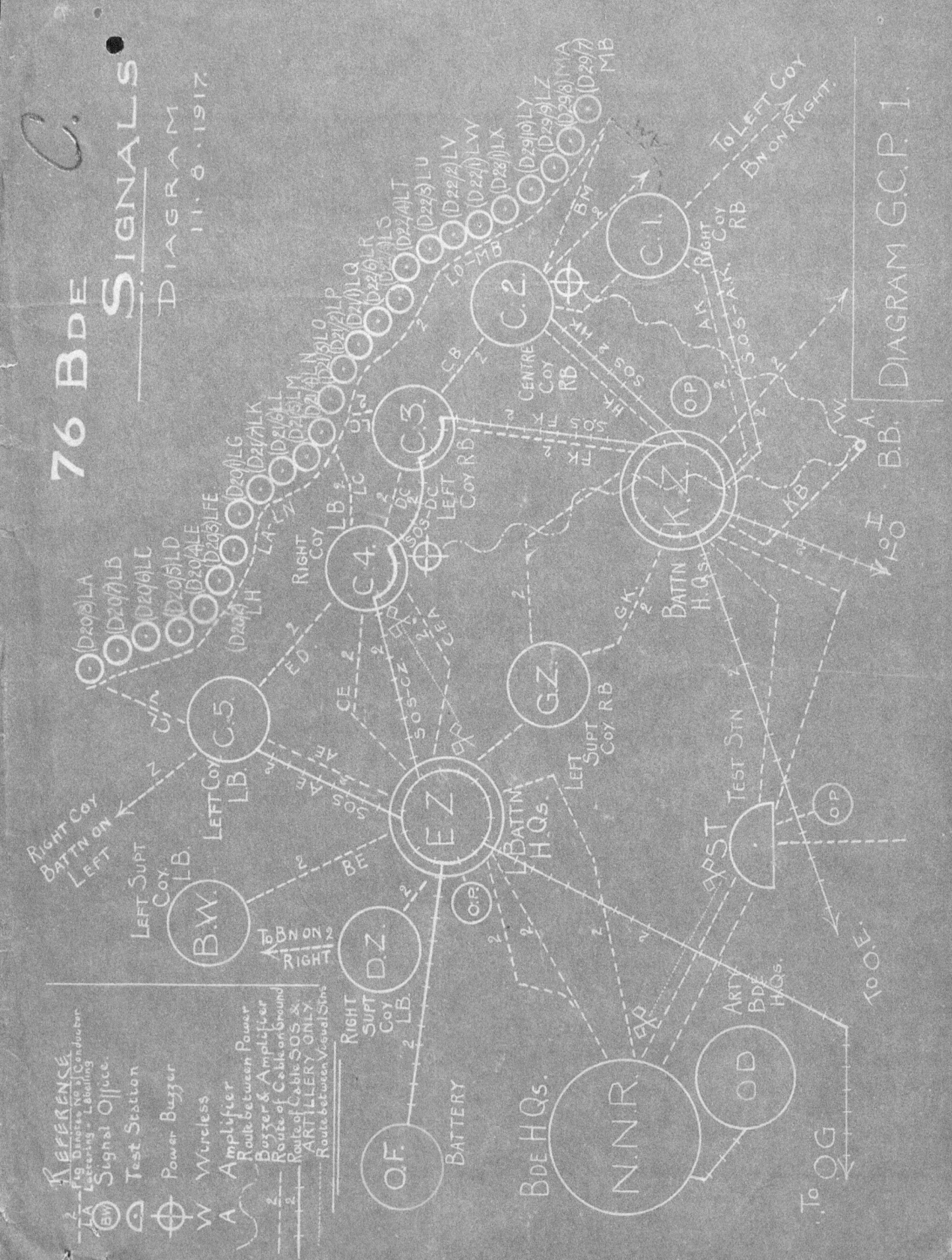

Army Form C. 2118.

WAR DIARY
or
INTELLIGENCE SUMMARY.
(Erase heading not required.)

3D Signals Vol 27

Place	Date	Hour	Summary of Events and Information	Remarks and references to Appendices
HAPLINCOURT	1st Septr		Active training. Started amn' for dug outs in Town Buzzin.	
	2nd		Reconnaissance	
	3rd			
	4,5,6th		'B' Section (men) to L.T. Laundry. Laying line for 9" Br area	
	5th		Section Everard new L. Bernby. Handed over to 56 "Sig Co at 6 am	
	6th		and carried on on his own in that area	
	7th		Duplex set coiled in two volumes. XI issued.	
	8th 15th 22nd		Company put Theo' post chowlists	
			Company Training. School broke up on 12th, all others O.P. return to their units.	
	12th		Lt C. SUTHERLAND accidentally injured to knees — evacuated No' CCS	
	13th		Lt W. DAWSON reported for duty from 61st Div. Sig. Co.	
	15th		N/A Holdsworth with Lt DAWSON returned with 3rd Div Arty	
			for V. Army	
	17		Company parade 7.30 am & entrained at CAPAUME for V Corps	

WAR DIARY
or
INTELLIGENCE SUMMARY.
(Erase heading not required.)

Army Form C. 2118.

Place	Date	Hour	Summary of Events and Information	Remarks and references to Appendices
PROVEN	18	10am	Arrived at PROVEN & went to rents. March to WATOU	
	18-22		Reconnoitred area of *YPRES*, arrange for stores etc	
	22		Sent by motor truck to POPERINGHE	
	19th		Lt. W. DAWSON and 2 O.R. Wounded near POTIZJE by shell fire	
	23rd		Relieved 1st front & appr. staff of 9th Army Dys	
	9th	10am	Communn'd Divis'l H.Q. BRANDHOEK Adv HQ RAMPARTS	
	26th		"Zero" at 5.50 am.	
			Lt. THOMAS, KSLI, att'd as Liason Officer to 76 T.D. - wounded	
			Lt. MORGAN - 42nd Arh. OD Sch. John - wounded at duty,	
			also 4 O.R. wounded.	
	1st Oct.		Command'n of Coys passed to 3rd Anck. Div.	
			3rd Gp. down to WINNEZEELE	
			Full report of Sqnd. Commanders attached	

R. Williams
Major Cdg. Gp. R.E.

Op. 38 wdy Cy

Army Form C. 2118.

WAR DIARY
or
INTELLIGENCE SUMMARY.
(Erase heading not required.)

3D Signals Vol 26

Place	Date	Hour	Summary of Events and Information	Remarks and references to Appendices
	October 1917			Appendix 'A' Report on Operations at YPRES, maps, etc.
YPRES	1st	10am	Handed over lines at Ypres to 3rd Cavl. Div. Sig. Coy. Company marched to WINNIZEELE and spent night at same hour.	
WINNIZEELE	2nd		Entrained all attached personnel.	
"	4th		Proceeded to RENESCURE by road march	
RENESCURE	5		At RENESCURE	
"	6	3am	Rest Coy to STOMER — Entrained for BAPAUME	
BAPAUME	6	8pm	Detrained at BAPAUME WEST and marched to old HQ at HARLINCOURT	
HARLINCOURT	7.8.9.10		Reconnaissance of area of 63rd Divt	
MONUMENT	12	10am	Took over command from 62nd Div Sig Coy	
	13–31		Nothing outstanding. Divisional lines continually patrolled, lengthen & repaired. A heavy rate of late censure along RAILWAY RESERVE, a cooking park of VII Corps sigsub being hit the telephone lines very often interrupted by low flying RE8's of the working parks the trenches came from the W end of Rly tram up to	

WAR DIARY
or
INTELLIGENCE SUMMARY.
(Erase heading not required.)

Army Form C. 2118.

Place	Date	Hour	Summary of Events and Information	Remarks and references to Appendices
At Bn Hdqtrs			H.Q. of Left Brigade. 50 prisoners (Rain)	
			Ampflep- in Shelters in D.O. at junction TANK ALLEY and R & Roads. Wiring of importance in view.	
	26th		Silent School: A School for about 60 gup'rls started at LIETTA	
			Hutting: Our ASTRIAN Rest for men & 2 missions will enrich, also two Rests for NCO's	
			Horse Lines: There were funerals of Colonel Hannaford	
	1st - 31st		Casualties: Nil Health Good	

G. Wilham Maj RE
O.C. 3rd Rest Lp Co.

Field Service Appendix RE

Army Form C. 2118.

WAR DIARY
or
INTELLIGENCE SUMMARY.
(Erase heading not required.)

Instructions regarding War Diaries and Intelligence Summaries are contained in F.S. Regs., Part II. and the Staff Manual respectively. Title pages will be prepared in manuscript.

Place	Date	Hour	Summary of Events and Information	Remarks and references to Appendices
MONUMENT	Oct- COMMENCE 1st/6th J*		November 1917	
			General maintenance work on roads. No burnt calls — 60 pairs —	
			Completed to Bay at 69 and test points installed	
			Field Kitchens sent on patrol were put into training all Sub over loaded	
	8th		Commenced + Part road parallel to BUCQUOY ECOURT ROAD	
			9 New Armoury guards from VAULTS to post Service at C&C	
	9th		Completed services and tested through to Railway Reserve	
	10-17		General maintenance & training	
	17/18 night		Laid 2 pairs from burnt work in Sydney St to Railway Reserve (Bay at No 69)	
	18/19 night		Commenced up all M.G. Positions to Batteries HQ's for "Z" Day	
	19/20 "		Took over visual station 8th & 9th Inf Bde. Moved up to NOREUIL & RAILWAY RESERVE respectively	
			holding Sounder at Batty H.Q.	
			Installed 3 Aircraft & 6 P.B. for use of 9th Div on Z Day	

A6945 Wt. W11422/M1160 350,000 12/16 D. D. & L. Forms/C/2118/14.

Army Form C. 2118.

WAR DIARY
or
INTELLIGENCE SUMMARY.
(Erase heading not required.)

Instructions regarding War Diaries and Intelligence Summaries are contained in F. S. Regs., Part II, and the Staff Manual respectively. Title pages will be prepared in manuscript.

Place	Date	Hour	Summary of Events and Information	Remarks and references to Appendices
	20	6.20	Zero. Our guns fell through. Our P.B. sent over both attacking trips and did good work. All S.O.S. signal sent & correctly received. Also Wr messages. Visual worked well. In trouble with communication except in London Sappers & Tower Support. Shot was Jewish shelled.	
			"Break down" Sany installed at ECOUST.	
	21		No attempts to fratise. Capt WRIGHT to VII Corps School. Lieut SPEIGHT in his place.	
	22-26		General manoeuvres. Withdraw "Breakdown" Sany on 26th.	
	28th		Laid 2 pair for VAULX to Bde Hq at LYENCOURT CROSS RDS for 9th Bde.	
	29.30		Manoeuvres.	
			Section gets better during TR mouth good. Gun good. Slate improved, want of wire, wires. Brass clippers	

Q Walkham Maj RE OC 3 Corps Coy.

Army Form C. 2118.

3rd Divisnl Signal Co R.E WAR DIARY
or
INTELLIGENCE SUMMARY.

Instructions regarding War Diaries and Intelligence
Summaries are contained in F.S. Regs., Part II.
and the Staff Manual respectively. Title pages
will be prepared in manuscript.

(Erase heading not required.)

Wt 30

Place	Date	Hour	Summary of Events and Information	Remarks and references to Appendices
(Sheet 57C) H.15.C. "the Monument"	Dec 1st		Telegraph and telephone circuit lines in good order. Maintenance parties patrolling routes.	
" "	2nd		Raising Permanent line Routes between H.15.C (Sheet 57c) the Monument and FAVREUIL.	
" "	3rd		Routine Work.	
" "	4th		Erection of Permanent line from the MONUMENT to BEUGNATRE. Repair of line between VAULX and L'HOMME MORT.	
" "	5th		Continuation of the work of the 5th.	
" "	6th		Further construction on line route from MONUMENT to BEUGNATRE	
" "	7th		Continuation of work of the 4th	
" "	8th		Ground lines laid between VAULX and NOREUIL.	
" "	9th		Lieut SOMERS-SMITH R.E (S.R) leaves this unit for 16th Divnl Sig Co. 3rd Army Signal Co. Lieut C.C. STRICK joins the 3rd Divn Sig Co R.E from the 3rd Army Signal Co R.E.	
			lines erected on Army Route W. of BAPAUME - ERVILLERS Road. Maintenance parties on other routes.	
	10th		Repair work on Perm. lines around MORY.	

2nd Division Signal Co. R.E.

WAR DIARY
or
INTELLIGENCE SUMMARY
(Erase heading not required.)

Army Form C. 2118.

Place	Date	Hour	Summary of Events and Information	Remarks and references to Appendices
H.Qs at THE MONUMENT H-15C (Sheet 57c)	Dec 11th		Cable laid from MORY tied bar to BEHAGNIES. (4D Div. H.Q.)	
	12th		Routine work.	
	13th		Wire work at BEHAGNIES.	
THE MONUMENT 14th		10am	H.Qs moved to BEHAGNIES. Several alterations made on lines leading to Brigades and other units to new H.Qs.	
BEHAGNIES.	14			
	15th		Maintenance work on lines between BEHAGNIES and MORY	
	16th		General Maintenance work on lines. Lieut C.S. BROADWOOD G.L. and to St Pol to take charge of Signal Section in place of Lieut C.H. MARTIN posted to H.Qs Section	
	18th-19th		Routine work	
	20th		Salvaging cable VAULX - LAGNICOURT district.	
	21st - 22nd		Erection of permanent lines forward of MORY.	
	23rd		do do	
	24th		Heavy snowstorm & frost. Several lines down on various routes. All communication through by noon	

A6945 Wt. W14422/M1160 350,000 12/16 D. D. & L. Forms/C./2118/14.

(3)

3rd Division Signal Coy R.E. **WAR DIARY**
or
INTELLIGENCE SUMMARY

Army Form 2118.

Place	Date	Hour	Summary of Events and Information	Remarks and references to Appendices
	Dec			
	24th		Portion of semi-perm: route damaged by shell fire. Necessary repairs made.	
	25th, 26th		Working Parties sent out to repair lines around VAULX	
	27th		Good traffic situation	
	28th		Maintenance Party on lines forward of MORY.	
	29th		Continuation of work of the 28th.	
	30th		Line work around MORY completed. Communications handed over to 40th Div	
	31st	9/30pm	Breakdown on corps trunks to DADOS and 283 M.G.Co. Repaired	

J.C.D. Phillips
Capt. R.E.
for O.C. 3rd Div. Sig. Co. R.E.

3 DIVISION SIGNAL COY.

1918 JAN — 1919 MAY

Box 1404

"3RD DIV. SIG. CO. R.E."

3rd Signal — Vol 31

Army Form C. 2118.

WAR DIARY
INTELLIGENCE SUMMARY

(Erase heading not required.)

Instructions regarding War Diaries and Intelligence Summaries are contained in F. S. Regs., Part II. and the Staff Manual respectively. Title pages will be prepared in manuscript.

Place	Date	Hour	Summary of Events and Information	Remarks and references to Appendices
	January			
BEHAGNIES.	1.		Routine Work.	
"	2		" "	
"	3		" "	
"	4		" "	
"	5		" "	
"	6		" "	
BEHAGNIES & GOMIECOURT.	7		Divl. HQs. closed at BEHAGNIES 12 noon and reopened same hour at GOMIECOURT.	
GOMIECOURT.	8		Routine Work.	
"	9		" "	
"	10		" "	
"	11		" "	
"	12		" "	
"	13		" "	
"	14		" "	
"	15		" "	
"	16		" "	

3rd Divn Sig: Co R.E.

WAR DIARY
or
INTELLIGENCE SUMMARY.
(Erase heading not required.)

Army Form C. 2118.

Place	Date	Hour	Summary of Events and Information	Remarks and references to Appendices
GOMIECOURT	JANUARY 17		Routine work	
"	18		" "	
"	19		" "	
"	20		" "	
"	21		" "	
"	22		" "	
"	23		" "	
"	24		" "	
"	25		" "	
"	26		" "	
"	27		" "	
"	28		" "	
"	29		Divl HQrs closed at GOMIECOURT at 10 am and opened same hour at BOISLEUX-AU-MONT	
BOISLEUX-AU-MONT	30		General Routine work and improving Camp.	
"	31		" " " " "	
"	FEB 1		" " " " "	

WAR DIARY
-of-
INTELLIGENCE SUMMARY.
(Erase heading not required.) 3RD DIV. SIGNAL COY. R.E.

Army Form C. 2118.

Vol 32

Instructions regarding War Diaries and Intelligence Summaries are contained in F. S. Regs., Part II. and the Staff Manual respectively. Title pages will be prepared in manuscript.

Place	Date	Hour	Summary of Events and Information	Remarks and references to Appendices
BOISLEUX -AU-MONT	FEBRUARY 1		Division H.Qs: Considerable trouble with Permanent lines owing to frost - Routine work	
	2		" " " " " "	
	3		" " " " " "	
	4		Repairs of Lines & routine work	
	5		Routine work. Renewal of Brigade lines	
	6		Routine work. Maintenance of lines etc	
	7		" " " " "	
	8		" " " " "	
	9		Laying Armd Cable E of Arras-Bapaume Road - Brigade to Div Comm"	
	10		" " " " "	
	11		" " " " "	
	12		" " " " "	
	13		" " " " "	
	14		" " " " "	
	15		" " " " "	
	16		" " " " "	

Sheet 2.

WAR DIARY
INTELLIGENCE SUMMARY.

(Erase heading not required.) 3RD. DIVISION SIGNAL Co R.E.

Army Form C.2118.

Place	Date	Hour	Summary of Events and Information	Remarks and references to Appendices
BOISLEUX -AU-MONT.	17		General routine work. Laying ground lines Divi to Bde.	
"	18		Testing Divi to Bde visual Signalling - Routine work. Laying ground lines to Divi Bde.	
"	19		" " " " " " "	
"	20		" " " " " " "	
"	21		Routine work. Line laying to new position of Bde HQs.	
"	22		" " "	
"	23		" " "	
"	24		" " "	
"	25		" " "	
"	26		" " "	
"	27		Routine Work. Building Dugout for Signal Office. Laying lines to new position for 9th Bde HQs.	
"	28		" " " " " " "	

J.C.O. Phillips
Capt RE
for O.C. 3rd Divl Sig Coy R.E.

3rd Divisional Engineers

3rd DIVISIONAL SIGNAL COMPANY R.E.

MARCH 1918

The D.A.G.
    3rd Echelon.

Herewith enclosed please find War Diary of this Unit for the month of March.

GCD Phillips
Capt R.E

for OC.

WAR DIARY
or
INTELLIGENCE SUMMARY.
(Erase heading not required.)

Army Form C. 2118.

3 Div Signal Coy
Sheet I

Place	Date 1916	Hour	Summary of Events and Information	Remarks and references to Appendices
BOISLEUX AU MONT	MARCH 1		Ordin: Work. Building Aug: but for Signal Office.	Fine - Frost
	2		"	"
	3		" { laying ground lines to hus Brigade Headquarters	"
	4		"	"
	5		"	"
	6		"	"
	7		"	"
	8		" { laying ground lines from M.G. Company Headquarters to Batteries.	"
	9		"	"
	10		"	"
	11		"	"
	12		"	"
	13		" tightening overhead lines at various points.	2nd Lt V. DYKES posted from 3rd Army Sig. C.
	14		"	Div. to BOE Nichol & buried communication maintained
	15		"	"
	16		" laying new Cope Buried trunk	"

Army Form C. 2118.

WAR DIARY
or
INTELLIGENCE SUMMARY.
(Erase heading not required.)

Sheet 2

Place	Date	Hour	Summary of Events and Information	Remarks and references to Appendices
BOISLEUX AU MONT	MARCH 17		Routine Work.	
	18		" " Laying new line Burial Route.	
	19		" "	
	20		" "	
	21		" " maintaining found lines and jointing new line Burial Route	
	22		" "	
BRETENCOURT	23		Move to Bretencourt.	
	24		Routine Work.	Division to Brigade Visual and Wireless communication maintained. From 3.29 pm 24th until landing over to KDG on the night 29th/30th wireless traffic was taken for the Guards Division to into Flanking Divisions and Guards Supply Dues.
	25		" " Laying and maintaining	
	26		" " ground lines to our	
	27		" " Brigade H.Q's.	
	28		" "	
	29		" "	
LUCHEUX	30		Move to Lucheux. Laying local lines.	
	31		Routine work. maintaining " " and recharging equipment.	

HCOPhillips
Captain R.E.
for O.C. 3rd Signal Co.

3rd Divisional Engineers

WAR DIARY

3rd DIVISIONAL SIGNAL COMPANY R. E.

APRIL 1918

Army Form C. 2118.

3rd DIVISIONAL SIGNAL COMPANY WAR DIARY R.E.   or   PAGE 1
INTELLIGENCE SUMMARY
(Erase heading not required.)

MAP REFERENCE SHEET (FRANCE) 36A S.E.
SHEET (FRANCE) 36A N.E.

Vol 34

3rd DIVISIONAL SIGNAL COY'S. R.E.

Place	Date	Hour	Summary of Events and Information	Remarks and references to Appendices
BRUAY	APRIL 1st		SIGNAL OFFICE closed at LUCHEUX and opened at BRUAY.	
LABEUVRIERE	2nd		Signal office closed at BRUAY and opened at LABEUVRIERE. Company moved to LABEUVRIERE	
"	3rd		maintaining local lines and overhauling equipment	
"	4th		Do.	
FOUQUIERES	5th		Signal Office closed at LABEUVRIERE, and opened at FOUQUIERES. Company moved to FOUQUIERES.	
"	6th		maintaining local lines. Company training at Horsemanship, Visual, Buzzers and general work.	
"	7th		Do.	
LABEUVRIERE	8th		Signal Office closed at FOUQUIERES and opened at LABEUVRIERE. Company returned to LABEUVRIERE	

Army Form C. 2118.

3rd DIVISIONAL SIGNAL COMPANY R.E.

WAR DIARY PAGE 2
or
INTELLIGENCE SUMMARY.

(Erase heading not required.)

Instructions regarding War Diaries and Intelligence Summaries are contained in F. S. Regs., Part II. and the Staff Manual respectively. Title pages will be prepared in manuscript.

MAP REFERENCES
SHEETS (FRANCE) 36A S.E. & 36 B N.E.

Place	Date	Hour	Summary of Events and Information	Remarks and references to Appendices
LABEUVRIERE	9		Maintained telelines. Company training - horsemanship, road, visual, cables and general instruction	
	10		Do. Do. Do.	
OBLINGHEM	11		Signal Office closed at LABEUVRIERE. Opened at OBLINGHEM. Laid this line back to Divisional aux Train Visual closed to 8th Brigade at 8 a.m. and LABEUVRIERE opened at 10 a.m. at TZA working to YCR thru this transmitter to YC. YC thru transmitter to MZL	
			Map Refs: YCR = W21.c.3.5 TZA (Bde.) = W14.a.2.5 MZL (Bde.) = W23.b.0.3	
	12		Laid lines mentioned. Visual communication maintained a.m. - pouring day.	
LABEUVRIERE	13	1pm	Power Exchange (YCR) opened at OBLINGHEM. (Officer i/c 2nd Lieut V. DYKES) and Divisional Headquarters established at LABEUVRIERE. Visual communication maintained	
	14		Lines laid back to YCR and Bdes. Visual communication in field	

3rd DIVISIONAL SIGNAL Coy R.E. Army Form C. 2118.

WAR DIARY
or
INTELLIGENCE SUMMARY

PAGE 3

MAP REFERENCES
SHEETS (FRANCE) 36.a S.E. & 36.0 N.E.

Place	Date	Hour	Summary of Events and Information	Remarks and references to Appendices
LAVENTIE	15		Lines maintained to Bdes and YCR. YCR moved to ANNEZIN. Visual signalling maintained.	(Div to Bde M.O.)
			W/T Sets opened location:-	
			Division D/S at D11 a 7.7 call AED. Ybt Bde at W.29 a 8.9 call UBC.	
			Gds Brigade E.5 c 7.7 call TEP. MAP LOCATION YCR = E.9 D.r.9	
	16		Special Radio works being W/T and visual communication maintained.	
	17		Do	Do
	18		Do	Do
	19		Do	Do
	20		Do	Do
	21		Do	Do

Army Form C. 2118.

WAR DIARY
or
INTELLIGENCE SUMMARY.
(Erase heading not required.)

3rd DIVISIONAL SIGNAL COMPANY R.E. PAGE 4

MAP REFERENCE SHEETS (FRANCE) 36 A S.E. & 36 B. N.E.

Instructions regarding War Diaries and Intelligence Summaries are contained in F. S. Regs., Part II. and the Staff Manual respectively. Title pages will be prepared in manuscript.

Place	Date	Hour	Summary of Events and Information	Remarks and references to Appendices
LAGEUVRIERE	22		Normal Routine work. Lines W/T and Visual communication maintained to Bdes. & YCR.	
	23		Do. Do. Do.	
	24		Company carrying on work as in preceding days. Physical drill &c.	
			Normal Routine work. Lines W/T and Visual communication maintained to Bdes. & YCR. Company having as preceding day.	
	25		Do. Do.	
	26		Do. Do.	
	27		Do. Do.	
			Lieut C.S. BROADWOOD O/C Signals 8th Bde returned to his Unit R M c A MATEER	
			Lieut C.S. BROADWOOD has [out] command No 5 Section (M.G. Bn.)	

A6945 Wt. W1142a/M1160 350,000 12/16 D. D. & L. Forms/C./2118/14.

Army Form C. 2118.

WAR DIARY
or
INTELLIGENCE SUMMARY.

(Erase heading not required.)

3rd DIVISIONAL SIGNAL COMPANY R.E.   PAGE 5.

MAP REFERENCE SHEETS (FRANCE) 36ᵃ S.E. & 36B N.E.

Instructions regarding War Diaries and Intelligence Summaries are contained in F. S. Regs., Part II. and the Staff Manual respectively. Title pages will be prepared in manuscript.

Place	Date	Hour	Summary of Events and Information	Remarks and references to Appendices
LABEUVRIERE	28		Quiet. Routine Work. Lines W/T and Visual Communications established to Bdes. & Y.C.R. Company training on previous days	
	29		Do Do Do Do	
			Lieut BARWOOD to Command of No 5 (M.G.) Section vice Lieut C.S. BROADWOOD	
			Lieut C.S. BROADWOOD to Y.C.R. relieving 2nd Lt. V. DYKES	
			2nd Lieut V. DYKES to Company H.Q.	
	30		Quiet Routine work. Lines W/T and Visual Communications maintained to Bdes and Y.C.R. Company training as previous days.	

J.C.O. Phillips
Captain R.E.
to O.C. 3rd Signal Company

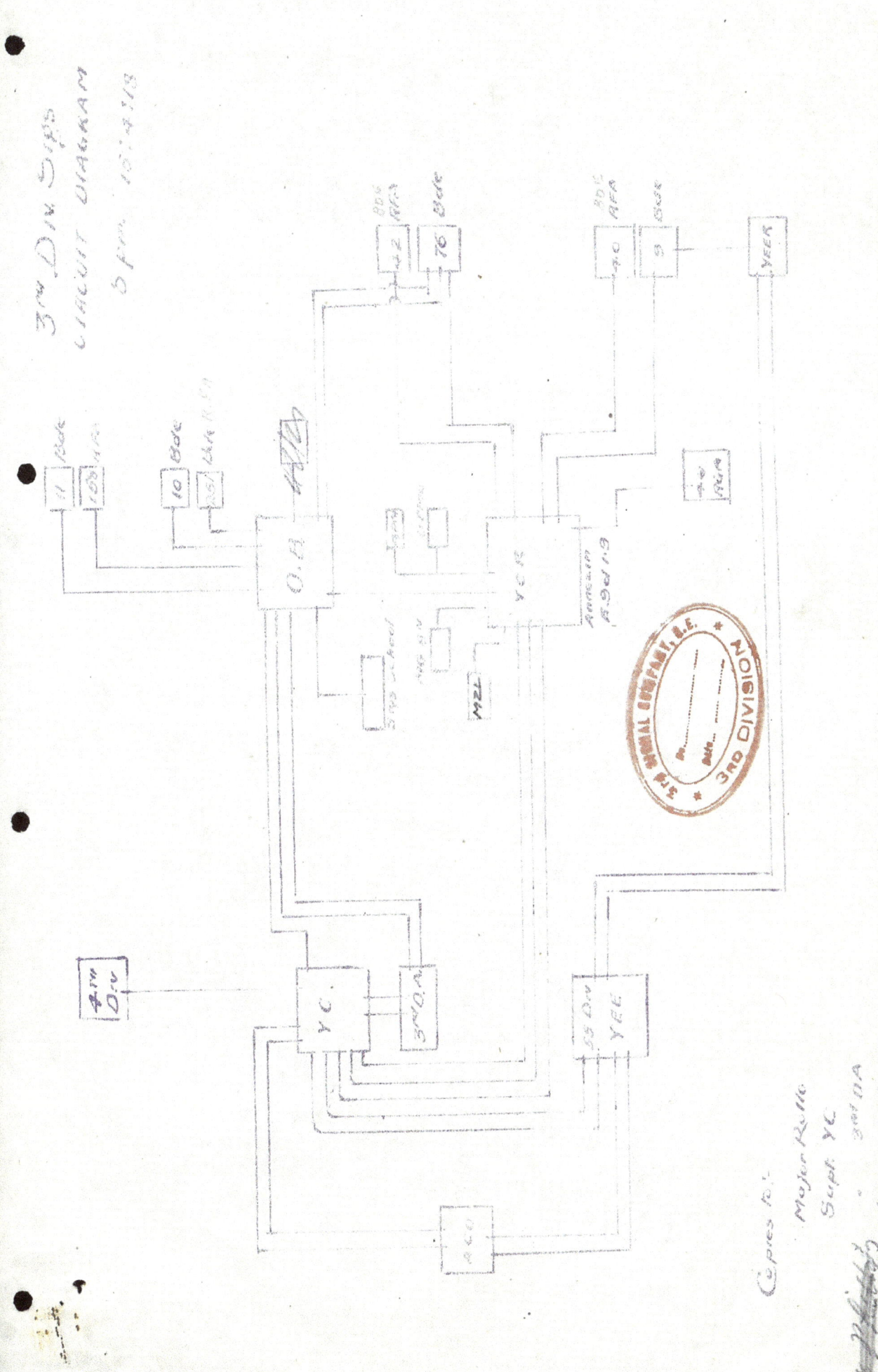

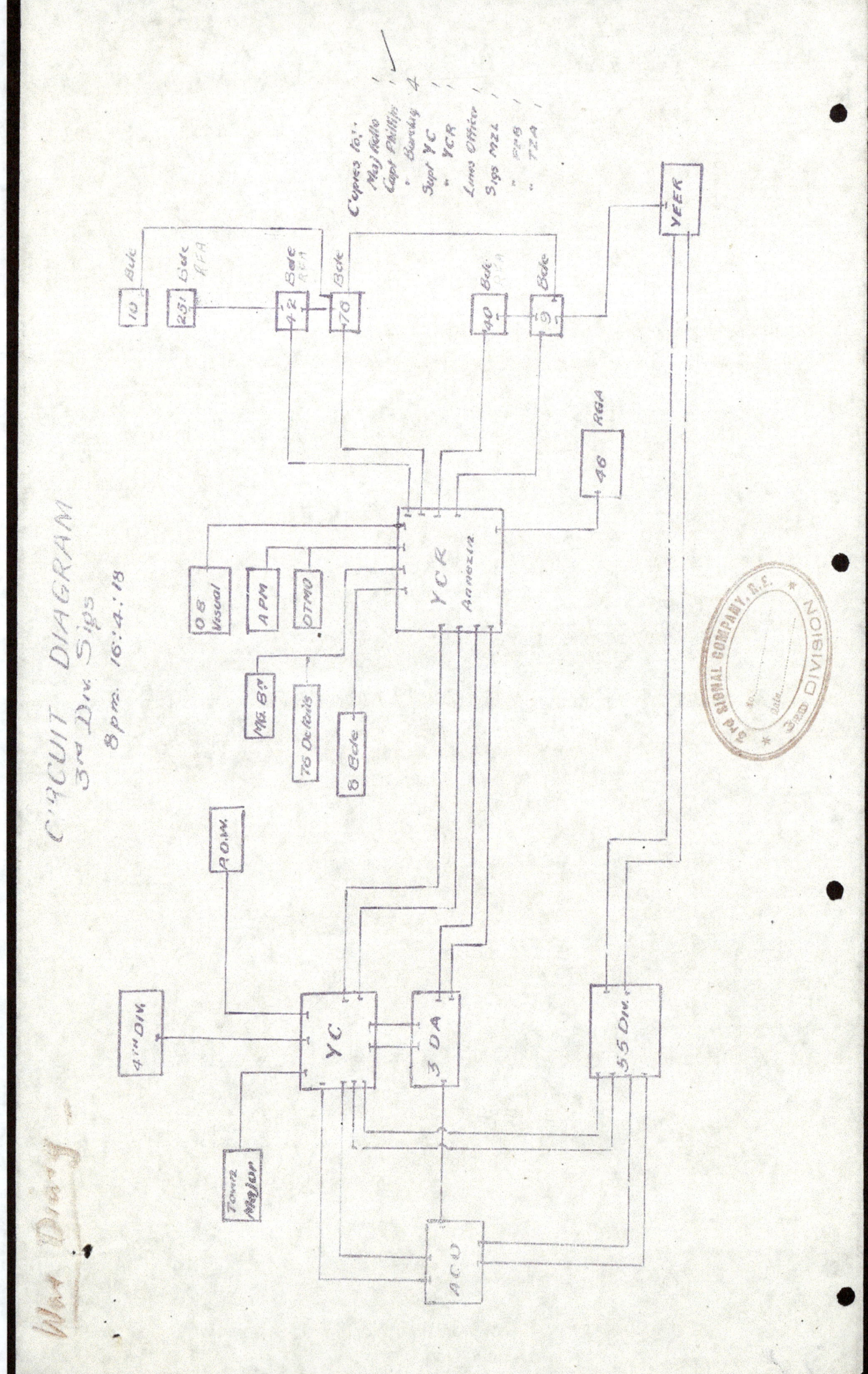

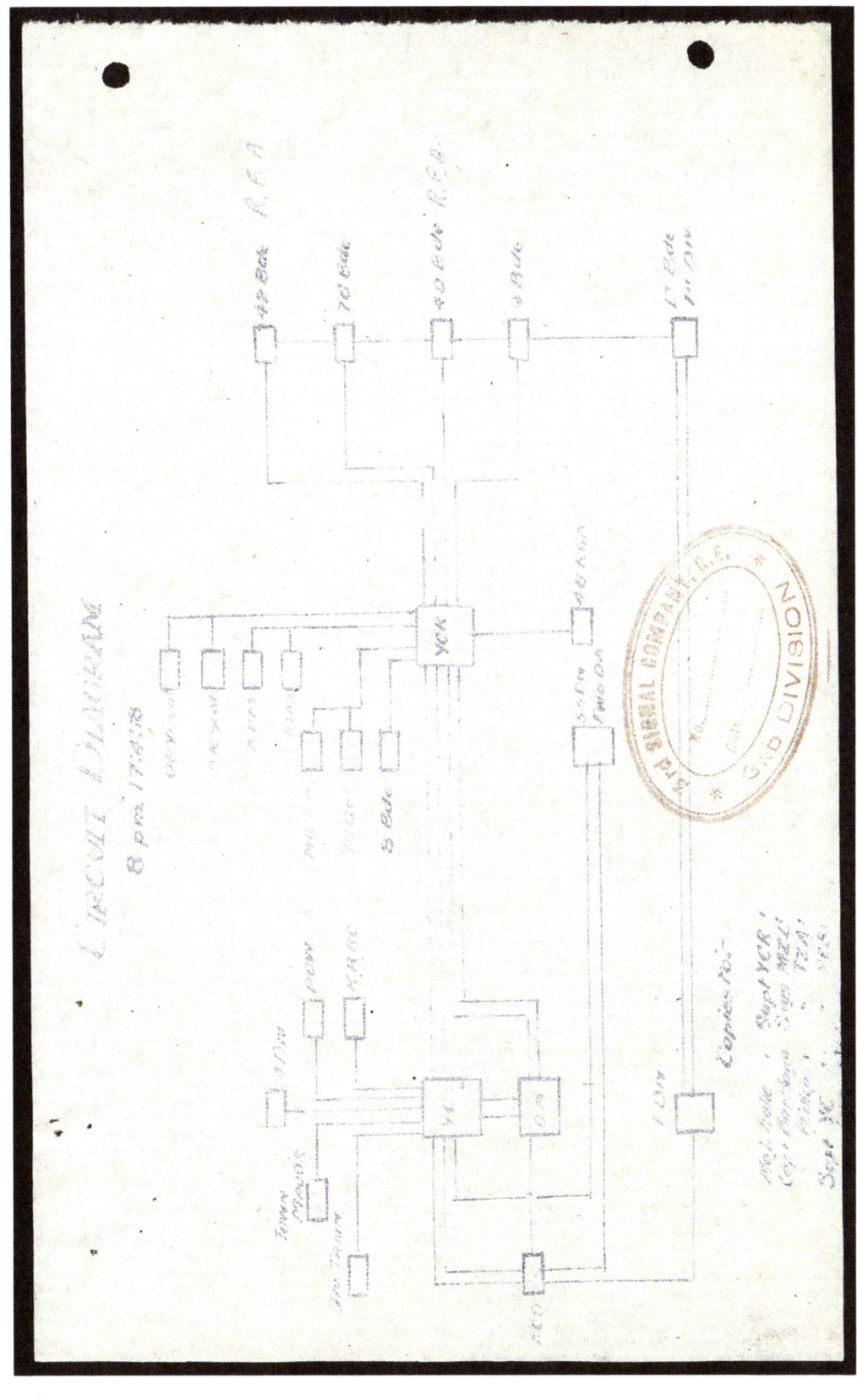

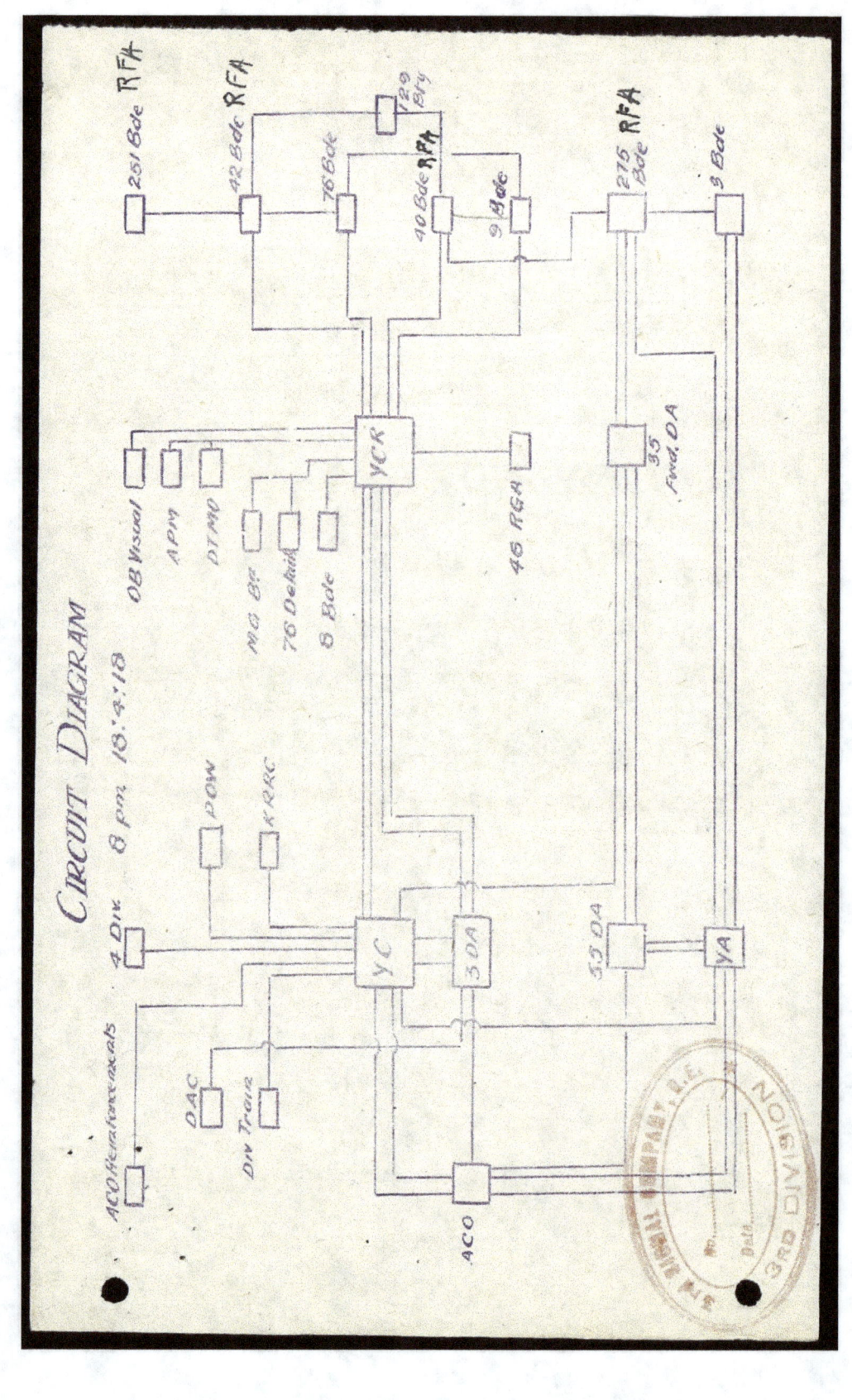

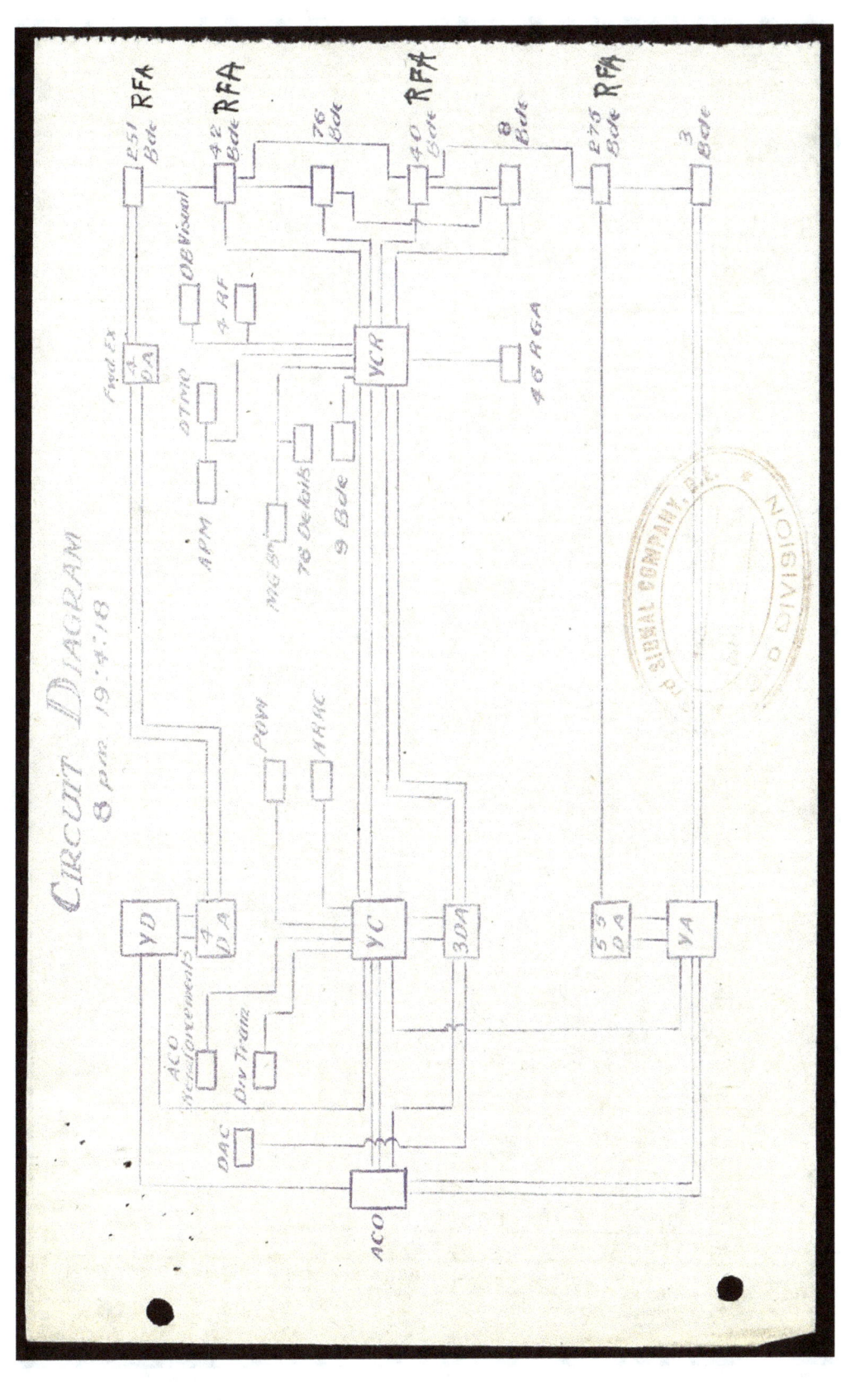

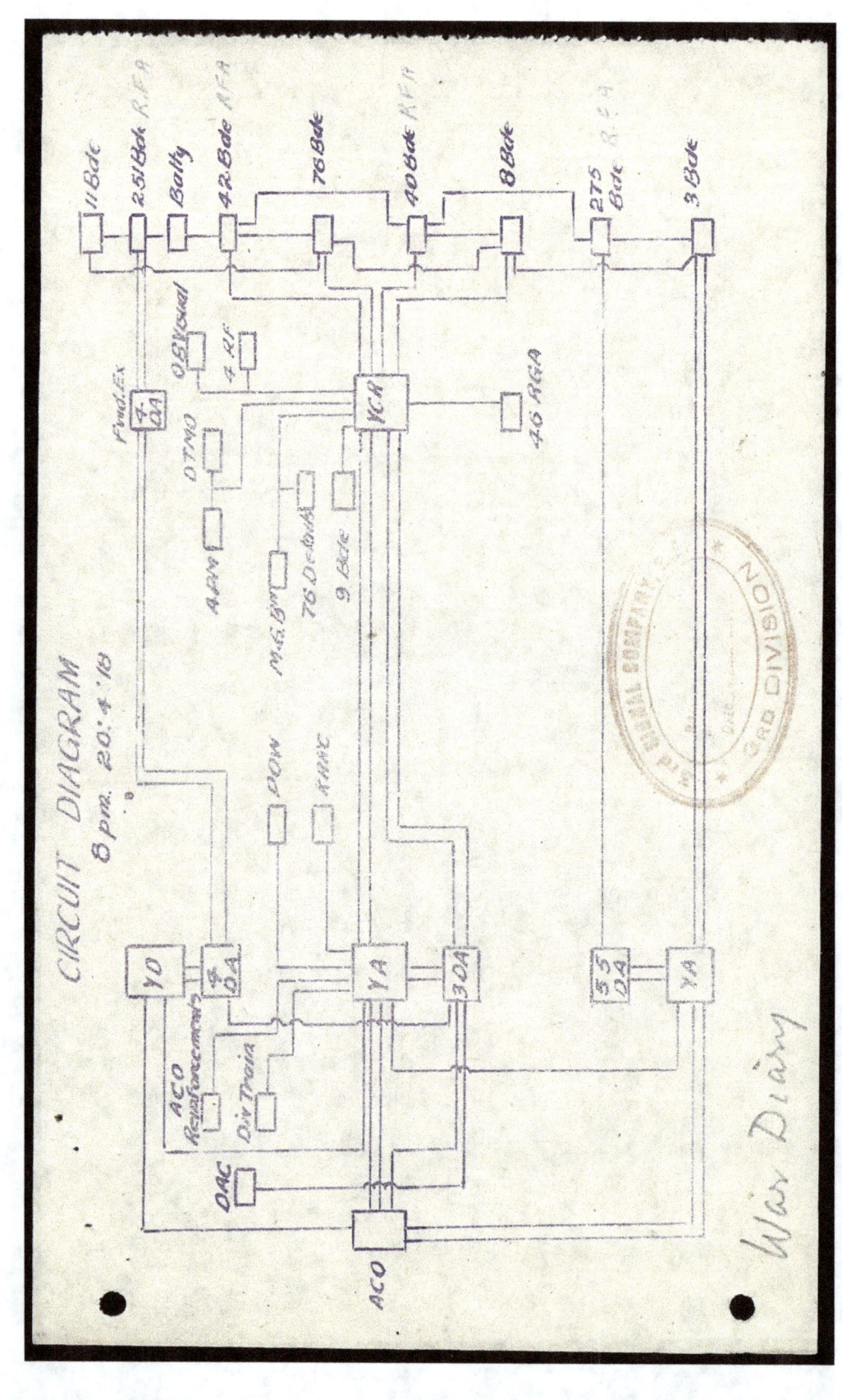

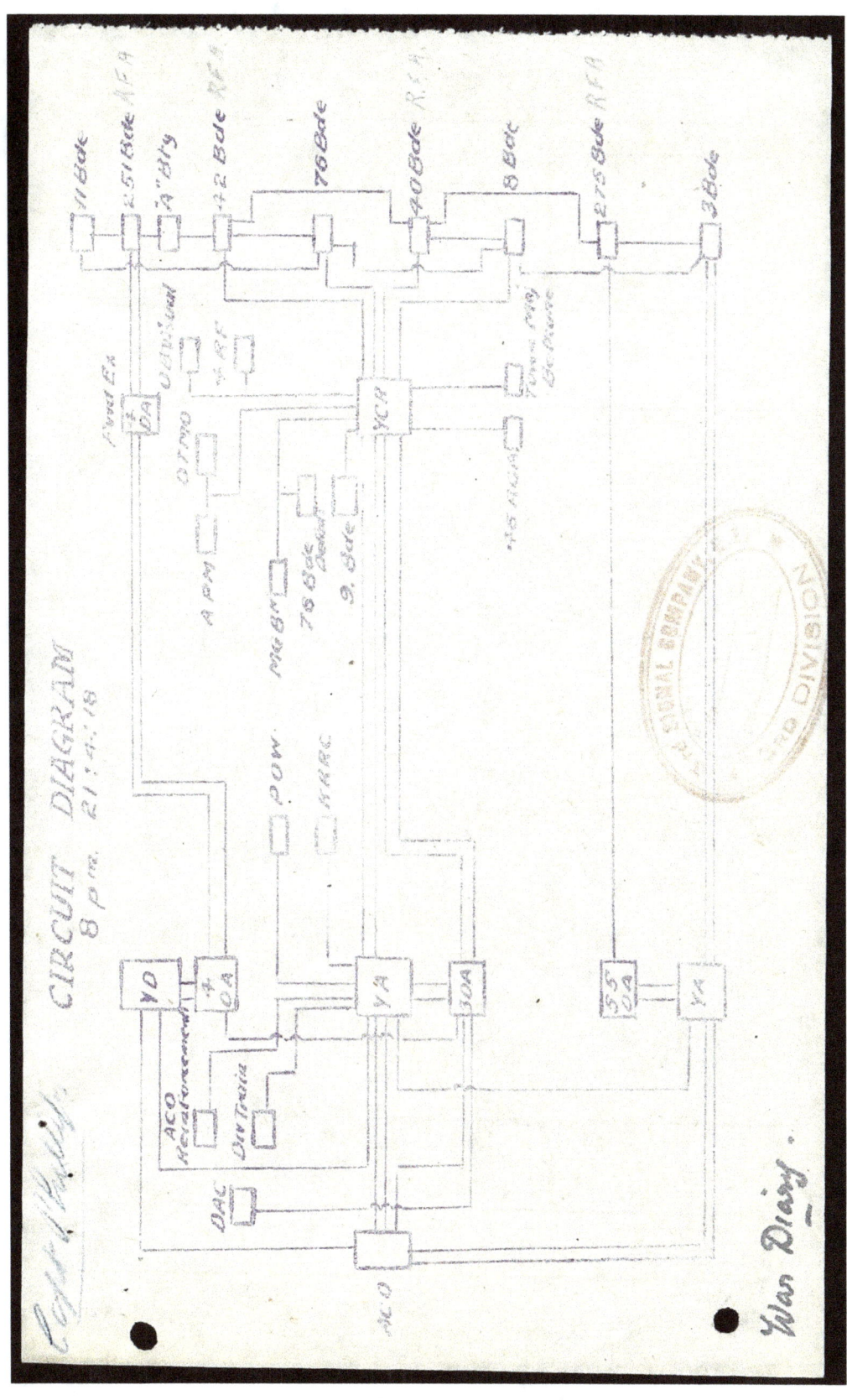

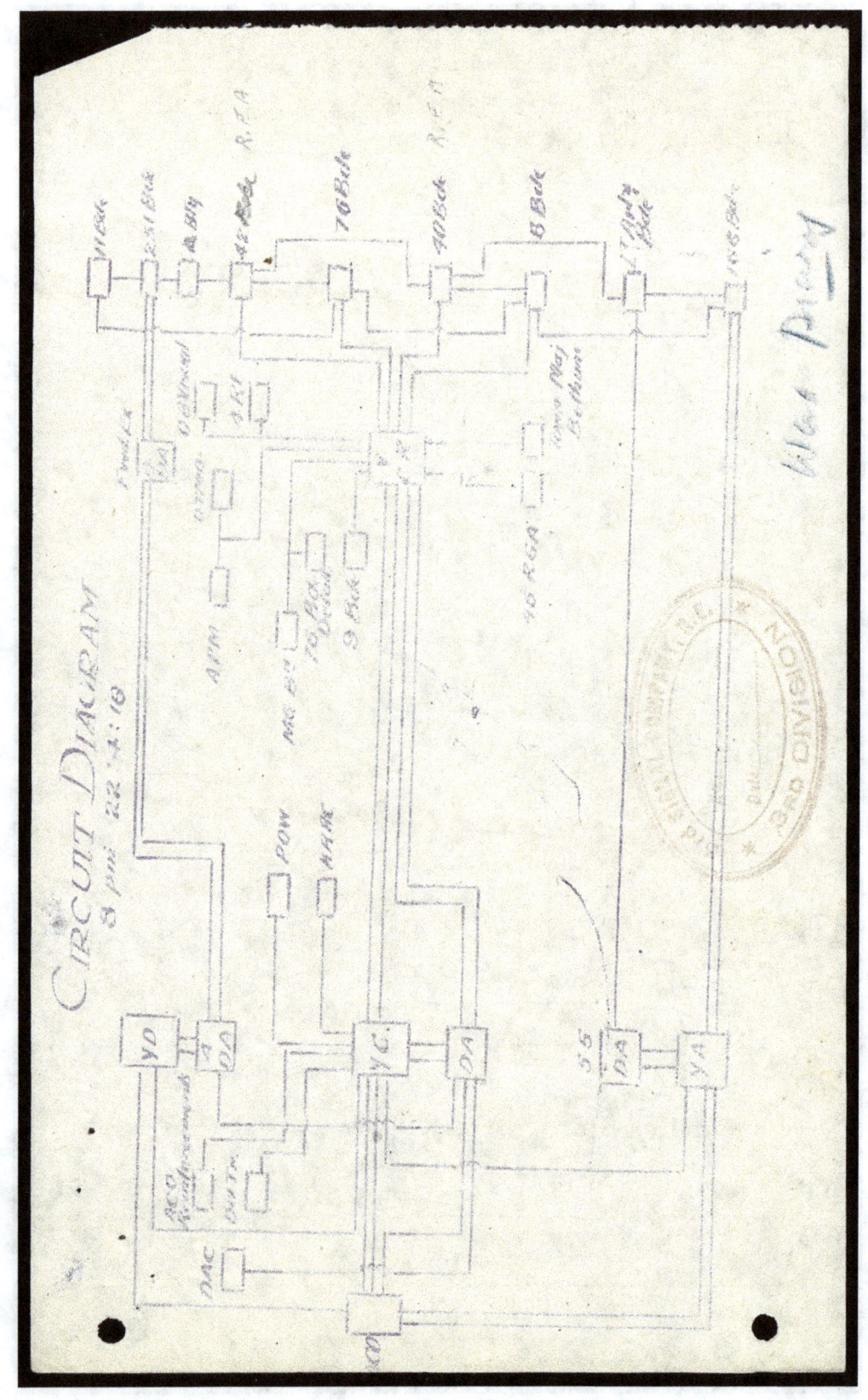

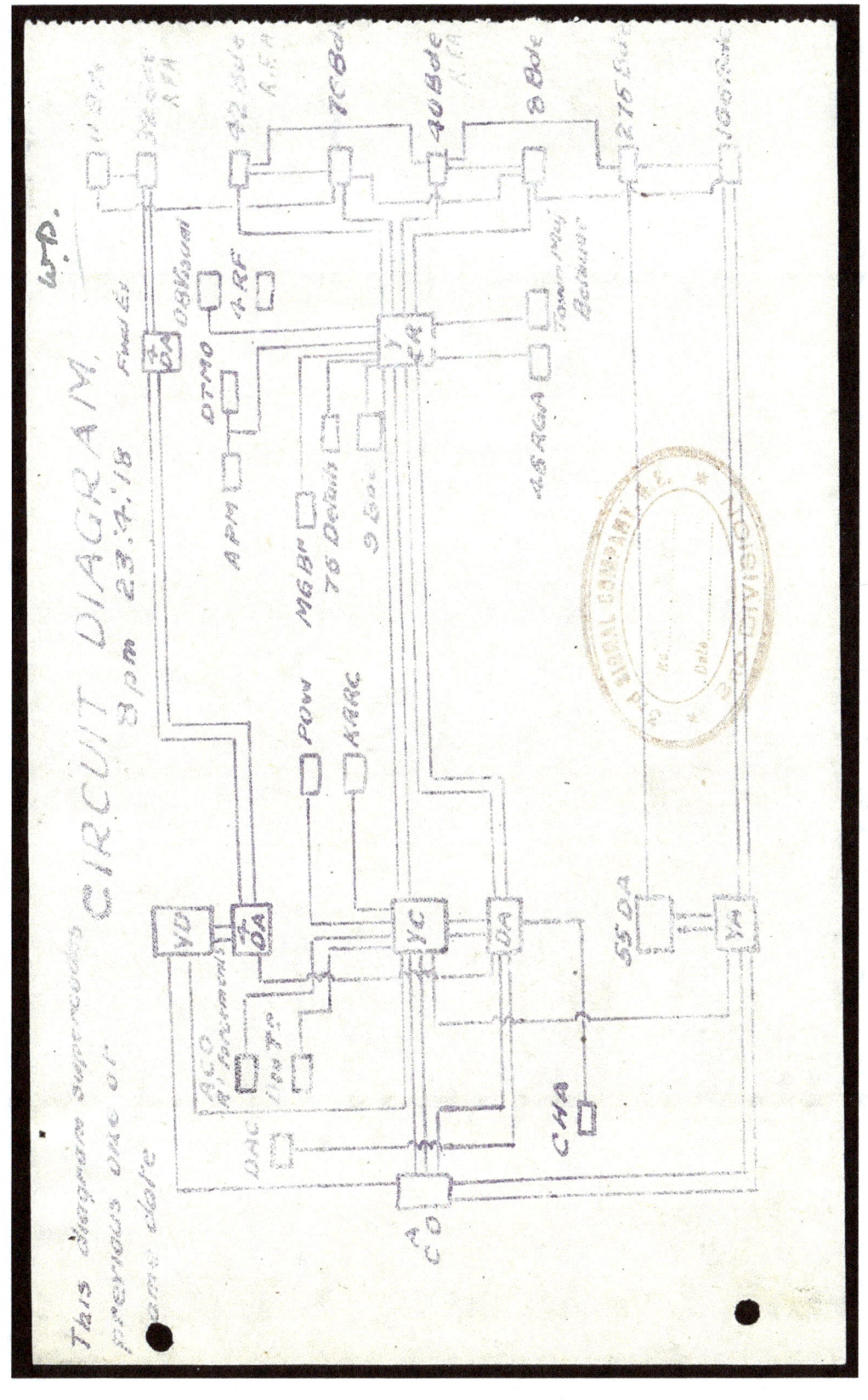

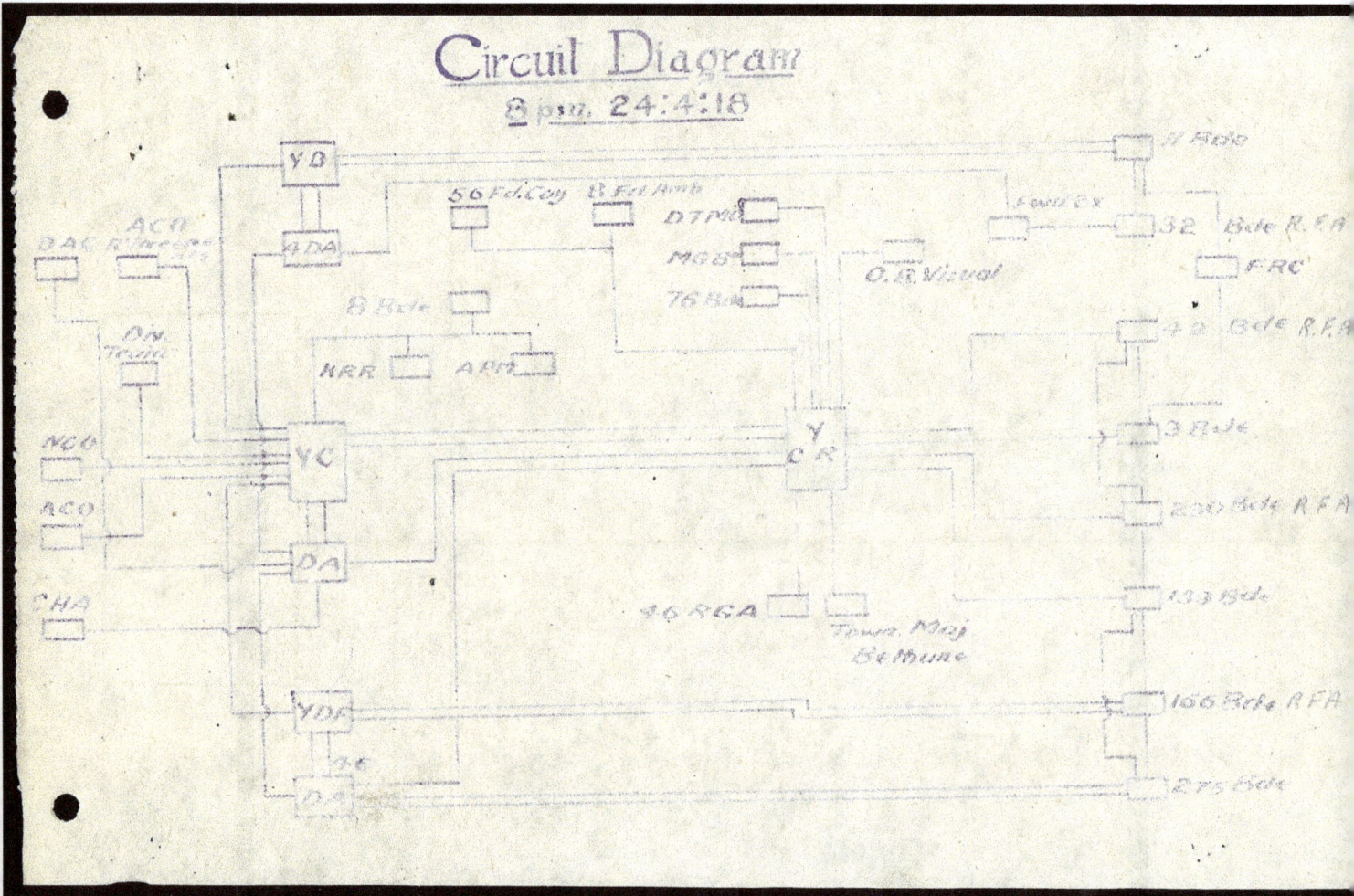

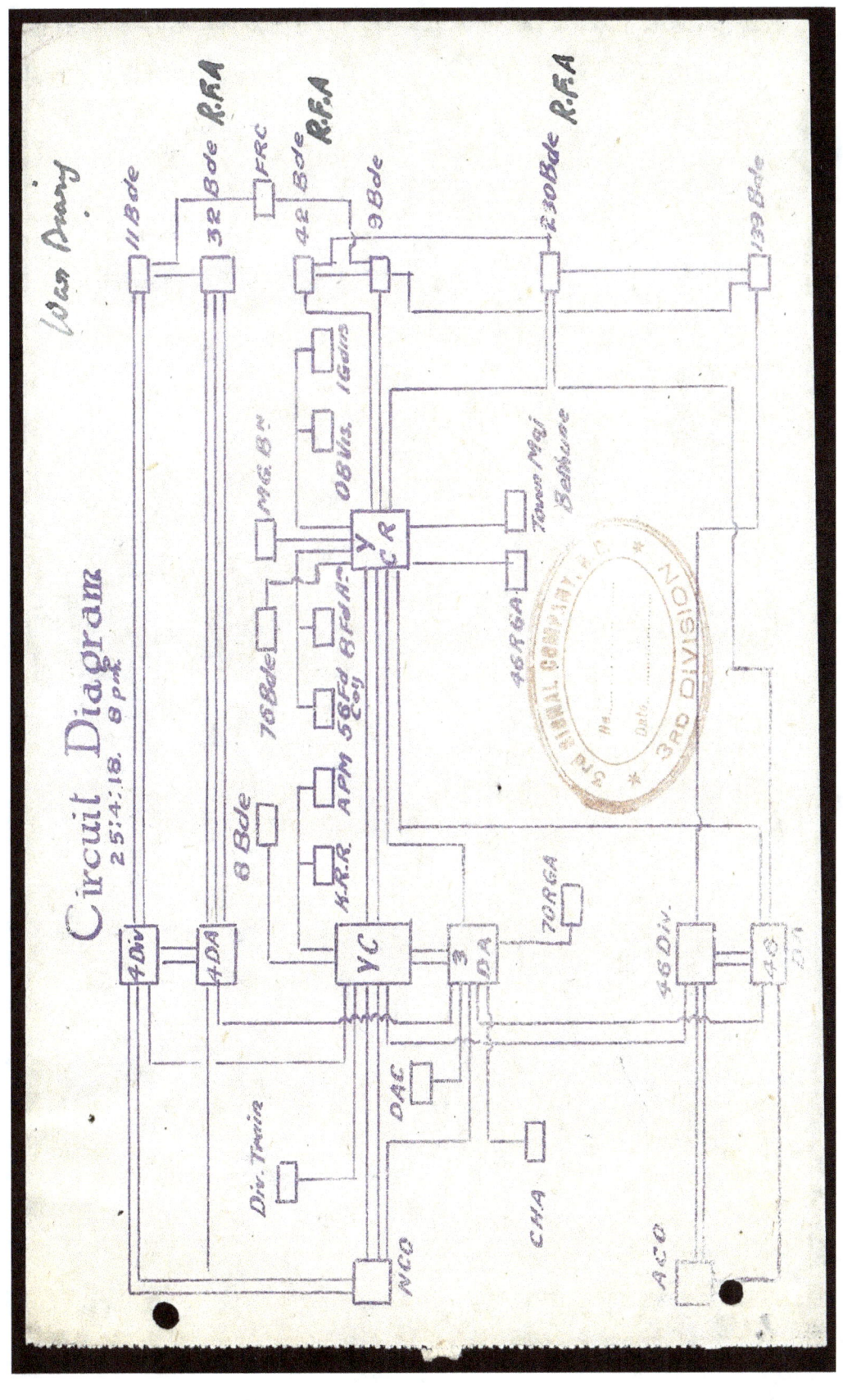

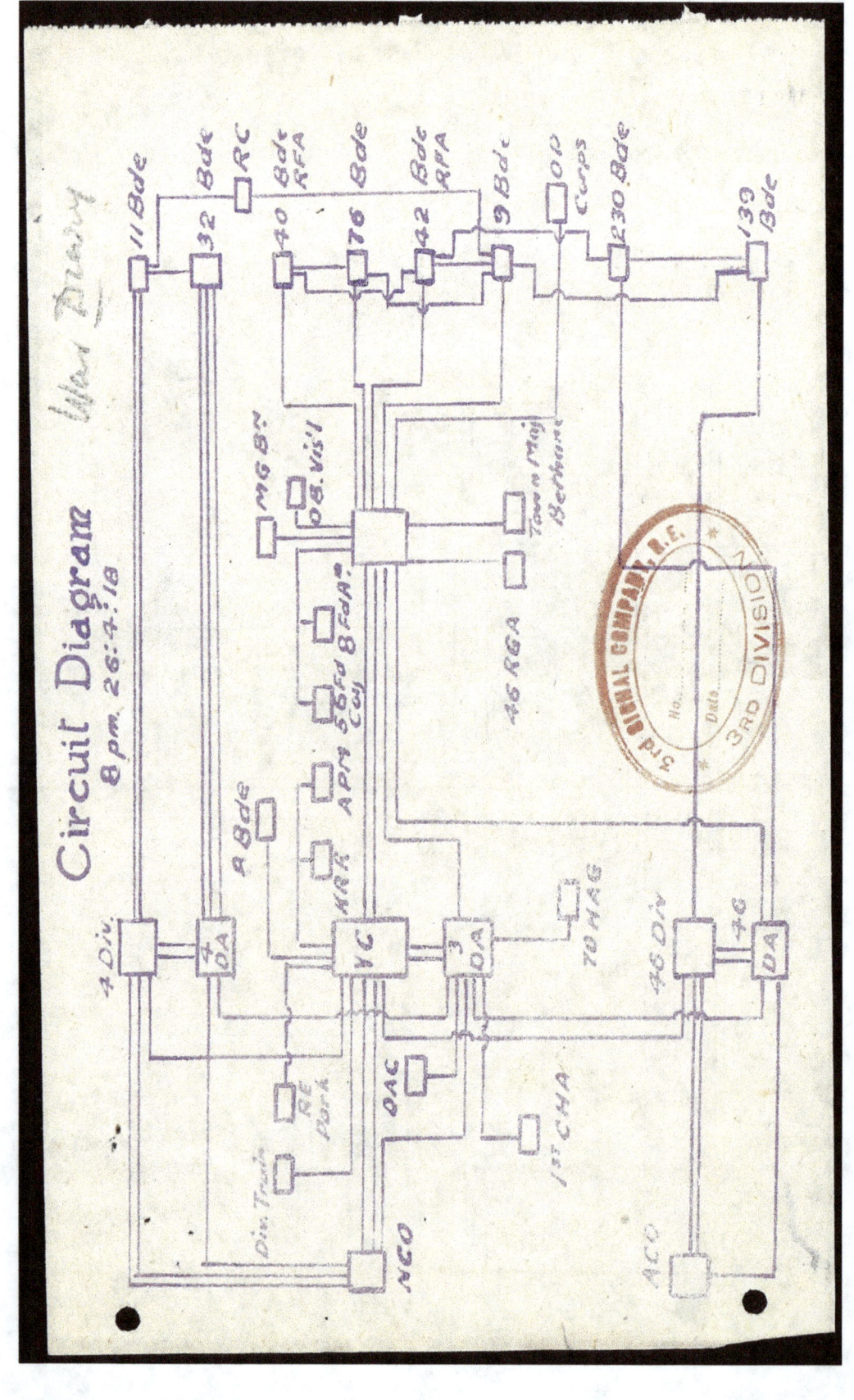

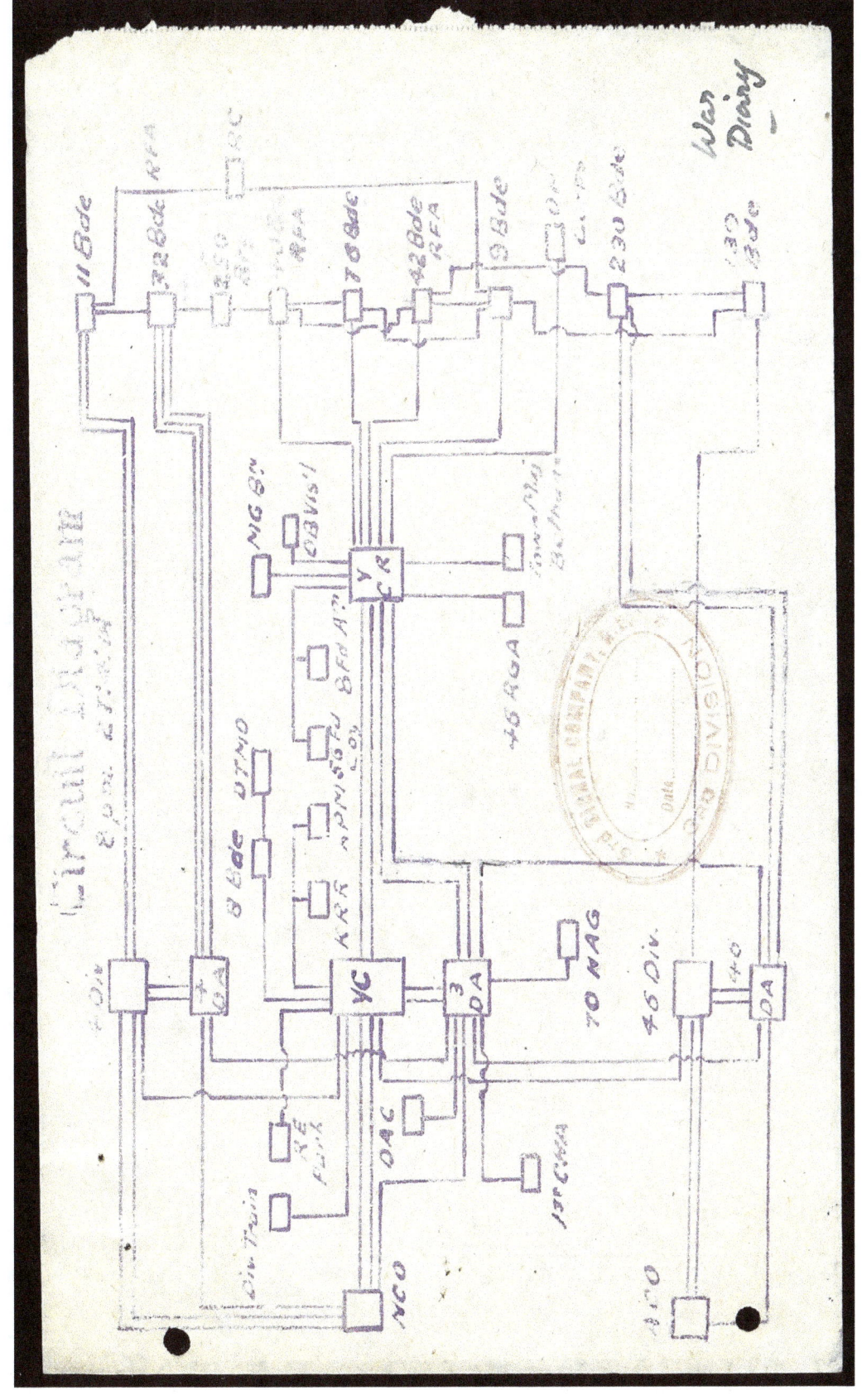

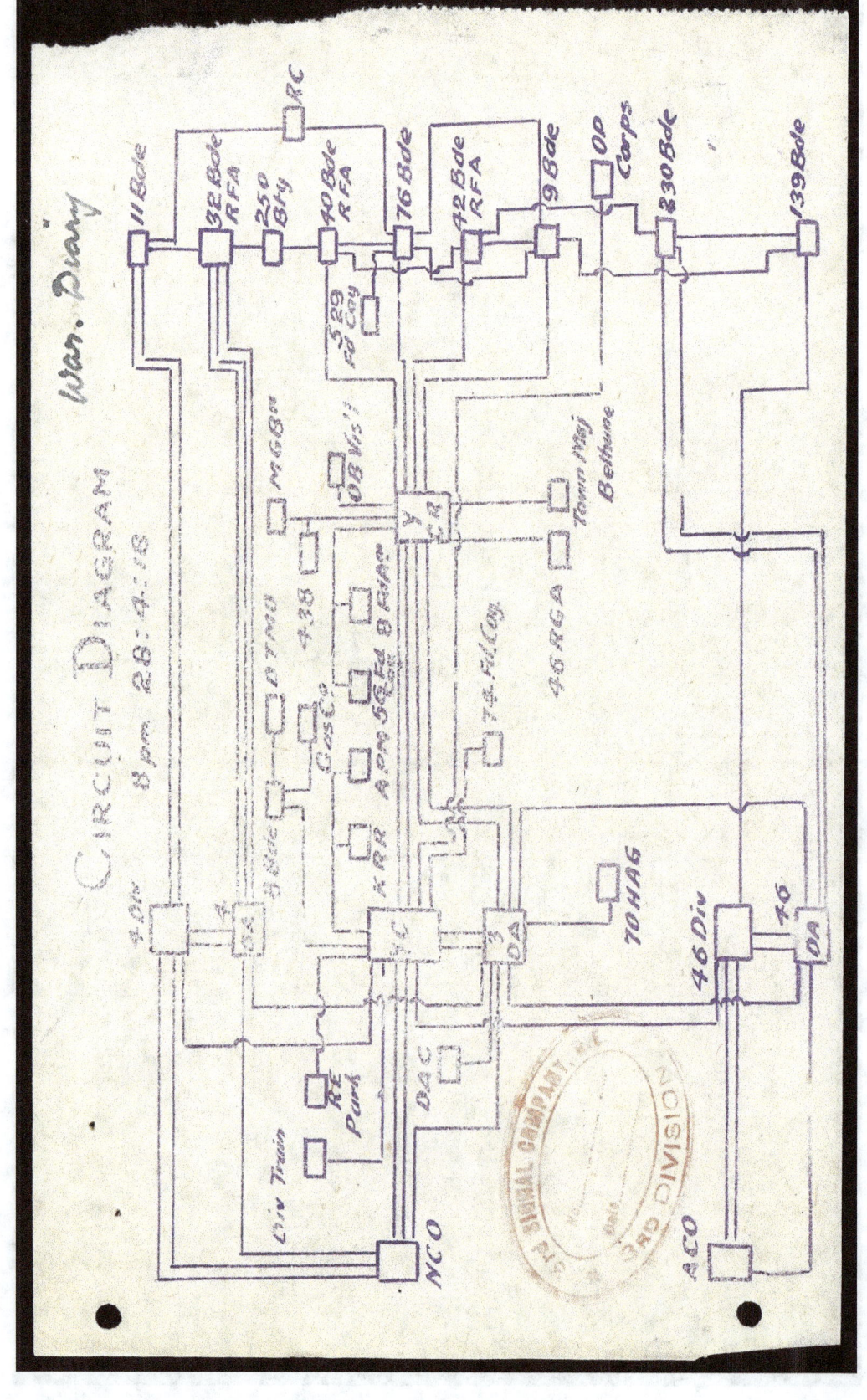

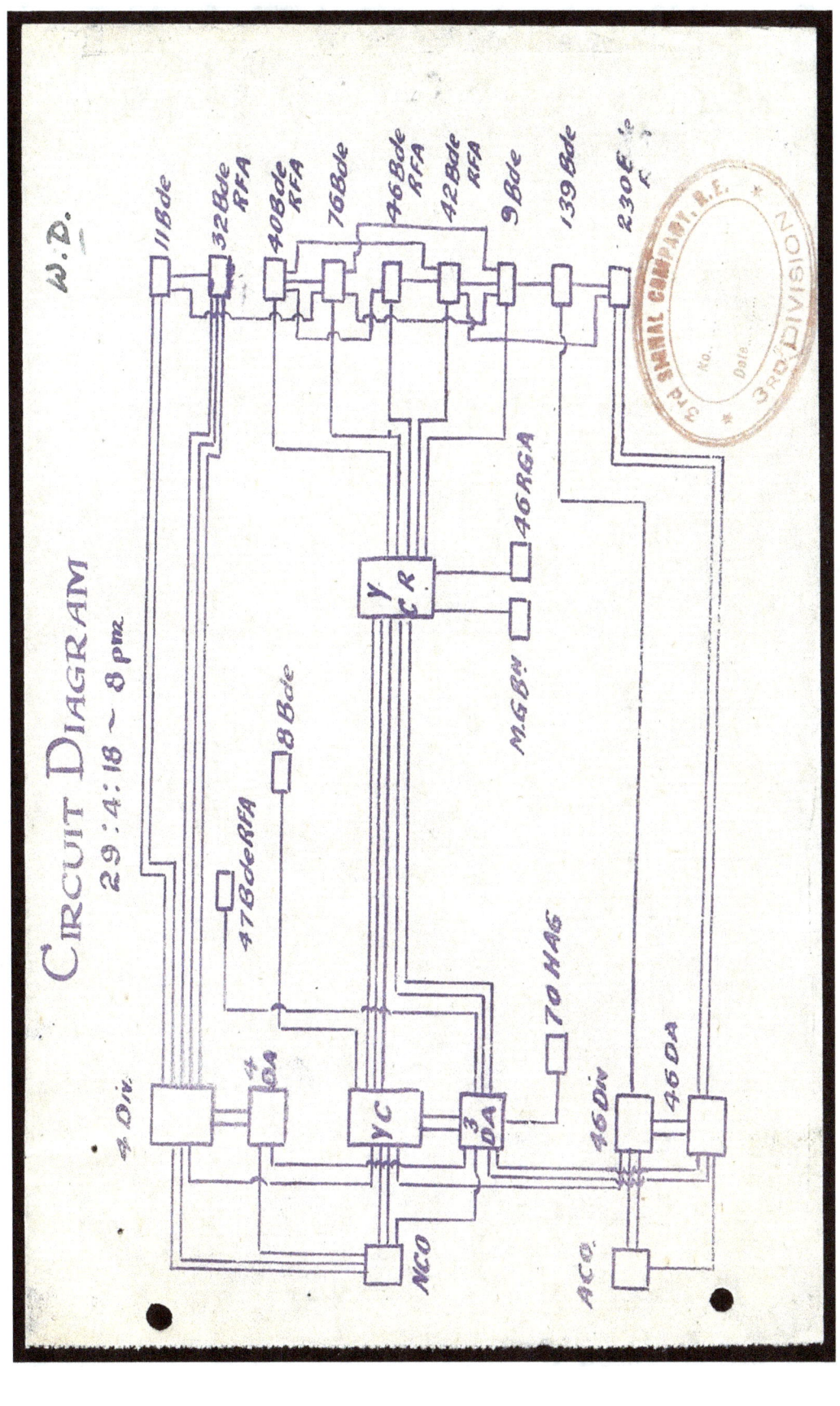

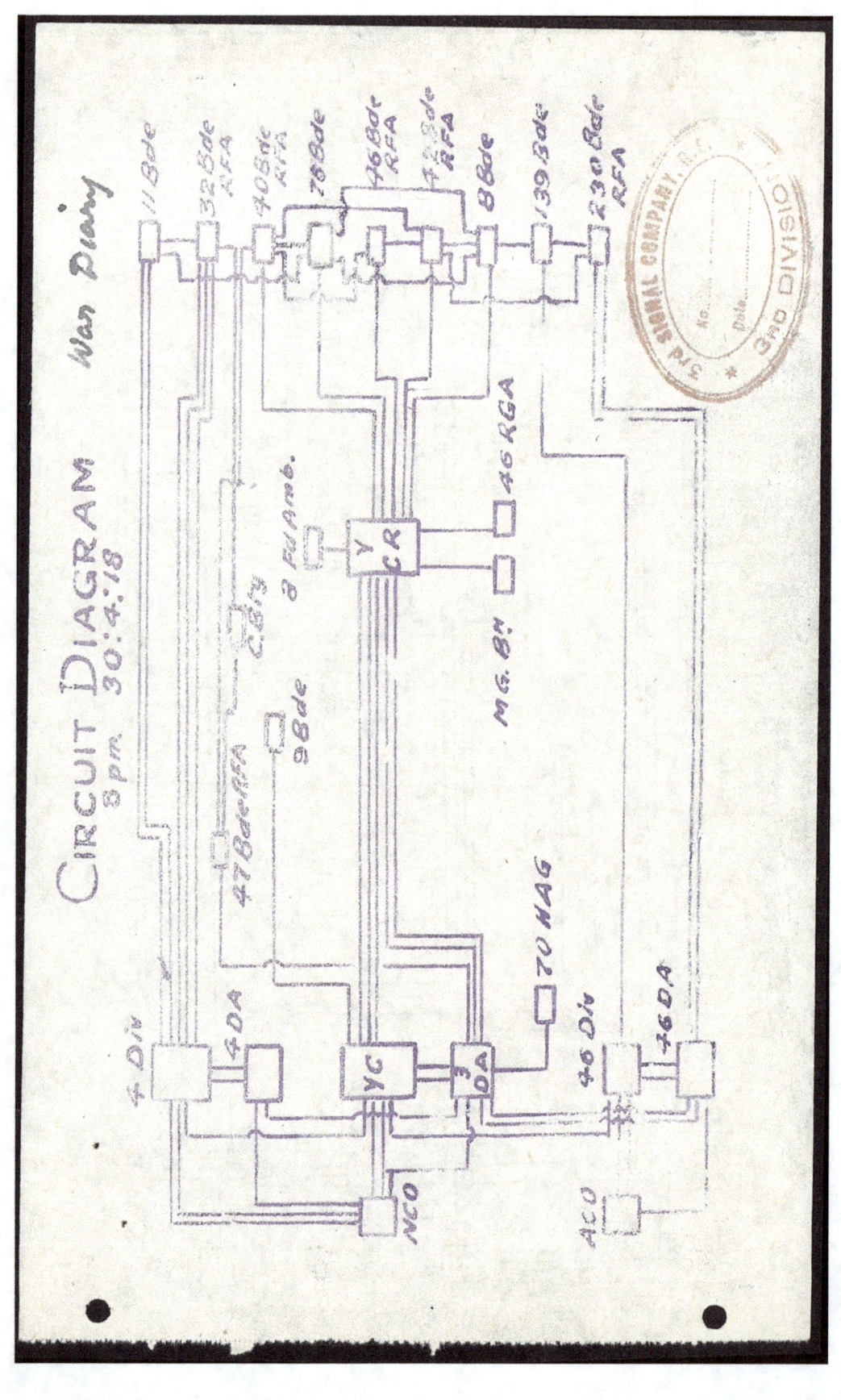

War Diary.

Diagram of Visual Communications as at 8pm 10·4·18
Sigs Y.C.

Links to:-
G.G. Sigs
Capt. Phillip
S. Bde
Pol. Pln
2nd Bn
1 Sig

4/B CV
E.16.c.25

4/B
Y.C.
Died 2.5.
Div. H.Qr.

4/B L B 4/B
Woodcote
Oosterghem

4/B
N.L.
R.19.6.5

4/B C.K.S
15.27.c.6.5

4/B
T.Z.M

4/B W.20.c.4.2
To 1 Bde

4/B P.E.D
65.c.7.9
3 Can

Reserve

Louberscretes

R. M. Arthur
Lieut.
16·4·18

War Diary

DIAGRAM OF VISUAL COMMUNICATIONS AS AT 5 P.M. 15.4.15
Sigs Y.C.

○ OP 1/A 76 Bde
○ OP W.23 d 4.8 ○ OP P58
                              9 Bde
                              E.5 c.7.1

○ OP OP
○ OP W.9 d 9.9

○ OP Cv D.6.W.9.5

○ OP YC Zillebeke
D 11 d 2.1

Copies for:-
O.C. Sigs
Capt Phillips
O.K. Div Visual
Sigs D.A.
  " 7th Bde RFA
  " 42 "
  76, 8, 9 Bdes
Sigs 3 Mtg Bde
1 Spare.

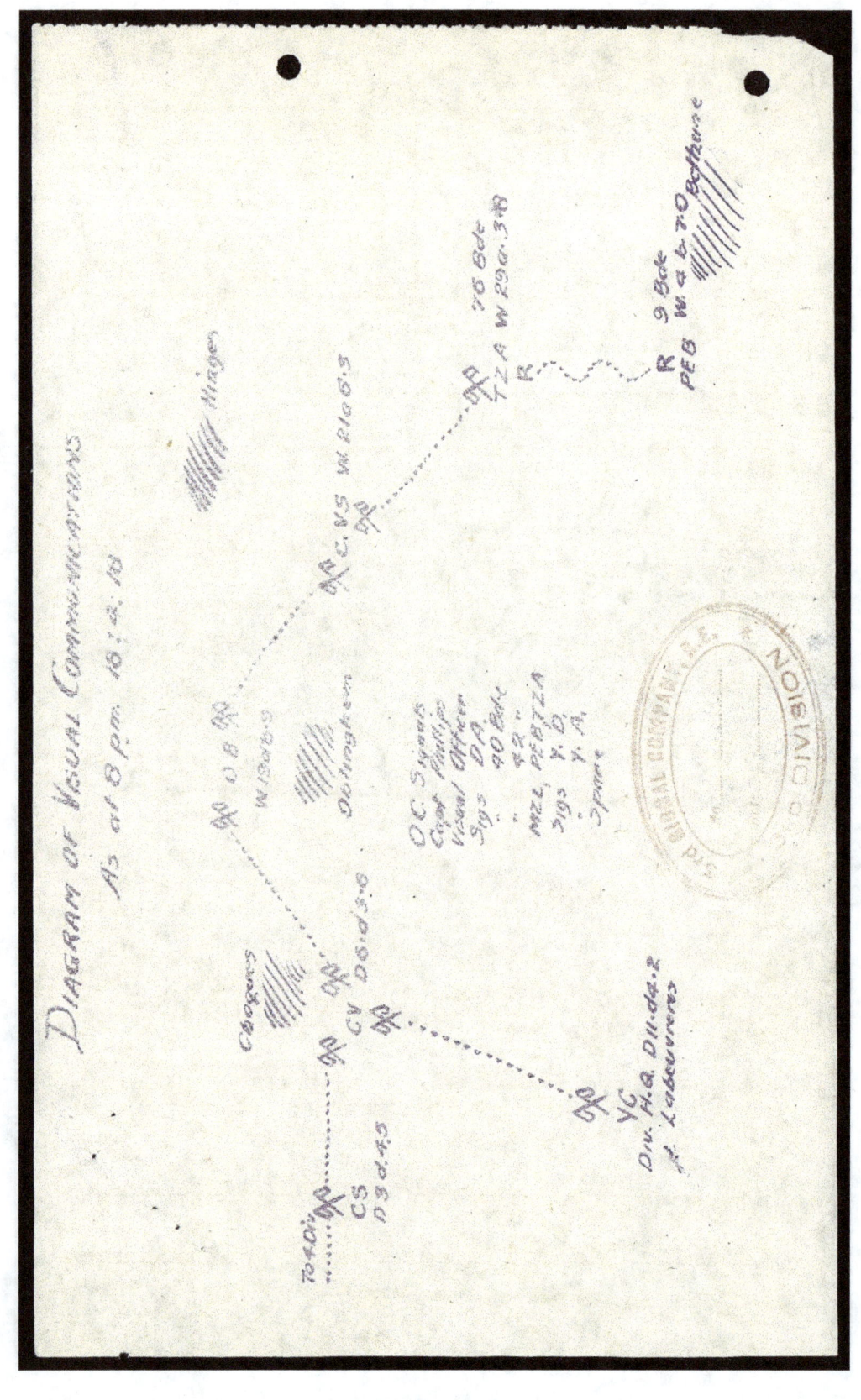

System of Visual Communications
As at 8 pm 13:4:18

Choques

OB W.19.d.8-3

Hinges

4 To 4 Div

C.S
D.3.d.4-5

CV D.6.d.3-6

Oblinghem

CVS W.21.d.6-3

BN
W.20.d.7.5

Copies to
O.C. Sigs
Capt Phillips
 „ Barclay
Visual Officer
Sigs 40 Bde
 „   42 „
 „   8 „
 „   9 „
 „   76 „
 „   V.D.
 „   V.A.

YC
Div. H.Q D.11.d.4.2
Labeuvrière

MZL 8 Bde
E.4 & 7.0

TZA 76 Bde
W.29.o.5.8

3rd Signal Co RE

WAR DIARY
or
INTELLIGENCE SUMMARY

Army Form C. 2118.

Instructions regarding War Diaries and Intelligence Summaries are contained in F. S. Regs., Part II. and the Staff Manual respectively. Title pages will be prepared in manuscript.

(Erase heading not required.) PAGE 1.

MAP REFERENCE
SHEETS (FRANCE) 36ᴬ S.E. and 36ᴬ N.E.

Vol 35

Place	Date 1918	Hour	Summary of Events and Information	Remarks and references to Appendices
LABEUVRIERE	MAY 1		GENERAL ROUTINE WORK. LINES, W/T and VISUAL Communication maintained to Brigades and YCR (MAP REF. Eg d.3.8.)	
	2		COMPANY TRAINING continued :- HORSEMANSHIP, VISUAL, and PHYSICAL TRAINING.	
	2		GENERAL ROUTINE WORK. LINES W/T and VISUAL Communication maintained to Brigades and YCR.	
			COMPANY TRAINING continued :- HORSEMANSHIP, VISUAL and PHYSICAL TRAINING.	
			LIEUT ARTHUR R.E. and VV CABLE SECTION from XIII Corps Signal Coy. attached for area work	
	3		GENERAL ROUTINE WORK. LINES, W/T and VISUAL Communication maintained to Brigades and YCR. ARMOURED CABLE laying in DITCHES	
	4		Do. do. do. do. do. do.	
	5		Do. do. do. do. do. do.	
	6		Do. do. do. do. do. do. ARMOURED CABLE laying in DITCHES	
	7		Do. do. do. do. do. do. do.	

A6945 Wt. W11422/M1160 350,000 12/16 D.D.& L. Forms/C/2118/14.

Army Form C. 2118.

WAR DIARY
or
INTELLIGENCE SUMMARY.
(Erase heading not required.)

PAGE 2. MAP REFERENCE SHEETS (FRANCE) 36A.S.E. and 36B.N.E.

Instructions regarding War Diaries and Intelligence Summaries are contained in F. S. Regs., Part II. and the Staff Manual respectively. Title pages will be prepared in manuscript.

Place	Date 1919	Hour	Summary of Events and Information				Remarks and references to Appendices
LABEUVRIERE	MAY 8th		GENERAL ROUTINE WORK. LINES, W.T. and VISUAL Communications maintained to Brigades and YCR. Armoured Cable laying in Ditches				
	9th		Do.	Do.	Do.	do.	
	10		Do.	Do.	Do.	do.	
	11		Do.	Do.	Do.	do.	
	12		Do.	Do.	Do.		
	13		Do.	Do.	Do.	Armoured Cable laying in Ditches	
	14		Do.	Do.	Do.	Do.	
	15		Do.	Do.	Do.	Do.	

A6945 Wt. W14422/M1160 350,000 12/16 D. D. & L. Forms/C./2118/14.

Army Form C. 2118.

WAR DIARY
or
~~INTELLIGENCE SUMMARY~~

(Erase heading not required.) PAGE 3

Instructions regarding War Diaries and Intelligence Summaries are contained in F. S. Regs., Part II. and the Staff Manual respectively. Title pages will be prepared in manuscript.

MAP REFERENCE SHEETS (FRANCE) 36A. S.E. and 36B. N.E.

Place	Date 1915	Hour	Summary of Events and Information	Remarks and references to Appendices
LABEUVRIERE	MAY 16		GENERAL ROUTINE WORK. LINES W/T and VISUAL Communications maintained to Bdes and Y.C.R. ARMOURED CABLE laying in Ditches	
	17		Do. Do. Do. Do.	
			A/MAJOR. (LIEUT) D. POPE 8th HUSSARS arrived to take over command of Company vice CAPT. (A/MAJOR) W.S. ROLLO R.E.	
	18		GENERAL ROUTINE WORK. LINES W/T and VISUAL Communications maintained to Brigades and Y.C.R. ARMOURED CABLE laying in Ditches	
	19		Do. Do. Do. NIGHT 19/20th {LIEUT C.S. BRADFORD G.L. Marindin (Gosson) 2nd LIEUT V. DYKES R.E. Do.	
	20		Do. Do. Do. ARMOURED CABLE laying in Ditches.	
			CAPTAIN (A/MAJOR) W.S. ROLLO R.E. (OFFICER COMMANDING.) LEFT FOR 2nd ARMY SIGNAL COMPANY. LIEUT (A/MAJOR) D. POPE 8th HUSSARS from 39th DIVISIONAL SIGNAL Coy R.E. assumed command. LIEUT G.K. FIRTH. R.E. to C.C.S. (Sick)	
	21		GENERAL ROUTINE WORK. LINES W/T and VISUAL Communication maintained to Brigades and YCR. ARMOURED CABLE laying in Ditches.	
			LIEUT J. KING (LINES REGT) arrived from 1st Div. Signal Company for duty, as Supernumerary Officer.	

Army Form C. 2118.

WAR DIARY
or
~~INTELLIGENCE SUMMARY~~
(Erase heading not required.)

Instructions regarding War Diaries and Intelligence Summaries are contained in F. S. Regs., Part II. and the Staff Manual respectively. Title pages will be prepared in manuscript.

PAGE 4.   MAP REFERENCE SHEETS (FRANCE) 36A. S.E. and 36A. NE

Place	Date 1919	Hour	Summary of Events and Information			Remarks and references to Appendices
LABEUVRIERE	MAY 22		GENERAL ROUTINE WORK. LINES W/T. and Visual Communication maintained to Bde. & YCR. Armoured Cable laying in Ditches.			
	23		Do. do. do. do. do. do.			
	24		Do. Do. Do.			
	25		Do. Do. Do.			Corps Recd'd Cable Bury
	26		Do. Do. Do.			Do.
	27		Do. Do. Do. 2nd Lieut A.B. Rorke R.E. from 39 Sgt. Div. Sig. C. for duty & posted to Corps Army Telecoms			Do.
	28		Do. Do. Do. ARMOURED CABLE LAYING IN DITCHES.			Do.
	29		Do. Do. Do.			Do.

WAR DIARY
or
INTELLIGENCE SUMMARY.

Army Form C. 2118.

MAP REFERENCE SHEETS (FRANCE) 36A.S.E and 36B.N.E

PAGE 5

Place	Date	Hour	Summary of Events and Information	Remarks and references to Appendices
LABEUVRIERE	1918 MAY 30		GENERAL ROUTINE WORK. LINES. W/T and VISUAL Communication maintained to Brigades & YCR. Buried Cable Laying in Ditches.	
	31		Do. Do. Do. Do. Do.	Cable laying in Cable Bay

H.C.O.Phillips
Captain R.E.
for Officer Commanding 3RD SIGNAL COMPANY R.E.

System of Visual Communication

Spm K:6:10

PEB — ⚑ D.5.c.7.8
PFI — ⚑ D.5.a.2.7
— ⚑ D.2.a.7.3
GV — ⚑ D.6.d.9.6
M.Y.C — ⚑ D.11.d.4.9
SV Wood — ⚑ 7.5
NEL — ⚑ E.A.6.7.0
Post Dr — ⚑
4th Div — ⚑ D.10.a.3.8

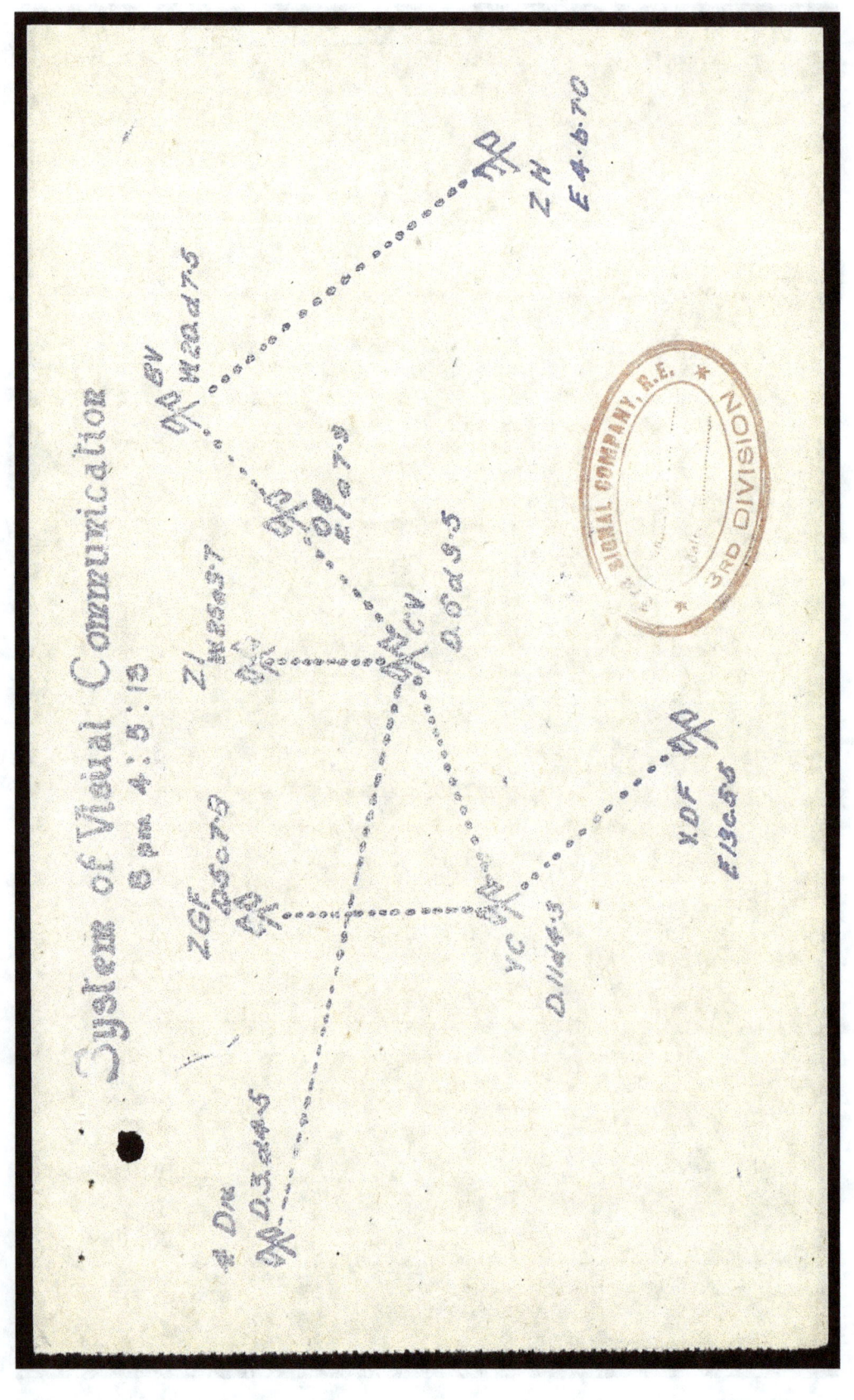

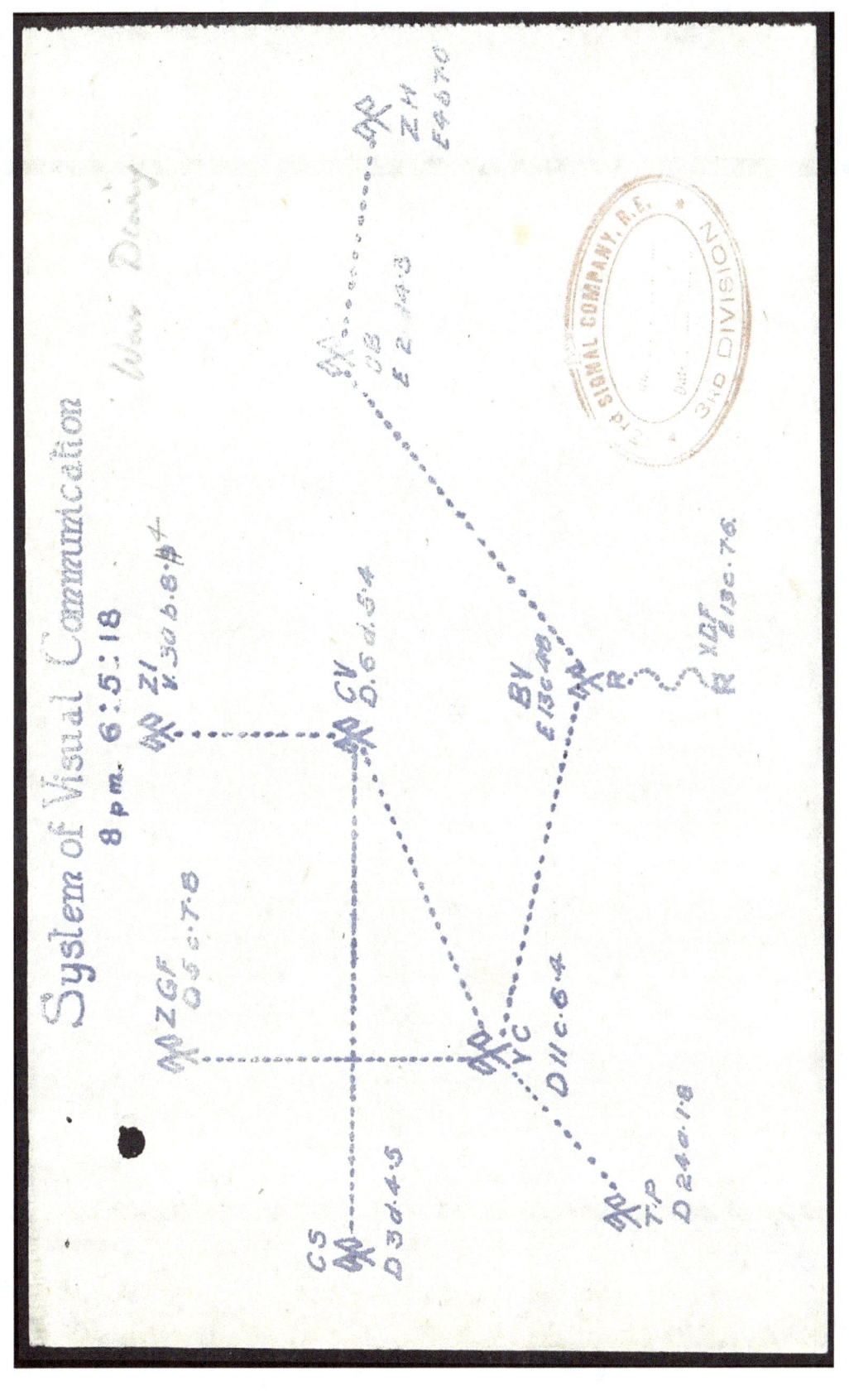

System of Visual Communication

8 pm. 9:5:18

```
                    ⚑ Z1
                    V 30 b 8·4


                                       OB
                                       ⚑
   CS ⚑ · · · · · · ⚑ CV · · · · · · · · · · ZGF
   D 3 d 4·5        D 6 d 5·4         E 2 d 4·3        ⚑
                                                       E 4 b 7·0


           YC ⚑
           D 11 c 5·4      BY
                           ⚑ E 13 c 4·8
                           R
                           ·
                           ·
                           R YDF
                           E 13 c 7·6
```

3rd SIGNAL COMPANY, R.E.
No.
Date
3RD DIVISION

3RD DIVISION SIGNALS
System of Visual Communication
8 pm 13:5:18

3RD DIVISION SIGNALS
System of Visual Communication
14:5:18

3RD DIVISION SIGNALS

System of Visual Communication
15:5:18

3RD DIVISION SIGNALS

Visual Communication
Sps 22:5:18

Wireless, PB-A & Visual Communication
3rd Division Signals
17:3:16

R.E. Signals Division
18-5-18
Wireless & Visual Communications.

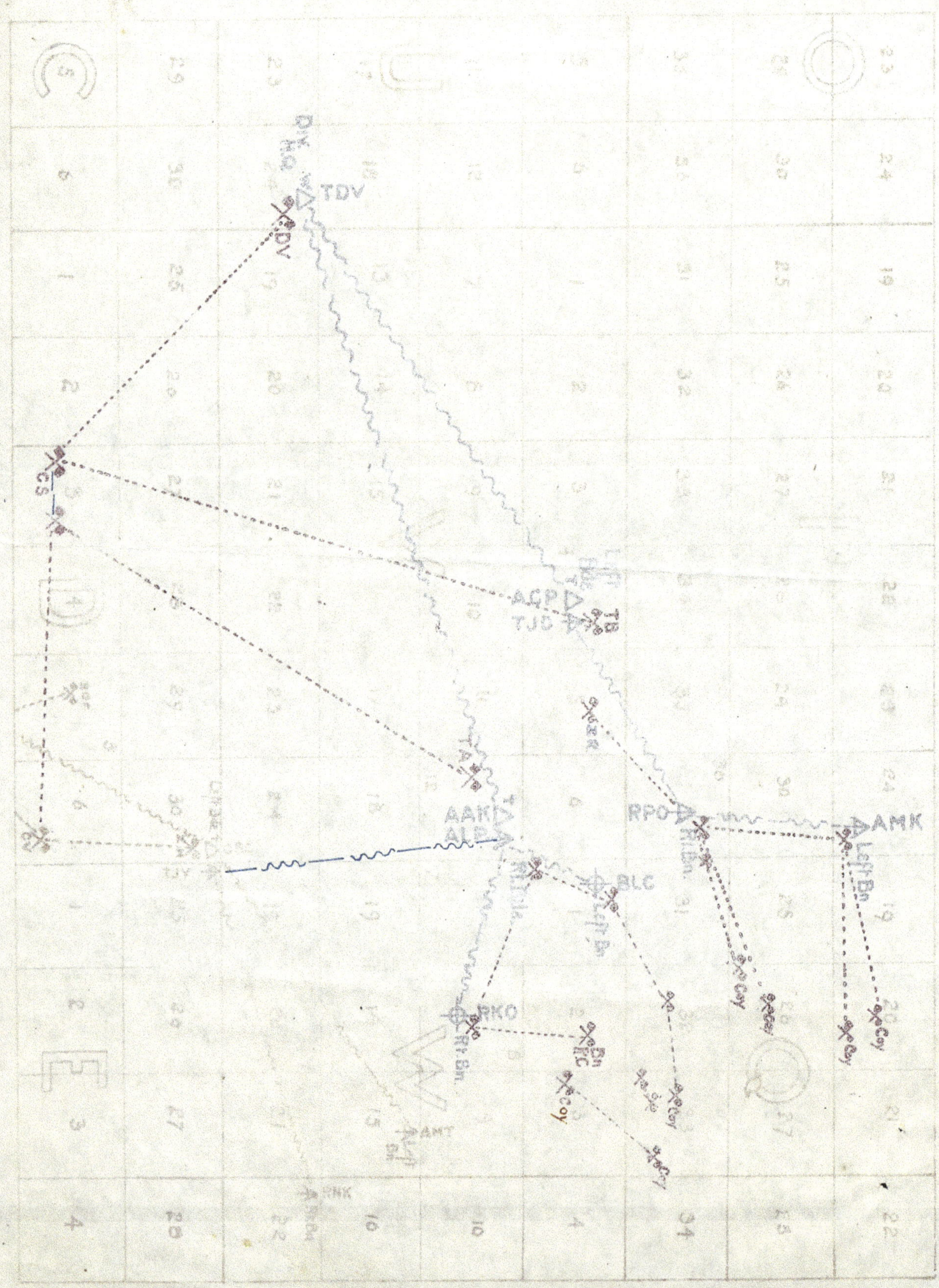

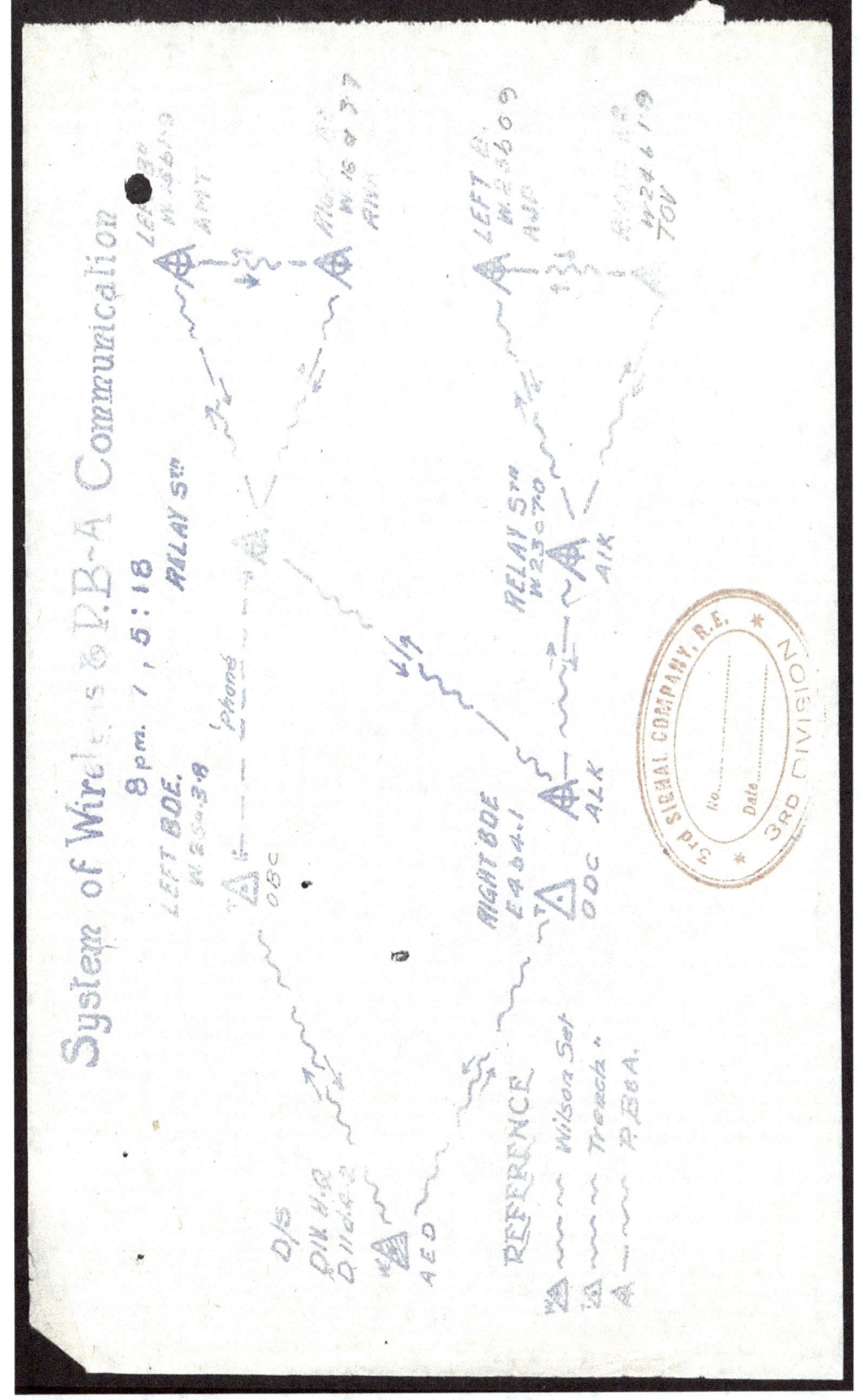

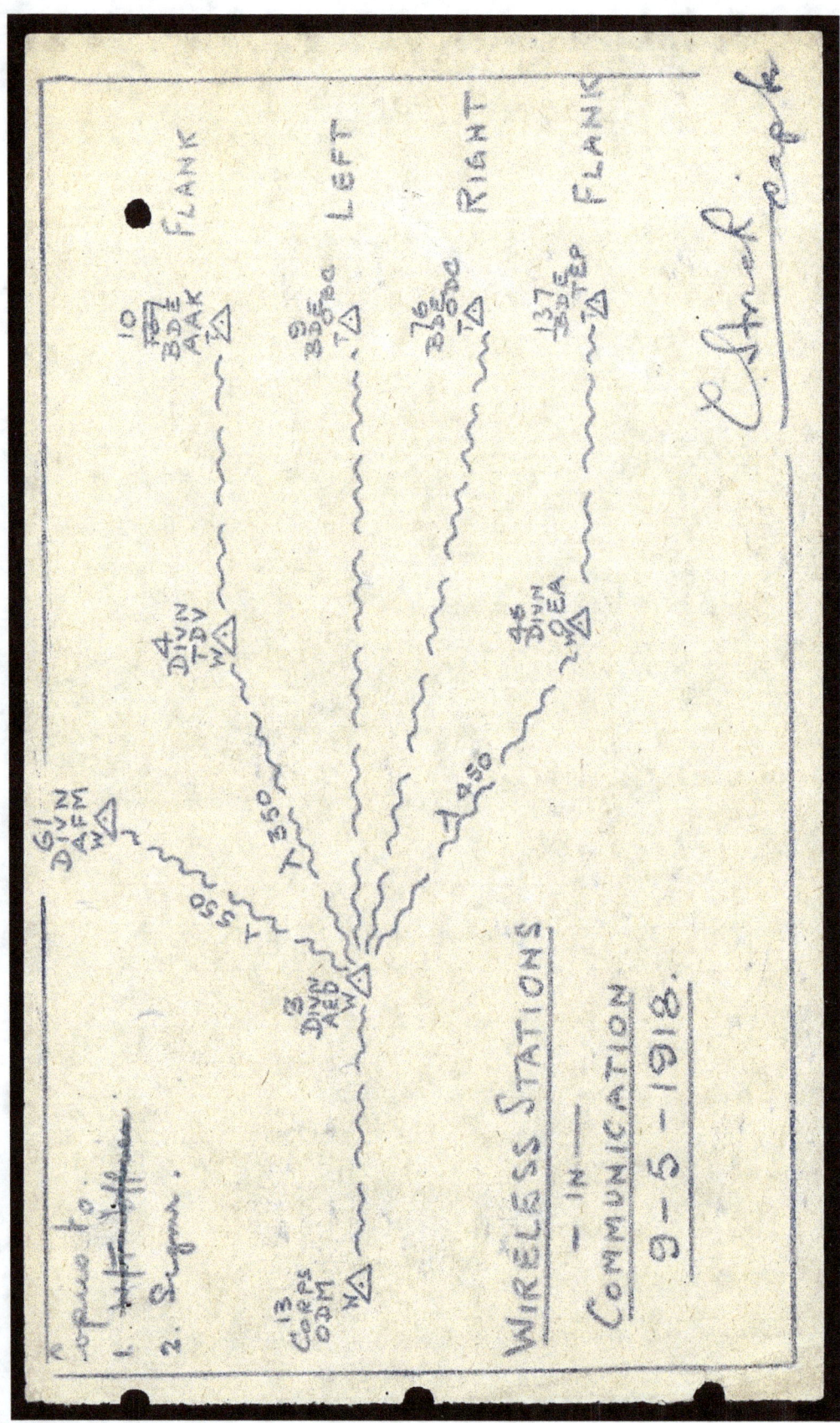

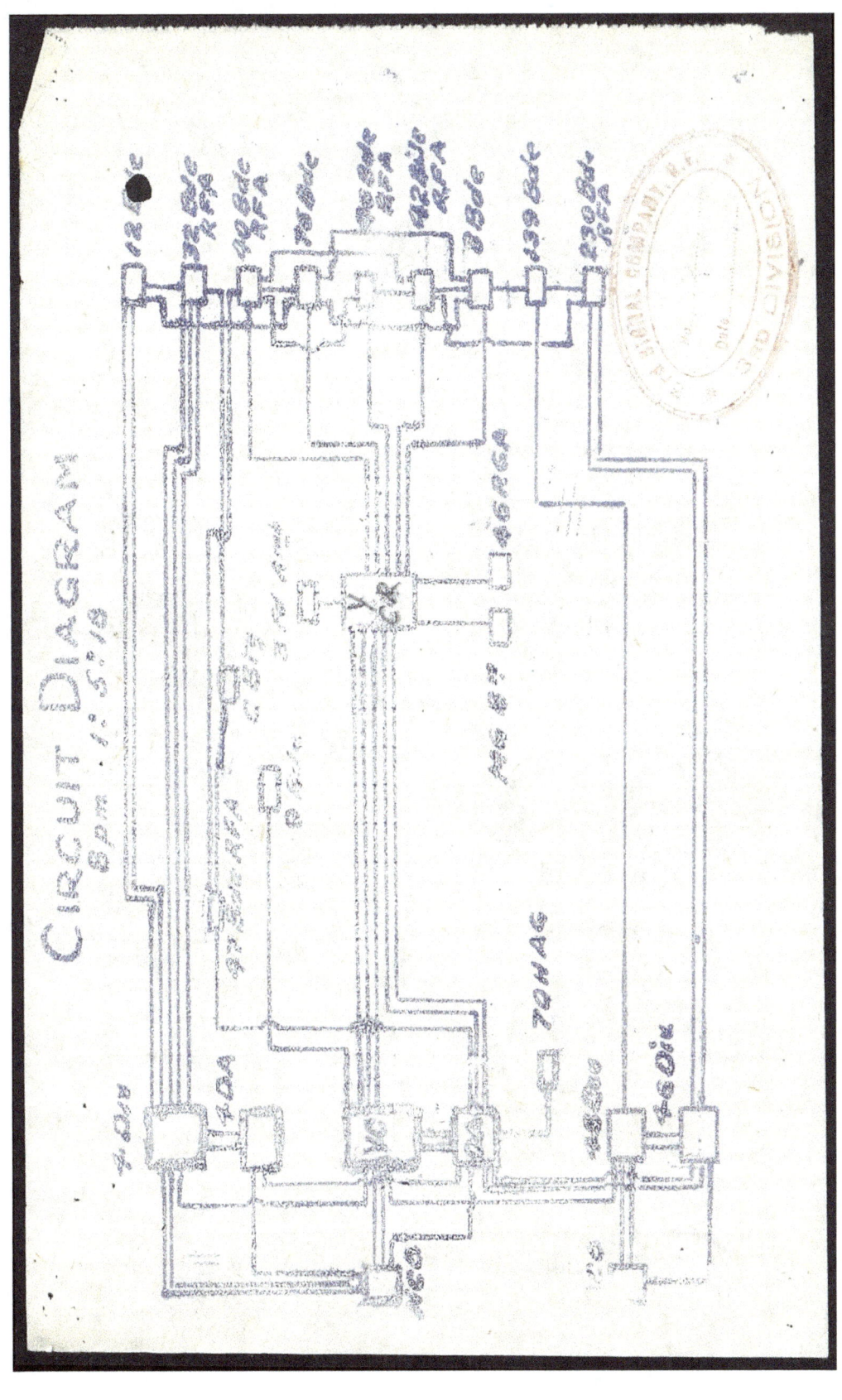

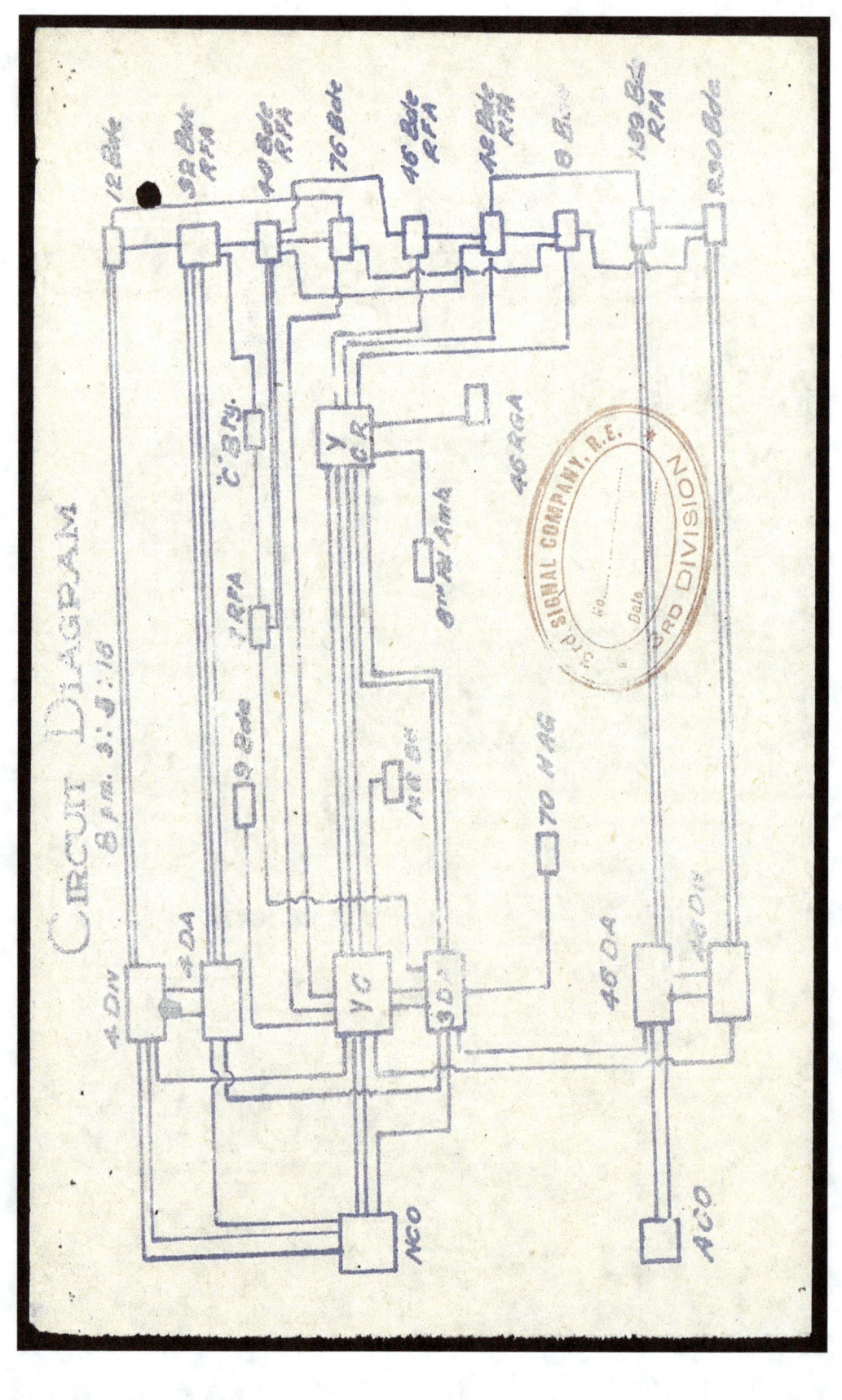

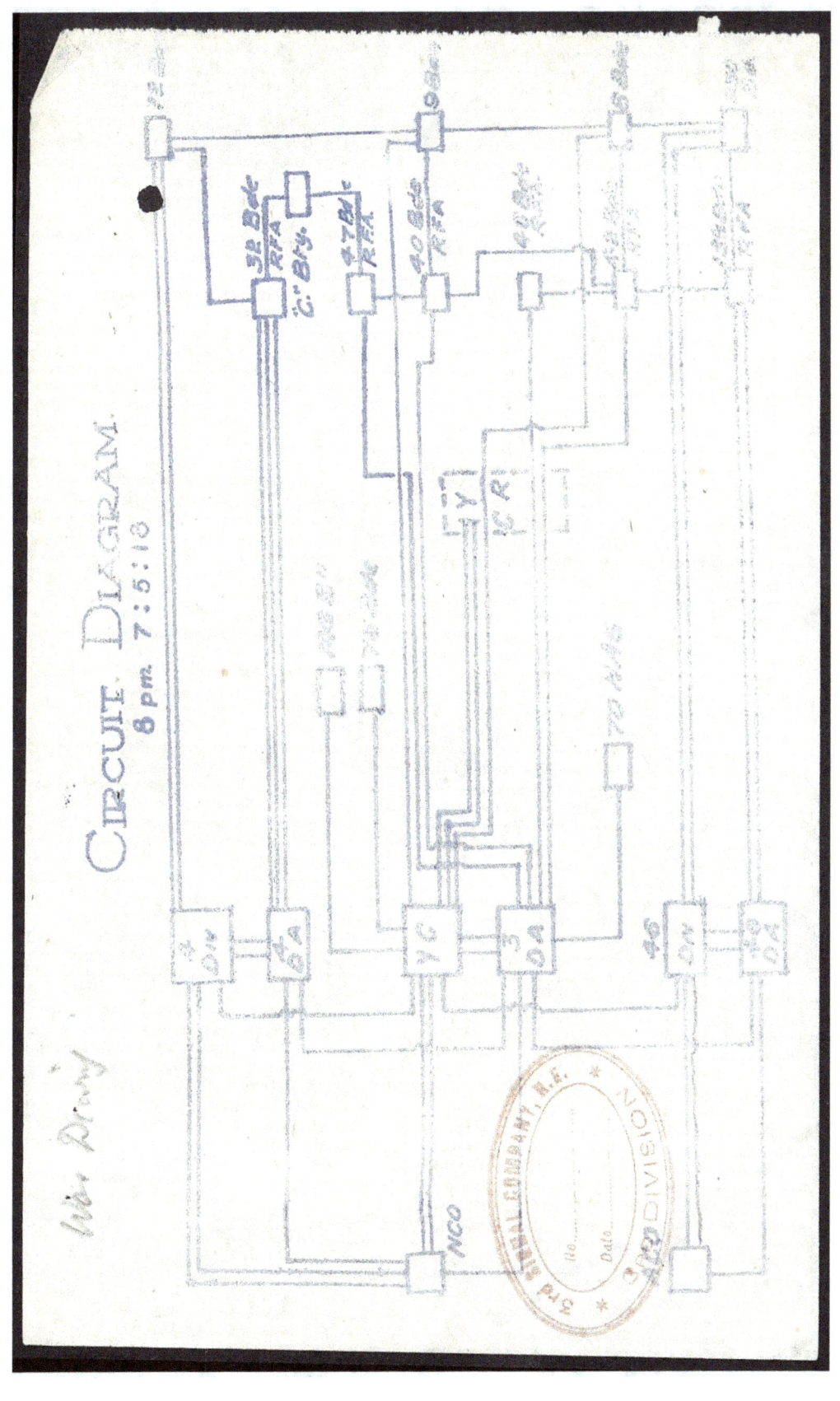

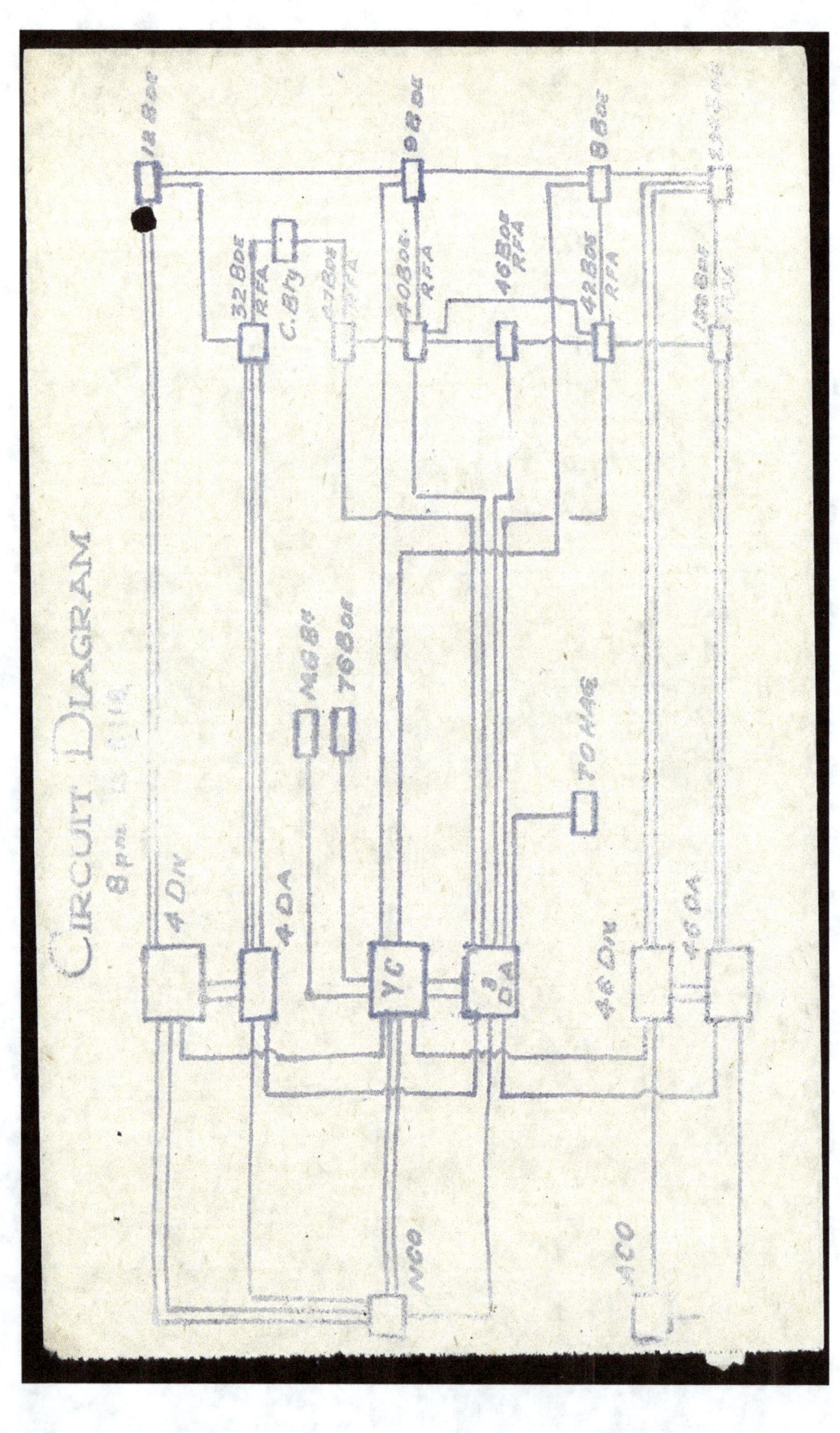

War Diary

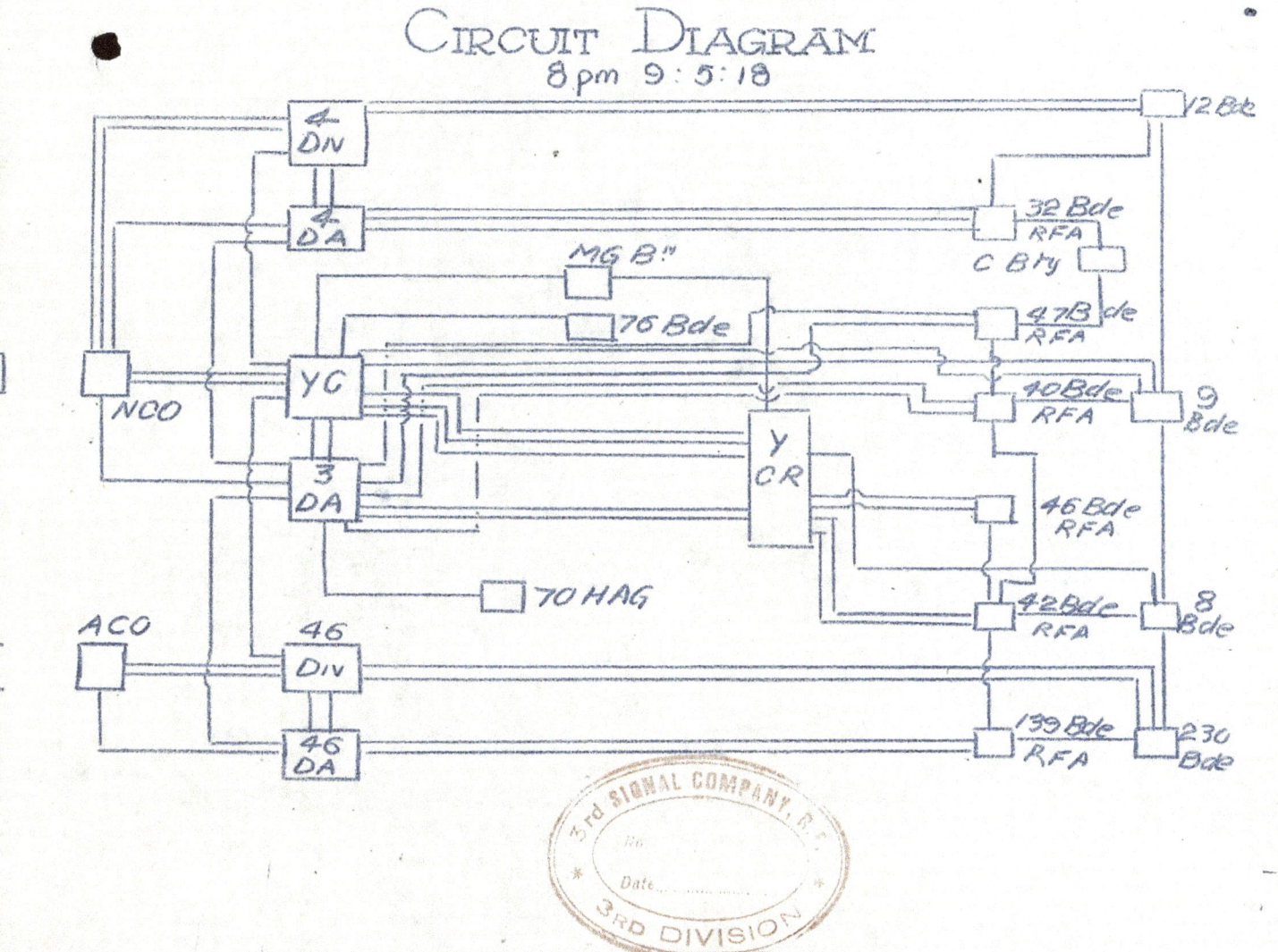

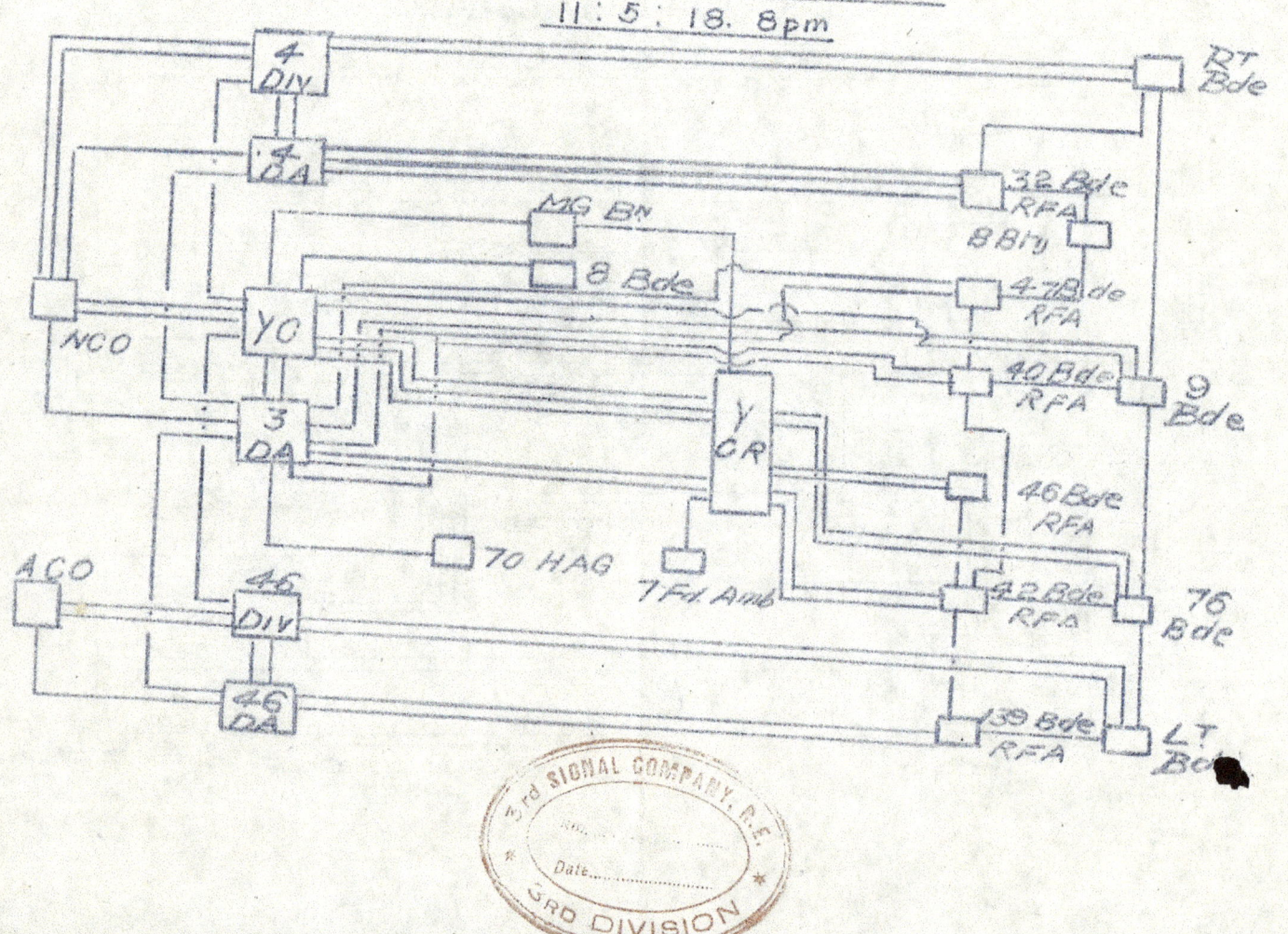

WIRELESS DIAGRAM
3RD DIVISION SIGNALS

Date 22/5/18

No 14

NOTE!
Wireless shewn in Red
R.E.-A. Blue
Battle Calls underlined

Scale 1:40,000

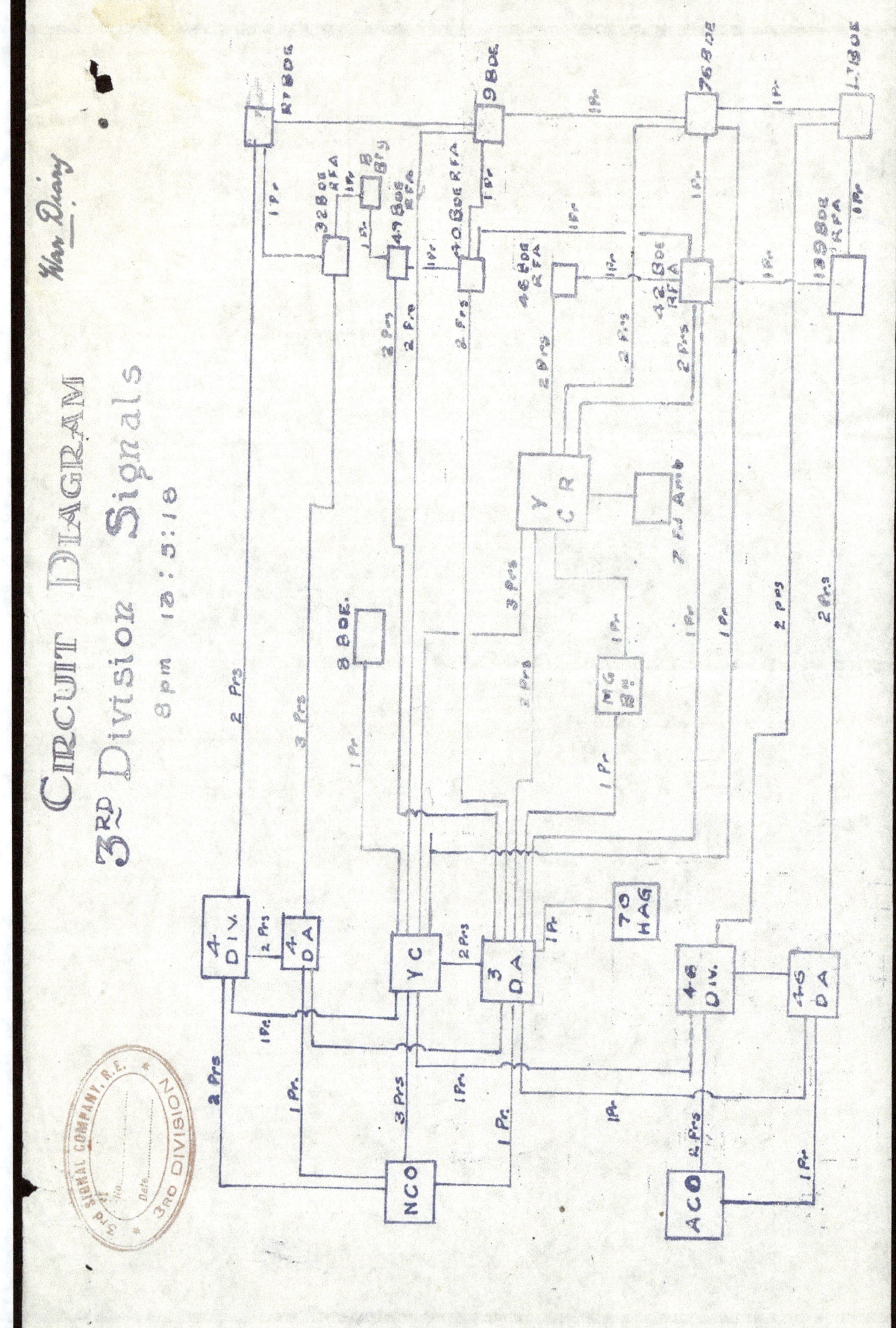

Army Form C. 2118.

3rd Signal Coy

WAR DIARY
or
~~INTELLIGENCE SUMMARY.~~

(Erase heading not required.)

Instructions regarding War Diaries and Intelligence Summaries are contained in F. S. Regs., Part II. and the Staff Manual respectively. Title pages will be prepared in manuscript.

Place	Date	Hour	Summary of Events and Information	Remarks and references to Appendices
Labeuvrière	June 1st.		General Routine Work. Lines, W/T and Visual Communication maintained to Brigades and YCR. Construction of Corps Armoured Cable bury and Armoured Cable route in Canals Streams and Ditches.	
	2nd.		" Lines, W/T and Visual Communication maintained to Brigades and YCR.	
	3rd.		" Lines, W/T and Visual Communication maintained to Brigades and YCR. Construction of Corps Armoured Cable Bury.	
	4th.		" Lines, W/T and Visual Communication maintained to Brigades and YCR. Construction of Corps Armoured Cable Bury.	
	5th.		" Lines, W/T and Visual Communication maintained to Brigades and YCR. Laying of Armoured Cable route in Canal Streams and Ditches.	
	6th.		" Lines, W/T and Visual Communications maintained to Brigades and YCR. Laying of Armoured Cable routes in Canal streams and Ditches. 2nd. Lt. A.Guthrie R.E. arrived from XIII Corps Signal Co for attachment.	
	7th.		" Lines, W/T and Visual Communications maintained to Brigades and YCR. Construction of Armoured cable Bury.(Corps).	

Army Form C. 2118.

WAR DIARY
or
~~INTELLIGENCE SUMMARY~~

(Erase heading not required.)

Instructions regarding War Diaries and Intelligence Summaries are contained in F. S. Regs., Part II. and the Staff Manual respectively. Title pages will be prepared in manuscript.

Place	Date	Hour	Summary of Events and Information	Remarks and references to Appendices
Labeuvriere	8th.		General Routine Work. Lines,W/T and Visual Communication maintained to Brigades and YCR. Laying of Armoured Cable in Canal Streams and Ditches.	
	9th.		" Lines,W/T and Visual Communications maintained to Brigades and YCR. Laying of Armoured Cable routes in Canal, streams and Ditches. Lieut. F.W.Deans R.E. from Supernumerary First Army Signal Company attached to 3rd. Div. Signal Coy.	
	10th.		" Lines,W/T and Visual Communication maintained to Brigades and YCR. Laying of Armoured Cable routes in Canal streams and Ditches.	
	11th.		" Lines,W/T and Visual Communications maintained to Brigades and YCR. Laying of Armoured Cable in Canal ,streams and ditches. Construction of Corps Armoured Cable Bury. Instruction Class for partly trained Battalion Signallers assembled at Noon. Total number 44 O.R. Duration of course, eight weeks. 2/Lieut A.Guthrie R.E. to 11th. Div. Signal Company as Wireless Officer.	
	12th.		" Lines,W/T and Visual Communication maintained to Brigades and YCR. Construction of Corps Armoured Bury. Laying of Armoured Cable in Canal,streams and Ditches.	

Army Form C. 2118.

WAR DIARY
or
INTELLIGENCE SUMMARY.
(Erase heading not required.)

Instructions regarding War Diaries and Intelligence Summaries are contained in F. S. Regs., Part II. and the Staff Manual respectively. Title pages will be prepared in manuscript.

Place	Date	Hour	Summary of Events and Information	Remarks and references to Appendices
Labeuvriere	13th.		General Routine Work. Lines,W/T and visual Communications maintained to Brigades and YGR. Laying of Armoured Cable routes in Canal, streams and Ditches.	
	14th.		" Lines,W/T and visual Communication maintained to Brigades and YGR. Laying of Armoured Cable route in Canal,streams and Ditches.	
	15th.		" Lines W/T and visual Communication maintained to Brigades and YGR. Laying of Armoured Cable routes in Canal, streams and Ditches.	
	16th.		" Lines W/T and visual Communication maintained to Brigades and YGR.	
	17th.		" Lines,W/T and visual Communication maintained to Brigades and YGR. Cable Salvage Parties commenced work on Forward Areas. Lieut R.M.Clarke,R.E. O.C. 9th.Bde. Sigs. to Hospital. Lieut F.W.Deans R.E. posted temporarily as O.C. 9th. Bde Sigs. vice Lieut R.M. Clarke R.E.	
	18th.		" Lines,W/T and visual communication maintained to Brigades and YGR. Cable Salvage Parties continued work on forward areas.	

Army Form 2118.

WAR DIARY
or
INTELLIGENCE SUMMARY
(Erase heading not required.)

Instructions regarding War Diaries and Intelligence Summaries are contained in F.S. Regs., Part II. and the Staff Manual respectively. Title pages will be prepared in manuscript.

Place	Date	Hour	Summary of Events and Information	Remarks and references to Appendices
Labeuvrière	19th.		General Routine Work. Lines, W/T and visual communication maintained to Brigades and YGK. Cable Salvage parties continued work on forward areas.	
	20th.		" Lines, W/T and visual communication maintained to Brigades and YGK. Cable Salvage parties continued work on forward areas. Corps Armoured Cable Bury construction continued.	
	21st.		" Lines, W/T and visual communication maintained to Brigades and YGK.	
	22nd.		" Lines, W/T and visual communication maintained to Brigades and YGK. Construction of Corps Armoured Cable Bury proceeded with.	
	23rd.		" Lines, W/T and visual communication maintained to Brigades and YGK.	
	24th.		" Lines, W/T and visual communication maintained to Brigades and YGK. Further construction of Corps Armoured Cable Bury. "Cable Salvage Party continued work on forward areas.	
	25th.		" Lines, W/T and visual communications maintained to Brigades and YGK.	

Army Form C. 2118.

WAR DIARY
or
INTELLIGENCE SUMMARY.
(Erase heading not required.)

Place	Date	Hour	Summary of Events and Information	Remarks and references to Appendices
Labeuvriere	26th.		General Routine Work. Lines, W/T and Visual communication maintained to Brigades and YOR. Captain C.H.Barcley R.E. O.i/c.Arty Signals left for fourteen days leave to United Kingdom.	
	27th.		" " Lines, W/T and Visual communication maintained to Brigades and YOR.	
	28th.		" " Lines, W/T and Visual communication maintained to Brigades and YOR.	
	29th.		" " Lines, W/T and visual communications maintained to Brigades and YCR. Cable Salvage Parties continued work on forward Areas.	
	30th.		" " Lines, W/T and visual Communication maintained to Brigades and YOR.	

G.C.O'Phillips
Captain R.E.
for O.C. 3rd. Div. Signal Company

30/ 6 / 1918.

Army Form C. 2118.

WAR DIARY
or
INTELLIGENCE SUMMARY.
(Erase heading not required.)

3rd Signal Coy
RE

Vol 37

Instructions regarding War Diaries and Intelligence Summaries are contained in F. S. Regs., Part II. and the Staff Manual respectively. Title pages will be prepared in manuscript.

Place	Date	Hour	Summary of Events and Information	Remarks and references to Appendices
Labeuvriere	JULY 1st.		General Routine Work. Lines,W/T, and Visual Communications maintained to Brigades and YCR. Construction of Armoured Cable Bury.	
	2nd.		General Routine Work. Lines,W/T, and Visual Communications maintained to Brigades and YCR. Construction of Armoured Cable Bury. Lieut. E.A.Adams to be Acting O. i/c 9th. Bde. Signals , vice Lieut R.M.Clark R.E. T.C. evacuated sick to United Kingdom.	
	3rd.		General Routine Work. Lines, W/T, and Visual Communications maintained to Brigades and YCR. Construction of Armoured Cable Bury. Cable Salvage Party employed in Labeuvriere. Laying of Armoured Cable in Canal, Streams and Ditches.	
	4th.		General Routine Work. Lines, W/T, and Visual Communications maintained to Brigades and YCR. Construction of Armoured Cable Bury. Laying of Armoured Cable in Canal, Streams and Ditches.	
	5th.		General Routine Work. Lines, W/T, and Visual Communications maintained to Brigades and YCR. Laying of Armoured Cable in Canal, Streams and Ditches.	
	6th.		General Routine Work. Lines, W/T, and Visual Communications maintained to Brigades and YCR. Laying of Armoured Cable in Canal, Streams and Ditches.	
	7th.		General Routine Work. Lines, W/T, and Visual Communications maintained to Brigades and YCR. Construction of Armoured Cable Bury. Capt.C.G.Strick. 91sm. Yeo. to United Kingdom for 14 days leave (O. i/c Wireless).	

Army Form C. 2118.

WAR DIARY
or
INTELLIGENCE SUMMARY.

(Erase heading not required.)

Instructions regarding War Diaries and Intelligence Summaries are contained in F. S. Regs., Part II. and the Staff Manual respectively. Title pages will be prepared in manuscript.

Place	Date July	Hour	Summary of Events and Information	Remarks and references to Appendices
Labeuvriere	8th.		General Routine Work. Lines,W/T, and Visual Communications maintained to Brigades and YCR. Construction of Armoured Cable Bury.	
	9th.		General Routine Work. Lines,W/T, and Visual Communications maintained to Brigades and YCR. Laying of Armoured Cable in Canal, Streams and Ditches.	
	10th.		General Routine Work. Lines,W/T, and Visual Communications maintained to Brigades and YCR. Construction of Armoured Cable Bury.	
	11th.		General Routine Work. Lines,W/T, and Visual Communications maintained to Brigades and YCR. Construction of Armoured Cable Bury. Capt. Barclay R.E. O.i/c Arty. Signals returned from 14 days leave to U.K. 2/Lieut V.P.Howells joined unit for duty(Supernumerary) from Fifth Army Signal Company.	
	12th.		General Routine Work. Lines,W/T, and Visual Communications maintained to Brigades and YCR.	
	13th.		General Routine Work. Lines,W/T, and Visual Communications maintained to Brigades and YCR. Construction of Armoured Cable Bury.	
	14th.		General Routine Work. Lines,W/T, and Visual Communications maintained to Brigades and YCR. Construction of Armoured Cable Bury.	
	15th.		General Routine Work. Lines,W/T, and Visual Communications maintained to Brigades and YCR.	

Army Form 2118.

WAR DIARY
or
INTELLIGENCE SUMMARY.
(Erase heading not required.)

Instructions regarding War Diaries and Intelligence Summaries are contained in F. S. Regs., Part II. and the Staff Manual respectively. Title pages will be prepared in manuscript.

Place	Date July	Hour	Summary of Events and Information	Remarks and references to Appendices
Labeuvrière	16th.		General Routine Work. Lines, W/T and Visual Communications maintained to Brigades and YCR. Construction of Armoured Cable Bury. One Sergeant and 8 O.R. attached to 8th.Bde. for constructing a dug-out for Buried Cable scheme.	
	17th.		General Routine Work. Lines, W/T and Visual communications maintained to Brigades and YCR. Laying of Armoured Cable in Canal, Streams and Ditches.	
	18th.		General Routine Work. Lines, W/T and Visual communications maintained to Brigades and YCR.	
	19th.		General Routine Work. Lines, W/T and Visual communications maintained to Brigades and YCR. Lieut F.W.Deans to Hospital (Sick).	
	20th.		General Routine Work. Lines, W/T and Visual Communications maintained to Brigades and YCR. Construction of Armoured Cable Bury. Lieut.H.G.Barwood M.G.Corps posted to 3rd. Div. Signal Co. as O. i/c No. 5 Section.	
	21st.		General Routine Work. Lines,W/T and Visual communications maintained to Brigades and YCR. Construction of Armoured Cable Bury. Capt.C.C.Strick.Glam. Yeo. O.i/c Wireless re-joined from leave to U.K.	
	22nd.		General Routine Work. Lines, W/T and Visual communications maintained to Brigades and YCR.	
	23rd.		General Routine Work. Lines, W/T and Visual communications maintained to Brigades and YCR. Construction of Armoured Cable Bury.	
	24th.		General Routine Work. Lines,W/T and Visual communications maintained to Brigades and YCR. joined Unit from Fifth Army Signal Co.(Supernumerary)	

Army Form C. 2118.

WAR DIARY
or
INTELLIGENCE SUMMARY.
(Erase heading not required.)

Instructions regarding War Diaries and Intelligence Summaries are contained in F. S. Regs., Part II. and the Staff Manual respectively. Title pages will be prepared in manuscript.

Place	Date	Hour	Summary of Events and Information	Remarks and references to Appendices
Labeuvriere.	July 25th.		General Routine Work. Lines, W/T and Visual communications maintained to Brigades and YCR. Lieut. F.W.Deans R.E. re-joined Unit from Hospital.	
	26th.		General Routine Work. Lines, W/T and Visual communications maintained to Brigades and YCR.	
	27th.		General Routine Work. Lines, W/T and Visual communications maintained to Brigades and YCR. 1 Corporal and 6 O.R. attached to 8th. Bde. for work on Buried Cable system. Armoured Cable laying in Canal, Ditches and Streams.	
	28th.		General Routine Work. Lines, W/T and Visual communications maintained to Brigades and YCR.	
	29th.		General Routine Work. Lines, W/T and Visual Communications maintained to Brigades and YCR. Forward Area parties employed on Armoured Cable Bury:- Jointing ,etc.	
	30th.		General Routine Work. Lines, W/T and Visual communications maintained to Brigades and YCR. Forward Area Parties employed on Armoured Cable Bury :- Jointing, etc.	
	31st.		General Routine Work. Lines, W/T and Visual communications maintained to Brigades and YCR. Forward Area parties employed on Armoured Cable Bury:- Jointing, etc. Armoured Cable laying in Canal, Streams and Ditches.	

J.C.S.Phillips
Capt.R.E.
for O.C. 3rd. Divisional Signal Co.R.E.

WAR DIARY
or
INTELLIGENCE SUMMARY.

3rd. Divl. Signal Co.
Sheet 1.
August 1918

Map References:—
Sheets 36B and 51C. FRANCE

(Erase heading not required.)

Instructions regarding War Diaries and Intelligence Summaries are contained in F. S. Regs., Part II. and the Staff Manual respectively. Title pages will be prepared in manuscript.

Place	Date	Hour	Summary of Events and Information	Remarks and references to Appendices
LABEUVRIERE Sheet 36B D11c.5.4	1st. to 5th.		(General Routine Work. Lines, W/T., and Visual Communications maintained to (Brigades and YCR. (Forward Area parties employed on Armoured Cable Bury;— Jointing, Test Boxes, &c.	
"	6th.		General Routine Work. Lines, W/T., and Visual Communications maintained to Brigades and YCR. 2nd.Lieut.H.J.IVISON Posted from Supernumerary 3rd.Div.Signal Co. to 19th. Div. Signal Co. Authy. D.D.Sigs. Fifth Army. JO 20. R.T.O.	
"	7th.		General Routine Work. Lines, W/T., and Visual Communications maintained to Brigades and YCR. at LABEUVRIERE until handed over to the 19th.Div.Signal Co. Divisional Signal Office closed at LABEUVRIERE at 10 am, opened at AUCHEL at the same hour.	
AUCHEL Sheet 36B C23a.1.7	8th.		General Routine Work. Local Lines maintained. Overhauling Wagons and equipment.	
"	9th.		(General Routine Work. Local Lines maintained. (Visual,W/T., Cable Drill, Horsemanship and Company training resumed.	
"	10th. to 12th.		(General Routine Work. Local Lines maintained. (Visual, W/T., Cable Drill, Horsemanship and Company training.	
BAVINCOURT Sheet 51C P 35a.2.4	13th.		Closed at AUCHEL, moved to BAVINCOURT by road (two days march). Signal Office opened at BAVINCOURT. Local lines maintained.	
"	14th.		General Routine Work. Local Lines maintained.	

Army Form C. 2118.

WAR DIARY
or
INTELLIGENCE SUMMARY.
(Erase heading not required.)

3rd.Divl.Signal Co.   Map References.
Sheet 2.   Sheets 36B. France.
Part II. August 1918.   51C.

Instructions regarding War Diaries and Intelligence Summaries are contained in F. S. Regs., Part II. and the Staff Manual respectively. Title pages will be prepared in manuscript.

Place	Date	Hour	Summary of Events and Information	Remarks and references to Appendices
BAVINCOURT. P35a.2.4 Sheet 51C	15th. to 19th.		(General Routine Work. Local lines maintained. (Visual, W/T., Cable Drill, Horsemanship and company training.	
POMMIERS W25c4.8 Sheet 51C.	20th.		General Routine Work. Closed at BAVINCOURT, opened at POMMIERS.	
"	21st.		General Routine Work. Lines, W/T., and visual communications maintained to Brigades and YCR. YCR office opened at F14c.8.5 Sheet AYETTE. Lieut.R.Mc.A.MATHER Genl.List. O.i/c.Sigs. 8th.Bde. to Hospital (gassed). Lieut.V.P.HOWELLS to O.i/c. Signals 8th. Bde. vice Lieut. R.Mc.A.MATHER. G.L.	
"	22nd.		General Routine Work. Lines, W/T., and Visual communications maintained to Brigades and YCR.	
"	23rd.		General Routine Work. Lines, W/T., and Visual communications maintained to Brigades and YCR. 2nd.Lieut.A.I.HAY R.E.T.C. joined unit as Supernumerary Officer, posted to take charge of Div. visual Signals.	
"	24th.		Closed at POMMIERS, opened at E4C2.4 (vicinity BIENVILLERS) Advanced H.Q'rs. Lines maintained to Bdes. and Flanking Divisions. General Routine Work. Overhauling wagons and equipment.	
Vicinity of BIENVILLERS E.4C2.4 Sheet 51C.	25th. to 27th.		(General Routine Work. Lines, W/T., and Visual communications maintained to (Brigades and flanking Divisions. (Overhauling wagons and equipment.	
BOIRY ST.MARTIN S20a.3.6 Sheet 51C.	28th.		Advanced Headquarters moved to BOIRY ST. MARTIN, closed at E4C2.4 at 4 pm. (sheet 51C.). General Routine Work. Lines maintained to Brigades.	

WAR DIARY
or
INTELLIGENCE SUMMARY.

(Erase heading not required.)

3rd.Divl.Signal Company
Sheet 3.
August.1918.

Place	Date	Hour	Summary of Events and Information	Remarks and references to Appendices
Vicinity HAMELINCOURT A 11b.7.8 Sheet 51C	29th.		Closed at BOIRY ST. MARTIN and moved to A.11b.7.8 (vicinity HAMELINCOURT) Sheet 51C. General Routine Work. Lines,W/T., and Visual communication maintained to Brigades and Flanking Divisions.	
"	30th.		General Routine Work. Lines,W/T., and Visual communication maintained to Brigades and YCR. Lieut.R.Mc.A.MATHER General List rejoined from Hospital and re-posted to O.i/c. 8th. Inf.Bde.Signals. 2nd. Lieut. V.P.HOWELLS re-joined H.Q'rs of Company as Supernumerary Officer.	
"	31st.		General Routine Work. Lines,W/T., and Visual communications maintained to Brigades and Flanking Divisions.	

NPPhillips
Captain R.E.
for O.C. 3rd. Divisional Signal Co.R.E.

Army Form C. 2118.

3 D Signal
WD 39

WAR DIARY
or
INTELLIGENCE SUMMARY.
(Erase heading not required.)

Map References Sheets 51C. and 57C.
France.

Page 1.

Instructions regarding War Diaries and Intelligence Summaries are contained in F. S. Regs., Part II. and the Staff Manual respectively. Title pages will be prepared in manuscript.

Place	Date September	Hour	Summary of Events and Information	Remarks and references to Appendices
HAMELINCOURT. A11b7.8 Sheet 51C.	1st. to 2nd.		General Routine Work. Lines,W/T. and Visual Communications maintained to Brigades and Flanking Divisions.	
Vicinity RAMSART. X13a.6.5 Sheet 51C.	3rd.		Closed at HAMELINCOURT, opened in vicinity of RAMSART. General Routine Work. Local Lines maintained.	
	4th. and 5th.		General Routine Work. Local Lines maintained. Overhauling Wagons and equipment. Company Training, Physical Drill etc.	
HUMBERCAMPS V29a.3.0	6th.		Closed at vicinity RAMSART opened at HUMBERCAMPS. General Routine Work. Local lines maintained.	
	7th.		General Routine Work. Local lines maintained. Company training resumed, Horsemanship,Cable Drill,Physical Drill etc. Lieut.R.Mc.A.MATHER G.L. O.i/c 8th.Bde. Signals to UK. for 14 days leave.	
	8th.		General Routine Work. Local lines maintained. Company training ie. Horsemanship, Cable Drill, Physical training. Captain C.C.STRICK Glam.Yeo. departed for ABBEVILLE ,posted as O.i/c P.E.L. ABBEVILLE Depot.	
	9th.		General Routine Work. Local lines maintained. Company training ie. Horsemanship, Cable Drill, Physical Drill etc. 2/Lieut. V.P.HOWELLS R.E.-C. from Supernumerary 3rd.Army Signal Co. attached 3rd. Div. Signal Co. posted to 3rd. Div. Signal Co. vice Captain C.C.STRICK to Signal Depot Abbeville. Authy. 3rd.Army A/A/903 dated 12/9/18.	
	10th.		General Routine Work. Local lines maintained. Company training ie. Horsemanship,Cable Drill, Physical Drill etc. Lieut.O.A.TAILOR O. i/c 76th. Bde. Signals to UK. for 14 days leave.	

WAR DIARY
or
INTELLIGENCE SUMMARY.

Page 2.

(Erase heading not required.)

Army Form C. 2118.

Map References.
Sheets 51D. and 57 C.
France.

Place	Date	Hour	Summary of Events and Information	Remarks and references to Appendices
GOMIECOURT. A30 a.6.9 Sheet 57D.	September 11th.		Closed at HUMBERCAMPS opened at GOMIECOURT. Local lines maintained. Lieut.C.H.LEFROY R.F.A. O.i/c 42nd.Bde.R.F.A.Signals to UK. for fourteen-days leave.	
	12th. to 14th.		Local lines maintained. Company training ie. Horsemanship, Cable Drill, Physical Drill etc. General Routine Work.	
BEUGNY. I 17a.8.9 Sheet 57D. N.W.	15th.		Closed at GOMIECOURT opened at BEUGNY. General Routine Work. Lines, W/T and visual communication opened to Bdes. 2/Lieut.F.G.HASLUCK R.E. joined unit from 3rd. Army Signal Co.	
	16th. to 21st.		General Routine Work. Lines, W/T and visual communication maintained to Brigades. Parties employed salvaging Cable and running running through salvaged Cable.	
	22nd.		General Routine Work. Lines,W/T and visual communications maintained to Brigades. Parties employed salvaging Cable and running through salvaged Cable. Lieut.R.McA.MATHER R.E. returned from leave to UK.	
	23rd. and 24th.		General Routine Work. Lines,W/T and Visual communications maintained to Brigades. Parties employed salvaging Cable and running through salvaged Cable.	
	25th.		General Routine Work. Lines, W/T and visual Communications maintained to Brigades. Parties employed salvaging Cable and running through salvaged Cable. Lieut.C.A.TAYLOR R.E. O.i/c 76th.Bde. Signals returned from leave to UK.	

Army Form C. 2118.

WAR DIARY
or
INTELLIGENCE SUMMARY.

Map References. Sheets 51C and 57C France

(Erase heading not required.)

Page 3.

Place	Date	Hour	Summary of Events and Information	Remarks and references to Appendices
BEUGNY I.17a.6.9 Sheet 57C. N.W.	September 26th.		General Routine Work. Lines W/T and visual communications maintained to Brigades. Divisional Advanced Signal Office opened at HERMIES J.24a7.4 Sheet 57C N.E. Lieut. C. LEROY R.F.A. O.i/c 42nd. Bde.R.F.A. Signals returned from leave to U.K. Parties employed on Cable Salvage and running through salvaged Cable.	
	27th.		General Routine Work. Lines, W/T and visual communication maintained to Brigades and YCR. Parties employed on Cable Salvage and running through salvaged Cable.	
	28th.		General Routine Work. Lines, W/T and visual communication maintained to Brigades and YCR. Parties employed on Cable salvage and running through Salvaged Cable. Lieut. J. KING Lincs.Regt. O.i/c 40th.Bde.R.F.A.Signals to UK for fourteen days leave.	
HERMIES. J24a.7.4	29th.		General Routine Work. Lines, W/T and Visual communication maintained to Brigades and YCR. Company moved to HERMIES. Captain J.O.D.PHILLIPS R.E.T.C. 2/i/c in Command to U.K. for fourteen days leave. Rear Office left with Divl. Rear H.Q. at BEUGNY.	
	30th.		General Routine Work. Lines W/T and visual Communication maintained to Brigades and Rear Office at BEUGNY.	

A.B.Rolla Lieut.R.E.
for O.C. 3rd. Divisional Signal Co.R.E.

Army Form C. 2118.

WAR DIARY
or
INTELLIGENCE SUMMARY.

Page 1.

(Erase heading not required.)

Map References.
FRANCE.
Sheets 57C.57B.51A.

Instructions regarding War Diaries and Intelligence Summaries are contained in F. S. Regs., Part II. and the Staff Manual respectively. Title pages will be prepared in manuscript.

Place	Date	Hour	Summary of Events and Information	Remarks and references to Appendices
FLESQUIERES L19a.5.6 Sheet 57C.	Oct. 1st.		Closed at HERMIES, opened at FLESQUIERES. Rear Office at BEUGNY closed. General Routine Work. Lines, W/T., and Visual communication maintained to Brigades and flanking Divisions.	
	2nd. to 5th.		General Routine Work. Lines,W/T., and Visual communication maintained to Brigades and flanking Divisions.	
	6th.		General Routine Work. Lines,W/T., and Visual communication maintained to Brigades and flanking Divisions. Parties employed Salving Cable and running through Cable on wagons. Lieut.G.H.BARWOOD M.G.C. O.i/c.Signals 3rd.Bn.M.G.C. to U.K. for 14 days leave.	
	7th.		General Routine Work. Lines,W/T., and Visual communication maintained to Brigades and flanking Divisions. Parties employed Salving Cable, and running through Cable on wagons. Lieut.G.H.BARWOOD M.G.C. O.i/c.Signals 3rd.Bn.M.G.C. transferred to General List for duty with Army Signal Service,dated 13/7/18.	
	8th.		General Routine Work. Lines,W/T., and Visual communication maintained to Brigades and flanking Divisions. Parties employed Salving Cable, and running through Cable on wagons.	
HERMIES J24a.7.4 Sheet 57C.	9th.		Closed at FLESQUIERES, opened at HERMIES. General Routine Work. Local lines maintained. Overhauling Wagons and equipment.	
	10th.		General Routine Work. Local Lines maintained. Overhauling Wagons and equipment.	

Army Form C. 2118.

WAR DIARY
or
INTELLIGENCE SUMMARY.
(Erase heading not required.)

Page 2.

Map References.
FRANCE.
Sheets 57C.57B.51A.

Instructions regarding War Diaries and Intelligence Summaries are contained in F.S. Regs., Part II. and the Staff Manual respectively. Title pages will be prepared in manuscript.

Place	Date Oct.	Hour	Summary of Events and Information	Remarks and references to Appendices
HERMIES. J24a.7.4 Sheet 57C.	11th.		General Routine Work. Local Lines maintained. Overhauling Wagons and equipment. 2/Lieut.V.P.HOWELLS R.E. to 62nd. Divisional Signal Co.	
	12th.		General Routine Work. Local lines maintained. Overhauling wagons and equipment. Lieut.J.KING Lincs.Regt. O.i/c.Signals 40th.Bde.R.F.A. returned from 14 days leave to United Kingdom.	
FLESQUIERES. L19a.5.6 Sheet 57C.	13th.		Closed at HERMIES, opened at FLESQUIERES. General Routine Work.Lines maintained to Brigades. Captain G.C.D.PHILLIPS 2/ in Command returned from 14 days leave to U.K. 2/Lieut.A.B.RORKE R.E. to United Kingdom for 14 days leave.	
	14th.		General Routine Work. Local lines maintained. Company Training resumed ie. Horsemanship,Cable Drill,Visual signalling etc.	
	15th.		General Routine Work. Local lines maintained. Company training ie. Horsemanship,Cable Drill,Visual Signalling etc. Parties employed salving Cable.	
	16th. to 19th.		General Routine Work. Local lines maintained. Company training ie. Horsemanship,Cable Drill,Visual Signalling etc. Parties employed salvaging Cable,and on camp improvements.	
CATTINIERES. H12c.8.9 Sheet 57B.	20th.		Closed at FLESQUIERES,opened at CATTINIERES. General Routine Work. Local lines maintained.	
	21st.		General Routine Work. Local lines maintained.	

Army Form C. 2118.

WAR DIARY
or
INTELLIGENCE SUMMARY.

(Erase heading not required.)

Map References
FRANCE
Sheets 57C.57B.57

Page 3

Instructions regarding War Diaries and Intelligence Summaries are contained in F. S. Regs., Part II. and the Staff Manual respectively. Title pages will be prepared in manuscript.

Place	Date Oct	Hour	Summary of Events and Information	Remarks and references to Appendices
QUIEVY D 13 c 7.0 57 b	22nd		Closed at CATTENIERES 17.00 Forward Signal Office opened at ST-PYTHON Sheet 51 a V 30 c Rear Signal Office at QUIEVY. General routing work. Lines, W/T and Visual Communications maintained to Bdes. and YCR. T2/Lt. A. W. Hay, R.E.T.C. attd. 3rd Div. Signal Coy. to 61st Div. Sig. Company (attd.)	
SOLESMES E 1 c 6.8 57 B	23rd		Closed at QUIEVY and ST-PYTHON at 13.15. Opened SOLESMES same hour. General routine work. Lines, W/T and Visual Communication maintained to Bdes. Lieut. C. d'Artois R.E. (Terr.) from 3rd Army Signal Co. as Supernumerary	
	24th		General Routine Work. Lines, W/T, and Visual Communication maintained to Bdes.	
	25th		General Routine Work. Lines, W/T, and Visual Communication maintained to Bdes.	
	26th		General Routine Work. Lines, W/T and Visual Communication maintained to Bdes.	
	27th		General Routine Work. Lines, W/T and Visual Communications maintained to Bdes.	
	28th		General Routine work. Lines, W/T and visual Communications maintained to Bdes. Parties employed salving cable and running through cable on wagons.	

Page 4.

WAR DIARY
or
INTELLIGENCE SUMMARY.
(Erase heading not required.)

Army Form C. 2118.

Map References
FRANCE
Sheets 57c 57b 57 a.

Place	Date	Hour	Summary of Events and Information	Remarks and references to Appendices
SOLESMES E 1 c 6.8	29th Oct		General Routine Work. Lines, W/T, and Visual communication maintained to Bdes.	
	30th		General Routine Work. Lines, W/T, and Visual communication maintained to Bdes. Lt. (A/Major) Rope* D. Pope, M.C. to United Kingdom for 14 days' leave. Closed at SOLESMES 11.00 and opened at QUIEVY same hour.	
QUIEVY D 13 c 7.0 57 B			General Routine Work. Lines maintained to Bdes.	

Medway Lt.
for O.C., 3rd Div. Signal Company.

3rd Signal Coy R.E.

Army Form C. 2118.

Instructions regarding War Diaries and Intelligence Summaries are contained in F.S. Regs., Part II. and the Staff Manual respectively. Title pages will be prepared in manuscript.

WAR DIARY
or
INTELLIGENCE SUMMARY.
(Erase heading not required.)

Page 1.

Map references.
FRANCE 57.B.
VALENCIENNES.
NAMUR & MARCHE.

Place	Date	Hour	Summary of Events and Information	Remarks and references to Appendices
Quievy D.19.a.1.6. 57.B.	1st Nov.		G.R.W. Lines, Communication maintained to Brigades. Remained QUIEVY. Lt. C. L'Artois to 2d Div. Sig. Coy.	
	2nd.		"	
	3rd.		"	
	4th.		" Forward Signal Office opened at ESCARLAIN W.5.c.8.8 57.B. 16.00 hours. Rear office remains open at QUIEVY.	
	5th.		G.R.W. Forward signal Office opens at RUESNES R.14.b.4.4. 57.B.	
	6th.		" Salving Cable at Y.C.R. and ORSINVAL.	
	7th.		" Rear office remains open at QUIEVY.	
	8th.		" " Fwd. Sig. Office opened at FRASNOY.	
	9th.		Rear Office closed at QUIEVY. Opened at FRASNOY 12 noon. T/2Lt. L.C.Voss R.E.T.C. joined Coy. As Supernumerary.	
	10th.		G.W.R. Forward signal Office opens LA LONGUEVILLE. Rear office remains FRASNOY.	
	11th.		G.R.M. Forward office opened at MAUBEUGE. Sheet Valenciennes 12. E.5. Rear office remains FRASNOY.	
	12th.		G.R.W. Forward Office remains MAUBEUGE, (Val. 12 E.3.) Rear office remains FRASNOY.	

Army Form C. 2118.

WAR DIARY
or
INTELLIGENCE SUMMARY.

(Erase heading not required.)

Instructions regarding War Diaries and Intelligence Summaries are contained in F. S. Regs., Part II. and the Staff Manual respectively. Title pages will be prepared in manuscript.

Place	Date	Hour	Summary of Events and Information	Remarks and references to Appendices
	13th.		G.R.W. Forward Office remains MAUBEUGE (Val.12.n.5.) Tea Office remains FLASNOY. No.1. Det. Rejoined from 62nd Division.	
	14th.		G.R.W. Forward Office remains MAUBEUGE (Val.12.L.3.) Tea Office remains FLASNOY.	
	15th.		G.R.W. Forward Office remains MAUBEUGE (Val. 12.L.3.) Major POPE rejoined from Leave.	
	16th.		G.R.W. Forward Office remains MAUBEUGE (Val.Q2.L.3.)1/Lt. Barwood to hosp. (accidentally injured).	
	17th.		G.R.W. Forward Office remains MAUBEUGE (Val.12.L.3.)	
	18th.		Div H.Q. closed FLASNOY 15.00 hrs. Opened SOUS LE BOIS 15.00 hrs. (Val.12)	
	19th.		Remains SOUS LE BOIS. Communication maintained to all Bdes. by W/T.	
	20th.		Div.H.Q. closed SOUS LE BOIS opened at COUSOLRE 12.00 hrs. Communication maintained to all Bdes. by W/T. (Namur 8. B.4.)	
	21st.		Div. H.Q. remain COUSOLRE G.R.W. Visual Section employed on reconnoitering roads.	
	22nd.		Div. H.Q. remains COUSOLRE G.R.W. Lt. Dean rejoined from leave.	
	23rd.		Div. H.Q. remains COUSOLRE G.R.W. Lt. Adam to U.K. on leave.	
	24th.		Div. H.Q. remain COUSOLRE 10.00 hrs. opened THUIN same hour. (Namur 8.)	

A6945 Wt. W14422/M1160 350,000 12/16 D. D. & L. Forms/C./2118/14.

WAR DIARY
or
INTELLIGENCE SUMMARY.
(Erase heading not required.)

Army Form C.2118.

Instructions regarding War Diaries and Intelligence Summaries are contained in F.S. Regs., Part II. and the Staff Manual respectively. Title pages will be prepared in manuscript.

Map References.
FRANCE 57.B.
VALENCIENNES.
NAMUR & MARCHE.

Page 6.

Place	Date	Hour	Summary of Events and Information	Remarks and references to Appendices
	25th.		Div. H.Q. Closed THUIN opened LOVERVAL noon (Namur 8.J.2.)	
	26th.		Div. H.Q. remained LOVERVAL	
	27th.		Div. H.Q. remained LOVERVAL.	
	28th.		Div. H.Q. Closed LOVERVAL opened BIOULE 15.00 hours, Communication by D.R. and W/T. (sheet Namur 8.J.2.)	
	29th.		Div. H.Q. remained BIOULE. Communication by D.R. and W/T.	
	30th.		Div. H.Q. Closed BIOULE opened EMPTINNE 15.00 hours. Communication by W/T. and D.R. (sheet Marches 5.2.)	

H. Mathully
Capt. R.E.
For O.C. 3rd Div. Sig. Coy. R.E.

Army Form C. 2118.

Map sheets
Marche 9.
Germany 1.M.
Germany 1.M.

WAR DIARY
or
INTELLIGENCE SUMMARY.
(Erase heading not required.)

Instructions regarding War Diaries and Intelligence Summaries are contained in F.S. Regs., Part II. and the Staff Manual respectively. Title pages will be prepared in manuscript.

Place	Date	Hour	Summary of Events and Information	Remarks and references to Appendices
December 1918.	1.st		Div. H.Q. remains EMPTINNE (sheet Marche 9.) S.B. 55.92. Commn. maintained to Bdes by W/T and D.R.	
	2.nd		Div. H.Q. remains EMPTINNE. Work - Cleaning of wagons etc. Visual Section on Road Reconnaisance.	
	3.rd		Div. H.Q. remains EMPTINNE. On Road Reconnaisance "	
	4.th		Div. H.Q. remains EMPTINNE. " Capt. Bruce Joined from 35th Div. Sig. Coy. R.E.	
	5.th		Div. H.Q. closed EMPTINNE 09.00hrs. Opened GRAND HAN (3.E. Marche) at 15.00hrs. Company at PTE ENILE. (3.E. Marche)	
	6.th		Div. H.Q. remained GRAND HAN. Coy at PT. ENILE. Commn. maintained by W/T and D.R.	
	7.th		Div. H.Q. remained GRAND HAN. Coy moved to OVERHEID. Lieut. H.C. Ref-Coy left for Sig. Sec. Tps. Genbre, Bedford. (CLERHEID - 3.H. Marche)	
	8.th		Div. H.Q. and Coy moved to SALM CHATEAU (3.K. Marche 9.) Opened 12.00hrs. Commn. maintained by W/T and D.R.	
	9.th		Div. H.Q. remains SALM CHATEAU. R.W. Marching Order Kit Inspection. (Marche 3.K.)	
	10.th		Div. H.Q. remains SALM CHATEAU. G.R.W. Visual Section Units of 9th and 76th. Bdes. rejoined Units.	
	11.th		Div. H.Q. remains SALM CHATEAU. G.R.W. Visual Section Units of 9th Bde. rejoined Units.	
	12.th		Div. H.Q. remains SALM CHATEAU. R.W.	
	13.th		Div. H.Q. remains SALM CHATEAU. R.W.	
	14.th		Div. H.Q. crossed SALM CHATEAU. 09.00hrs. Opened 15.00hrs. Factory near LOSHEIM (G.I. Germany 1.M.) Coy. moved to SETZ (Germany 1.M.)	
	15.th		Div. H.Q. remained at Factory near LOSHEIM. Coy move to factory nr. LOSHEIM	
	16.th		Div. H.Q. opened at Factory near LOSHEIM 09.00hrs. Opened EUSKIRCHEN 15.00hrs. (G.O. Germany 1.M.) Coy. moved from Factory near LOSHEIM to BLANKENHEIM. (G.M. Germany)	

Army Form C. 2118.

WAR DIARY
or
INTELLIGENCE SUMMARY.
(Erase heading not required.)

Instructions regarding War Diaries and Intelligence Summaries are contained in F. S. Regs., Part II. and the Staff Manual respectively. Title pages will be prepared in manuscript.

Place	Date	Hour	Summary of Events and Information	Remarks and references to Appendices
	17.th		Div. H.Q. remains EULKIRCHEN. Coy. moved from BLANKENHEIM to EULKIRCHEN. (S.O. Germany l.r.)	
	18.th		Div. H.Q. remains EUSKIRCHEN. Coy. remained EUSKIRCHEN. (S.O. Germany l.r.)	
	19.th		Div. H.Q. moved to DUREN. Coy. moved to DUREN. (S.O. Germany l.r.) open 12.00hrs. Comm. by W/T and D.R.	
	20.th		Div. H.Q. remained DUREN. G.R.W. Comm. by W/T and D.R. and Sounder	
	21.st		"	
	22.nd		"	
	23.rd		"	
	24.th		"	
	25.th		"	
	26.th		"	
	27.th		"	
	28.th		"	
	29.th		"	
	30.th		"	
	31.st		"	

for O.C. 3rd Div. Sig. Coy. A. and Division

Army Form C. 2118.

WAR DIARY
or
INTELLIGENCE SUMMARY.
(Erase heading not required.)

3D Signal Corps
Vol 43

Place	Date	Hour	Summary of Events and Information	Remarks and references to Appendices
	1st Jan.		Div. Hq. remains DUREN, GRW, commn by W/T, Sounder and D.R.L.S. Div. to Inf. Bdes. & Arty. Groups	
	2nd		" "	
	3rd		" "	
	4th		" "	
	5th		" "	
	6th		" Company Training Commences	
	7th		" Capt Bruce-Leave to U.K. 7/1/19 to 21/1/19	
	8th		" Company Training Continues	
	9th		" "	
	10th		" "	
	11th		" T/2/Lieut Adams E.A. Demobilized	
	12th		" Company Training Continues	
	13th		" "	
	14th		" "	
	15th		" "	
	16th		" "	

Army Form C. 2118.

WAR DIARY
or
INTELLIGENCE SUMMARY.
(Erase heading not required.)

Instructions regarding War Diaries and Intelligence Summaries are contained in F. S. Regs. Part II. and the Staff Manual respectively. Title pages will be prepared in manuscript.

Place	Date	Hour	Summary of Events and Information	Remarks and references to Appendices
	17th Jan		Div.Hq.remains DUREN,GRW,commn by W/T, Sounder and D.R.L.S to Inf.Bdes. & Arty.Gps. Company Training Continues	
	18th		"	
	19th		"	
	20th		"	
	21st		"	
	22nd		"	
	23rd		"	
	24th		"	
	25th		"	
	26th		" Marching Order and Inspection Parade	
	27th		Company Training Continues	
	28th		"	
	29th		"	
	30th		"	
	31st		"	

Capt. R.E.
for O.C. 2nd Div. Sig. Co.

Army Form C. 2118.

WAR DIARY
or
INTELLIGENCE SUMMARY.
(Erase heading not required.)

Instructions regarding War Diaries and Intelligence Summaries are contained in F. S. Regs., Part II. and the Staff Manual respectively. Title pages will be prepared in manuscript.

Place	Date	Hour	Summary of Events and Information	Remarks and references to Appendices
DUREN	1919 Feb 1st		General Routine Work, Commn. to Bdes., R.A., Sounder, W/T., D.R.L.S. Company Training Continues.	
"	2nd		T/Lieut. J.G. Riddell posted to Company.	
"	3rd		Lieut. Adams demobilized. Company Training continues.	
"	4th		"	
"	5th		Lieut. J.B. Le Gros posted to Company. Company Training continues.	
"	6th		"	
"	7th		"	
"	8th		T/Lieut. Barwood granted Leave to U.K. Company Training continues.	
"	9th		"	
"	10th		T/Lieut. Rorke granted Leave to U.K. Company Training continues.	
"	11th		"	
"	12th		A/Capt. Phillips granted Leave to U.K. Company Training continues.	
"	13th		"	
"	14th		"	
"	15th		T/2Lieut. C.A. Taylor to U.K. for Demobilization Company Training continues.	
"	16th		"	

Army Form C. 2118.

- Sheet 2 -

WAR DIARY
or
INTELLIGENCE SUMMARY.
(Erase heading not required.)

Place	Date	Hour	Summary of Events and Information	Remarks and references to Appendices
DUREN, Feb.	17th		General Routine Work, Comm. to Bdes,R.A.,Sounder, W/T.,D.R.L.S	A/Major Pope to England on Duty.
"	18th		"	Company Training continues.
"	19th		"	T/Lieut F.W.Deans in Command of Company. Company Training continues.
"	20th		"	"
"	21st		"	"
"	22nd		"	"
"	23rd		"	A/Major Pope returns off Duty and resumes Command of Company. Company Training continues
"	24th		"	Company Training continues.
"	25th		"	"
"	26th		"	"
"	27th		"	"
"	28th		"	(T/Lieut F.W.Deans proceeds on Special Leave (T/Lieut H.G.Barwood returned from Leave to U.K (T/Lieut .Rorke returned from Leave.

Major,
O.C. 3rd Div. Signal Company.

WAR DIARY or INTELLIGENCE SUMMARY

Army Form C. 2118.

Place	Date	Hour	Summary of Events and Information	Remarks and references to Appendices
(Indenthal) COLOGNE.	Mch 1919. 1st		Div H.Q. moved from "Duren" to Cologne (Indenthal) and relieved Guards Divn.	
	2		General Routine work by Sounder Drls, Company and Training continues.	
	3		"	
	4		A/Capt G.D.C.Phillips. returned from leave.	
	5		"	
	6		Lt R McB Mather to England for Demobilization.	
	7		"	
	8		"	
	9		W/T Comm established to all Bdes.	
	11		"	
	12		"	
	13		"	
	14		"	
	15		L/T F.V.Miller posted to Coy from 2nd Sig Constn Co 2nd Army Autny C.S.O. 2nd Army 0232 D/14/3/19.	

Army Form C. 2118.

WAR DIARY
or
INTELLIGENCE SUMMARY.
(Erase heading not required.)

Place	Date	Hour	Summary of Events and Information	Remarks and references to Appendices
lindenthal) Cologne.	Mch 1919 16		Div H.Q. at Cologne (lindenthal) G.W.R., Comms by Sounder, DRls, Wireless, Company Training and Educational Training continues.	
"	17		"	
"	18		" T/Lt F.W.Deans returned from leave resumes duties as O/I/C lines.	
"	19		"	
"	20		" Major D.Pope.M.C. leave to U.K.	
"	21		" " " "	
"	22		" " " "	
"	23		" " " "	
"	24		" T/Lt J.C.King to be acting Capt whlst empld as O/I/C Sigs 3rd Div appvd by C.I.C. 1st army 9.3.18. North Div letter A 43/61 6th Corps C/105/184 d/21/3/19	
"	25		" T/Lt F.G.Hasluck from leave resumes duty by Scunder D.A.I.S.	
"	26		" "	
"	27		" "	
"	28		" Company & Eductnl Training continues.	
"	29		" "	
"	30		" "	
"	31		" "	

[signature] Capt R.E.
for O.C. 3rd Div Signal Coy R.E.

Army Form C. 2118.

WAR DIARY
or
INTELLIGENCE SUMMARY.
(Erase heading not required.)

Place	Date	Hour	Summary of Events and Information	Remarks and references to Appendices
LINDENTHAL COLOGNE	APRIL 1919.			
	1.		Div H.Q. at (Lindenthal) Cologne. General routine work. Communications by Brigades & R.A. by Squadron W/T + D.R.L.S.	
	2	"	Company training + Educational Work continues.	
	3	"	Lt. Q.B. Porter granted Special Leave 3-4-19 to 17-4-19.	
	4	"	"	
	5	"	Major R. Pope. Ext. leave to 13-4-19. Auth. W.O. A642. D/25-3-19. 2nd Rt. R.A. No 33. granted leave to U.K. 5-4-19 to 19-4-19.	
	6	"	Lt. G. Whalley Baxter joined this unit from 17th Signal Coys. Auth. 3rd Army. A/A/2553/53 and 3rd Corps. I/A/790/186. D/26-3-19.	
	7	"	Lt. E.W. Baker posted to 76th Inf. Bde. for duty. Lt. P. Rivenne joined this unit from 19th Divr Sig Coy.	
	8	"	Auth. A.G. 10336/3.S.R. D/7-4-19. Lt. G.R. Porter joined this unit from 20th Div. Sig Coy. Auth. 3rd Army A/A/2553/71. D/29-3-19 and commences duty as O/C. W/T.	
	9	"	CONTINUED.	

Army Form C. 2118.

WAR DIARY
or
INTELLIGENCE SUMMARY.
(Erase heading not required.)

3rd SIGNAL COMPANY R.E.
3rd DIVISION

Place	Date	Hour	Summary of Events and Information	Remarks and references to Appendices
COLOGNE	APRIL 1919			
			Div. H.Q. at (LINDENTHAL) Cologne. G.R.W. Com. to Bas. + R.A. Bde. W/T: DRLS + Solrs.	
	10		Cadre of 3rd. Div. Sig. Coy formed. Lt. R.V. Muller A/S(1) O/C	
	11		Lt. E.G. Sams joined this unit from 186 Bde. R.F.A.	
	"		To 74 Bde. R.F.A. for duty.	
	12		Pt. R.C. Voss rejoined from leave to duty as O/C G.P.O. of Bde. Sigs	
	"		P. Dunne to "D" Corps Sig Coy as Wireless Instructor (Temp/s.)	
	13		G.R.W. Coms by S. W/T. DRLS.	
	14		" " Coy Colrs. wire continued.	
	15		Major D. Pope from leave to duty as O.C. of D.H. Signalling.	
	16		Capt. A/Major C.H. WALSH M.C. 1/5 Connaught Rangers Joined from 17th Corps Signals Cadre. Rhine Army. A 307/634 - 6 May 25. A.A./1/19.	
	"		Acts. takes over Command of this unit. Vice Lt. A/Major D Pope M.C.	
	17		Lt. R.H. Nisbett joined from 2nd Army Signal Coy.	
	18		Auth. AG.10 336/15R. 21/23:3·19. To Mil. Div. Sig. School as O/C	
	19		Lt. A.B. Rorke returned from Leave to duty as O/C	
			'A' Section of this Company	
			Continued	

WAR DIARY or INTELLIGENCE SUMMARY

Army Form C. 2118.

Place	Date	Hour	Summary of Events and Information	Remarks and references to Appendices
COLOGNE	APRIL 1919		Div. H.Q. at LINDENTHAL. COLOGNE. G.R.W. Comms. to Bdes. & RA. By Sounder W/T. & DRLS. Coy & F.D. Work continues	
	20		"	
	21		Cadre formation moves to NIPPES - COLOGNE.	
	22		"	
	23		Major D. Pope M.C. To U.K. duty. Auth. W.O. 100/gen/6184. (M.S.I.A.)	
	24		"	
	25		Lt. P. Dunne returned from "D" Corps. W/T. Course	
	26		"	
	27		Lt. R.J. Sims granted leave to U.K. 27-4-19 – 11-5-19	
	28		Q.R. Patten to 73 Bde. RFA Sigs Vice Lt. R.J. Sims	
			Major C.H. Walsh leave to U.K. 28-4-19 to 12-5-19.	
	29		General Routine Work. Communications to Brigades, RA, & H.Q's by Sounder W/T & DRLS	
	30		Education & Company Training continue	

H.J.Ph. Major
a/ O.C. Northern Divisional Signal Coy.

J.R.C. Capt. R.E.

WAR DIARY 3rd Divl Signal Co RE.
or
INTELLIGENCE SUMMARY. Cadre.

Army Form C. 2118.

Place	Date	Hour	Summary of Events and Information	Remarks and references to Appendices
COLOGNE	1.5.19		General Routine work. Communication maintained with Northern Div. by phone & W/S.	
"	2.5.19		"	
"	3.5.19		"	
"	4.5.19		"	
"	5.5.19		"	
"	6.5.19		"	
"	7.5.19		"	
"	8.5.19		"	
"	9.5.19		"	
"	10.5.19		"	
"	11.5.19		"	
"	12.5.19		1/Lt L.V. Miller granted leave to the U.K. 12.5.19 to 26.5.19.	
"	13.5.19		General Routine work. Communication maintained with Northern Div. by phone & W/S.	
"	14.5.19		"	
"	15.5.19		"	
"	16.5.19		"	

Army Form C. 2118.

WAR DIARY 3rd Div Signal Co R.E. Ca. &c.
or
INTELLIGENCE SUMMARY.
(Erase heading not required.)

Place	Date	Hour	Summary of Events and Information	Remarks and references to Appendices
NIPPES Cologne	17.5.19		General Routine work. Communication maintained with Northern Div by phone r DR.LS	
	16.5.19		T/Lt A/Capt J King Lincolnshire Regt assumed command of Company	
	19.5.19		Cadre entrained at Cologne 0900 hrs en route for St Omer to pick up stores. 2 officers, 148 OR. of 31st Div Sig C.o R.E. to complete Cadre. Stages one night in Charleroi.	
	20.5.19		Proceeded from Charleroi and arrived at St Omer to find 31st Div Sig Co had moved to Dunkirk. Journey continues to Calais. Same night arriving there 0300 hrs 21st	
Dunkirk	21.5.19		Left Calais for Dunkirk and packed up 2 off/s and 48 OR 31st Div Sig Co RE. - (T/Lt A/Capt O.S. Webb, T/2/Lt J.W. Robertson R.E.)	
Dunkirk	22.5.19		All vehicles moved to docks and guards mounted	
"	23.5.19		Vehicles remain at docks under guard.	
	24.5.19		Vehicles loaded on board S.S. Mogileff	
		17.30 hrs	Embarked for Southampton arriving 12 noon 25th inst.	

Donating Capco.
OC 3rd Div Signal Co R.E.

3rd Division
War Diaries

1/1st East Riding Field Coy R.E.

August to December

1916

To France Sep 1915
When war diaries first Aug '16

3rd <u>Divisional Engineers</u>

<u>1/1st EAST RIDING FIELD COMPANY R. E.</u>

<u>AUGUST 1 9 1 6</u>

WAR DIARY

1/1st EAST RIDING FIELD Co. R.E. Army Form C. 2118.

INTELLIGENCE SUMMARY
(Erase heading not required.)

Place	Date	Hour	Summary of Events and Information	Remarks and references to Appendices
MERICOURT	1.8.16		Training. Pontoon and Trestle Bridging over the River ANCRE, and Section Drill. E.W.S.	
MERICOURT	2.8.16		Training. Pontoon and Trestle Bridging over the River ANCRE, and Section Drill. A reinforcement of two men joined the Company from the Base. E.W.S.	
MERICOURT	3.8.16		Training. Pontoon and Trestle Bridging over the River ANCRE, and Section Drill. O.O. Inspected reinforcement of two men arrived yesterday and gave them instructions. C.O. Mr. Major WATKINS the Commandant of the Captured Prisoners Camp at MERICOURT to select a site and arrange for the erection of an additional camp. E.W.S.	
MERICOURT	4.8.16		Training. Pontoon and Trestle Bridging over the River ANCRE, and Section Drill. 2nd Lieut HAITHWAIT set out to prepare new camp for German Prisoners. E.W.S.	

Army Form C. 2118.

WAR DIARY 1/1ᵐᵗ EAST RIDING FIELD Co. R.E.

INTELLIGENCE SUMMARY.

(Erase heading not required.)   Sheet 2.

Instructions regarding War Diaries and Intelligence Summaries are contained in F. S. Regs., Part II. and the Staff Manual respectively. Title pages will be prepared in manuscript.

Place	Date	Hour	Summary of Events and Information	Remarks and references to Appendices
MERICOURT	5.8.16		Motored from MERICOURT to CARNOY and arranged for work to be done on C.R.E. with C.R.E. 3rd Division, and D. lines of defence East of MONTAUBAN and South of BERNAFAY and TRONES WOOD, Returned by motor to MERICOURT and immediately marched out with the Company and transport complete to the CITADEL where the Company was accommodated in huts ready to carry out the work as arranged with the C.R.E. in the morning. 800 Infantry from the 76th Infantry Brigade and 400 of the 2nd Division Pioneers (Kings Royal Rifles) were put under the command of the C.O. for this work. E.W.S.	
THE CITADEL	6.8.16		Took Officers of the 1/1ᵐᵗ EAST RIDING FIELD Co. R.E. up to the trenches and explained the work to be carried out on the C and D. lines of defence. The Officers set at the work. Met the Officers who would be with the Infantry Working Parties and explained to them on the ground the work to be done by their men. Infantry paraded in two for the Infantry Working Parties, two parties each of 200 men at 9.30 P.M. and two parties each of 200 men to parade at 2.0 A.M. a section of the 1/1ᵐᵗ EAST RIDING FIELD Co. R.E. to work with each Infantry Working Party. E.W.S.	

WAR DIARY

INTELLIGENCE SUMMARY

Army Form C. 2118.

1/1st EAST RIDING FIELD Co. R.E.

Sheet 3.

Place	Date	Hour	Summary of Events and Information	Remarks and references to Appendices
THE CITADEL	7.8.16		Work on C defence line as yesterday. 10 R.E. with 80 Infantry and 10 Pioneers making gun emplacements and shelters for the Royal Artillery. E.W.P.	
THE CITADEL	8.8.16		Work as yesterday. No. 465 Sapper COYNE. E.W. Wounded. E.W.P.	
THE CITADEL	9.8.16		Work on C defence line as yesterday. E.W.P.	
THE CITADEL	10.8.16		Work on C defence line as yesterday. E.W.P.	
THE CITADEL	11.8.16		Work on C defence line as yesterday. No. 921 Sapper MARSHALL. J.W. Wounded. E.W.P.	
THE CITADEL	12.8.16		Work on C defence line as yesterday. No. 425. Lance Corporal ANNIS.T.A. Wounded. E.W.P.	
THE CITADEL	13.8.16		The whole of the Company marched to VILLE SUR ANCRE for baths. Interview with G.O.C. 76th Infantry Brigade at his Head Quarters at the SAND PIT with reference to immediate operations to be carried out by the 76th Infantry Brigade, also with G.O.C. 76th Infantry Brigade and Staff to 3rd Division Head Quarters at the FORKED TREE to see G.S.O. (Lieut-Colonel DE BRETT) then motored to CARNOY ① my visits with G.O.C. 76th Infantry. E.W.P.	

WAR DIARY

INTELLIGENCE SUMMARY

1/2nd EAST RIDING FIELD Co. R.E.   Sheet H

Army Form C. 2118.

Place	Date	Hour	Summary of Events and Information	Remarks and references to Appendices
THE CITADEL	13/6/16 (contd.)		9/6th Infantry Brigade and Hors the two Brigadiers who were handing over the Trenches to be occupied by the 9/6th Infantry Brigade for the forthcoming operations.	
		8.30 P.M.	N.I.T. to 3rd (Sunton) Head Quarters for conference with C.R.E. to arrange for work to be done in connection with forthcoming offensive operations, arranged to commence work immediately on dugouts for Brigade Head Quarters in CHIMPANZEE COMMUNICATION TRENCH. Returned to quarters at 12.30 A.M. E.W.T.	
THE CITADEL	14/6/16	11.0 A.M.	Rode to CARNOY (Smeyents met G.O.C. 9/6th Infantry Brigade (Brig-Gen KENTISH) and Staff and went up to the Trenches in connection with the forthcoming Offensive operations. Commenced work on new dugouts for Brigade Head Quarters in CHIMPANZEE TRENCH. R.E. to work with working parties of Infantry, work to be carried on continuously until complete. E.W.T.	

WAR DIARY 1/1st EAST RIDING FIELD Co R.E.

INTELLIGENCE SUMMARY Sheet 5.

Army Form C. 2118.

Place	Date	Hour	Summary of Events and Information	Remarks and references to Appendices
THE CITADEL	15/6/16	5.0 AM	Visited works proceeding at new dugouts for Brigade Head Quarters in CHIMPANZEE Trench.	
		3.30 PM	Marched Company with transport complete from the CITADEL to MINDEN POST and took over the camp vacated by the 2/1st WEST LANCASHIRE FIELD Co.R.E. (Fig. C.B.5). No 3 Section proceeded to dugouts in CARNOY VALLEY to be at the disposal of the G.O.C. 76th Infantry Brigade for the offensive operations. E.W.	
MINDEN POST	16/6/16	6.15 AM	Took 2nd Lieutenant PICKERSGILL round the trenches and explained to him the scheme of offensive operations to be carried out by the 76th Infantry Brigade and the work to be carried out by his No 8 Section. No 2 Section moved from CARNOY dugouts to CHIMPANZEE Trench, reinforcing their section in Divisional Reserve at MINDEN POST E.W.	
MINDEN POST	17/6/16	8.0 Wp	At the trenches all day and night, as at the request of the G.O.C. 76th Infantry Brigade arranged for work to be done to consolidate trenches and ground gained from the Germans in the attack yesterday and for another attack. Set out a tape in front of the front line trench for the Infantry (R.W.C.) to form up on for the attack. 2nd Lieutenant STONE 1/1st EAST RIDING FIELD Co R.E. who helped to set out the tape did not return when this job E.W.D.	

WAR DIARY 1/1st EAST RIDING FIELD Co. R.E. Sheet 6. Army Form C. 2118.

INTELLIGENCE SUMMARY.

(Erase heading not required.)

Instructions regarding War Diaries and Intelligence Summaries are contained in F.S. Regs., Part II. and the Staff Manual respectively. Title pages will be prepared in manuscript.

Place	Date	Hour	Summary of Events and Information	Remarks and references to Appendices
	17/8/16		was completed. No 2. Section with an Infantry Working Party dug a new communication Trench from our original front line trench to connect up with the length of trench captured from the Germans near the Ravine. E.M.P.	
MINDEN POST	18/8/16		No 1. Section with 2nd Lieutenant J A RIGGALL went up to the trenches to relieve No 2. Section. E.M.P.	
MINDEN POST	19/8/16		C.O. at the trenches all day. No 1. Section worked during the day clearing CHIMPANZEE and DUNCAN ALLEY, Communication Trenches and at night with an Infantry Working Party dug a new communication Trench to connect our original front line trench to LONELY TRENCH captured from the Germans and then on to GORDON TRENCH a new trench dug by the Gordon Highlanders on the ground gained by them, and then returned to camp at MINDEN POST. E.M.P.	
MINDEN POST	20/8/16	2.45 P.M.	C.O. rode to the HAPPY VALLEY to arrange for moving the Company there. Marched from MINDEN POST to the HAPPY VALLEY with the Company and transport complete, accommodated in tents. E.M.P.	

Army Form C. 2118.

WAR DIARY 1/1st EAST RIDING FIELD Co. R.E.

INTELLIGENCE SUMMARY. Sheet 7

(Erase heading not required.)

Instructions regarding War Diaries and Intelligence Summaries are contained in F. S. Regs., Part II. and the Staff Manual respectively. Title pages will be prepared in manuscript.

Place	Date	Hour	Summary of Events and Information	Remarks and references to Appendices
HAPPY VALLEY	21-8-16	8.0.AM	Marched from HAPPY VALLEY to MORLANCOURT where the men were accommodated in huts and the Officers billeted in a farm. E.M.N.	
MORLAN- COURT	22-8-16		Section Drills. Joiners employed fitting up billets as requested by the Town Major.	
		10.15.AM	Captain P. de H. HALL and 2nd Lieut. HAITHWAIT marched off with the Cyclists, Mounted portion of the Company and all Transport and joined the 76th Infantry Brigade Transport on the march to BERTANGLES. E.M.N.	
MORLAN COURT	23-8-16	4.15.AM	Received orders to entrain dismounted portion of the Company at MERICOURT at 6.0AM	
		4.45.AM	Loaded dismounted portion of the Company and marched off to MERICOURT, entrained and proceeded to CANDAS where the men detrained and marched to OCCOCHES where a halt was made for a meal, then marched to billets at MONPLAISIR, men were billeted in the farm buildings and the Officers in the farm house, Captain P. de H. HALL and 2nd Lieutenant HAITHWAIT rejoined with the transport at MONPLAISIR. E.M.N.	

WAR DIARY 1/1ᵗʰ EAST RIDING FIELD Co. R.E.

INTELLIGENCE SUMMARY.

Army Form C. 2118.

Sheet 6.

(Erase heading not required.)

Instructions regarding War Diaries and Intelligence Summaries are contained in F. S. Regs., Part II. and the Staff Manual respectively. Title pages will be prepared in manuscript.

Place	Date	Hour	Summary of Events and Information	Remarks and references to Appendices
MONPLAISIR	24/8/16		Inspection of Arms, Ammunition, Tools, Helmets, Iron Rations and K. C.O. called at Head Quarters, 76ᵗʰ Infantry Brigade at LE MEILLARD, and at offices of C.R.E. 3ʳᵈ Division at BERNAVILLE. E.W.S.	
MONPLAISIR	25/8/16		Marched from MONPLAISIR through OUTREBOIS — MEZEROLLES — RUNEN LEGRAND — FORTEL — VACQUERIE LE BOUCQ to LIGNY SUR CANCHE with the 76ᵗʰ Infantry Brigade Group. The road was hilly and the weather very hot. Many Infantry fell out, but no men of this unit fell out, before the completion of the march the Infantry Battalions were halted for a rest, this was not halt but continued the march independently. The Sappers were marching well. The Sappers marching names of the Sappers was due to the fact that the Sappers were wearing shorts and marched with bear games and there was a system of the legs and cadence. Men G. ??? killed on farm, Officer under a wagon shot in an orchard. E.W.S.	|||
LIGNY SUR CANCHE.	26/8/16		Marched from LIGNY SUR CANCHE through HAUTECOTE — ECOIVRES to GRAND RIEZ man OEUF with 76ᵗʰ Infantry Brigade Group. Very heavy rain during the march. Women fell out. Men billeted in farm buildings, Officers under a wagon shed on orchard. V. not night. E.W.S.	

WAR DIARY

1/1st EAST RIDING FIELD Co. R.E.   Army Form C. 2118

INTELLIGENCE SUMMARY

(Erase heading not required.)   Sheet 9.

Instructions regarding War Diaries and Intelligence Summaries are contained in F.S. Regs., Part II. and the Staff Manual respectively. Title pages will be prepared in manuscript.

Place	Date	Hour	Summary of Events and Information	Remarks and references to Appendices
GRAND RIEZ	27/6/16		Marched from GRAND RIEZ through BEAUVOIS–PIERRMONT–WAVRANS–MONCHY CAYEUX–ANVIN–PETIT ANVIN–BERGUENEUSE–NEUCHIN to FONTAINE LEZ BOULANS. Heavy rain during the march. Men billeted in a farm buildings, Officers in a Château. E.M.S.	
FONTAINE LEZ BOULANS	28/6/16		Marched from FONTAINE LEZ BOULANS through SAINS LEZ PERNES to TANGRY. Men billeted in barns, Officers in houses and a tent. E.M.S.	
TANGRY	29/6/16		Marched from TANGRY through PRESSY LES PERNES– PERNES–CHAMBLAIN– CHATELAIN–BRUAY to HEDIGNEUL. Very heavy rain and thunderstorm during the march. Directed for the night in W.D.H. etc previously occupied by Artillery. The huts were in a filthy condition when taken over. E.M.S.	

WAR DIARY 1/1st EAST RIDING FIELD CO. R.E.

INTELLIGENCE SUMMARY.
(Erase heading not required.)

Sheet 10.

Army Form C. 2118.

Place	Date	Hour	Summary of Events and Information	Remarks and references to Appendices
NESDIGNEUL	30.8.16		O.O. and Officers rode through HOUCHIN – NOEUX LES MINES – MAZINGARBE to PHILOSOPHE, took over from the 152nd Field Co. R.E. and next found the trenches. Captain R. H. HALL and 2nd Lieutenant HAITHWAIT followed with the Company and took over quarters in PHILOSOPHE and horse lines in MAZINGARBE, the quarters taken over were in a very filthy state. Very wet day. A Reinforcement of 12 men arrived from the Base and joined the Company.	EMN
PHILOSOPHE	31.8.16		Cleaning up and repairing quarters. C.O. rode to MINX to arrange to take over water supply to trenches from O.C. 31st Co. R.E. Afternoon. Transport also inspected pumping plant containing at FOSSE 7, and met G.O.C. 76th Infantry Brigade with reference to future work. C.R.E. 3rd Division called at these quarters to discuss and arrange for future work.	E. M. Newell Lieut. Col. R.E. O.C. 1/11st East Riding Field Co. R.E.

1 September 1916.

3rd Divisional Engineers.

1/1ST EAST RIDING FIELD COMPANY R.E.

SEPTEMBER 1 9 1 6.

Army Form C. 2118.

1/1st EAST RIDING Field Co RE

September 1916 Sheet 1. Vol 2

WAR DIARY
of
INTELLIGENCE SUMMARY
(Erase heading not required.)

Instructions regarding War Diaries and Intelligence Summaries are contained in F. S. Regs., Part II. and the Staff Manual respectively. Title pages will be prepared in manuscript.

Place	Date	Hour	Summary of Events and Information	Remarks and references to Appendices
PHILOSOPHE	1.9.16		Repairing and cleaning quarters at PHILOSOPHE. Took over pumping plant at FOSSE 7 and water supply to the trenches from the 31st Army Troops Company R.E. G.W.D.	
"	2.9.16		Repairing and cleaning quarters at PHILOSOPHE. Detachments from Nos 3 and 4 Sections went up to the trenches and took over arrangements for the R.E. to live in. G.W.D.	
"	3.9.16		Repairing and finishing cookhouses and latrines at quarters at PHILOSOPHE. Nos 3 and 4 Sections less detachments already in the trenches, proceeded to dug outs in the trenches and commenced work on deep dug outs in the front line east of NORTHERN Vr. C. T. Church Parade in the evening for No 1 and 2 Sections. G.W.D.	

WAR DIARY
INTELLIGENCE SUMMARY

1/1 8th East Riding of C of RE
September 1916
Sheet 2

Army Form C. 2118.

Place	Date	Hour	Summary of Events and Information	Remarks and references to Appendices
PHILOSOPHE	8.9.16		No 2 Section proceeded to dug-outs in the trench area, making three sections quartered in the trenches for work. No 1 Section repairing quarters and making cookers shelter, latrines and improving quarters at PHILOSOPHE. Nos 3 and 4 Sections in the trenches repairing communication trenches, making deep dug-outs in the front lines and of NORTHERN VR. C.T and making trench Mortar Emplacements. E.M.N.	
PHILOSOPHE	9.9.16		Works as yesterday. E.M.N.	
PHILOSOPHE	10.9.16		Works as yesterday. Announced in 2nd Divn Orders that No.209 Sergeant B.L. DUGGLEBY, No. 507 Lance Corporal STEELE and No. 956 Lance Corporal G. GOODEVE had been awarded the Military Medals in connection with the operations at LONGUEVAL. E.M.N.	
PHILOSOPHE	11.9.16		Works as yesterday. E.M.N.	

WAR DIARY
INTELLIGENCE SUMMARY

(Erase heading not required.)

Army Form C. 2118.

1/1st East Riding R.E.
Sheet 3   September 1916

Place	Date	Hour	Summary of Events and Information	Remarks and references to Appendices
PHILOSOPHE	8.9.16		No.133. Corporal LOCKWOOD.F. appointed Acting Sergeant. E.W. Work as yesterday.	
PHILOSOPHE	9.9.16		No.1 Section relieved No.H. Section in the Trenches. With as yesterday, in addition work commenced on the construction of a dug out for the Field Ambulance in the trenches. (G.21.d.) and making new horse standings in site of old ones at the Huts. E.W.	
MAZINGARBE CHATEAU				
PHILOSOPHE	10.9.16		Work as yesterday, in addition work commenced on forming special horses in front line parapet for "C" Company Special Battalion R.E. E.W.	
PHILOSOPHE	11.9.16		Work as yesterday. E.W.	
PHILOSOPHE	12.9.16		Sapper HOWSON C. proceeded to the First Army Rest Camp at the Base for a fortnight. Work as yesterday, forming special horses in front line parapet for "C" Company Special Battalion R.E. complete. E.W.	

WAR DIARY
INTELLIGENCE SUMMARY

Army Form C. 2118.

11th East Riding of Co. R.E.

September 1916

Sheet 1.

Place	Date	Hour	Summary of Events and Information	Remarks and references to Appendices
PHILOSOPHE	13.9.16		No. 1 Section relieved No. 3 Section in the Trenches. Work the same as yesterday, less repairs known front line parapet completed, and in addition POSEN ALLEY and CHALK PIT ALLEY C.T.s were deepened and cleaned. E.W.N.	
PHILOSOPHE	14.9.16		Work as yesterday, except that no workmen class on POSEN ALLEY and CHALK PIT ALLEY C.T. no workers parties being available. E.W.N.	
PHILOSOPHE	15.9.16		Military Medal Ribbon presented by the C.R.E. 3rd Division (Colonel Elliott) to 2nd Corporal GOODEVE and Lance Corporal STEELE. Work as yesterday in addition POSEN ALLEY C.T. were repaired. E.W.N.	
PHILOSOPHE	16.9.16		No. 314 Sapper ATKINSON proceeded to BETHUNE to proceed to England to be employed on Munition Work. Leave for the men recommenced. No. 630 Driver APPLEBY H.R. proceeded to England on leave. Work as yesterday. E.W.N.	

Army Form C. 2118.

1/1st East Riding of G RE
September 1916 Sheet 5

WAR DIARY
INTELLIGENCE SUMMARY
(Erase heading not required.)

Instructions regarding War Diaries and Intelligence Summaries are contained in F.S. Regs., Part II. and the Staff Manual respectively. Title pages will be prepared in manuscript.

Place	Date	Hour	Summary of Events and Information	Remarks and references to Appendices
PHILOSOPHE	17.9.16		No 3 Section relieved No 2 Section in the Trenches. No Sig 2nd Corporal PALMER W.S. appointed Temporary Corporal. No. 268 Lance Corporal HIELD S. H.V. appointed Temporary 2nd Corporal. Work are yesterday and in addition CHALK PIT ALLEY C.T. was cleared and deepened. E.W.	
PHILOSOPHE	18.9.16		Work as yesterday, except that no further work was done on CHALK PIT ALLEY C.T. no working party being available. E.W.	
PHILOSOPHE	19.9.16		Announced in 3rd Division Orders that the Military Medal had been awarded to No 197 Sergeant W. KEYWORTH, No. 203 Sergeant N. HARRISON and No 133 Sergeant F. LOCKWOOD in connection with operations at MALTZ HORN FARM RIDGE E.W. Work as yesterday.	
PHILOSOPHE	20.9.16		Work as yesterday and in addition work commenced at night mining round the CHALK PIT and clearing the support lines. No. 896 Sapper GREENER proceeded to England on leave. E.W.	

Army Form C. 2118.

11th East Riding F.C. R.E.
Sheet 6 September 1916

WAR DIARY
INTELLIGENCE SUMMARY.
(Erase heading not required.)

Place	Date	Hour	Summary of Events and Information	Remarks and references to Appendices
PHILOSOPHE	19.9.16		Handed over to the 231st Co. R.E. Officers blown round the trenches and all work in hand. No 1 Section returned to quarters at PHILOSOPHE from dug outs in the trenches. No 3 and 4 Sections remained in the trenches to complete mining round the CHALK PIT. E.M.C.	
PHILOSOPHE	22.9.16		No 3 and 4 Sections returned to quarters at PHILOSOPHE from the trenches	
		3.0 P.M	The Company with all transport marched to NOEUX-LES-MINES & when it was billeted for the night. E.M.C.	
NOEUX-LES-MINES	23.9.16	9 A.M	The Company with Transport marched from NOEUX-LES-MINES to AUCHEL where it was billeted for the night. E.M.C.	
AUCHEL	24.9.16	8.15 A.M	The Company with transport marched from AUCHEL to LIGNY-LEZ-AIRE where billets were taken. Great difficulty was experienced in finding accommodation, all horses being filled up even. Marched past Major General DEVERELL G.O.C. 3rd Division. E.M.C.	
LIGNY-LEZ-AIRE	25.9.16		Training commenced. E.M.C	

WAR DIARY
INTELLIGENCE SUMMARY.
(Erase heading not required.)

Army Form C. 2118.

Instructions regarding War Diaries and Intelligence Summaries are contained in F. S. Regs., Part II. and the Staff Manual respectively. Title pages will be prepared in manuscript.

1/1 8th East Riding 8th Co. R.E. Sept. 1916

Place	Date	Hour	Summary of Events and Information	Remarks and references to Appendices
LIGNY-LEZ-AIRE	26.9.16		Training. Section Drill. Lectures on Organization and Duties of a Field Co. R.E., Equitation. Mounted Detachment at Riding and Driving exercise. E.W.D.	
LIGNY-LEZ-AIRE	27.9.16		Training. Instruction in Pontoon Bridging, Weldon Trestle Bridging, Explosives and Demolitions; Riding and Driving. E.W.D.	
LIGNY-LEZ-AIRE	28.9.16		Training. Marched to training area with all transport, carried out digging operations to test efficiency of (a) 2 men digging independently, (b) gang of 3 men, one digger 2 shovellers, while the three men rested. (c) gang of 3 men, two in turn digging (d) 1 man digging while one man rested. The results were strongly in favour of (a), 1 man digging independently. E.W.D.	
LIGNY-LEZ-AIRE	29.9.16		Training. Instruction in Pontoon Bridging, Weldon Trestle Bridging, Explosives and Demolitions; Riding and Driving. E.W.D.	
LIGNY-LEZ-AIRE	30.9.16		Training. Marched to the Training area with all Transport and took part with the 76th Infantry Brigade in a March Past, Inspection and Presentation of medal ribbons by the Brigadier General KENTISH D.S.O. afterwards marched back to billets at LIGNY-LEZ-AIRE.	

I. B. Stoker 1916
E. M. Newell
Lieut. 1/1 East Riding Field Co. R.E.
O.C. 1/1 1st East Riding Field Co. R.E.

3rd Divisional Engineers.

1/1ST EAST RIDING FIELD COMPANY R.E.

OCTOBER 1916.

1/1 E R Fd Coy R E
Army Form C. 2118.

WAR DIARY
INTELLIGENCE SUMMARY
(Erase heading not required.)

Sheet No 1.   Vol 3

Place	Date	Hour	Summary of Events and Information	Remarks and references to Appendices
LIGNY-LEZ-AIRE	1.10.16	1.0 A.M. (Zero)	Winter Time came into force, clocks put back one hour. Sunday. Ordered to have day of rest from Training.	
		9.00 A.M.	Inspection of Arms, Ammunition and Web Helmets. Church Parade, Chaplain from 3rd Suffolk Regiment took the service.	
		2.0 P.M.	The Commanding Officer attended the conference held by the G.O.C. 3rd Division on the Training ground to discuss the scheme of attack to be carried out during the next few days Training. E.W.W.	
		6.0 P.M.	Pay Parade.	
LIGNY-LEZ-AIRE	2.10.16	7.0 A.M.	No 1 Section with Tool cart marched to the training area to mark ground for Brigade operations.	
		9.30 A.M.	The Company marched with transport from LIGNY-LEZ-AIRE through CUHEM — ERNY ST JULIEN to the Training Ground near DELETTE, seven miles, to take part in a practice attack with the 76 Infantry Brigade, owing to the very wet day the operations were cancelled for that day, cooked dinners on the ground and marched back to LIGNY-LEZ-AIRE billets by the same route. E.W.W.	

Army Form C. 2118.

WAR DIARY

INTELLIGENCE SUMMARY.

(Erase heading not required.)

Instructions regarding War Diaries and Intelligence Summaries are contained in F. S. Regs., Part II. and the Staff Manual respectively. Title pages will be prepared in manuscript.

Place	Date	Hour	Summary of Events and Information	Remarks and references to Appendices
LIGNY-LEZ-AIRE	3/10/16	7.0 AM	No. 2 Section with Inf. cart marched seven miles to the training area to mark the ground for the 76th Infantry Brigade operations.	
		9.0 AM	The Company ready to march off to the training area for operations, message received to say that operations were cancelled for the day owing to very wet weather. Section instructed in knots and lashings. E.W.N.	
LIGNY LEZ-AIRE	4/10/16	8.0 AM	The Company marched seven miles to the training area with rations, transport and then took part in Divisional operations, consolidating positions captured and erecting strong points, after the operations witnessed a bombardment with 18 dive guns, covered dinner on the ground then marched back to billets at LIGNY-LEZ-AIRE, 7 seven miles. A very wet day. E.W.N.	
LIGNY LEZ-AIRE	5/10/16 10.45 AM		Marched from billets at LIGNY-LEZ-AIRE through WESTREHEM - FONTAINE-LEZ-BOULANS - HEUCHIN to BERGUENEUSE where billets were taken. Marched past G.O.C. 3rd Division.	

Army Form C. 2118.

WAR DIARY
or
INTELLIGENCE SUMMARY

(Erase heading not required.)

Sheet No. 3.

Instructions regarding War Diaries and Intelligence Summaries are contained in F. S. Regs., Part II. and the Staff Manual respectively. Title pages will be prepared in manuscript.

Place	Date	Hour	Summary of Events and Information	Remarks and references to Appendices
BERGUENEUSE.	6.10.16	8.0 AM	Mounted Standard, cyclists and all Transport under Captain P de H HALL and 2nd Lieut J H ALDEN marched from BERGUENEUSE to proceed South by road through ANVIN — WAVRANS — ST POL — MONCHEAUX — HOUVIN to REBREUVE.	
		12.0 Midnight	Dismounted men remained at BERGUENEUSE. 2nd Lieutenant J WADSLEY with billeting party were picked up by a 76th Infantry Brigade Motor Lorry passing through BERGUENEUSE and conveyed to ST POL Railway Station where they entrained for ACHEUX. E.M.N.	
BERGUENEUSE.	7.10.16	9.30 AM	Sections paraded for Physical Drill.	
		7.30 PM	The Dismounted portion of the Company paraded and marched to ST POL to entrain. Thence on arrival at ST POL at 10.55 PM informed by R.T.O. that train would not leave until next morning. Put men into huts at the rest camp and Officers put up at the Officers Rest House, ST POL. The Company was rationed up to tea time. All rations were expended on arrival. The Railway Station Rations had been asked for by me to meet this contingency, expecting from previous experience that there would be delay. This ration asked for was not considered necessary by Higher Authority. E.M.N.	

2353 Wt. W2344/7434 700,000 5/15 D. D. & L. A.D.S.S./Forms/C. 2118.

Army Form C. 2118.

WAR DIARY
INTELLIGENCE SUMMARY.
(Erase heading not required.)

Sheet No. 4

Place	Date	Hour	Summary of Events and Information	Remarks and references to Appendices
ST. POL	8.10.16	7.30.A.M	Left Into at the Rest Camp and marched to the Railway Station to entrain. Found an A.S.C. Store near the Railway Station, obtained rations for the men. The train left ST. POL at 8.36.A.M. and proceeded slowly South through DOULLENS – GEZAINCOURT, train held up at GEZAINCOURT for about 2 hours then proceeded South by a new track to ACHEUX where it arrived at about 7.30.P.M. some twelve hours late. Detrained and the men had a full meal which had been prepared for them, the Transport having arrived by road, then marched to MAILLY-MAILLET and went into their billets on further unrecorded instructions. G.M.W.	
MAILLY-MAILLET	9.10.16		Conference with C.R.E. 3rd Division at Cheshire Field Co. R.E. billet, with reference to work to be done. Took over from O.C. 1st East Anglian Field Co. R.E., my Officers went round sections of the Trench area with Officers of the 1st East Anglian Field Co. R.E. and took over men and commenced work at midnight. G.M.W.	

Army Form C. 2118.

WAR DIARY

INTELLIGENCE SUMMARY.

(Erase heading not required.)

Sheet No 5.

Instructions regarding War Diaries and Intelligence Summaries are contained in F. S. Regs., Part II. and the Staff Manual respectively. Title pages will be prepared in manuscript.

Place	Date	Hour	Summary of Events and Information	Remarks and references to Appendices
MAILLY MAILLET	10.10.16		All four sections employed in the Trenches, mostly night work, with have Infantry working parties. No.1 Section. Stokes Gun Emplacements behind the front line. No.2 Section. Wind Dugouts in ROB ROY TRENCH. No.3 Section. 7th Infantry Brigade Head Quarter Dugouts in RAILWAY AVENUE. No.4 Section. Repairing Communication Trenches and Assembly Trenches. 1/2 Companies of Pioneers 20th King's Royal Rifles attached for work. E.W.	
MAILLY MAILLET	11.10.16		Work the same as yesterday. E.W.	
MAILLY MAILLET	12.10.16		Work the same as yesterday. E.W.	
MAILLY MAILLET	13.10.16		Work the same as yesterday, in addition commenced to carry up material for forward R.E. Dumps. A Man from the 1st Gordon Highlanders and 3 Men from the 10th Royal Welsh Fusiliers arrived to be attached to this Company to be trained as Sappers for working parties. E.W.	

Army Form C. 2118.

WAR DIARY
INTELLIGENCE SUMMARY.
(Erase heading not required.)

Instructions regarding War Diaries and Intelligence Summaries are contained in F. S. Regs., Part II. and the Staff Manual respectively. Title pages will be prepared in manuscript.

Sheet. No 6.

Place	Date	Hour	Summary of Events and Information	Remarks and references to Appendices
MAILLY MAILLET	14.10.16		Work the same as yesterday. EWN	
MAILLY MAILLET	15.10.16		Work the same as yesterday. EWN	
MAILLY MAILLET	16.10.16		Conferred with C.R.E. 3rd Division at Head Quarters of 1/1st EAST RIDING FIELD Co. R.E. C.O.'s of 56th Field Co. R.E. Cheshire Field Co. R.E. and 208 K.R.R. (Pioneers) present with reference to work to be done during pending operations. 86 carnochan test moist in making note of 8th K.O.R.L. at working in CAMPION TRENCH, due to evening shell fire. W.O. on arrival by opts in ROBROY trench to supervise on account of shortage of labour and material. EWN	
MAILLY MAILLET	17.10.16		Recent orders to move the Company to COURCELLES-AU-BOIS, sent 2nd Lieutenant A PICKERSGILL to obtain billets, he sent back to report that there were no billets available and would not be any until tomorrow, so arranged with the 3rd Division to remain in present billets at MAILLY-MAILLET tonight. EWN	

2353 Wt. W 2344/1454 700,000 5/15 D. D. & L. A.D.S.S./Forms/C. 2118.

Army Form C. 2118.

WAR DIARY
INTELLIGENCE SUMMARY
(Erase heading not required.)

SHEET No. 7.

Place	Date	Hour	Summary of Events and Information	Remarks and references to Appendices
MAILLY-MAILLET	18.10.16	11.15.A.M	The dismounted portion of the Company with Infantry detachments attached for work marched from MAILLY-MAILLET to COURCELLES-AU-BOIS and took over huts from the Highland Field Co. R.E. accommodation for the Infantry detachments in part there in an empty canvas shed in the R.E. Camp at COURCELLES-AU-BOIS. No entraining parties except Pioneers and Infantry detachments attached available for work in the trenches. E.M.N.	
COURCELLES AU-BOIS	19.10.16		Work in the trenches as before. E.M.N.	
COURCELLES AU-BOIS	20.10.16		Work in the trenches as before in addition commenced work on a dugout at NORTHERN AVENUE for a Regimental Aid Post for the 3rd Australian Inf. Bde. Regt. O.C. accompanied G.O.C. 76th Infantry Brigade round the trenches last night and recommend the front line which was badly knocked about. E.M.N.	
COURCELLES AU-BOIS	21.10.16		Work in the trenches as yesterday. E.M.N.	
COURCELLES AU-BOIS	22.10.16		Work in the trenches as yesterday. Very heavy rain last few days. E.M.N.	
COURCELLES AU-BOIS	23.10.16		Work in trenches as yesterday. Dulled weather all morning was still strong in front of SERRE. Shelling trenches especially OBSERVATION WOOD (K.28.b.3.4.) The enemy's artillery more active than usual. E.M.N.	

Army Form C. 2118.

WAR DIARY

INTELLIGENCE SUMMARY

(Erase heading not required.)

SHEET No. 8

Instructions regarding War Diaries and Intelligence Summaries are contained in F. S. Regs., Part II. and the Staff Manual respectively. Title Pages will be prepared in manuscript.

Place	Date	Hour	Summary of Events and Information	Remarks and references to Appendices
COURCELLES AU-BOIS	24.10.16		Work suspended except in dug-outs owing to wet weather making digging operations impossible. E.W.N	
COURCELLES AU-BOIS	25.10.16		Work again held up except in dug-outs owing to continuous heavy rain. E.W.N	
COURCELLES AU-BOIS	26.10.16		One Section employed on revial heights for 76th Infantry Brigade in the trench area, and three sections employed draining and repairing trenches. E.W.N	
COURCELLES AU-BOIS	27.10.16		Cleaning, draining and revetting trenches, this work became necessary owing to the continuous heavy rain. Instructions received from C.R.E. 3rd Division to send Captain P. de H. HALL to join Office to carry on duties of C.R.E.'s adjutant. The C.O. instructed to take second in command of the Company, being there taken away to a soft job which can easily be done by any R.E. Officer of average intelligence, at a time when the Company was expecting to go into action at any moment and it would mean that the Company was one Officer short. There being no supernumeraries, no have use of Officers also demanded which was also among the Officers having being for the and a man also demanded. Officers having duties with the Company. Tests of no avail the efficiency of the Company must suffer. E.W.N	

Army Form C. 2118.

WAR DIARY
INTELLIGENCE SUMMARY

SHEET No. 9.

(Erase heading not required.)

Instructions regarding War Diaries and Intelligence Summaries are contained in F. S. Regs., Part II. and the Staff Manual respectively. Title Pages will be prepared in manuscript.

Place	Date	Hour	Summary of Events and Information	Remarks and references to Appendices
COURCELLES AU-BOIS	28.10.16		Work on Trenches the same as yesterday.	
COURCELLES AU-BOIS	29.10.16	4.0 P.M.	Captain P. de H. HALL went to C.R.E.'s Office to act as adjutant. The interests of the C.O. of no avail the efficiency of the Company must suffer. E.W.N. Work on The Trenches the same as yesterday, in addition clearing and draining Northern Avenue Westward of Euston Road. Church R aside. E.W.N.	
COURCELLES AU-BOIS	30.10.16		Clearing and watching Trenches and making approaches out of Communication Trenches. Major General DEVERELL, G.O.C. 3rd Division inspected the Company's quarters. A very wet day. E.W.N.	
COURCELLES AU-BOIS	31.10.16		Work continued as yesterday. A fine clear day.	

E.W. Newell
R.E. (T)
O.C. 1/1st EAST RIDING FIELD COMPANY, R.E.

3rd Divisional Engineers.

1/1ST EAST RIDING FIELD COMPANY R.E.

NOVEMBER 1916.

Army Form C. 2118.

WAR DIARY
INTELLIGENCE SUMMARY
(Erase heading not required.)

Instructions regarding War Diaries and Intelligence Summaries are contained in F. S. Regs., Part II. and the Staff Manual respectively. Title Pages will be prepared in manuscript.

Sheet No 1

Place	Date	Hour	Summary of Events and Information	Remarks and references to Appendices
COURCELLES AU-BOIS	1.11.16		No 1. Section making dug-outs at RAILWAY AVENUE Communication Trench and improving trench damaged by continuous wet weather.	
			No 2. do. NORTHERN AVENUE	
			No 3. do. CENTRAL AVENUE and making covered dug-out in camp.	
			No 4. (S)tanding Camp. E.U.T.	
- do -	2.11.16		Nos 1 and 2 Sections cleaning and draining NORTHERN AVENUE Communication Trench which was badly flooded and damaged by heavy rains.	
			No 3 Section making a deep dug-out in camp.	
			No 4 Section (S)tanding Camp. E.U.T.	
- do -	3.11.16		Work the same as yesterday.	
			No 886 Sapper R. GREENER proceeded to ACHEUX to report to the Camp Commandant.	
			V Corps for work as Engine (D)river.	
			12 men from each of the following Infantry Battalions attached to this Company for work reported this Evening. 5th King's Own Royal Lancaster Regiment: 10th Royal Welsh Fusiliers: 1st Ayrshire Highlanders: 3rd Jäger Regiment: 12 men from each Battalion still retained for work. E.U.T.	

Army Form C. 2118.

WAR DIARY
or
INTELLIGENCE SUMMARY
(Erase heading not required.)

Sheet 1

Instructions regarding War Diaries and Intelligence Summaries are contained in F. S. Regs., Part II. and the Staff Manual respectively. Title Pages will be prepared in manuscript.

Place	Date	Hour	Summary of Events and Information	Remarks and references to Appendices
COURCELLES AU BOIS	4.11.16		Work flow same as yesterday. E.M.S.	
— do —	5.11.16		Sunday. Inspection of all Arms, Ammunition, Equipment, Clothing and Sanitation. E.M.S.	
— do —	6.11.16		No. 2 Section marched to VAUCHELLES with Tool Carts and R.E. Sunder Wagon to erect NISSEN HUTS. E.M.S. Clearing, levelling and repairing NORTHERN AVENUE, C.T. & ENTRANCE, C.T. ROB ROY Fire Trench and Champion CAMPION Fire Trench. No. 3 Section resting huts at VAUCHELLES. E.M.S.	
— do —	7.11.16		Work the same as yesterday, but very little done on account of continuous very heavy rain. No. 2 Section resting huts at VAUCHELLES. E.M.S. No. 797. Sapper BARNES. H.M. proceeded to England on leave.	
— do —	8.11.16		No. 1 Section marched to VAUCHELLES to cut knotwood for making hurdles for revetting, to stamp the weights into existence by No. 2. Section. No. 2 Sand & Sections getting up material to the front line ready for revetting and Camp Drainage. No. 3 Section resting huts at VAUCHELLES. E.M.S.	

2449 Wt. W14957/Mgo 750,000 1/16 J.B.C. & A. Forms/C.2118/12.

Army Form C. 2118

WAR DIARY
or
INTELLIGENCE SUMMARY

(Erase heading not required.)

Sheet 3.

Instructions regarding War Diaries and Intelligence Summaries are contained in F.S. Regs., Part II. and the Staff Manual respectively. Title Pages will be prepared in manuscript.

Place	Date	Hour	Summary of Events and Information	Remarks and references to Appendices
COURCELLES AU BOIS	9.11.16		No. 1 Section cutting brushwood at VAUCHELLES for making hurdles for revetting ROB ROY Trench. No. 2 Section cutting NISSEN huts at VAUCHELLES. Nos. 3 and 4 Sections clearing and draining NORTHERN and CENTRAL AVENUES, C.T.s.	E.W.T.
— do —	10.11.16		No. 1 Section repaired the Company at COURCELLES AU BOIS with three Paridjing Wagons loaded with brushwood. No. 1 Section making hurdles. No. 2 Section cutting NISSEN huts at VAUCHELLES. Nos. 3 and 4 Sections clearing and draining NORTHERN and CENTRAL AVENUES, C.T.s and distributing hurdles in the Trenches. No. 2 Section rejoined the Company at COURCELLES AU BOIS to be ready for revetting of previous operations.	E.W.T.
— do —	11.11.16		No. 1 Section making hurdles. Nos. 2, 3 and 4 Sections clearing and draining NORTHERN & CENTRAL AVENUES.	E.W.T.
— do —	12.11.16		All men paraded for kit battles at the 3rd Camerons Baths on arriving there there was no one in attendance, no hot water and another unit claimed the baths, so baths were not had. B.O. with 2nd Lt P.C.RANSWICK & 2nd Lieut WADSLEY and No 1 Section went up to dugouts in the valley for previous operations. No 2 Section remained at COURCELLE AU BOIS in dugouts near the road.	B.W.T.

2449 Wt. W14957/Mgo 750,000 1/16 J.B.C. & A. Forms/C.2118/12.

Army Form C. 2118.

WAR DIARY
or
INTELLIGENCE SUMMARY

(Erase heading not required.)   Sheet 4

Instructions regarding War Diaries and Intelligence Summaries are contained in F.S. Regs., Part II. and the Staff Manual respectively. Title Pages will be prepared in manuscript.

Place	Date	Hour	Summary of Events and Information	Remarks and references to Appendices
COURCELLES AU BOIS	13.11.16		Headquarters and No 4 Section standing to in the Trenches ready to go forward and consolidate and make strong points in German Trenches in case trench during the attack on SERRE by the 7th Infantry Brigade, the Infantry attack not having successful. With one Section Gun supplements and stores, stored ROB ROY Trench. No 3 Section went up to the Trenches at 5.0 PM to assist in the work. No 1 and 3 Sections in Divisional Reserve in quarters at COURCELLES AU BOIS.	E.M.W.
do	14.11.16		Headquarters and No 4 Section in dugouts in Trenches. No 3 and 4 Sections worked in ROB ROY Trench and cleared NORTHERN AVENUE and CENTRAL AVENUE which had been filled in. No 1 and 2 Sections in Divisional Reserve in quarters at COURCELLES AU BOIS during the morning. The Infantry Battalion of 1st Gordon Highlanders attached to this Company to make good communication trenches in the trenches against SERRE. No 1 and 2 Sections came up to ROB ROY Trench at night and cleared the trench and made gristeps.	E.M.W.
do	15.11.16		Headquarters and No 4 Section in dugouts in Trenches. T of A No 4 Section on wiring front line in front of MATTHEW COPE trench in by night, machine gun fire and trench mortar fire. No 1, 2 and 3 Sections widening by night in ROB ROY Trench clearing and making firesteps. C.O. received instructions to proceed to G.H.Q. to hurry up E.M.T. No. Sapper MARTIN proceeded on leave to England. E.M.W.	
do	16.11.16		Headquarters and No 4 Section returned from dugouts in the Trenches to quarters at COURCELLES AU BOIS. Nos 1, 2, and 3 Sections wiring in front of Front line at night.	E.M.W.

Army Form C. 2118.

WAR DIARY
or
INTELLIGENCE SUMMARY

Sheet 5.

(Erase heading not required.)

Instructions regarding War Diaries and Intelligence Summaries are contained in F. S. Regs., Part II. and the Staff Manual respectively. Title Pages will be prepared in manuscript.

Place	Date	Hour	Summary of Events and Information	Remarks and references to Appendices
COURCELLES AU BOIS	17.11.16		Nos 1, 2, 3 and 4 Sections with Infantry attached reconstructing ROB ROY Trench, revetting with frames and putting in fire steps and Traverses tonight. E.W.N.	
—do—	18.11.16		Work the same as last night. E.W.N.	
—do—	19.11.16		Work the same as last night. E.W.N.	
—do—	20.11.16		Two Sections working at ROB ROY Trench, the same as last night. Two Sections making improvements to quarters for winter. E.W.N.	
—do—	21.11.16		Two Sections improving quarters by day. Two Sections with Infantry attached working in ROB ROY Trench at night. E.W.N.	
—do—	22.11.16		No 1 and 4 Sections worked in ROB ROY Trench by day. E.W.N.	
—do—	23.11.16		No 1 and 4 Sections worked in ROB ROY Trench by day. No 3 Section Camp improvements. No 2 Section with 2nd Lieut A.E. ?? and R.E. Stores Wagon proceeded to Bus to erect NISSEN Huts. 2nd Lieut A.PICKERSGILL and No 841 Driver COATES proceeded on leave to England.	
—do—	24.11.16		No 1 and 4 Sections working on reconstruction of ROB ROY Trench. Following Temporary promotions and appointments made. No 5076 2nd Corporal STEELE, J. E. to be A/Corporal. No 1459 A/2nd Corporal BOYCE F.H. to be A/2nd Corporal. No 403 A/2nd Corporal WHITING, H. to be A/2nd Corporal. [No 863]	

2449 Wt. W14957/Mg0 750,000 1/16 J.B.C. & A. Forms/C.2118/12.

Army Form C. 2118.

WAR DIARY
INTELLIGENCE SUMMARY
(Erase heading not required.)

Place	Date	Hour	Summary of Events and Information	Remarks and references to Appendices
COURCELLES AU BOIS (continued)	24/11/16		No. 363 Unpaid A/Lce Corporal BRIGGS. R. To be paid A/Lce. Corporal. No. 320 Sapper DIMBERLINE. A. To be unpaid A/Lce Corporal. No. 2669 Sapper RAYNER. K. To be unpaid A/Lce Corporal. No. 403 Sapper WITTY. J.F. To be unpaid A/Lce. Corporal. No. 440 Sapper McNALLY. P. To be unpaid A/Lce. Corporal. No. 630 Driver APPLEBY. N.R. To be unpaid A/Lce. Corporal. No. 676 Driver PIERCY. E.H. To be unpaid A/Lce. Corporal. Transfers. No. 507 A/Corporal STEELE. To No. 2 Section from No. H. Section. No. 4169 A/Corporal BOYCE. F.A. To No H. Section from No. A Section. No. 903 A/Corporal WHITING. H. To No 1 Section from No H Section. No. 863 A/Lce. Corporal BRIGGS. W. To No 2 Section from No 1 Section. No. 70 Sapper HUNT. G.L. To Head Quarters Establishment from No H. Section. No. 459 Sapper GLENTON. C.E. To Head Quarters Establishment from No 3 Section. No. 861 Sapper SKELTON. R.W. To Head Quarters Detachment from No 1 Section.	E.M.S.
—do—	25/11/16		No 1 and 2 Sections working on the reconstruction of ROB ROY Tunnel. No H. Section at BUS resting huts. No 3 Section in Camp.	E.M.S.

/ Army Form C. 2118.

WAR DIARY
INTELLIGENCE SUMMARY

Sheet 7.

(Erase heading not required.)

Place	Date	Hour	Summary of Events and Information	Remarks and references to Appendices
COURCELLES AU BOIS	26.11.16		Summary. No. 1 Section working on the reconstruction of ROB ROY Trench by day. No. 4 Section erecting Huts at BUS. No. 162 Sapper CARR. 6. No. 574 ⓦ Driver POTTER J.W. No. 670 ⓦ Driver KEITH H. proceeded on leave to England. E.W.N.	
—do—	27.11.16		No. 1 and 2 Sections working on the reconstruction of ROB ROY Trench by day. No. 3 Section taking over material and erecting material for five NISSEN HUTS from the Cheshire Field Co. R.E. to be erected for their Company's Head Quarters and Officers Quarters, the Quarters now occupied which were erected for the R.E. are being taken over as Brigade Head Quarters. No. 4 Section erecting Huts at BUS. E.W.N.	
—do—	28.11.16		Nos. 1, 2 and 3 Sections commenced to erect NISSEN HUTS for new Company Head Quarters and Officers Quarters. No. 4 Section at BUS erecting Huts.	
—do—	29.11.16		Nos. 1, 2 and 3 Sections and Carpenters attached, hard at work erecting Huts Company for new Quarters. E.W.N. No. 4 Section at BUS erecting Huts.	
—do—	30.11.16		Sapper FOUND, Sapper PENROSE, Sapper RUSSELL and Driver BLENAINDOP J. proceeded to England on leave. E.W.N. No. 1, 2 and 3 Sections erecting Huts for new Quarters. No. 4 Section marched to BUS with Tool Carts and R.E. Limber Wagon and Carts are unloading huts and necessary building from No. 4 Section returned to Head Quarters. E.W.N.	

Lieut: Col. R.E.(T)

3rd ~~Divisi~~onal Engineers.

1/1ST EAST RIDING FIELD COMPANY R.E.

DECEMBER 1916.

WAR DIARY
or
INTELLIGENCE SUMMARY

Army Form C. 2118.

Sheet No 1.

Place	Date	Hour	Summary of Events and Information	Remarks and references to Appendices
COURCELLES AU BOIS	1.12.16		Nos 3 and 4 Sections erecting Nissen Huts for new Head Quarters and Officers Quarters. No 2 Section, reconstruction of ROB ROY TRENCH by night. No 1 Section erecting NISSEN HUTS at BUS. E.U.S.	
— do —	2.12.16		Nos 3 and 4 Sections erecting NISSEN HUTS as above in the morning. No 4 Section continued erecting huts during the afternoon. No 2 Section, reconstruction of ROB ROY TRENCH by night. E.U.S. No 1 Section erecting NISSEN HUTS at BUS. 620 Cyc. Rgt's. 217 Bgn. BIMBERLINE. E. 656 Bgn BINNSINI mountain bart. E.U.S.	
— do —	3.12.16		Sunday. Inspection of arms, ammunition, tube helmets and iron rations. Nos 2 and 4 Sections Church Parade. No 3. Section, reconstruction of ROB ROY TRENCH by night. No 1 Section, erect'g. NISSEN HUTS at BUS. E.U.S.	
— do —	4.11.2.16		Nos 3 and 4 Sections erecting NISSEN HUTS for new Head Quarters and Officers Quarters. No 4 Section, reconstruction of ROB ROY TRENCH by night, and making Stokes Gun emplacements behind front line. No 1 Section, erecting NISSEN HUTS at BUS. E.U.S.	
— do —	5.12.16		Nos 2 and 3 Sections, erecting NISSEN HUTS. No 2 and 4 Sections, reconstruction of ROB ROY TRENCH and making Stokes Gun emplacements behind Front Line by night. No 1 Section, erecting NISSEN HUTS at BUS. E.U.S.	

No 844. Sgn. MOODY. J. No 197. Pte KEYWORTH. W.
No 646. Sgn. BARNABY. F. No 672 Sgn WRIGHT. S. proceeded on leave.

Army Form C. 2118.

Sheet No. 2

WAR DIARY
or
INTELLIGENCE SUMMARY
(Erase heading not required.)

Instructions regarding War Diaries and Intelligence Summaries are contained in F. S. Regs., Part II. and the Staff Manual respectively. Title Pages will be prepared in manuscript.

Place	Date	Hour	Summary of Events and Information	Remarks and references to Appendices
COURCELLES AU BOIS	6.12.16		No. 2 and 3 Sections, reconstruction of ROB ROY TRENCH and making Stokes Gun Emplacements behind the front line, by night. No. 3. Section, draining the camp and making "duck board" paths. No 1 Section, erecting NISSEN HUTS at BUS.	
do —	7.12.16		No 3. Section, reconstruction of ROB ROY TRENCH and making Stokes Gun Emplacements behind the front line, by night. No 4 Section, draining and repairing the camp. No 1 Section, erecting NISSEN HUTS at BUS.	
do —	8.12.16		No. 2 and 4 Sections, camp improvements during the morning. Reconstruction of ROB ROY TRENCH and making Stokes Gun Emplacements behind the front line by night. No 1 Section, erecting NISSEN HUTS at BUS. No. 863 Sapper BRIGGS. R. No 580 Driver WILLIS. A.H. No 693 Sapper HOULSON. C. proceeded on leave.	
do —	9.12.16		Nos 2, 3, and 4 Sections, reconstruction of ROB ROY TRENCH, making Stokes Gun Emplacements behind front line, and draining NORTHERN AVENUE into STAFF COPSE by night. No 1 Section making hutted camp at BUS.	

2449 Wt. W14957/M90 750,000 1/16 J.B.C. & A. Forms/C.2118/12.

Army Form C. 2118.

WAR DIARY
or
INTELLIGENCE SUMMARY

(Erase heading not required.)

Sheet No 3.

Instructions regarding War Diaries and Intelligence Summaries are contained in F. S. Regs., Part II. and the Staff Manual respectively. Title Pages will be prepared in manuscript.

Place	Date	Hour	Summary of Events and Information	Remarks and references to Appendices
COURCELLES-AU-BOIS	10.12.16		Nos 2, 3 and 4 Sections reconstruction of Rob Roy trench and making Stokes Gun Emplacements behind the front line by night, and during Northern Avenue into Staff Copse. No 1 Section making hutted camp at Bus. P.C.	
— do —	11.12.16		Nos. 2, 3 and 4 Sections Inspection of Arms Ammunition and Tube Helmets. No 1 Section making hutted camp at Bus. Wet day. P.C.	
— do —	12.12.16		No 4 Section working on Camp improvements. No working parties in forward area, as S.O.S. tests were being carried out at night. No 1 Section making hutted Camp at Bus. No 429 Su/Cpl Dorsett. J. No 840 Sapr Skerrow H, No 638 Driv Fuller C. proceeded on leave. P.C.	
— do —	13.12.16		No 4 Section working on Camp improvements by day. Nos 2 and 3 Section, reconstruction of Rob Roy Trench. P.C. No 1 Section making hutted camp at Bus.	
— do —	14.12.16		Nos 2 and 3 Sections reconstruction of Rob Roy Trench night work. No 4 Section commenced work on M.G. Emplacements in Candion Trench, night work. No 1 Section making hutted camp at Bus. P.C.	
— do —	15.12.16		No 4 Section commenced continuous work on two M.G. Emplacements in Candion Trench, with rate of 4 & one hour reliefs for 24 hours. Nos 2 and 3 Sections Reconstruction of Rob Roy Trench and drawing Northern Avenue into Staff Copse night work. No 1 Section making hutted camp at Bus. No 901 Sapper Sedgley. L. " 1359 " Andrew. F. } Proceeded on leave. P.C. " 873 " Ferguson. R.	

Army Form C. 2118.

WAR DIARY
or
INTELLIGENCE SUMMARY

(Erase heading not required.)

Sheet No. 4.

Instructions regarding War Diaries and Intelligence Summaries are contained in F. S. Regs., Part II and the Staff Manual respectively. Title Pages will be prepared in manuscript.

Place	Date	Hour	Summary of Events and Information	Remarks and references to Appendices
COURCELLES AU-BOIS	16.12.16		No 4 Section continued work on M.G. Emplacements in CAMPION TRENCH. No 1 Section making hutted camp at BUS. Had to destroy a mule which was hit by a piece of an H.E. shell at EUSTON DUMP. P.C.	
—do—	17.12.16		Sunday. Nos 2 and 3 Sections Church Parade 10.30 A.m. No 4 Section work as yesterday. Nos 2 & 3 Sections Reconstruction of ROB ROY TRENCH, draining NORTHERN AVENUE into STAFF COPSE, and work on Boffin's Gun Emplacements behind front line, (daylight work). Very foggy day. P.C. No 1 Section making hutted camp at BUS.	
—do—	18.12.16		No 4 Section work as yesterday. This section had to cease work from 9. P.m. 17/12/16 till 5.P.m to-day, 18/12/16 on account of shortage of material. Trenches very slippery to-day - patrols. Nos 2 and 3 Sections reconstruction of ROB ROY trench, draining NORTHERN AVENUE into STAFF COPSE. 1 Corporal and 4 Sappers supervising Infantry working party cutting slits and "scrapes" to drain CABER TRENCH, night work. No 1 Section making hutted camp at BUS. P.C.	
—do—	19.12.16		No 3 Section marched to BUS and relieved No 1 Section and took over work on huttec camp. No 4. Section work on M.E. Emplacements as yesterday. No 2 Section reconstruction of ROB ROY night work. 1 Corporal and 4 Sappers supervising drainage of CABER TRENCH (night work). P.C.	

2449 Wt. W14957/Mg0 750,000 1/16 J.B.C. & A. Forms/C.2118/12.

WAR DIARY
or
INTELLIGENCE SUMMARY

Army Form C. 2118.

Sheet No 5

Place	Date	Hour	Summary of Events and Information	Remarks and references to Appendices
COURCELLES AU BOIS	30.12.16		No 4 Section work on M.G. Emplacements as yesterday continuous. No 1 Section reconstruction of ROB ROY TRENCH, night work. 1 Corporal and 2 Sappers supervising drainage of CABER TRENCH night work. No 3 Section making hutted Camp at BUS. Very hard frost. J.C. No 451 Pioneer Sergt GILSOY C.E. No 203 Sergt HARRISON H. } Proceeded on leave. No 338 Driver ALLEN W.	
do	21.12.16		No 4 Section work on M.G. Emplacements as yesterday continuous. Nos 1 & 2 Sections reconstruction of ROB ROY trench night-work. 2 Sappers supervising cutting of drains in CABER TRENCH night work. No 3 Section erecting NISSEN HUTS at BUS. No 133 Sergt LOCKWOOD F. Proceeded on leave. J.C.	
do	22.12.16		No 4 Section work on M.G. Emplacements continuous. No 2 Section was sent out at 4 P.M. to clear a dug-out on ROB ROY trench which had been blown in by shell fire, and to extract some of the trench garrison. They worked until 2 A.M. by which time they had got all the line men out of the dug-out. This dug-out was 16 feet below ground level & the roof and a section of it about 10 feet long was blown completely in, which was partly due to not being strongly enough reinforced and the construction i.e. much prones to pr [shapes?] and hardly dud, to the shell and trench mortar holes, not being filled in on top of the dug-out. (By the garrison of the trench). A 5 men were killed and 6 or 7 injured as the result of this. 1 Corpor. and 4 Sappers supervising draining of CABER TRENCH, night work. No 3 Section erecting NISSEN HUTS at BUS. Very wet night. Lieut: Col: E.M NEWBY No 676 Driver PIERCE E.H. } Proceeded on leave. J.C.	

Army Form C. 2118.

WAR DIARY
or
INTELLIGENCE SUMMARY
(Erase heading not required.)

Sheet No 6.

Place	Date	Hour	Summary of Events and Information	Remarks and references to Appendices
COURCELLES-AU-BOIS	23.12.16		No 4 Section work on M.G. Emplacements continued. No 2 Section resumed work on the dugout in Rob Roy which was blown in yesterday. Work to be continuous with 4 hour reliefs for 24 hours. No 3 Section erecting Nissen huts at BUS. Very wet night, heavy rain. P.C.	
do	24.12.16		No 4 Section work on M.G. Emplacements continuous. No 2 Section work on damaged dug out - as yesterday continuous. 1 Corporal and 3 Sappers salvaging drainage of CABER TRENCH - night work No 3 Section erecting Nissen huts at BUS. Very wet night. P.C.	
do	25.12.16		XMAS DAY. No work. Nos 1, 2 and 4 Sections Church Parade 2.30.P.M. No 3 Section at BUS. No work. No 652 Sapper THOMPSON W. No 814 " BARRETT R.W. } Proceeded on leave. No 631 " Driver WALKER R.W. P.C.	
do	26.12.16		Nos 2o and 4 Sections resumed work at 1 A.M. on the dugout and M.G. Emplacements as before. No 1 Section reconstruction of Rob Roy trench night work No 3 Section erecting Nissen huts at BUS. P.C.	
do	27.12.16		Nos 2 and 4 Sections continuous work as yesterday No 1 Section reconstruction of Rob Roy trench night work 1 Corporal and 8 Sappers supervising drainage of CABER TRENCH for new drains started. No 3 Section erecting Nissen huts at BUS. P.C.	

Army Form C. 2118.

WAR DIARY
or
INTELLIGENCE SUMMARY

(Erase heading not required.)

Instructions regarding War Diaries and Intelligence Summaries are contained in F. S. Regs., Part II. and the Staff Manual respectively. Title Pages will be prepared in manuscript.

Sheet No 7.

Place	Date	Hour	Summary of Events and Information	Remarks and references to Appendices
COURCELLES-AU-BOIS	28.12.16		No. 4 Section had to cease work for 24 hours from 3 P.M. as no Infantry were available for carrying away all earth excavated. No. 2 Section continuous work as yesterday. No. 3 Section erecting Nissen huts at BUS. No. 100 Sapper PARRISH G. } Proceeded on leave. No. 305 " LYON A. } P.C.	
—do—	29.12.16		No. 4 Section resumed continuous work on M.C. Emplacements at 3 P.M. No. 2 Section continues work on dug out as yesterday. No. 3 Section erecting Nissen huts at BUS. P.C.	
—do—	30.12.16		Nos 2 and 4 Sections as yesterday. No. 1 Section driving R.O.B. Roy. (Corporal and 3 Sappers) Enquiring into accident in CANADIAN TRENCH. No. 3 Section erecting Nissen huts at BUS. P.C.	
—do—	31.12.16		No. 2 Section as yesterday. No. 4 Section. M.C. Emplacements, dug out and repairing dugout in CABARET WOOD by night. No. 1 Section driving R.O.B Roy Subway. No. 3 Section erecting Nissen Huts at BUS. No. 940 Sapper WRIGHT. E. proceeded on leave.	

Philip Cranwick Lieut
for Lieut. Col. R.E. (T)
O.C. 1/1st EAST RIDING FIELD COMPANY, R.E.

2449 Wt. W14957/M90 750,000 1/16 J.B.C. & A. Forms/C.2118/12.

2nd Division
War Diaries

529th/T. East Riding Field Coy.

From 1st January, To 31st December

1917

WAR DIARY or INTELLIGENCE SUMMARY

Army Form C. 2118.

Sheet No 1.

Place	Date	Hour	Summary of Events and Information	Remarks and references to Appendices
COURCELLES-AU-BOIS	1.1.17		No 1 Section driving ROB ROY TRENCH night-work. No 2 Section continuous work on additional dug-out in ROB ROY trench work carried on at the rate of 4 six-hour reliefs for 24 hours. No 4 Section continuous work on M.G. Emplacements and CAMPION TRENCH and dug-out in CABER TRENCH, working at the rate of 4 six-hour reliefs for 24 hours. No.3 Section erecting huts at BUS. P.C.	
COURCELLES-AU-BOIS	2.1.17		Nos 2 and 4 Sections work as yesterday. No.3 Section erecting huts at BUS. O.C. went over to BUS to see the C.R.E. re preliminary orders for handing over and relief. P.C.	
COURCELLES-AU-BOIS	3.1.17	8.0am	New hours assumed of ROB ROY trench night work. 2nd Lieut A. PICKERSGILL with 14.50 and 10 sappers proceeded to CANAPLES by motor lorry to take over [illegible] the RED [illegible] 252 [illegible] That area [illegible] B.W. No 2 Company BORDER L.I. [illegible] not [illegible] to leave B.W.	P.C.
COURCELLES-AU-BOIS	4.1.17		All available men employed working [illegible] days repairing dug-outs	B.W.
COURCELLES-AU-BOIS	5.1.17		All available men repairing dug-outs	B.W.
COURCELLES-AU-BOIS	6.1.17		All available men sparring dug-outs as yesterday	B.W.
COURCELLES-AU-BOIS	7.1.17		Nos 2 and 3 Sections repairing dug-outs	B.W.
COURCELLES-AU-BOIS	8.1.17		No 1 took what men could Bridging. Way was ready to move	B.W.

Army Form C. 2118.

WAR DIARY
INTELLIGENCE SUMMARY
(Erase heading not required.)

SHEET No. 2

Instructions regarding War Diaries and Intelligence Summaries are contained in F. S. Regs., Part II. and the Staff Manual respectively. Title Pages will be prepared in manuscript.

Place	Date	Hour	Summary of Events and Information	Remarks and references to Appendices
COURCELLES AU-BOIS	9.1.17		Coy. Hqrs. moved to PUCHEVILLERS (10½ miles) Sections Pulcheviller, South of it, Halloy and North of it	
PUCHEVILLERS	10.1.17		Sub-Coy. marched to PERNOIS (13 miles) through TALMAS & NAOURS via BERTES, HEZNEUX CANAPLES, HALLOY, no billets ready at PERNOIS. No 1 and 2 on ROAD repair & broken from the A.D. Hqrs. of R.E. the remainder of the men in tents.	
PERNOIS	11.1.17		Inspection of Stores and Documents. Sections placed under and hoods training in the camp.	
PERNOIS	12.1.17		No 1, 2, 4 Sections military drill No 3 Section erecting NISSEN huts and new BATH HOUSE at PIEFFES.	
PERNOIS	13.1.17		No 1 Section making horse shelter. Nos 2, 4 Sections erecting NISSEN huts and Rubethras, and loading timber at PIEFFES, on which to be brought to the R.E. dumps at CANAPLES and HALLOY. No 3 & 4 Sections working on the lines to laid in reinforcement of tramp to PERNOIS Railway Station. Where No 1 and 2 sections at NIGHT put jointing with A.M.E. Section & Army Signals for 2½ miles, and military Section marched by Lines from 7½ miles Brigade in respect over the Railway Station.	
PERNOIS	14.1.17		No 1 Section marching hutted Shelters at HALLOY. No 2 Section N.C.O. and 18 men returned out and loading R.E. material from PIEFFES to CANAPLES, remainder of section erecting NISSEN HUTS at 6 HALLOY No 3 Section guttering, hut to such at billets at PERNOIS Railway Station No 4 Section erecting NISSEN HUTS at HALLOY. G.O.C. Inspected all Officers of the 3rd Division.	
PERNOIS	15.1.17		Nos 1 & 4 Sections. Inspection of huts, tube huttents and war notions. No 3 Section building horse shelters at HALLOY, and No 4 Section in common to PERNOIS Railway Station. No 4 Section erecting NISSEN HUTS at HALLOY.	

2449 Wt. W14957/M90 750,000 1/16 J.B.C. & A. Forms/C.2118/12.

Army Form C. 2118.

WAR DIARY
INTELLIGENCE SUMMARY
(Erase heading not required.)

SHEET No 3

Instructions regarding War Diaries and Intelligence Summaries are contained in F.S. Regs., Part II. and the Staff Manual respectively. Title Pages will be prepared in manuscript.

Place	Date	Hour	Summary of Events and Information	Remarks and references to Appendices
PERNOIS	16.1.17		No 1 and 4 Sections Physical Drill, section Drill and instruction in the use of the Pipe Pushing Plant. Recreational Training in the afternoon.	
PERNOIS	17.1.17		No 3 and 4 Sections work the usual Oxy-Acetylene outfit. No 2 Section MADSEY Bridging. No 1 and 4 Sections, instruction in the use and experiences on the Pipe Pushing Plant. Recreational Training in the afternoon. Mr Miller replaces Mr PERNOIS Railway Station completed No 5 and H Sections work the usual as yesterday. Mr Miller replaces Mr PERNOIS Railway Station completed No 3 and H Sections moved into billets from H.Q.	G.W.
PERNOIS	18.1.17		No 1. Section MILLER Trestle Bridging. No 2. Section Pontoon Bridging. No 3. Section erecting NISSEN huts at the Horse Lines HALLOY for the Divers No 4. Section erecting NISSEN huts at HALLOY The Company Marched by detachments on the afternoon and marched to St OVEN (?) for Baths	G.W.
PERNOIS	19.1.17		No 1. Section Pontoon Bridging. No 2. Section MILLER Trestle Bridging. No 3 and H Sections work the same as yesterday. Recreational Training in the afternoon. Lieutenant R. CRANSWICK rejoins the Company from leave. Frost during the night.	G.W.
PERNOIS	20.1.17		No 1 and H Sections instruction in the use and care of the new tools. Baths for No 2 and 3 sections in the morning.	G.W.
PERNOIS	21.1.17		The O.C. Lieut-Colonel E.M. NEWELL proceeded to No 2 a G.H.Q. R.E School of Instruction at LE PARCQ for a two days course. Fatigue day. No H. Section Inspection and Church Parade.	G.W.

Army Form C. 2118.

WAR DIARY
or
INTELLIGENCE SUMMARY

(Erase heading not required.)

SHEET No 4

Place	Date	Hour	Summary of Events and Information	Remarks and references to Appendices
PERNOIS	22.1.17		Nos 1+2 Sections erecting Nissen huts, joining up Revival Canvas and fixing oil engine + sawmill. Nos 3+4 sections, Training, Section Drill (in the morning, Recreation & Bathing in the afternoon.)	
"	23.1.17		As yesterday.	
"	24.1.17		Nos 1+2 Sections erecting Nissen huts, joining oil engine + sawmill, fixing Amplify Plant for Divisional Baths at Fieffes. Nos 3+4 section Training. Morning Canteen Building. Afternoon Recreational training.	
"	25.1.17		Nos 1+2 Section as yesterday. Nos 3+4 Sections Training. Morning Lewis Trench Drill Bayonet. Afternoon Recreational training.	
"	26.1.17		Nos 1+2 Sections erecting Nissen huts, joining volumes, fixing Amplify Plant for baths and completing Lewis standings. Nos 3+4 Sections Training. Morning Wiring Drill for early afternoon bore, Afternoon Recreational training.	
"	27.1.17		Nos 1+2 Sections strengthening of nissen fields for Cavalry Depot. Nos 3+4 Sections collecting Stores + supplies & necessary items for R.E. Park S.Q. as per instruction in O.O. No. 4 of Div Park S.O.	
"	28.1.17		Completion of Arms, Ammunition + Tool Holders for Mobile Company. The Company formed in Marching Order unit Transport at 10-30A.m and marched from PERNOIS-LES-AMIENS to AMPLIER, starting at 11.15 P.M, via route:- CANAPLES, FIEFFES, MONTRELET, BONNEVILLE, BEAUVAL, FRESNILETTE. Distance 13½ miles. Billets in AMPLIER very poor.	

WAR DIARY
or
INTELLIGENCE SUMMARY

(Erase heading not required.)

Army Form C. 2118.

SHEET No 5.

Place	Date	Hour	Summary of Events and Information	Remarks and references to Appendices
AMPLIER	29/1/17		The Company paraded in Marching Order with Transport at 11.15 A.M. and marched from AMPLIER to BARLY arriving 4.15 P.M. Route, AUTHIEUX, DOULLENS, RANSART distance 8 miles. The march was very slow owing to the Company being in rear of the Brigade column, and the roads and very slippery on the hill tops all waggons having to double teams to get up the steep hill East of BARLY	
BARLY	30/1/17		The Company marched from BARLY to SÉRICOURT. Route, BONNIÈRES, FREVENT. Left BARLY 8.30 A.M. arrived SÉRICOURT 12-noon. distance 8 miles. The Transport with 2nd Lieutenant PICKERSGILL, went via NEUVILLETTE, BOUQUEMAISON, FREVENT	
SÉRICOURT	31/1/17		The Company marched from SÉRICOURT to CAUCOURT. Leaving SÉRICOURT at 9.45 A.M. arrived CAUCOURT 5 P.M. distance 16 miles. Route BISIVILLE, BUNVILLE, TERNAS, LIGNY -ST- FLOCHEL, TINQUES, VILLERS BRULIN, BETHONSART. The roads were very slippery, which necessitated double teams to get the Transport up a steep hill on the SIRIVILLE BONE VILLE road. 2nd Lieutenant WAGSBY was unable to proceed with the disconsolate branch + went to wait for the Transport. The Transport followed the same route as the Company as far as TINQUES, and they went round by BARLY and BETHON -SART keeping off the main roads, and arrived at CAUCOURT at 9 P.M.	

E.W. Newell
Lieut Col R.E.G1.
O.C. 1/1st East Riding Field Co R.E.

Army Form C. 2118.

WAR DIARY
INTELLIGENCE SUMMARY
(Erase heading not required.)

Instructions regarding War Diaries and Intelligence Summaries are contained in F. S. Regs., Part II. and the Staff Manual respectively. Title pages will be prepared in manuscript.

Place	Date	Hour	Summary of Events and Information	Remarks and references to Appendices
GAUCOURT	1.2.17		The Company marched from GAUCOURT to AMBRINES through BETHONSART, SAVY, MONCHEL and VILLERS SIRE SIMON 9½ miles. Billeted at AMBRINES for the night. No.676 A/Lance Corporal PIERCY. E.R. found dead in bed, suffocated by fumes from a brazier which had been burning in the room when the door & the windows lived. No bodies. MOODY who slept in the same room were found unconscious. Inquest has first made worked with proper room. The Company remained at AMBRINES. (S)id worker for the Town Major resting huts and improvements	JMJ
AMBRINES	2.2.17			JMJ
AMBRINES	3.2.17		The Company less N°1 and 2 sections marched from AMBRINES to WARLUS (10½ miles) through GIVENCHY, LE NOBLE, AVESNES, HAUTEVILLE and WANQUETIN great difficulty was experienced in getting billets at WARLUS though instructions had been given that billets had been arranged nothing had been done until the billeting party arrived and made that arrangements they could. No 1 and 2 sections remained at AMBRINES fitting timber known as great Kempel.	JMJ
			Promotions made to date from 29th January 1917. 2nd Lieutenant J. ALDEN proceeded on leave to England.	
			358 2nd Corporal HIELDS. H.J to be A/Corporal.	
			2nd Lance Corporal BUCHANAN. D to be A/2nd Corporal.	
			130 Lance Corporal DIMBERLINE.A to be A/2nd Corporal.	
			490 Lance Corporal (acting) McNALLY.P. to be A/Lance Corporal (paid)	JMJ

Army Form C. 2118.

WAR DIARY
INTELLIGENCE SUMMARY

SHEET No 2

(Erase heading not required.)

Instructions regarding War Diaries and Intelligence Summaries are contained in F. S. Regs., Part II. and the Staff Manual respectively. Title pages will be prepared in manuscript.

Place	Date	Hour	Summary of Events and Information	Remarks and references to Appendices
WARLUS	4.2.17		Nos 1 and 3 Sections at AMBRINES, making frames for Nissen huts at 14th	
WARLUS	5.2.17		Nos 2 and 4 Sections erecting NISSEN huts in 3rd Division Head Shelters. V. laun gard. G.W.J.	
			Work the same as on the 4th inst.	
			Appointments made to date from the 29th January 1917.	
			403 A/Lance Corporal (unpaid) WITTY.J. to be A/Lance Corporal (paid)	
			709 A/Lance Corporal (unpaid) RAYNER.K. to be A/Lance Corporal (paid) G.W.J.	
			No 634 Driver BURDASS F. proceeded on leave to England. G.W.J.	
WARLUS	6.2.17		Work the same as on the 5th inst. G.W.J.	
WARLUS	7.2.17		Work the same as on the 6th inst.	
WARLUS	8.2.17		Work the same as on the 7th inst. No 646 Driver GRANTHAM. J.W. proceeded on leave to England. G.W.J.	
WARLUS	9.2.17		Work the same as on the 8th inst. G.W.J.	
WARLUS	10.2.17		Work the same as on the 9th inst. G.W.J.	
WARLUS	11.2.17		Work the same as on the 10th inst. The 3rd Division moved into the huts erected for their shelter. G.W.J.	
WARLUS	12.2.17		Nos 1 and 3 Sections at AMBRINES, making frames in barns as before, little progress made on account of shortage of material.	
			Nos 3 and 4 Sections forming partitions in huts for 3rd and 14th Division Head shelters and finishing off. G.W.J.	

Army Form C. 2118.

WAR DIARY

SHEET No. 3.

INTELLIGENCE SUMMARY.

(Erase heading not required.)

Instructions regarding War Diaries and Intelligence Summaries are contained in F. S. Regs., Part II. and the Staff Manual respectively. Title pages will be prepared in manuscript.

Place	Date	Hour	Summary of Events and Information	Remarks and references to Appendices
WARLUS	13.2.17		Work the same as on the 12th inst.	
WARLUS	14.2.17		Work the same as on the 13th inst.	
WARLUS	15.2.17		No 149 Lance Corporal DRESSER J.A. proceeded to be drilled as a bugler for the Forming Battalion.	E.M.N. / BMN
			No 1 Section moved from AMBRINES to LIENCOURT	
			No 2 Section moved from AMBRINES to WANQUETIN to erect huts and bunks.	
			Nos 3 and 4 Sections erecting huts, Camp accessory buildings and laying trench tracks at WARLUS	BMN
WARLUS	16.2.17		No 1 Section at LIENCOURT. No 2 Section at WANQUETIN.	
			Nos 3 and 4 Sections erecting NISSEN huts for our sappers.	
WARLUS	17.2.17		No 1 Section at LIENCOURT. No 2 Section at WANQUETIN. Little work done on account of shortage of material.	
			Nos 3 and 4 Sections. Work as yesterday in the morning.	
	5.30PM		Head Quarters and Nos 3 and 4 Sections marched to ARRAS and went into billets in the French Infantry Barracks. Offices in a large house quite inhabitable, badly damaged by shell fire.	BMN
ARRAS	18.2.17		No 1 Section at LIENCOURT. No 2 Section at WANQUETIN.	
			Nos 3 and 4 Sections commenced work on new deep dugouts for 76th Infantry Brigade Battle Head Quarters.	BMN

Army Form C. 2118.

WAR DIARY
INTELLIGENCE SUMMARY.

SHEET No. 4

(Erase heading not required.)

Instructions regarding War Diaries and Intelligence Summaries are contained in F.S. Regs., Part II. and the Staff Manual respectively. Title pages will be prepared in manuscript.

Place	Date	Hour	Summary of Events and Information	Remarks and references to Appendices
ARRAS.	19.2.17		No 1 Section at LIENCOURT. No 2 Section at WANQUETIN. Little work done on account of shortage of material. Nos. 3 and 4 Sections working extensively in shifts on dugouts for 76th Infantry Brigade Battle Head Quarters. E.W.	
ARRAS	20.2.17		Work the same as on the 19th inst.	
ARRAS	21.2.17		Work the same as on the 20th inst. In addition commenced to reconstruct the support line of trenches working from IMPERIAL STREET Northward, and 1 N.C.O. and 3 sappers detailed to assist the Artillery in the construction of gun emplacements.	
ARRAS	22.2.17		Work the same as on the 21st inst. Officers moved from billet in No 36 RUE GAMBETTA to billet in smaller house at No 2 RUE de L'ARSENAL E.W.	
ARRAS	23.2.17		Work the same as on the 22nd inst. E.W. Dull, not cold day.	
ARRAS	24.2.17		Work the same as on the 23rd inst. G.O.C. 3rd (D)ivision inspected horses and mules of the three (D)ivisional Field Companies R.E. complimented the O.C. on the good condition of the 1/1st East Riding Field Co. R.E. animals. E.W.	

Army Form C. 2118.

WAR DIARY
or
INTELLIGENCE SUMMARY

SHEET No 5

(Erase heading not required.)

Instructions regarding War Diaries and Intelligence Summaries are contained in F. S. Regs., Part II and the Staff Manual respectively. Title pages will be prepared in manuscript.

Place	Date	Hour	Summary of Events and Information	Remarks and references to Appendices
ARRAS	25.2.17		Work the same as on the 24th inst. E.W.D.	
ARRAS	26.2.17		Work the same as on the 25th inst. Bombing touch Ratt: of 76th Brigade attached for work on Brigade dumps. E.W.D.	
ARRAS	27.2.17		Nos 1 and 2 Sections on same as on the 26th inst. No working parties available for Nos 3 and 4 Sections. Sections inspection and children in the use of the Box Respirator and Tube Helmet and revalved for but with E.W.D.	
ARRAS	28.2.17		Work resumed as on the 26th inst: working parties supplied by the 8th Infantry Brigade. From the 7th Kings Own Shropshire Light Infantry. Little progress made owing to shortage of materials.	

1. March 1917.

E. W. Newell
Lieut RE
O.C. 1/1st EAST RIDING FIELD COMPANY, R.E.

Vol 8

WAR DIARY.

For month ending 31st March 1917.

UNIT: 529th (E. Riding) Field Company R.E.

Army Form C. 2118.

WAR DIARY
or
INTELLIGENCE SUMMARY.

(Erase heading not required.)

Sheet No 1.

Place	Date	Hour	Summary of Events and Information	Remarks and references to Appendices
ARRAS	1.3.17		No 1 Section erecting huts and Lundry frames and improvements to billets at LIBECOURT	
	2.3.17		No 2 Section erecting Nissen huts at WARLUS	
			No 3. Sand & Section making deep dugouts for 76th Infantry Brigade Battle Head Quarters and reconstructing the support line of trenches between IMPERIAL STREET C.T. and the CAMBRAI Road. BWF	
	3.3.17		Work the same as on the 1st inst. BWF	
	4.3.17		do BWF	
	5.3.17		do BWF	
	6.3.17		do BWF	
	7.3.17		do BWF	
			Reinforcements posted. No 425. Lance Corporal ANNIS. T. H. to Head Section. No 88 Sapper HUDSON. H. and No 4476 Sapper CARLIN. P. to No 1 Section. No 6547 & Sapper HOLLIDAY. E. W. from the LONDON. R.E. to No 2 Section. No 1097 Sapper PETRIE. L. G. to No 3 Section. BWF	
	8.3.17		Work the same as on the 7th inst. Promotion and Appointment No 6443. A/Lance Corporal ROBSON. P. to be A/2nd Corporal. No 576. Sapper LILLEY. E. to be A/Lance Corporal (Paid). BWF	
	9.3.17		Work the same as on the 8th inst. BWF	

Army Form C. 2118.

Sheet No. 2

WAR DIARY
INTELLIGENCE SUMMARY.
(Erase heading not required.)

Instructions regarding War Diaries and Intelligence Summaries are contained in F. S. Regs., Part II. and the Staff Manual respectively. Title pages will be prepared in manuscript.

Place	Date	Hour	Summary of Events and Information	Remarks and references to Appendices
ARRAS	10.3.17		No. 1 section building, breaking, leaves and improving shelters in LIEN COURT area. No. 2 section existing NISSEN huts at WANQUETIN. Nos 3 and 4 sections making deep dugouts for 76th Infantry Brigade Battle Head Quarters and reconstructing the support line of Trenches between IMPERIAL STREET and the CAMBRAI ROAD.	E.M.N.
ARRAS	11.3.17		Work the same as on the 10th inst.	
ARRAS	12.3.17		Work the same as on the 10th inst. Lieut Colonel E.A. NEWELL appointed C.R.E. 58th Division. Captain P. de H. HALL took over the Command of this unit.	P.
ARRAS	13.3.17		Work the same as on the 10th inst.	P.
ARRAS	14.3.17		Work the same as on the 10th inst. Promotions and Appointments: Captain P.de H. HALL to be Acting MAJOR. T/Lieut P. CRANSWICK to be Acting CAPTAIN, approved by G.O.C. 3rd Division.	P.
ARRAS	15.3.17		Work the same as on the 10th inst	

Army Form C. 2118.

WAR DIARY
or
INTELLIGENCE SUMMARY
(Erase heading not required.)

Sheet No. 3

Place	Date	Hour	Summary of Events and Information	Remarks and references to Appendices
ARRAS	16.3.17		No 1 Section hutting, trenching drains, and reinforcing billets in LIEVRCOURT AREA. No 2 Section erecting NISSEN Huts at WANQUETIN. No 3 & 4 Sections finishing dug outs August Pass 76th Infantry Brigade Battle Headquarters and strengthening entrance and approaches to same. Reporting safe from *Bernack guard to four sewers. C.	× Cpl Brush 11/3/17 Posthumously awarded DCM Died of wounds ARRAS 7 R. 51 S NW 3
ARRAS	17.3.18		Work the same as on Febr 16th inst. C.	
ARRAS	18.3.18		Ditto	
ARRAS	19.3.18		Work the same as on the 16th inst. 1 Officer and 43 O.R. were attached to this company as a permanent working party from the 28th of February. 76th Inf. Brigade C.	
ARRAS	26.3.17		No 1 Section hutting, trenching tramrails in LIEVRCOURT AREA. No 2 Section erecting NISSEN huts at WANQUETIN. No 3 Section making dug outs for 76th Inf. Bge. B.H.Q. and laying light tramway (double track) at C.28, d, 9, 3. No 4 Section working on 76th Inf. Bge. B.H.Q. dugouts and strengthening tunnel. Opening out from Basin to sewer to Four Sewers. No 1 Section (2nd Lieut R.A. Riddell) joined the company in ARRAS Sewery through A.2.0/21" from LIEVCOURT. C.	

Army Form C. 2118.

WAR DIARY
or
INTELLIGENCE SUMMARY. Sheet 4.

(Erase heading not required.)

Instructions regarding War Diaries and Intelligence Summaries are contained in F. S. Regs., Part II. and the Staff Manual respectively. Title pages will be prepared in manuscript.

Place	Date	Hour	Summary of Events and Information	Remarks and references to Appendices
ARRAS	21.3.17		No 1 Section clearing cellars + erecting WELDON TRESTLE Gear. No 2 Section erecting NISSEN huts at WANQUETIN. No 3 Section fitting out 76" Brigade H.Q. dugouts and strengthening tunnel. Laying light tramway track at G.38. d.9.3.5. No 4 Section making hutches for 76" Brigade H.Q. dugouts and strengthening tunnel. Repairing exit from Boons to front to town sewer forming advanced Brigade dump of R.E. stores at G.35. A.B.1. for forthcoming operations. (C)	Cut map ARRAS 7 A Sheet 51B HK3
ARRAS	22.3.17		Work the same as yesterday 21st inst. (C)	
ARRAS	23.3.17		No 1 Section preparing cellars for occupation during Operations. Repairing tank on top of water tower at G.38. No 2 Section erecting NISSEN huts at WANQUETIN. No 3 Section strong shoring tunnel to 76" Bde B.H.Q. dugouts, making hutches and laying light tramway track up G.38. d.9.3. No 4 Section making hutches for 76" Brigade B.H.Q. and strengthening tunnel. Carrying got. for Barrack yard to town sewer. Forming advance dump of R.E. stores at G.35. B.3.1. for forthcoming operations. Nothing notes + ammunition dumps for 76" Brigade in Tunnel. (C)	
ARRAS	24.3.17		Work same as on 23rd inst. (C)	
ARRAS	25.3.17		—— ditto —— (C)	
ARRAS	26.3.17		—— ditto —— (C)	

A.5834. Wt W4973/M687. 750,000 8/16 D. D. & L. Ltd. Forms/C.2118/13.

Army Form C. 2118.

WAR DIARY
or
INTELLIGENCE SUMMARY.

Sheet No 5

(Erase heading not required.)

Instructions regarding War Diaries and Intelligence Summaries are contained in F. S. Regs., Part II. and the Staff Manual respectively. Title pages will be prepared in manuscript.

Place	Date	Hour	Summary of Events and Information	Remarks and references to Appendices
ARRAS	27/3/17		No 1 Section fitting gas proof curtains to cellars to be occupied by 76th Brigade. No 2 Section erecting NISSEN huts at WARRUS TIN. No 3 Section making dugouts in tunnel & reentered at 76th Brigade R.H.Q. No 4 Section making latrines, kitchens and sister dug/t & store at 76th Brigade R.H.Q. Forming reinforcement. R.E. dump at G.35.b.8.1.	M.A. Ref/- A22 28 3rd-31st/1443
ARRAS	28/3/17		Work same as on the 27th inst.	
ARRAS	29/3/17		No 1 Section fitting gasproof curtains to cellars to be occupied by 76th Brigade. No 2 Section erecting NISSEN huts at WARRUS TIN. No 3 Section making latrines in tunnel and in trench at 76th B.R.Q. No 4 Section making kitchens, latrines and sisters dugout & store for 76th Bde R.H.Q. Forming reinforced R.E. dump at G.35.b.8.1. Working on entrance to SAUVEUR TUNNEL at Rue de PASTEUR. 2nd Lieut R.V. TAYLOR. 2nd Lieut A. PICKERSGILL at NAVALETIN. 2nd Lieut. N POWERSGILL arrival for MC O's from No 2 Section joined the Company in ARRAS & reconné & getting ready work the Sauveur area.	
ARRAS	30/3/17		Nos 1, 2, and 4 Sections employ the same at yesterday 29/3 inst. No 3 Section making latrines in tunnel at B.H.Q. and repairing shaft in comms Jo the Rue D'AMIENS.	
ARRAS	31/3/17		Nos 1 + 2 Sections work the same as on the 29th inst. No 3 Section finishing latrines in tunnel at R.H.A. and making for the seven screens, Rue D'Amiens at R.S. France to ARRAS No 4 Section making latrines, and dumps at 76 Bdge B.H.Q. and working on entrance to St SAUVEUR TUNNEL at Rue PASTEUR.	

Reference M/2/1/17 Major R.E.

OC 329 (Midd/-) Tyle R.E.

WAR DIARY.

For month ending April 30th 1917.

UNIT. 529th (E. Riding) Field Company R.E.

Army Form C. 2118.

WAR DIARY
or
INTELLIGENCE SUMMARY

(Erase heading not required.)

Sheet No. 1.

Instructions regarding War Diaries and Intelligence Summaries are contained in F.S. Regs., Part II. and the Staff Manual respectively. Title pages will be prepared in manuscript.

Place	Date	Hour	Summary of Events and Information	Remarks and references to Appendices
ARRAS	1.4.17		No 1 Section fitting gas proof curtains to cellars to be occupied by 76th Inf Brigade. No 2 Section erecting MSS as huts at HANNAV-TIN. No 3 Section erecting screens at the entrance to ARRAS along the RUE DE DOUVRES to screen traffic from enemy observation ballon. Digging assembly trench for two sections N.W. in Potnichery (?) operational. No 4 Section making latrines & dumps in front of 76th Inf Brigade B.H.Q. at G 35.b.1.7,7. Entrance to St. Sauveur tunnel through the sewer in Rue Pasteur. Digging slits and shelters for 7th M.G.C. positions in German old line at G 36 d. One officer supervising construction of assembly trenches for 76th Inf Brigade in Potnichery Operations	Reference WAR. ARRAS 7A. West 3 & NW 3.
ARRAS	2.4.17		No 1 Section fitting gas proof curtains to be occupied by 76th Inf Brigade. WELDON TRESTLE and short lengths of bridging for carrying up to girder bridge brought during the night. Nos 2 and 3 Section work same as yesterday afternoon. No 4 Section making latrines and Thompson Tunnel for 76th Belge S.A.A. Digging slits & shelters for 76th M.G.C. positions in German old line at G 36 d. One officer supervising construction of assembly trenches for 76th Inf Brigade.	
ARRAS	3.4.17		No 1 Section fitting gas proof curtains to cellars to be occupied by 76th Inf Brigade. Nos 2, 3 and 4 Sections work same as yesterday 2nd inst.	
ARRAS	4.4.17		No 1 Section laying flooring in CRINCHON sewer. No 2 Section erecting Nissen huts at HANQUIN during morning. Afternoon developing pits & gas clothing in storage place at HANQUIN. 2nd Lieut TAPPER R.E. and No 2 Section joined the Company. Wares at 11 a.m. Nos 3 and 4 Sections busting. The sappers from No 4 Section dismantled a burst of steel telegraph standard at G 28.c.8.6. at 11.45 p.m. 30 slabs of guncotton was used and the standard was a complete success.	

Army Form C. 2118.

WAR DIARY or INTELLIGENCE SUMMARY

Sheet No 2.

(Erase heading not required.)

Instructions regarding War Diaries and Intelligence Summaries are contained in F. S. Regs., Part II. and the Staff Manual respectively. Title pages will be prepared in manuscript.

Place	Date	Hour	Summary of Events and Information	Remarks and references to Appendices
ARRAS	5.4.17		All sections resting. 3 Sappers helping 7th M.R.C. to dig shelters in front line. Inspection of arms & ammunition for winter & talk by Belmont.	Map Ref Sheet 51ᵇ NW3
ARRAS	6.4.17		Company resting, each section had an hours physical drill.	
ARRAS	7.4.17		Company resting.	
ARRAS	8.4.17		Company resting, each section had an hours physical drill. Also section had an hours digging & entrenching.	
ARRAS	9.4.17		ZERO day. Company allotted as follows for operations No 1 Section - Bridging Nest on Cambrai Road with WELDON Trestle. No 2 Section - Divisional Reserve Attached to 76th Inf. Brigade for work on stony ground.
		12.15 A.M.	3rd Lieut. M. J. WADLEY with half No 4 Section and Lieut. H.C. MUTTER with O.C. Platoon 28th Suffolk Regt moved off from ARRAS and assembled in Tunnel I.54
		5.30 A.M. ZERO hour	New Zealand Tunnelling Coy Blew up North pipe to form C.T. and Lieut H.C. MUTTER with their parties commenced to improve this entrance from a C.T. and lay down trench boards.
		7.0 A.M.	2nd Lieut. J.H. ALDEN with No 3 Section half No 4 Section and one platoon 2nd Suffolk Regt (standing by in ARRAS) ordered forward for making stony points.
		9.5 A.M.	3rd Lieut WADLEY and ALDEN with No 3 and 4 Sections went forward from 76th Inf. Brigade Bomb H.R. to form stony points at: G.36 d. 4.9 ; G.36 b.5.4. and G.36 b.8.7. Very little enemy shelling but a fair amount of sniping. [signed]

A 5834 Wt.W4973/M687 750,000 8/16 D.D.& L.Ltd. Forms/C.2118/13.

Army Form C. 2118.

WAR DIARY
or
INTELLIGENCE SUMMARY
(Erase heading not required.)

Sheet W.2.5

Place	Date	Hour	Summary of Events and Information	Remarks and references to Appendices
ARRAS	9-4-17 (cont)		and M.G. fire from Tilloy and N. of CAMBRAI road.	MAP REF Sheet 51.S N.W.3
		1.30 P.M.	76th Inf. Brigade ordered to reinforce 8th Inf. Brigade. Orders received to stop work on strong points. Lieut. NUTTER and his party remained work on C.T. and ordered forward to join 2nd Lieut. WADSLEY at DEVILS WOOD. Orders received for mobile party to stand by.	
		3.35 P.M.	2nd Lieut J.L. RIDDOCK with No.1 Section moved up from ARRAS to build a track bridge over a pit in the CAMBRAI road at H.31.a.8.5. Bridge complete and section returned by 6 P.M.	
		6.15 P.M.	2nd Lieut A. PICKERSGILL with No.2 Section moved from ARRAS to north on R.E. trolley tracks, and strengthen bridge where the track crosses the German front line trench system. Party returned at (1.15.a.m. 10th inst.).	
		8.15 P.M.	Orders received to consolidate GARRICK trench and form a strong point at G.36.d.0.9. Nos 3 and 4 Sections and attached Infantry ordered to garrison. Moved at once.	
			CASUALTIES. No. 474200 Sergt. GUY T. No. 474339 Sapper RUSSELL T. No. 414427 " CLARKE B.O. } Wounded No. 474440 " BOLD L. No. 474536 " CRISP. E.A. No. 474381 " CARR S. Also three attached Infantry wounded.	

A5831 Wt.W4973/M687 750,000 8/16 D.D.&L.Ltd. Forms/C.2118/13.

Army Form C. 2118.

WAR DIARY
or
INTELLIGENCE SUMMARY. Sheet 4.
(Erase heading not required.)

Place	Date	Hour	Summary of Events and Information	Remarks and references to Appendices
ARRAS	10.4.17	5 A.M.	Work on strong point 6 complete and party ordered back to old British outpost line to rest.	MAP REF: Sheet 51c NW3 ARRAS 7h.
		9 A.M.	White party brought back to billets in ARRAS	
		3 P.M.	Transport moved from WARLUS to EAST of ARRAS Company standing by to entrain with 76th Inf. Brigade.	
ARRAS	11.4.17	2.15 A.M.	Orders received. Company to assist next 9th Inf. Brigade at BOIS DES BOEUFS, made Officer of C.R.E. 5 A.M. Company arrived BOIS DES BOEUFS standing by all day. Transport moved back to West of ARRAS. Sever storm in the evening. 2nd Lieut. R.V. TAYLOR attached for duty with 51st Field Coy. R.E.	
			CASUALTY No 474100 Sapper CHRISTIE H Wheel.	
ARRAS	12.4.17	1-0 P.M.	Company moved back to billets in ARRAS.	
ARRAS	13.4.17		Company with attached infantry working on Scout Artillery Road "C"	
ARRAS	14.4.17		Ditto. Reburial. Company resting. Transport moved back to WARLUS "C"	
ARRAS	15.4.17		Company resting. One hour Regimental drill. Wet day. "C"	
ARRAS	16.4.17		Same as yesterday 15th inst. "C"	
ARRAS	17.4.17		Ditto. Reinforcements. 5 Drivers from Base. "R"	
ARRAS	18.4.17		Rifle exercises and Route till Jonny nights with Scorps. "R"	
ARRAS	19.4.17		Rifle exercises and Lecture on Bridging + Anchoring by Section Officers. Reinforcements - Two Sappers from No 5 Reinforcement Company. "R"	

Army Form C.2118.

WAR DIARY
or
INTELLIGENCE SUMMARY
Sheet No 5.
(Erase heading not required.)

Instructions regarding War Diaries and Intelligence Summaries are contained in F.S. Regs., Part II. and the Staff Manual respectively. Title pages will be prepared in manuscript.

Place	Date	Hour	Summary of Events and Information	Remarks and references to Appendices
ARRAS	20.4.17		Section Drill, Lecture on explosives by Section Officers. P	MARKER Sheet 57 1/4/1917
ARRAS	21.4.17		Section Drill 10.30 A.M. to 12.30 P.M. P	
ARRAS	22.4.17	11.30 A.M.	Church Parade 11.30 A.M. Half No.3 Section marches to WARLUS to wash and clean bridging gear. Harness inspection for drivers. P	
ARRAS	23.4.17		Company standing to all day. First line transport went up to in the Divisional transport area W. of ARRAS in C.20.c. at 9 A.M. and bivouacked. P	
ARRAS	24.4.17	10.30 A.M.	C.O. attends C.R.E.'s conference, and received orders to move Company from 1.30 P.M. The C.O. and Nos 1, 2, 3 and 4 sections with their transport and field cookers move up to NEVILLY TRENCH about N.I.d.4.18. 5.30 P.M. Batteries outlying waggons moved up to transportation W. of ARRAS (empty). One section attached to each Battalion of 76th Inf. Brigade for work at night. Bd trenches E 7 M onwards. Very little work done owing to Divisional Relief being in progress. P	
			LE-PREUX	
ARRAS	25.4.17		Company moved from N.I.d.4.8, NEVILLY TRENCH, to TILLOY QUARRY. Nos 1 + 2 sections work on communication up PICK TRENCH and SHRAPNEL TRENCH, Support line No 3 Section construction of TWIN copses No 4 Section construction of SHRAPNEL TRENCH. P	
ARRAS	26.4.17		Nos 1, 2 and 4 sections same as yesterday 25 inst. being too late start else to operations on right of Divl. front, very little work was done and No 3 Section did not reach their job. P	
ARRAS	27.4.17		No 1 Section with a Strong Point near Copse at O.8. central (Sht-51B). Nos 2, 3 and 4 Sections work on C.T. from Support to Front line. Drill work done owing to heavy bombardment. All transport moved from WARLUS to G.20.d W. of ARRAS Wassendal. 2nd Lieutenant A. PICKERSGILL

CASUALTIES Killed No. 474434 Sapper BROWN G.H.

A5834. Wt.W4973/M687 730000 8/16 D.D. & L. Ltd. Forms/C.2118/13.

WAR DIARY
or
INTELLIGENCE SUMMARY

Plat No 6.

(Erase heading not required)

Army Form C. 2118.

Place	Date	Hour	Summary of Events and Information	Remarks and references to Appendices
ARRAS	28/4/17		Nos 1, 2 and 3 Sections work on track from SHRAPNEL TRENCH North to MORCHY-LE-PREUX. CASUALTIES Wounded 2nd Lieutenant J.H. ALDEN.	MAP REF Sheet 51.B. 1/40000
ARRAS	29/4/17		Nos 1 & 2 Sections digging extension to FRONT LINE trench. No 4 Section construction of SHRAPNEL trench. 2nd Lieutenant R.V. TAYLOR rejoined unit from 565 Field Co R.E. AWARDS. a/Sergt. GON GUY R.E.m. The Military Medal.	
ARRAS	30/4/17		Nos 1 & 2 Sections work on connecting PICK trench and SHRAPNEL trench. No 3 Section construction of trench in TWIN COPSES. No 4 Section construction of SHRAPNEL trench. CASUALTIES. Wounded, No 474074 Sapper MERRIKIN. E.B.	

Philip Garwick
Capt. R.E. (T)
1/5/17

for O.C. 529th (E. Riding) F/A Coy R.E. (T)

WAR DIARY.

for month ending. 31st May 1917.

529th (E. Riding) Field Co. R.E.

Army Form C. 2118.

WAR DIARY
or
INTELLIGENCE SUMMARY

Sheet No. 1.

(Erase heading not required.)

Instructions regarding War Diaries and Intelligence Summaries are contained in F. S. Regs., Part II. and the Staff Manual respectively. Title pages will be prepared in manuscript.

Place	Date	Hour	Summary of Events and Information	Remarks and references to Appendices
ARRAS	1.5.17		Company resting in shelters at Tilloy Quarry. No 474 Sapper BARTLE E. proceeded to England for a Cadets Course. P.	Map Ref Sheet 51B 1/40,000
ARRAS.	2.5.17.		No work. Resting. Company moved to old German Strong Point at about H.31.b.8.3 just N.W. of CAMBRAI-ARRAS road. P. Company resting. P.	
ARRAS.	3.5.17.		Company resting. P.	
ARRAS.	4.5.17.		All 4 sections digging C.T. from S.E. end of MONCHY-LE-PREUX to DRAGOON LANE about O.7.A.2.7. 600 yards of trench dug average depth 3 feet. Working Party 340 O.R. 1st GORDON HIGHLANDERS. P.	
ARRAS.	5.5.17.		All 4 sections digging continuation of C.T. commenced last night. 800 yards of trench dug average 3 feet work. 1 and 3 platoons. Working Party 620 O.R. 1st GORDON HIGHLANDERS and 1 BN. K.O.R.L. Driver FRENHAM F.O. granted special leave. P.	
ARRAS	6.5.17.		All 4 sections working on C.T. as on 4th inst. Working Party 620 O.R. 1st GORDON HIGHLANDERS and 1 BN. K.O.R.L. P.	
ARRAS	7.5.17.		All 4 sections working on C.T. as on 4th inst. C.T. cut through HUSSAR LANE & met bridge put over trench across roadway. CASUALTY. No 474 538 Sapper ALLMAN. J.H. wounded. Remained at duty. P.	
ARRAS	8.5.17.		Nos. 2, 3, and 4 Sections strengthening wire in front of SHRAPNEL TRENCH under intermittent M.G. shelling. P.	
ARRAS	9.5.17.		Nos 1, 3, and 4 sections strengthening wire in front of SHRAPNEL TRENCH Party heavily shelled during whole work. No 474 471 Lce Cpl ROWE C. wounded. No 174080 2/Cpl BUCHANAN D. SHELL SHOCK. 2nd Lieutenant M.J. WADLEY. P.
			CASUALTIES. KILLED. No 474 375 Sapper BARNES (remained at duty).	

Army Form C. 2118.

WAR DIARY
or
INTELLIGENCE SUMMARY
(Erase heading not required.)

Sheet N° 2

Place	Date	Hour	Summary of Events and Information	Remarks and references to Appendices
Tilloy	10.5.17		Nos 1, 2 and 4 sections strengthening wire in front of SHRAPNEL TRENCH. 2nd Lieut. J.A. RIDDALL proceeded to Head Quarters in ARRAS for Lewis Duty. Captain P. CROMWELL proceeded to Tilloy to assist Company in trench area. C.	Pt. MAP LENS II. 1/10,000
Tilloy	11.5.17		Company resting.	
Tilloy	12.5.17		REINFORCEMENTS. 3 O.R. from No. 5 Reinforcement Company. C. No. 2 section attached 76th Infantry Brigade for consolidation on DEVILS TRENCH. 4 men of No. 1 section and 4 men of No. 2 section attached 76? M.G.C. to assist in making entanglements in DEVILS TRENCH. Attached did not reach its objective, so parties are now resting but the M.G.C. detachments were kept later. Rest of Company resting. CASUALTIES. KILLED N° 474504 Pte BERRE J.C. WOUNDED. N° 474623 Pte CUMMING. R.W., N° 474385 Pte FOWND W.E., N° 474489 L/cpl. MASON J.E. N° 470386 Pte MILESTONE F. (remained on duty) N° 474500 Pte BOOTH F. (remained on duty) C.	
Tilloy	13.5.17		Nos 3 & 4 sections strengthening wire to SHRAPNEL TRENCH. C.	
Tilloy	14.5.17		Handed over to the 455 (W. Riding) Field Co. R.E.?. Transport under 2nd Lieut J.A. RIDDALL moved from ARRAS to DUISSANS at 2.30 P.M. Company marched from Tilloy to DUISSANS at Tilloy 8.30 P.M., arrived DUISSANS 10.45 P.M. Route Tilloy - THINNES - DUISSANS. C.	
Duissans	15.5.17		Resting. 10 A.M. Kit Inspection. C.	
Duissans	16.5.17		9. A.M. Inspection of Arms, Ammunition and respirators. Rifle Exercises and Physical drill. Rifle exercises for the recruit section in the afternoon. C.	

Army Form C. 2118.

WAR DIARY
or
INTELLIGENCE SUMMARY.
(Erase heading not required.)

Sheet No. 3.

Place	Date	Hour	Summary of Events and Information	Remarks and references to Appendices
DUISSANS	17.5.17		Company moved up DUISSANS 10.15 A.M. arriving HOPLISETTE 12.15 P.M. Route HENEZ - COURAS - MAISNICOURT - HASTROIS. Billeted in huts.	Remark
HOPLISETTE	18.5.17		Reinforcements 3. O.R. from No. 6. Reinforcement Company. 2nd Lieut R.W. PICKLES R.E. joined company as reinforcement. Company detailed for work at the village of WANQUETIN. Annaleur Church. O.C. met C.E. XIII Corps at WANQUETIN repairing huts damaged by enemy.	LEWIS II. 1/100-III
WANQUETIN	19.5.17		Company marched out from HOPLISETTE at 2.30 P.M. arriving WANQUETIN 3.10 P.M. at 12 noon for orders re work. Nos 1, 2, 3 & 4 Sections repairing buildings all day. Square drill in afternoon.	C
WANQUETIN	20.5.17		Nos 1 & 2 Sections repairing buildings all day. Square drill in afternoon. Drivers spent time Nos 3 & 4 Sections repairing buildings — morning. Square drill in afternoon. No 474300 Driver RAWLINGS 9. granted Leave to ENGLAND	C
WANQUETIN	21.5.17		all four Sections working on buildings	C
WANQUETIN	22.5.17		do	
WANQUETIN	23.5.17		All four sections working on buildings in morning. Afternoon recreational training No 4/4 driver JLEE Wooden spare on leave.	C
WANQUETIN	24.5.17		Nos 1 & 2 Sections work on buildings all day. Nos 3 & 4 Sections work on buildings in morning afternoon Section Drill. Drivers shoeing on Shot up at Range N.E. of VERNON.	C
WANQUETIN	25.5.17		All four sections working on buildings morning. 1 and 2 Sections Square drill in afternoon 3 and 4 repairing buildings. Drivers shoeing in afternoon. No 5 Reinforcing Company Reinforcements 5 O.R. from 1 Driver posted to Event.	C
WANQUETIN	26.5.17		No 1 & 2 Section working on billets all day. Nos 3 and 4 Section working on billets in morning. Afternoon rifle section shooting. No 3 Section shooting. Reinforcements 2nd Lieutenant J.H. PARKIN. No 5 Section 2nd Lieutenant + O. Coles joined company for duty.	5 O.R. from

A 5834. Wt. W4973/MG87. 750,000 8/16 D.D. & L. Ltd. Forms/C.2118/13.

Army Form C. 2118.

WAR DIARY
or
INTELLIGENCE SUMMARY

2nd Lieut No 4.

(Erase heading not required.)

Instructions regarding War Diaries and Intelligence Summaries are contained in F.S. Regs., Part II and the Staff Manual respectively. Title pages will be prepared in manuscript.

Place	Date	Hour	Summary of Events and Information	Remarks and references to Appendices
WANQUETIN	27-5-17		No 2, 3, 4 Sections repairing buildings & improving. No 1 Section shooting. 2nd Lieut J.A. Riddle transferred to 5th Bn Divn as Adjutant MGC. R.E. 58th Division. Anthony A.G. No A/23358/583. 2nd Lieut R.C.W. Pickles to No 1 Section. 2nd Lieut J.H. Parkin to No 3 Section. 2nd Lieut H.T. Cook to No 1 Section	REF MAP LENS II 1/40,000
WANQUETIN	28-5-17		No 1 Section work in billets in morning. Inoculation in afternoon. No 2 Section ———— do ———— Inoculation in afternoon. No 3 Section Inoculation. No 4 Section work in billets all day.	
WANQUETIN	29-5-17		No 1 and 3 Sections attending billets all day. No 2 Section Inoculation No 4 Section work in billets in morning. Shooting in afternoon. H/Q H.Q. Section Inoculation	
WANQUETIN	30-5-17		No 1, 2, and 3 Sections work on billets all day. No 4 Section Inoculation. REINFORCEMENTS. 13 O.R. from No 6 Reinforcement Company H/Q H.Q. Section Inoculation	
WANQUETIN	31-5-17		No 1, 2, 3 and 4 Sections worked in billets in morning. Warm Reveille Training Capt P Lamswick went on leave to England.	

Signed
Major R.E.
O.C. 517th (Kent) 7th C.E.R.E.

Vol XI 30th June

WAR DIARY.

For Month ending 30th June 1917.

UNIT. 529th (E. Riding) Field Company R.E.

Army Form C. 2118.

WAR DIARY
or
INTELLIGENCE SUMMARY
(Erase heading not required.)

Instructions regarding War Diaries and Intelligence Summaries are contained in F.S. Regs., Part II. and the Staff Manual respectively. Title pages will be prepared in manuscript.

Place	Date	Hour	Summary of Events and Information	Remarks and references to Appendices
WANQUETIN	1-6-17		Sections 1.2.3+4 repairing buildings in morning. Pay Parade 2·30 p.m.	MAP REF: Sheet 51 B.
"	2·6·17	9 a.m.	Lieut Taylor and 10 cyclists as advanced party left WANQUETIN at 9 a.m. arrived HOULETTE WORK at 11 a.m. Took over from WEST RIDING R.E. FIELD COMPANY, including work in DUGOUTS at points E+D VINE TRENCH and the repairs & extension of EAST TRENCH also Bumph at TILLOY & workshop at ARRAS. Sections 1.2.3+4 Left WANQUETIN at 1·30 p.m. arrived at HOULETTE WORK 5·30 p.m. 2/Lt PARKIN with an Officer of the WEST RIDING R.E. sketched a tape for continuation of DALE TRENCH. Leaving HOULETTE WORK at 7 p.m.	Sheet № 1.
HOULETTE WORK.	3-6-17		No 3+4 Section on DUGOUTS at points E+D " 2 Section Dismantling Dugouts in the HOLT area TILLOY. " 1 Section Repairing EAST TRENCH. No 474357 Driver FLETCHER J.M. proceeded on leave.	
"	4-6-17		2/Lt PALETHORPE. G.M. joined the 529th Field Coy for duty. No 1 Section Repairing EAST TRENCH " 2 " Dismantling Dugouts in the HOLT area " 3+4 " working on DUGOUTS at points E+D.	

Army Form C. 2118.

WAR DIARY
or
INTELLIGENCE SUMMARY. Sheet N° 2.
(Erase heading not required.)

Place	Date	Hour	Summary of Events and Information	Remarks and references to Appendices
HOULETTE WORK	5-6-17		N° 1 Section working on EAST TRENCH.	MAP REF Sheet 51B.
			" 2 " " " " "	
			3+4 " Dismantling dugouts in HOLT area. At night began with O.P. at D. post VINE LANE.	
			" " working on dugouts at points E + D.	
			AWARDS. MAJOR P. DE HAVILLAND HALL. Military Cross.	
"	6-6-17		N° 1 Section working on EAST TRENCH. Sgt. Milestone hurt by the explosion of a shell.	
			" 2 " " O.P's EAST of D POST.	
			" 3+4 " " dugouts at points E + D.	
			N° 474.013. C.S.M. Bean E. proceeded on leave.	
"	7-6-17		N° 1 Section working on EAST TRENCH.	
			" 2 " " O.P's EAST of D POST.	
			" 3+4 " " dugouts at points E + D.	
"	8-6-17		N° 1 Section working on EAST TRENCH.	
			" 2 " " O.P's EAST of D POST.	
			" 3+4 " " dugouts at points E + D.	
"	9-6-17		N° 1 Section working on EAST TRENCH.	
			" 2 " " O.P's EAST of D POST.	
			" 3+4 " " dugouts at points E + D.	

Army Form C. 2118.

WAR DIARY
or
INTELLIGENCE SUMMARY Book No 3
(Erase heading not required.)

Instructions regarding War Diaries and Intelligence Summaries are contained in F.S. Regs., Part II. and the Staff Manual respectively. Title pages will be prepared in manuscript.

Place	Date	Hour	Summary of Events and Information	Remarks and references to Appendices
TILLOY	10-6-17		No 1 Section working on EAST TRENCH	Map 25E Map 51SE
			2 " " " OPs EAST OF D POST	
			3+4 " " " Dugouts at points E+D.	
"	11-6-17		No.4 74237 Batt CARLIN P. returned on leave.	
			No 1 Section working on EAST TRENCH	
			2 " " " OPs EAST OF D POST	
			3+4 " " " Dugouts at points E & D.	
"	12-6-17		No 1 Section working on Dugouts and OPs Captain P. CROMWELL returned from leave	
			2 " " " OPs East of D Post	
			3+4 " " " Dugouts at points D.	
"	13-6-17		Nos 1.2.3+4 Section working at D.Post on OPs & Dugouts	
"	14-6-17		Nos 1+2 Working on C.T. between HILL + HOOK Trenches NORTH	REINFORCEMENTS
			" 3+4 " " " " " " " SOUTH	2nd Lieut H. HAITHWAITE
			" " " " " ADA + HOOK " NORTH	2nd " J. BRODIE
"	15-6-17		Nos 1+2 Working on C.T. between HILL + HOOK Trenches NORTH	2 " C.B FUNNELL } P.
			3+4 " " " " " " " SOUTH	
			" " " " " ADA + HOOK " SOUTH	
			2/Lt R.V.TAYLOR went on leave to England.	2nd Lieut C.G FUNNELL attached to 458th (Clerine)
"	16-6-17		All Sections remained in Camp.	Field Coy R.E. for Duty

WAR DIARY
or
INTELLIGENCE SUMMARY Sheet No 4

Army Form C. 2118.

Place	Date	Hour	Summary of Events and Information	Remarks and references to Appendices
TILLOY	17.6.17 / 18.6.17		On the night of 17th/18th No 1 Section working on new junction trench, starting from HOOK TRENCH and running NORTH. Nos 2, 3 & 4 Sections on H.C.T. between HOOK and LONG ARCADES. 12.30 A.M. the enemy heavily bombarded all front line defences in that area, until about 3 A.M. when he attacked the positions. The Company assisted the 76th Inf Brigade to resist this attack, which was successfully accomplished. Nos 2, 3 & 4 Sections suffered heavy casualties during the bombardment. No 1 Section returned to camp at 8 A.M. Nos 2, 3, & 4 Sections, with 2nd Lieut H. HATHWAITE returned to camp at 2 P.M., the Officers of 3 & 4 Section having become casualties. CASUALTIES. KILLED 2nd Lieut H.J. PARKIN, and 11 other ranks. WOUNDED. 2nd Lieut R.E.W. PICKLES and 16 other ranks. WOUNDED. (Remained at Duty) 2 O.R. MISSING. 2 O.R.	MAP REF. Sheet 51B
TILLOY	19.6.17		2nd Lieut H.J. COOK attached to 56th F.E. Co. R.E. for duty. Company resting. 3.30 P.M. Company marched to billets in ARRAS. OC RE took over billets.	
ARRAS	20.6.17		3.15 A.M. The Transport and cyclists move off from ARRAS arriving 10.30 A.M. ROUTE. BEAUMETZ—LAMERLIÉRE—MONDICOURT—POMMERA—HALLOY. The dismounted body of the Company left ARRAS on motor busses at 4.45 P.M. and CHOMESNIL 6.45 P.M. ROUTE as above. Capt. PARKER Proceeded on Leave.	MAP REF. LENS 11.

Army Form C. 2118.

WAR DIARY
or
INTELLIGENCE SUMMARY
(Erase heading not required.)

Instructions regarding War Diaries and Intelligence Summaries are contained in F.S. Regs., Part II. and the Staff Manual respectively. Title pages will be prepared in manuscript.

Plat No 5.

Place	Date	Hour	Summary of Events and Information	Remarks and references to Appendices
CAUMESNIL	21.6.17	10 A.M.	Inspection Arms, Ammunition, Gas Respirator and Kit.	MAP: REF. LENS 11.
			POSTINGS. 1st Lieut H. HAITHWAITE to No. 1 Section. 2nd Lieut C.W. PALETHORPE to No. 3 Section. 1st Lieut J. BRODIE to No. 3 ". 3rd Lieut C.G. FUNNELL to No. 4 ".	R
CAUMESNIL	22.6.17	9 A.M.	Physical Drill. 10.30 A.M. Sword Drill. 12 Artillery to 12.30 P.M. M.G.O.'s Communication Drill.	R
CAUMESNIL	23.6.17		ditto	R
CAUMESNIL	24.6.17		1st Lieut C.G. FUNNELL separate company. No 474303 drive PAWSON O' sent to Lear.	R
CAUMESNIL	25.6.17	9 A.M.	Inspection of Arms and Equipment. 5.30 P.M. Church Parade.	R
CAUMESNIL	26.6.17		Physical Drill and Musketry training. Nos 1 and 2 Sections Firing Practice on Range. Nos 3 + 4 Sections Physical drill and Musketry. No 3 and 4 Sections Firing Practice on Range. No 1+2 Section Physical Exercise Musketry.	R
CREMESSE	27.6.17	9-10 A.M.	Physical Drill.	R
			2nd Lieut R.W. TOPER returns from Leave.	
CAUMESNIL	28.6.17	9 A.M.	Company marched to 76th Brigade training ground and marched over 76th Brigade for future of laying Molab's prepared by Major J.A.L. HOLDMS DSO II Corps Commander. AWARDS No 474381 A/Cpl EDMONDS G; 474089 Pte RAYNOR R; 474405 Cpl PARKER J.W; No 474545 Pte FINNEY W; No 479375 Pte BARKER H.H; No 479453 Pte NOROAS G. Awarded M.M. for rest of Gallantry in the Field in operations of 7/18 June 1917 at SACRIFICE HILL. C.R.O No 2352 D/f 28.8.17.	

Army Form C. 2118.

WAR DIARY
or
INTELLIGENCE SUMMARY

(Erase heading not required.)

Sheet N° 6.

Instructions regarding War Diaries and Intelligence Summaries are contained in F. S. Regs., Part II. and the Staff Manual respectively. Title pages will be prepared in manuscript.

Place	Date	Hour	Summary of Events and Information	Remarks and references to Appendices
CAMBLAIN	30.6.17		Physical drill. Squad drill. No Parade in afternoon. N°474697 Sapper Roberts proceeded on leave.	Ref. Map LENS 11.

Tennican
Major R.E. in
O.C. 529th (E. Riding 2) Fd Cy R.E.

30/6/17

A 5834 Wt. W4973/M637 750,000 8/16 D. D. & L. Ltd. Forms/C.2118/13.

Vol 12

WAR DIARY.
For month ending 31st July 1917.

UNIT. 529th (E. Riding) Field Company R.E.(T).

Army Form C. 2118.

WAR DIARY
or
INTELLIGENCE SUMMARY

Sheet No. 1.

(Erase heading not required.)

Instructions regarding War Diaries and Intelligence Summaries are contained in F. S. Regs., Part II and the Staff Manual respectively. Title pages will be prepared in manuscript.

Place	Date	Hour	Summary of Events and Information	Remarks and references to Appendices
ACHIET-LE-PETIT	1.7.17		Company moved to ACHIET-LE-PETIT. Attacked Martin left CARVOSSIEL at 5 A.M and marched with 76th INF. Brigade Advanced Group, arriving ACHIET-LE-PETIT at 2 P.M. ROUTE ORVILLE — THIEVRES — AUTHIE — BUS — BERTRANCOURT — BEAUSSART — MAILLY-MAILLET — SERRE — PUISIEUX — BUCQUOY. Distance 20 miles. Dismounted portion of Company proceeded to DOULLENS. Route HALLOY — BEAUREPAIRE and then entrained. Detrained at ACHIET-LE-GRAND and marched to ACHIET-LE-PETIT. No. 474957 Lieutenant M.J. WADSLEY joined Company from hospital. Lieut. HUSSEY. G. proceeded on leave.	MAP. REF. LENS 11.
LEBUCQUIERE	2.7.17		Company moved to LEBUCQUIERE. C.O. and Lieut. M.J. WADSLEY went on ahead to fix up Horse Standings. Company arrived 1½ from ACHIET-LE-PETIT at 1 P.M. arriving LEBUCQUIERE at 4.45 P.M. ROUTE ACHIET-LE-GRAND — BIHUCOURT — BIEFVILLERS — BARASTRE — FREMICOURT. Distance 11 miles. Took over work from 474 (S. MIDLAND) Field Company R.E. Nos 1 + 3 Sections Officers + Sergeants went up the Line to take over works.	MAP REF. FRANCE Sheet 57 C.
LEBUCQUIERE	3.7.17		Nos 2 and 4 Sections working on billets. No. 1 Section commenced continuous work on dug outs at I.12 D 2/0 and D.20.C.5.5 at 8.P.M. and carried out in 6 hour reliefs. No. 3 Section commenced continuous work on dug outs at K.7.C.0.5. and K.7.06.0.5 at 8.P.M. Work carried out in 6 hour reliefs.	
LEBUCQUIERE	4.7.17		Nos 1 + 3 Sections continuous work on dug outs. 2nd Lieut. M.J. WADSLEY attached to CRS for duty. Nos 2 + 4 " Cant. improvements. No. 474341 2nd Corpl. COUPLAND proceeded on leave.	
LEBUCQUIERE	5.7.17		do	
LEBUCQUIERE	6.7.17		do	
LEBUCQUIERE	7.7.17		Nos 1,3,2 Sections as yesterday. No. 4 Section work on C.T. running from E.7th Road at K.7.C.85 to K.7.C.0.5. REINFORCEMENTS. 18 O.R. from No. 5 Reinforcement Company.	
LEBUCQUIERE	8.7.17		do. Major R. de. H. HALL proceeded on Leave.	

MAJOR R. de. H. HALL

Army Form C. 2118.

WAR DIARY
or
INTELLIGENCE SUMMARY

Year No 2

(Erase heading not required.)

Instructions regarding War Diaries and Intelligence Summaries are contained in F. S. Regs., Part II. and the Staff Manual respectively. Title pages will be prepared in manuscript.

Place	Date	Hour	Summary of Events and Information	Remarks and references to Appendices
LEBUCQUIÈRE	9.7.17		Nº 1 & 3 Sections working on dug outs. Nº 4 Section working on C.T. at K.7.c.8.9. Nº 2 Section Camp Improvements. REINFORCEMENTS. 3 O.R. from Nº 5 Reinforcement Coy.	M.I.P.REF. SS.1-57.C C.
LEBUCQUIÈRE	10.7.17		Work as on the 9th inst: Nº 474367 Sergt. PAPES and Nº 474635 Sapper SMITH.R Invalided on Leave through fall from horse. 11th inst: 2nd Lieut M.J. WADSLEY to Hospt: Fractured pelvis sustained through fall from horse. 11th inst.	C
LEBUCQUIÈRE	11.7.17		Ditto	
LEBUCQUIÈRE	12.7.17		Nº 1 Section work on dug outs. Nº 2 Section work on dug out at K.7.d.1.1 and C.T. leading to it. Nº 3 Section Camp Improvements. Nº 4 Section erecting high wire entanglement N.E. of DOIGNIES. AWARDS. II Lieut: GEORGE WILLIAM PALETHORPE. 7th MILITARY CROSS. II Lieut: REGINALD CLARENCE WIFFRET PICKLES HR/582 dated 7/7/17. II Corps C/1/38/256 dated 7/7/17. Authority (Third Army Reinforcing Coy.) C.	
LEBUCQUIÈRE	13.7.17		Work as on the 12th inst: REINFORCEMENT. 22 O.R. from Nº 7 Reinforcing Coy. Nº 474385 Driver BARNABY proceeded on Leave.	C.
LEBUCQUIÈRE	14.7.17		Ditto	
LEBUCQUIÈRE	15.7.17		G.O.C. inspected Lines.	C.
			Nº 1 Section dug. dugouts. Nº 2 Section dug dugout and C.T. Nº 3 Section new dug dugout for Gunners and 7 men working in Camp. Nº 4 Section erecting high wire entanglement N.E. of DOIGNIES. II Lieutenant R.V. TAYLOR proceeded to IV Corps School BOVES for a course of Infantry Traing. Nº 474298 Driver BARNES T. proceeded on Leave.	
LEBUCQUIÈRE	16.7.17		Work as on 15th inst.	C.
LEBUCQUIÈRE	17.7.17		Nos 1, 2 and 4 sections same as yesterday. Nº 3 Section dug dugouts and erecting Dinium C Cinema at I.30.a.3.4. Nº 474397 Sapper COLLINSON J. and Nº 246031 Sapper HYDG.J. proceeded on Leave	C.

Army Form C. 2118.

WAR DIARY
or
INTELLIGENCE SUMMARY

(Erase heading not required.)

Sheet No 3.

Place	Date	Hour	Summary of Events and Information	Remarks and references to Appendices
LEBUCQUIÈRE	18.7.17		No 1 Section working on dug outs, and sinking 2 wells at C.30.b.9.9. No 2 Section & 4 Section working on C.T. Lebrun D.21.d, 9.4 & D.27.a, 2, 3. No 3 Section tapping a dug-out and erecting division Cinema. This unit had a definite area allotted it, on the Gricourt Road for work, and took over all work in that area which was not at present in hand. (P.) No 474455 Sapper Moody J. and No 474019 C. S. M. S. Bramald.	MAP REF Sheet 57 C
LEBUCQUIÈRE	19.7.17		Work same as on 18th inst. No 4 Proceeded on Leave. (P.)	REINFORCEMENTS 1 O R. from
LEBUCQUIÈRE	20.7.17		Work same as on 18th inst. Major P. de H. Hall returned from Leave. (P.) 87th Field Coy RE (Transferred).	
LEBUCQUIÈRE	21.7.17		No 1, 2, and 3 Section work same as on 18th inst. (P.) No 4 Section resting.	
LEBUCQUIÈRE	22.7.17		No 1 Section work on dug outs and C.T. No 2 Section work on C.T. No 3 Section work on a dug out and erecting Cinema. No 4 Section work on dug outs in Intermediate line trees & laying trench tramway in C.T. No 474259 Sapper Clarke H.E. proceeded on Leave. (P.)	
LEBUCQUIÈRE	23.7.17		Work same as on 22nd inst. (P.)	
LEBUCQUIÈRE	24.7.17		Nos 1, 3, & 4 Section work on dug outs. No 2 Section resting. No 474633 Sapper Skelton R.W.S. proceeded on Leave. (P.)	
LEBUCQUIÈRE	25.7.17		Nos 1, 3, & 4 Section work on dug outs. No 2 Section work on C.T. (P.)	
LEBUCQUIÈRE	26.7.17		Work same as on 25th inst. No 474362 2/C. Sharpe H. proceeded on Leave. (P.)	

Army Form C. 2118.

WAR DIARY
or
INTELLIGENCE SUMMARY
(Erase heading not required.)

Instructions regarding War Diaries and Intelligence Summaries are contained in F.S. Regs., Part II. and the Staff Manual respectively. Title pages will be prepared in manuscript.

Sheet No. 4

Place	Date	Hour	Summary of Events and Information	Remarks and references to Appendices
LEBUCQUIÈRE	27-7-17		Nos 1, 3, & 4 Sections working on deep dugouts Nº 3 Section commenced new dugout on Post 29 LACMICOURT LINE. Nº 1 Section working well also. Nº 2 Section Winch on C.T.	Map. Ref: Sheet 57 C
LEBUCQUIÈRE	28-7-17		Work same as on the 27th inst. Nº 474218 Sapper KITSON W. & Nº 474458 Sapper MORDACE G. proceeded on leave.	
LEBUCQUIÈRE	29-7-17		Ditto	
LEBUCQUIÈRE	30-7-17		Nº 1 Section working two deep dugouts, West, and shoring & reshoring Post 27 Doignies-LEBUCQUIERE Line. Nº 2 Section work in C.T. Nº 3 & 4 Sections same as on 27th inst. Nº 474502 L/C RADKLEY A. & Nº 474438 Sapper ELLIS H.J. proceeded on leave. Major P.D.G. HALL attached to C.R.E. for duty.	
LEBUCQUIÈRE	31-7-17		Nº 1 Section work on two deep dugouts & well, August 1st Inst. 1712 completed. Nº 2 Section work on C.T. No night work owing to heavy rain. Nos 3 & 4 Sections same as on 27th Inst. Nº 474456 Sapper ASHTON F. proceeded on leave	

Philip Cranswick
Capt. R.E. Co.
per Payor, O.C. 529th (E.Rudby)
Field Coy R.E. (T)

1st August 1917.

WAR DIARY. For month ending 31st August 1917.

UNIT. 529th (E. Riding) Field Company R.E.

Army Form C. 2118.

WAR DIARY
or
INTELLIGENCE SUMMARY. Sheet N° 1
(Erase heading not required.)

Instructions regarding War Diaries and Intelligence Summaries are contained in F. S. Regs., Part II. and the Staff Manual respectively. Title pages will be prepared in manuscript.

Place	Date	Hour	Summary of Events and Information	Remarks and references to Appendices
LEBUCQUIÈRE	1.8.17		No 1 Section working deep dugout at J.7.d.9.9. Well at C.30.b.9.9. No 2 Section resting. No 3 Section working on deep dugout at I.12.b.2.5 and ditto at Post 29 Intermediate Dry-out at I.12.b.2.5. Completed. No 4 Section nothing in two Deep dugouts in Posts 27 + 28 Intermediate line Major P.DE H. HALL rejoined Company from C.R.E. 3rd Division.	MAP REF Sheet 57 c
LEBUCQUIÈRE	2.8.17		No 1 Section work on deep dugout, Well, and cutting drain from Post 27 Intmo Line No 2 Section work on C.T. to Post L.38 No 3 Section work on deep dugout in Post 29 No 4 Section work in dugouts in Posts 27 + 28. No 474353 Driver BANOS G. proceeded on leave.	C.
LEBUCQUIÈRE	3.8.17		Work same as yesterday. #28" inst.	C.
LEBUCQUIÈRE	4.8.17		No 1 Section work on dugout, Well, and mining Intermediate line No 2,3, + 4 Section same as 2nd inst.	C.
LEBUCQUIÈRE	5.8.17		Work same as on 4th inst. No 474067 Corporal DIMBERLINE A.E. proceeded on leave.	C.
LEBUCQUIÈRE	6.8.17		Ditto. No 474911	C.
LEBUCQUIÈRE	7.8.17		Ditto. No 474329 L/Cpl ROBSON P. and Sapper TAYLOR J. proceeded on leave.	C.
LEBUCQUIÈRE	8.8.17		Ditto.	C.
LEBUCQUIÈRE	9.8.17		Ditto. No 474081 Bergt. GOODEVE G., No 474251 Spr NORMAN E. + No 474 Spr JOCT A.H. proceeded on leave.	C.
LEBUCQUIÈRE	10.8.17		Ditto. No 474007 Sapper HUDSON H. (carpenter) + No 48823 Sapper WINTER E. proceeded on leave.	C.
LEBUCQUIÈRE	11.8.17		Ditto.	C.
LEBUCQUIÈRE	12.8.17		Ditto.	

Army Form C. 2118.

WAR DIARY
or
INTELLIGENCE SUMMARY

Sheet N°. 2.

(Erase heading not required.)

Instructions regarding War Diaries and Intelligence Summaries are contained in F. S. Regs., Part II. and the Staff Manual respectively. Title pages will be prepared in manuscript.

Place	Date	Hour	Summary of Events and Information	Remarks and references to Appendices
LEBUCQUIÈRE	13.8.17		No 1 Section. Work on Well. Cock dugout & Wiring between Posts 27 & 29 in J.1.R. & J.3.a. No 2 Section. Work on C.T. and digging C.T. & firebench at Posts 27 & 28 in J.3.a. No 3 Section. Work on Cook dugout & Repairing Douchies - Lagnicourt Road. No 4 Section. Work on Reft dugouts. No 474384 Driver LAMMING R.D. & No 474 Driver WARDLE E. proceeded on Leave.	MAP REF. Sheet 57 C.
LEBUCQUIÈRE	14.8.17		Work same as yesterday. 1st instr. ∧ No 474049 L/C DICK E. & No 474301 Pnr HELME T. proceeded on Leave. E.	
LEBUCQUIÈRE	15.8.17		do. do. No 474030 Cpl GUBBET J. proceeded E	
LEBUCQUIÈRE	16.8.17		ditto. No 474089 L/Cpl HUNT G. & No 474306 Cpl DENT C. proceeded E	
LEBUCQUIÈRE	17.8.17		Nos 1, 3, & 4 Sections same as above. (Driver HUNT proceeded new appointment Leave) E No 2 Section Wiring. 2nd instr. R. V. TAYLOR aspirant sergt from I Corps School.	
LEBUCQUIÈRE	18.8.17		No 2, 3, 4 Section as above. No 474241 Spr JENNINGS E. & No 474503 L/Cpl FORD C.E. proceeded on Leave. No 1 Section Wiring. (On Festubert in the new Egyptian Leave) E	
LEBUCQUIÈRE	19.8.17		No 1 Section. Work on Well. Cook dugouts Wiring. No 3 Section. Work on C.T. & Post 27 & 28 (a). No 4 Section. Work on Reft dugouts & repairing Douchies - Lagnicourt Road. No 474214 S/Sgt McDOUGALL E. & No 679. Cpl KEMMERCHAM F. proceeded No 3 Section. Work on Reft dugouts. on Leave. E	
LEBUCQUIÈRE	20.8.17		Work same as yesterday. 19th instr. No 474012 Cpl BAINSBURY E. & No 474025 C.Cpl McNALLY P.	
LEBUCQUIÈRE	21.8.17		ditto (C/S RAINSBURY) No 474 Driver KEVERN D. & No 474091 Spr HARRISON K. proceeded on Leave. E	
LEBUCQUIÈRE	22.8.17		ditto	
LEBUCQUIÈRE	23.8.17		ditto. No 4/5056 Driver BROOK F.R. & No 134995 L/Cpl ATRESTER L. proceeded on Leave. E	
LEBUCQUIÈRE	24.8.17		ditto	
LEBUCQUIÈRE	25.8.17		ditto. No 474178 Cpl DENNIS K. R. proceeded on Leave E	

Army Form C. 2118.

WAR DIARY
or
INTELLIGENCE SUMMARY
(Erase heading not required.)

Sheet No 3.

Instructions regarding War Diaries and Intelligence Summaries are contained in F. S. Regs., Part II. and the Staff Manual respectively. Title pages will be prepared in manuscript.

Place	Date	Hour	Summary of Events and Information	Remarks and references to Appendices
LEBUCQUIÈRE	26-8-17		No 1 Section. Wiring Intermediate Line & sinking Well. No 2 Section. Working on Posts in Intermediate Line & making dugouts. No 3 Section. Making out dugouts. Post 29 & 28S. No 4 Section. Finishing dugouts. Posts 27, 28. No 474 Sapper Booth W. proceeded on Leave. C	M.D. Res. Sheet 57C
LEBUCQUIÈRE	27-8-17		Work same as yesterday 26th Inst. No 474 299 L/C Torset & No 474 789 2/Cpl Ropper K proceeded on Leave. C	
LEBUCQUIÈRE	28-8-17		No work owing to wet night.	
LEBUCQUIÈRE	29-8-17		Work same as on 26th Inst. No 474 338 A/2nd/Cpl Ellwood G. + No 474 208 Sapper Arundel G. Ditto proceeded on Leave. C	
LEBUCQUIÈRE	30-8-17		Ditto. No 474 068 Sapper Wickinson I. proceeded on Leave.	
LEBUCQUIÈRE	31-8-17		Ditto.	

1/9/17

M Laurence
Major R.E. G.
O.C. 529th Field Company R.E. G.

Vol 14

WAR DIARY.

For month ending 30th September 1917.

UNIT. 529th (E. Riding) Field Company R.E.

Army Form C. 2118.

WAR DIARY
or
INTELLIGENCE SUMMARY

Sheet No 1.

(Erase heading not required.)

Instructions regarding War Diaries and Intelligence Summaries are contained in F. S. Regs., Part II. and the Staff Manual respectively. Title pages will be prepared in manuscript.

Place	Date	Hour	Summary of Events and Information	Remarks and references to Appendices
LEBUCQUIERE	1.9.17		No 1 Section working in WELL at C.30.b.9.9. and wiring bottom of Intermediate Line. No 2 Section working on Posts 28 + 33 and wiring deep dugouts with M.C. Enbankment (Intermediate Line). No 3 Section work on deep dugout in POST 29 (Intermediate Line). No 4 Section work on deep dugouts in POSTS 38 + 37 (Intermediate Line). Mentioned in despatches London Gazette dated 18/5/17. No 474367 Sergt. CAPES J.S. No 474035 Sapper ASPLT GILBOY C.F.	M.V.P. Ref. Sheet 57C. FRANCE
LEBUCQUIERE	2.9.17		Work same as yesterday 1st inst: No 474346 Driver DORSEY T. + No 498118 Sapper JEFFRIES J proceeded on leave. No 474033 Sapper HODSON L.S. and No 474390 Driver KIRKHAM S.T. Proceeded on leave. Sapper Hodgson 1 months reengagement leave 1 O.R. returned to No 6 Reinforcement depot (on full to assimilate.)	(F) (F)
LEBUCQUIERE	3.9.17		─── Ditto ───	(F)
LEBUCQUIERE	4.9.17		─── Ditto ───	
LEBUCQUIERE	5.9.17		Company meeting, loading up waggons and cleaning camp etc. 1 Lieut. PALETHORPE G.M. & No 474090 Corporal WITT J.F. proceeding Leave. Handed over to 416th Army Coy RE. (56th Division) Company arrived in JUA marched to BARASTRE leaving 11.45 A.M. with transport at 10 A.M. and marched to BARASTRE via HAPLINCOURT. No 474360 Driver PARKER G.F. + No 474085 Sapper BRIERS J.W. and No 474316 Sapper HARGREAVES W proceeded on leave.	(F)
BARASTRE	7.9.17	9 am to 12.30 PM	Nos 1,2,3 + 4 Sections Squad drill + Physical Training + 7 Shrapnel Loading + Inclosing Bridle way + nozzles drill.	(F)
BARASTRE	8.9.17		Training - Morning Squad Drill + Musketry, Afternoon Military Engineering.	(F)
BARASTRE	9.9.17		Church Parade + Lecture by the O.C. No 474307 Sapper SMITH A. proceeded on leave.	(F)
BARASTRE	10.9.17		No 1 Section working in Rifle Range near BAPAUME No 2,3,4 Sections Training Musketry Engineering + drill. No 474431 Sapper NOBLE B.E. proceeded on leave.	(F)

Army Form C. 2118.

WAR DIARY
or
INTELLIGENCE SUMMARY

(Erase heading not required.)

Sheet N° 2

Instructions regarding War Diaries and Intelligence Summaries are contained in F. S. Regs., Part II. and the Staff Manual respectively. Title pages will be prepared in manuscript.

Place	Date	Hour	Summary of Events and Information	Remarks and references to Appendices
BARASTRE	11.9.17		Trainings. Drill Musketry and Building Engineering	MAP REF SH57872
BARASTRE	12.9.17		Training - do - do -	
BARASTRE	13.9.17		Training - do - do - N° 474086 Sapper CARTER J.L. proceeded on Leave E	
BARASTRE	14.9.17		Training - do - N° 474289 Sapper MOTT H.B. and N° 474317 Sapper CHARNEY proceeded on Leave	
BARASTRE	15.9.17		Training - do - N° 474224 Sapper SMITH E. proceeded on Leave E	
BARASTRE	16.9.17		Resting - N° 479308 Driver WILLIAMSON A. + N° 174 Sapper WALLER P. proceeded on Leave E	
BARASTRE	17.9.17		N° 474 365 Sapper L/C MODELL E. proceeded on Leave E	
			Bath and Company drill in Morning	
BARASTRE	18.9.17		Company paraded in Marching Order at 4.30 P.M. and proceeded to BAPAUME arriving at 6.15 P.M. ROUTE HAPLINCOURT - BANCOURT. Entrained at BAPAUME WEST. N° 474655 Sergt. Thompson W.E. + N° 142CY Sapper RIGBY R.A. proceed on Leave.	
VLAMERTINGHE	19.9.17		Arrived at GODENSVELDE 7.30 A.M. and detrained and marched to VLAMERTINGHE arriving at 4.45 P.M. Joined at H.Q. L.E. of VLAMERTINGHE. Moved off at 10.45 P.M. and E Company billeted and joined at H.Q. L.E. ROUTE BUSSEBOE, WESTOUTRE ROBENIN-HEIST E. of VLAMERTINGHE. Billeted L/C RE V CORPS TROOPS for work on NISSEN HUTS.	MAP REF Sh28 N.W. BELGIUM
VLAMERTINGHE	20.9.17		Company making School - and erecting NISSEN HUTS. N° 474483 2/C.M. MCMURDO N.B.F. + N° 47045/C. DIGSP A.E. proceeded on Leave.	
VLAMERTINGHE	21.9.17		Erecting NISSEN HUTS. 2nd Lieut. G.M. PALETHORPE returned from Leave E	
YPRES	22.9.17		Company (Company Orders) moved off at 1 P.M. to Ypres and took over work of 2" Canadian Coys. H.Q. at I.7. d.3.8. N° 470448 L/C SHAW. C. proceeded on Leave E	

Army Form C. 2118.

WAR DIARY
or
INTELLIGENCE SUMMARY
(Erase heading not required.)

Sheet No. 3.

Instructions regarding War Diaries and Intelligence Summaries are contained in F.S. Regs., Part II. and the Staff Manual respectively. Title pages will be prepared in manuscript.

Place	Date	Hour	Summary of Events and Information	Remarks and references to Appendices
YPRES	23.9.17		No. 1 Sect. work on Gullets Nos. 2, 3, & 4 Sections work on Tracks to Grown Line & sections in squares D.26 & D.27. All organisation work. Operations for the 15th September Transfer Personnel Section arrived back to Ypres G.H.Q. Section.	MAP REF Sheet 28NW (Belgium)
YPRES	24.9.17		1 Section wiring track from CAMBRIDGE ROAD to KIT KAT. 1 Section forming track from KIT KAT to ALL HOT. (Regiment) No. 474497 L/Cpl Wilkinson E. 2 sections ditto track from southside of KIT KAT to NE corner of HANNEBECK WOOD (wounded) G. Hare 1 section repairing track WIT KIT KAT WEST of LAKE FARM.	
YPRES	25.9.17		Nothing. No. 474174 7/c Timson F. proceeded on Leave	
YPRES	26.9.17		No. 1 Section detailed for work on track from D.26. d.u.s. to St. JOSEPHS INSTITUTE. Also Reserve was further into Belge Reserve & was unable to go to work. No. 3 Section detailed to make track from ZIMMEREG ROAD to MUHLE. No. 3 Section with 14 Lost Platoons 20 R.R.R.C. & unable per... At St JOSEPHS INSTITUTE. All during 30th received Heule 40. Gas Shell & compelled Cpl. & Section and reserve Brick to ... No. 4 Section with 3 Platoons 30 K.R.R.C. detailed to make track from D.27 h.g.o. got-tut - 60 of Ypres L Infantry Aid Sta. etc to working on a front of 200 x. WOUNDED Lieut C.R.S.	
YPRES	27.9.17		1 Section working on track from D. 26 4.4.5 to St JOSEPHS INSTITUTE. 1 Section working on track from KIT KAT to MUHLE. 1 Section working on BATT HQ ROGER H.Q. 1 Section working on dugouts. Bgn. started working on BRICK KILN. Enemy Gunners ... No. 474397 Sgt Coconnen T and No. 474757 L/Cpl Fish E proceeded on Leave	

Army Form C. 2118.

WAR DIARY
or
INTELLIGENCE SUMMARY   Sheet No 4.
(Erase heading not required.)

Instructions regarding War Diaries and Intelligence Summaries are contained in F. S. Regs., Part II. and the Staff Manual respectively. Title pages will be prepared in manuscript.

Place	Date	Hour	Summary of Events and Information	Remarks and references to Appendices
YPRES	28.9.17		1 Section working BATT & Bde H.Q.S. 1 Section repairing road J. 3. c. + a. 1½ Sections + 3 Platoons repairing & enlarging NORTHERN duckwalk track. Casualties. 1 O.R. and 1 O.R. wounded at duty. WOUNDED 1 O.R.	MAP REF. Sheet 28NW (Belgium)
BRANDHOEK	29.9.17		Company relieved by 11th Australian Field Coy: R.E. Company left YPRES at 4.0.P.M. and marched to camp at + track H.27.c.4.5. being intercept bombed shrapnel at night. Casualties. Killed No.4774 Sapper HARGREAVES.W. WOUNDED 3.O.R. (1 committed duty) No.474479 Sapr BRIDGE.R.A. and No. 4796187 Sapr CURTIS.T. proceeded to base.	
WINNEZEELE	30.9.17		Company moved to WINNEZEELE areas. Transport under CAPT. P. PARMENTIER left Bde. General at 12.30 P.M. and marched to New H.Q. at D.6.a.2.4 arriving 4.10 P.M. Route: + units or C.S. O1. D1. D2 (which with Lieut CORNEL PEREGRIMUS SAWYER-ISSUE) Company (dismounted section) left camp at BRANDHOEK with the 3rd Section for WITTOU - 1 units on J.12.a.8. and arrived camp 5.0.P.M. Same route as Transport. Belleface via France.	MAP REF Sheet 27 (Belgium and France)

A. Bawarah Capt R.E. 4th
Jnr Major D.A. 329 (Army) J.K. 32
R.E. (1)

Army Form C.2118.

WAR DIARY
or
INTELLIGENCE SUMMARY

(Erase heading not required.)

529TH (E. RIDING) FIELD COMPANY, R.E.

Date: October 1917

Vol 15

Place	Date	Hour	Summary of Events and Information	Remarks and references to Appendices
WINNEZEELE	1-10-17		Completion of ammunition & kit. Company ready. W. 47467 & M. Petterson C.4. brought to base.	MAP REF Sheet 31 (Belgium & Part 2) J.6.a.07
— do —	2-10-17		Section order. Physical exercises. Bayonet parade.	
— do —	3/10/17		Company attended Ceremonial Parade of 76 & 77 & 78 & 130. Children by G.O.C. 3rd Division.	
— do —	4/10/17	9.30 am	Transport moved to entrain Lieut WHITEWAY & journal 8 O.R. & 1 Cob Group marched to ARQUES (S.10.a.3.9) VIA HARDIFORT, WISMAERS-CAPPEL & LES TROIS ROIS.	
		12.30 p	Dismounted Personnel marched off from 78 & 4 R.E. Group entrained.	
			ARQUES via CASSEL & BAVINGHOVE.	
		5.30 p	Transport arrived.	
		9.0 p	Bivouacked better arrival. Very wet day. Billeted for night under canvas.	
MALHOVE	5/10/17	8.0 pm	Company & Transport moved off. 13 entrained WIZERNES for BAPAUME.	
		10.15 p	Arrived WIZERNES & troops at hand for train. All wagons & animals entrained in 45 minutes.	
WIZERNES	6/10/17	1.44 a	Train left for BAPAUME.	
BAPAUME	6/10/17	12 midday	Train arrived at 13 BAPAUME. Raining hard. Marched to BARASTRE. Camp at O.16.c.2.7. Very cold night.	MAP REF Sheet 57.C

WAR DIARY of INTELLIGENCE SUMMARY

Army Form C.2118.

529th (E. Lancs) F.Coy R.E.

October 1917 Sheet No. 2

(Erase heading not required.)

Instructions regarding War Diaries and Intelligence Summaries are contained in F. S. Regs., Part II. and the Staff Manual respectively. Title pages will be prepared in manuscript.

Place	Date	Hour	Summary of Events and Information	Remarks and references to Appendices
BARASTRE	7/10/17		Very wet windy weather. Church parade cancelled.	Map Ref. Sheet 57^d
— do —	8/10/17	9 am	Section Drill	
		11.30 am	Camouflage of horse standings near BARASTRE	
		4 pm	Lecture R.E. & Corps Troops	
— do —	9/10/17	8 am	Advance Party under BRODIE & PALETHORPE & L.Cpl. STRONELL to FAVREUIL H.16.d.3.6 & 10 an-to 13 aug. put. on road near ECOUST C.8.a.2.3 to take over work from 468 & 74 Coy R.E. 6th Division.	
		9 am 10/12 midday	Section Drill + Physical Training ?	
— do —	10/10/17	9.30 am	Company moved up to take over Billets at FAVREUIL H.16.d.3.6 from 468 & 74 Coy R.E. Very good billets & Hutch.	
FAVREUIL	11/10/17	5 pm	Los 1 & 3 Sections moved up to forward billets near ECOUST C.8.a.2.3 work to be carried out by 3 sections as ECOUST H.Q. impracticable owing to company pleased under Orders of G.O.C. 7th R.A. Bde for work.	Forest good November water
FAVREUIL			No 1 Section making small break lodge for light Railway in Sulgrave Avenue C.7. No 2 Section working on Gordon Support and Chimp Line. No 3 Section working on Tower Support & Tower Redoubt. No 4 Section working. Parties on ? ? bullets and Dug-outs R	

Army Form C. 2118.

WAR DIARY
or
INTELLIGENCE SUMMARY
(Erase heading not required.)

Instructions regarding War Diaries and Intelligence Summaries are contained in F. S. Regs., Part II. and the Staff Manual respectively. Title pages will be prepared in manuscript.

Unit No ...

Place	Date	Hour	Summary of Events and Information	Remarks and references to Appendices
ECOUST	12-10-17		N° 1 Section working on Trestle Bridge for Light Railway over BULLECOURT AVENUE O.T.	
			N° 2 Section working on CORDON BLANCAT and CHINA LANE	
			N° 3 Section working on MADE LANE and SUNKEN ROAD O.T.	
			N° 4 Section working - improving road bullets	
ECOUST	13-10-17		Work same as yesterday 12 inst.	
ECOUST	14-10-17		Ditto	
ECOUST	15-10-17		Ditto	
ECOUST	16-10-17		N° 1 Section relieved N° 1 Section	
			N° 2 Section. On fatigues, resting	
			N° 3 Section working on CHINA LANE	
			N° 3 Section working on CORDON LANE, MADE LANE, and Trestle Railway maintenance of BULLECOURT AVENUE O.T.	
			N° 4 Section working on Sunken - Ecoust road - Spring - Arnings	
ECOUST	17-10-17		Work same as yesterday 16th inst.	
ECOUST	18-10-17		Ditto	
			Lieut R.V. TAYLOR attached permanent R.E.A.	
ECOUST	19-10-17		Ditto	
ECOUST	20-10-17		Ditto	
			N° 1 Section relieved N° 2 Section	

Army Form C. 2118.

WAR DIARY
or
INTELLIGENCE SUMMARY.
(Erase heading not required.)

Instructions regarding War Diaries and Intelligence Summaries are contained in F. S. Regs., Part II. and the Staff Manual respectively. Title pages will be prepared in manuscript.

Place	Date	Hour	Summary of Events and Information	Remarks and references to Appendices
ECOUST	21-10-17		No 1 Section Training and mining. CHINA LANE and mouth of BULLECOURT AVENUE Ext.	Map Ref. 51c.J-51.O
			No 2 & 4 " Repairing Roads & Dugouts	
			No 3 " "	
			No 4 Section Repairing and upkeep CAUCHY LANE, DARE LANE, and Front Trenches.	
ECOUST	22-10-17		No 4 Section Ropes to Dugouts ECOUST ROAD	Different
			Work done as yesterday. Ditto.	
ECOUST	23-10-17		Ditto	
ECOUST	24-10-17		Ditto	
ECOUST	25-10-17		Ditto	
ECOUST	26-10-17		No 1 Section Mined No 3 Leitrim	
			No 1 Section Familying and working CHINA LANE and maintenance of BULLECOURT AVENUE	
			No 2 Leitrim Ditto	
			No 3 Section Revetting DARE LANE Sunken Lanes and Tank Railway Dumps	
			No 4 " Repairs to ECOUST ROAD	
ECOUST	27-10-17		Work done Repairing 81" "MIX" ECOUST ROAD	
ECOUST	28-10-17		Ditto	
ECOUST	29-10-17		Ditto	
ECOUST	30-10-17		No 3 Section Relieved by No 1 Canadian	
ECOUST	31-10-17		No 1 Section Training and mouthing CHINA LANE	
			No 2 Section Familying and mouthing MARE LANE, CAUCHY LANE, and Front Trenches maintenance	
			No 3 Section Repairs to Dugouts - ECOUST ROAD	
			New Section Raw Recruits	Officer Commanding No 1 Company
				1st November 1917. For Major O.C. 529th Field Co R.E.M.

WAR DIARY. For month ending 30th November 1917.

UNIT. 529th (E. Riding) Field Company. R.E.

WAR DIARY
or
INTELLIGENCE SUMMARY

Army Form C. 2118.

(Erase heading not required.)

Place	Date	Hour	Summary of Events and Information	Remarks and references to Appendices
ECOUST	1-11-17	No 1 Section	Training and rectifying CHINA LANE + programme of BULLECOURT AVENUE	MAP REF. Sheet 57.C. Bullecourt and Mt BULLECOURT
		No 2 Section	Training and wiring MARE LANE + CRUCIFIX LANE + extending 1 Brick Trench	
		No 3 Section	Repair to SUNKEN - ECOUST TRACK - Mt & support to ATHYORPS RANGE B	
		No 4 Section	Back Billets	
BIEFVILLERS	2-11-17		Work same as yesterday reliefs	
ECOUST	3-11-17		ditto	
ECOUST	4-11-17		ditto	
ECOUST	5-11-17	No 4 Section relieved No 1 Section Back Billets		
		No 1 Section	O.R. working party (Support + repair)	
		No 2 Section	Training and wiring MARE LANE + CRUCIFIX LANE	
		No 3 Section	Repair to SUNKEN BULLECOURT AVE	
		No 4 Section	Training and wiring SUNKEN LANE	Mt B. Support + SUNKEN Support and wire Sunken Track ahead
ECOUST	6-11-17		Work same as yesterday 5th Each	
	7-11-17		ditto	
	8-11-17		ditto	
ECOUST	9-11-17		No 1 Section relieved No 2 Section	
ECOUST	10-11-17	No 1 Section	Training + wiring MARE LANE road Town Buffets	Casualties
		No 2 Section	Back Billets (15.O.R. on Bieuvillers field cable)	wounded 1 O.R.
		No 3 Section	Repairs to ECOUST - BULLECOURT road	
		No 4 Section	Training + wiring OSTRICH AVE on STRONGE REDOUBT + right half of BULLECOURT AVE	
ECOUST	11-11-17		ditto	
ECOUST	12-11-17		ditto	
ECOUST	13-11-17		ditto	
ECOUST	14-11-17		No 2 Section relieved No 3 Section	

Army Form C. 2118.

WAR DIARY
or
INTELLIGENCE SUMMARY.
(Erase heading not required.)

Sheet No. 2.

Instructions regarding War Diaries and Intelligence Summaries are contained in F. S. Regs., Part II. and the Staff Manual respectively. Title pages will be prepared in manuscript.

Place	Date	Hour	Summary of Events and Information	Remarks and references to Appendices
ECOUST	15-11-17		No 1 Section Erecting and mending Tower Support & Trench Tramway maintenance	Wind & rain
			No 2 Section Erecting and repairing Gordon Support	Strong wind
			No 3 Section. Bush Billets.	Cold & dull
			No 4 Section Erecting and mending CHINA LANE Supports.	Wind & rain
			REINFORCEMENTS 1 O.R. from R.E. CASUALS	Bullecourt
ECOUST	16-11-17		No 1, 3, & 4 Sections same as yesterday	
			No 2 Section mending Gordon Support and mending R.A.P at HACKNEY MARSHES. C	
ECOUST	17-11-17		No 4 same as yesterday 16 Nov.	
ECOUST	18-11-17		No 1 Section Repairing Dugout and clearing MARE LANE	
			No 2 Section Cleaning CHINA LANE and Gorbes. R.A.P. at HACKNEY MARSHES.	
			No 3 Section Bush Billets	
			No 4 Section Burying CHINA LANE	
			No 3 Section above No 4 Section	
ECOUST	19-11-17		Sections resting.	
ECOUST	20-11-17		No 4 Section Standing by for orders from 7th Inf Brigade	
			Nos 1, 2, & 3 Section cleaning Ecoust – Bullecourt road.	
ECOUST	21-11-17		Same as yesterday 20 Nov.	Bullecourt visit of observers of Ecoucourt (rifle-marsh)
ECOUST	22-11-17		Nos 1, 2, & 3 Sections cleaning road from BULLECOURT Church to Boy-Line trenches.	
ECOUST	23-11-17		No 4 Section same as yesterday.	
			Same as yesterday. C	
ECOUST	24-11-17		Work done as 23 Nov. from Railway Reserve Park to ECOUST	
			CASUALTIES: WOUNDED No 474814 Corpl. GREENWOOD. F	

WAR DIARY
or
INTELLIGENCE SUMMARY.

(Erase heading not required.)

Army Form C. 2118.

Instructions regarding War Diaries and Intelligence Summaries are contained in F. S. Regs., Part II. and the Staff Manual respectively. Title pages will be prepared in manuscript.

Place	Date	Hour	Summary of Events and Information	Remarks and references to Appendices
Ecoust	25-11-17		Billets resting.	Map Ref. France Sheet 57c edition 3A of Bullecourt
Ecoust 57c	26-11-17		Do.	
Ecoust	27-11-17		No. 1 Section cleaning & burying spoil-lane and Gordon support. No. 2 Section Repairing to Ecoust & Bucquoi road. No. 3 Section Clearing & repairing Mireltake Crucifix-Lane. No. 4 Section Stock Bullets. Advance MG 1 Section	
Ecoust	28-11-17		No. 1 Section Stock Bullets. No. 2 Section Repairs to Lagnicourt Ecoust road. No. 3 Section Clearing Mire Lane and clearing Fork Lane. No. 4 Section Clearing Gordon support and Gordon Ave Cuthbert Ave and clearing and widening Fokker Lane.	
Ecoust	29-11-17		Nos. 1, 2, 3, 4 Sections Same as yesterday. No. 3 Section clearing Marconer and Joy Ride support.	
Ecoust	30-11-17		Nos. 1, 2, & 3 Sections same as 29th Nov. No. 3 Section clearing Mire Lane &c.	

1st December 1917

P Keith Granville Major R.E. for Major O.C. 2/1st F. & C 1st R.E. T.F.

WAR DIARY.

For month ending 31st December 1917.

UNIT. 529th (E. Riding) Field Company R.E.

Army Form C. 2118.

WAR DIARY
or
INTELLIGENCE SUMMARY.
(Erase heading not required.)

Sheet No 1.

Instructions regarding War Diaries and Intelligence Summaries are contained in F.S. Regs., Part II. and the Staff Manual respectively. Title pages will be prepared in manuscript.

Place	Date	Hour	Summary of Events and Information	Remarks and references to Appendices
Ecoust	1-12-17		No 1 Section Bath Billets. No 2 Section Return to Ecoust - Suzanne road. No 3 Section Maintenance of Maze Lane - Truck support and widening New Pelican Avenue. No 4 Section Clearing and widening China Lane (Gordon Support) and widening Saddle Lane.	Map Ref: France Shut 57B and Shut 57C Bullecourt
Ecoust	2-12-17		Work carried out yesterday by No 1 No 1 Section relieved No 2 Section.	
Ecoust	3-12-17		No 1 Section Repairs to Dugout - Suzanne road. No 2 Sitting. Bath Billets. No 3 Section Maintenance of Maze Lane + Truck Support + widening New Pelican Avenue. ongoing on Stanhope Redoubt No 4 Section Maintenance of Garden Support + China Lane widening New Pelican Avenue with Lane, and Carry dugout in Bovis Kraal	C
Ecoust	4-12-17		Work same as yesterday.	C
Ecoust	5-11-17		Ditto	C
Ecoust	6-12-17		Ditto	C
Ecoust	7-12-17		Ditto	
Ecoust	8-12-17		No 1 & 2 Section relieved No 3 Section. No 1 Section Return to Ecoust - Suzanne road. No 2 Section Maintenance Maze Lane and Truck Supplies forming New Pelican Avenue. work on dugouts Stanhope Redoubt. No 3 Section Bath Billets. No 4 Section Work on Garden Support, China Lane, Saddle Lane and dugouts in Bovis Trench.	C
Ecoust	9-12-17		Work same as yesterday	C

Army Form C. 2118.

WAR DIARY
or
INTELLIGENCE SUMMARY.

(Erase heading not required.)

Skel- N° 2

Place	Date	Hour	Summary of Events and Information	Remarks and references to Appendices
ECOUST.	10-12-17		N° 1 Section. Repairs to ECOUST - LUCERIS road. N° 2 Section. Work on MAELANE, TOWER SUPPORT, BULLECOURT AVENUE, NEW PELICAN AVENUE, and dugout in STANHOPE REDOUBT. N° 3 Section. Back billets. N° 4 Section. Work on GORDON SUPPORT, CHINA LANE, SADDLER LANE, NEW FOX TROT m.m. junction on BOYS TRENCH.	MAP REF GRENAY 57 c
ECOUST.	11-12-17		W/k. Carrd on as yesterday.	
ECOUST.	12-12-17		Company stood to on Early Warning from 6.15 a.m to 8 a.m Enemy put down b.g.a.m - 7.30 a.m on Stanhope Company stood to on Early Warning from 6.15 a.m to 8 a.m CASUALTIES. WOUNDED LIEUT F.W. FALCONER M.C. (2nd Lieut GIBSON TURNER and others HARRINGTON. H. N° 3 Section wounded, N° 4 section	
ECOUST.	13-12-17		N° 1 Section, repairs to ECOUST - LUCER 15 road. N° 2 Section, work on New Pelican Ave: Tower Support, MacELANE + dugout in STANHOPE redoubt. N° 3 Section. Work on GORDON SUPPORT, CHINA LANE, SADDLER LANE + Trench Tramway. N° 4 Section Back billets. CASUALTIES WOUNDED. I.O.R.	
ECOUST.	14-12-17		Work same as yesterday.	
ECOUST.	15-12-17		Ditto. H.Q. + transport moved to new near billet at MORY. B.22.b.2.6.	
ECOUST.	16-12-17		Work same as on 13th inst.	

Army Form C. 2118.

WAR DIARY
or
INTELLIGENCE SUMMARY
(Erase heading not required.)

No. Sheet No 3

Instructions regarding War Diaries and Intelligence Summaries are contained in F. S. Regs., Part II. and the Staff Manual respectively. Title pages will be prepared in manuscript.

Place	Date	Hour	Summary of Events and Information	Remarks and references to Appendices
ECOUST.	17-12-17.		No 1 Section. Repairs to Ecoust-Bullecourt Rd. No 2 Section. Work on Pelican Avenue, Tower Support, Swan Lane, & Dugout in STANHOPE REDOUBT. No 3 Section. Work in Gordon Support, China Lane, Saddler Lane & Tunnel Tramway maintenance. No 4 Section. Back Billets. C. No 4 Section relieved No 1 Section. C.	Sheet 57C (FRANCE) and Trench Map of Bullecourt.
ECOUST.	18-12-17.		Work same as yesterday 17th inst. C.	
ECOUST.	19-12-17.		Ditto. CASUALTY. Wounded. Lieut. BRODIE. J. REINFORCEMENT. 2nd Lieut. MULLER H.F. and 7 O.R. from Base Rouen.	
ECOUST.	20-12-17.		Ditto. C.	
ECOUST.	21-12-17.		Ditto. C.	
ECOUST.	22-12-17.		Ditto. C.	
ECOUST.	23-12-17.		No 1 Section relieves No 2 Section. No 1 Section. Dugout in STANHOPE REDOUBT, and Dugouts in Billets, maintenance of BULLECOURT AVE. No 2 Section. Back Billets. No 3 Section. Putting GORDON and LONDON Supports and SADDLER LANE, framing dugout No 161. No 4 Section. 3 wiring gun curtains, maintenance of trial tramway. C.	
ECOUST.	24-12-17.		Work same as yesterday 23rd inst. C.	
ECOUST.	25-12-17.		No work. Company resting. REINFORCEMENT. 2nd Lieut. CHAPMAN F.W. Base Rouen.	
ECOUST.	26-12-17.		Work same as on 23rd inst. Officers from 231st Field Coy 40th Division, came to take over work in the Line and all billets.	

WAR DIARY
or
INTELLIGENCE SUMMARY

Army Form C. 2118.

Sheet N° 4.

(Erase heading not required.)

Place	Date	Hour	Summary of Events and Information	Remarks and references to Appendices
HAMELINCOURT	27-12-17.		N°s 1, 3 & 4 Sections moved up from forward billets to rear billets. Company paraded for Deft billets at HAMELINCOURT. March off 11-35 A.M. (route ERVILLERS). Line to B 31st Field Coy R.E. ☙	MAP REF: LENS 11.
HAMELINCOURT	28-12-17.		9.30 A.M. Inspection of Arms, ammunition, Clothing etc. N° 2 Section proceeded to HENDICOURT-LES-RANSART to note on camps of 76th Inf: Brigade. N° 1 Section work in camp and Labs at MOYENNVILLE. N°s 2 & 3 Sections section drill, Musketry, Hygiene & Reconnect Training. ☙	
HAMELINCOURT	29-12-17.		MASTER R.D.M. H. HALL M.C. proceeded on leave to U.K. ☙	
HAMELINCOURT	30-12-17.		Same as yesterday 29th instt. ditto	
HAMELINCOURT	31-12-17.			

1st January 1918.

Chilch Cranwich, Capt R.E. Co.
for Major O.C. 529th Field Coy R.E. 91.

3rd Division

Wm Dranan

529th East Riding Field Coy.

~~January 1st to 31st December~~

~~1918~~

1918 JAN. — 1919 SEP

War Diary.

For month ending 31st January 1918.

Unit. 529th East Riding Field Company R.E.

Army Form C. 2118.

WAR DIARY
or
INTELLIGENCE SUMMARY.
(Erase heading not required.)

Sheet No. 1.

Instructions regarding War Diaries and Intelligence Summaries are contained in F. S. Regs., Part II. and the Staff Manual respectively. Title pages will be prepared in manuscript.

Place	Date	Hour	Summary of Events and Information	Remarks and references to Appendices
HAMELINCOURT	1-1-18		Company Muster. 12-noon. Reinforcements & O.R. rejoined Base depot	MAP REF LENS II
HAMELINCOURT	2-1-18		No 1 Platoon - Route march	
			No 2 Platoon - at Headquarters - bathing	
			No 3 & 4 Platoon - Training & Organisation of Company	
			Base reinforcements 2 O.R.	
HAMELINCOURT	3-1-18		Ditto	
HAMELINCOURT	4-1-18		Ditto	
HAMELINCOURT	5-1-18		Ditto	
HAMELINCOURT	6-1-18		Company Training	
HAMELINCOURT	7-1-18		Company Training	
			No 1 & 2 Platoons Training	
			No 3 & 4 Platoons Lectures. Lewis Gun & Gas. No Men Sick Reinforcements	
HAMELINCOURT	8-1-18		Ditto 2 O.R.	
HAMELINCOURT	9-1-18		Ditto	
HAMELINCOURT	10-1-18		Ditto	
HAMELINCOURT	11-1-18		Ditto	
HAMELINCOURT	12-1-18		Battalion paraded & marched to Ransart	
HAMELINCOURT	13-1-18		Battalion marched to Berles-au-Bois Reinforcements	
			1 NCO 2 O.R.	

Army Form C. 2118.

SHEET No 2.

WAR DIARY
or
INTELLIGENCE SUMMARY.
(Erase heading not required.)

Instructions regarding War Diaries and Intelligence Summaries are contained in F.S. Regs., Part II. and the Staff Manual respectively. Title pages will be prepared in manuscript.

Place	Date	Hour	Summary of Events and Information	Remarks and references to Appendices
HAMELINCOURT	14/1/18		Nos 1 2 & 4 Sections training & recreational training. No 3. Working at Div. H.Q. "2/Lt H.F. MILLER attached R.F.A. MA	MAP REF LENS. II.
— do —	15/1/18		Nos. Do Do Reversions on ceding	
			ranks. No 474410 A/Cpl. G.W. BULLOCK to be ¾ Cpl from 29-12-17. No 474 G/G A/Cpl. L.G. PETRIE to be L/Cpl.	
			as from 29-12-17. ESTABLISHMENT. No 474,214 Cpl. F. GREENWOOD is absorbed vice ¾Cpl. G.W. BULLOCK 29-12-17	
			PROMOTIONS. L/Cpl. (vp) A. RACKLEY. to be L/Cpl (paid) as from 11-1-18. 2/Lt R.W. TAYLOR returned from R.F.A. MA	
— do —	16/1/18		Nos 1, 2, 3 & 4 Sections same as 15th. MA	
— do —	17/1/18		Nos 1, 2 & 4 Sections. Work on camp improvements. No 3 Section working at Div. H.Q. MA	
— do —	18/1/18		Nos 2, 3 & 4 Sections — do — No 1. Section — do — MA	
— do —	19/1/18		— do — — do — MA	
— do —	20/1/18		Company parade (less No 1. Section) Inspection. No 1 Section work at Div. H.Q. Church Parade 4 pm.	
			No 241759 Sapp. HOLLAND C. admitted to hospital. Capt. GRANSWICK attached for course at M MA	
			R.E. School of instruction at BLENDECQUES	
— do —	21/1/18		All sections parade for work. camp improvements. MA	
— do —	22/1/18		— do — — do — MA	
— do —	23/1/18		AWARDS:- No 474,447. Sapp. HEPWORTH. E.	
			14 days F P No 1. ("Insolence to an Officer") No 474296 Dr WILLIS. Forfeits 4 days pay & 2 days pay under R W MA	
			4 O.R. Joined Company as reinforcements. No 522839 Sapp. James H.G. to hospital. (absent without leave) MA	
— do —	24/1/18		Nos 1, 3 & 4 Sections parade for work. Camp improvements. No 2. Section. Working at Div. H.Q. MA	

A.S.834 Wt.W4973/M687 750,000 8/16 D.D. & L. Ltd. Forms/C.2118/13.

Army Form C. 2118.

WAR DIARY
or
INTELLIGENCE SUMMARY.
(Erase heading not required.)

SHEET N° 5

Instructions regarding War Diaries and Intelligence Summaries are contained in F. S. Regs., Part II. and the Staff Manual respectively. Title pages will be prepared in manuscript.

Place	Date	Hour	Summary of Events and Information	Remarks and references to Appendices
HAMELINCOURT	25/1/18		All sections parade for work. Camp improvements. N° 474409 Sapp. STAINFORTH G.A. admitted to hospital. MH	MAP REF LENS 11
— do —	26/1/18		N° 225796. A/cp/Lce/Cpl. CLARKE.S.L. reestablishd appn HS do	
— do —	27/1/18		Company parade. Inspection. MH	
— do —	28/1/18	9.30 a.m.	Company moved forward to BOIRY – BECQUERELLE. Route via BOYELLES. Very good billets and stables. MAP REF: T11 C 56. 2 p.m. N°s 2,3 & 4 Sections moved up to forward fields near WANCOURT N.22.c.9.5. (SHEET 51B S.W.) Poor billets. Work to be carried out by 3 sections forward of lat BOIRY - BECQUERELLE, under White Company parised under orders for Nos 4 & 5 Inf Bde. In work. MH	
BOIRY – BECQUERELLE	29/1/18		N° 2 Section cleaning & revetting SHIKA AVENUE. N° 5 Section deepening out in KEY'S SUPPORT N° 4 Section deepening out in EGRET trench. N° 1 Section resting. MH	
WANCOURT	30/1/18		Same as 29th inst. MH	
— do —	31/1/18		Same as 30th inst. MH	

During the month 1 Officer and 41 O.R. proceeded on leave to U.K. 99

1st February 1918

MKirkwood Lt R.E (H)
for Major O.C. 529 (32) Ltd 30 RE

529 M Coy
9/7/19

War Diary

For month ending 28th February 1918.

Unit 529th (East Riding) Field Company R.E.

Army Form C. 2118.

WAR DIARY
or
INTELLIGENCE SUMMARY.
(Erase heading not required.)

SHEET No. 1.

Instructions regarding War Diaries and Intelligence Summaries are contained in F.S. Regs., Part II. and the Staff Manual respectively. Title pages will be prepared in manuscript.

Place	Date	Hour	Summary of Events and Information	Remarks and references to Appendices
WANCOURT	1 2/18		No 2 Section clearing and revetting SHIKAR AVENUE No 5 Section deep dug-out in KEY RESERVE. No 4 Section deep dug out in EGRET TRENCH. No 1 Section resting. REWARDS - 474082 Sgt. SHIELDS H. Belgian Croix de Guerre (Routine Orders by 4.D.D. 3rd Div. 20/1/18) K.R.	MAP REF. LENS II
— do —	2 2/18		No 2 Section clearing and revetting SHIKA AVENUE No 5 Section deep dug out in KEY RESERVE and clearing & revetting SOUTHERN AV. No 4 Section deep dug out in EGRET TRENCH. No 1 Section resting. No 1 Section moved forward to where No 2. K.R.	
— do —	3 2/18		No 1 Section clearing and revetting SHIKA AVENUE. Nos 3 & 4 same as 2nd inst. No 2 resting K.R.	
— do —	4 2/18		Nos 1, 3 & 4 Sections. Dug out in EGRET TRENCH. Revetting EGRET TRENCH, SHIKAR AV. & LION TRENCH & SOUTHERN AV. Dug out in KEY RESERVE. Repair b'road N22a. K.R. No 2. resting	
— do —	5 2/18		Nos 1, 3 & 4 Sections work same as 4th. No 2 Section resting. K.R.	
— do —	6 2/18		Nos 1, 3 & 4 Sections work same as 5th. No 2 Section resting. K.R.	
— do —	7 2/18		Nos 1, 3 & 4 Sections work same as 6th. No 2 Section resting. No 2 moved forward relieved No 3. K.R.	
— do —	8 2/18		Nos 1, 2 & 4 Sections work same as 7th. No 3 Section resting. K.R.	
— do —	9 2/18		Nos 1, 2 & 4 Sections work same as 8th. No 3 Section resting. K.R.	
— do —	10 2/18		Nos 1, 2 & 4 Sections work same as 9th. No 3 Section resting. K.R.	
— do —	11 2/18		Nos 1, 2 & 4 Sections work same as 10th. No 3 Section resting. K.R.	

Army Form C. 2118.

WAR DIARY or INTELLIGENCE SUMMARY.

(Erase heading not required.)

SHEET N°. 2.

Instructions regarding War Diaries and Intelligence Summaries are contained in F. S. Regs., Part II. and the Staff Manual respectively. Title pages will be prepared in manuscript.

Place	Date	Hour	Summary of Events and Information	Remarks and references to Appendices
WANCOURT	12/2/18		N°s 1,2 & 4 sections. Dug out in EGRET TRENCH. Revetting EGRET TRENCH, SHIKAR AV.	MAP REF LENS 11.
			LION TRENCH & SOUTHERN AV. DUG OUT IN KEY RESERVE. Repairs to road N22A.	
—do—	13/2/18		N° 3 section resting. N° 5 section moved forward, relieved N° 4. HX	
—do—	14/2/18		N°s 1,2 & 5 sections work same as 12th. N° 4 section resting. HX	
—do—	15/2/18		N°s 1,2 & 5 sections Dug out EGRET TRENCH. Revetting SHIKAR AV. & SOUTHERN AV. Dug out in KEY RESERVE. Repairs to road N22A. N° 4 section resting. HX	
—do—	16/2/18		N°s 1, 2 & 3 sections work same as 14th also using Willey pledge at N22a31. N°4 section resting. HX	HX
—do—	17/2/18		N°s 1, 2 & 3 sections — do —	
—do—	18/2/18		N°s 1, 2 & 3 sections Dug out in EGRET TRENCH. Revetting SHIKAR AV & SOUTHERN AV. Dug out in	
			KEY RESERVE. Repairs to road at N22A. Shelter to M.G.C. HQ. O.P. SHOVEL TRENCH. N°4 section on N°1. HX	
—do—	19/2/18		N°s 2,3 & 4 sections work same as 17th. N°1 section resting. HX (i.k.k. C.G.Funnell rummed to hospital) HX	
—do—	20/2/18		— do — HX	
—do—	21/2/18		— do — HX	
—do—	22/2/18		— do — HX	
—do—	23/2/18		— do — N°1 section relieved N°2. HX	
—do—	24/2/18		N°2 section resting — do —	KEY RESERVE HX
—do—	25/2/18		N°s 1,3 & 4 sections. Dug out in EGRET TRENCH. Revetting SHIKAR AV. Dug out in SHOVEL TR. O.P. HX	SHOVEL TR. O.P. HX
—do—			Repairs to road N22A. Shelter M.G.C. HQ. Dam at COJEUL RIVER N°2 section resting HX	
—do—	26/2/18		N°s 1,3 & 4 sections. Dug out in EGRET TRENCH. Revetting EGRET TRENCH & SOUTHERN AV. Dug out KEY RESERVE	KEY RESERVE
			Repairs to road WANCOURT. Shelter M.G.C.HQ. N°2 section resting HX.	

Army Form C. 2118.

WAR DIARY
or
INTELLIGENCE SUMMARY.
(Erase heading not required.)

SHEET N° 3

Instructions regarding War Diaries and Intelligence Summaries are contained in F. S. Regs., Part II. and the Staff Manual respectively. Title pages will be prepared in manuscript.

Place	Date	Hour	Summary of Events and Information	Remarks and references to Appendices
WANCOURT	27/3/18		N°s 1.3 & 4 sections. Dug outs in EGRET TRENCH. Ravening EGRET TRENCH & SOUTHERN AVENUE. Dug out KEY RESERVE. Repairs to road WANCOURT. Sheen M.G.C. H.Q. Dam across COJEUL RIVER. N° 2 Section relieved N° 3.	MAP REF LENS II.
do	28/3/18		N°s 1, 2 & 4 sections ——— do ——— N° 3 Section resting.	
			During the month 2 Officers & 26 O.R. proceeded on leave to U.K.	

Killican
Major R.E.
O.C. 529th (E. Riding) F.C.C. R.E.

3rd Divisional Engineers

529th (East Riding) FIELD COMPANY R.E.

MARCH 1918

Name Dranil

For month ending 31st March 1918

Unit. 529th (East Riding) Field Company R.E.

Army Form C. 2118.

WAR DIARY
or
INTELLIGENCE SUMMARY
(Erase heading not required.)

Instructions regarding War Diaries and Intelligence Summaries are contained in F. S. Regs., Part II. and the Staff Manual respectively. Title pages will be prepared in manuscript.

Sheet No. 1.

Place	Date	Hour	Summary of Events and Information	Remarks and references to Appendices
NAMPCOURT	1-3-18		Nos 1, 2 and 4 Sections work in trench area No 3 Section resting	Major R.E.F.J. Sgt-M.2.d.w 2nd Lens H.
do	2-3-18		do	
do	3-3-18		do	
do	4-3-18		do	
do	5-3-18		Nos 1, 2 & 3 Sections work in trench area No 4 Section resting	
do	6-3-18		do	
do	7-3-18		do	
do	8-3-18		do	
do	9-3-18		do	
do	10-3-18		Nos 2, 3 & 4 Sections work in trench area, No 1 Section resting	
do	11-3-18		do	
do	12-3-18		do	
do	13-3-18		Moved forward Sections from H.23.a.6. Sr to Auger Trench Cutting at M.23.a.54. No. 1 Coy. Aux on 10½ in Ry	
do	14-3-18		ditto	
do	15-3-18		Nos 3 and 4 Sections work in trench area No 1 & 2 Sections resting	
do	16-3-18		do	
do	17-3-18		do	
do	18-3-18		do	
do	19-3-18		do	
do	20-3-18		Nos 1 and 2 Sections work in trench area Nos 3 & 4 Sections resting. Capt. P. Cranswick returned from leave.	
do	21-3-18		Nos 1 & 2 Sections work in forward area, No 3 & 4 Sections resting	
do	22-3-18		Nos 1 & 2 Sections in PARCLET. Enemy attacked H.R. and near Rest 9½" Mine Co-opera front at 1 r.e. P.M. Transport moved to M.73.d. 90.70 3 Section moved to hatch near Beaurains- Mercatel. Max. E. No. 3 & 4 Sections dug a trench at M.23.a. No. E. 14 Mercatel. Lt. & Lieut. H.F. Miller proceeded on leave to U.K.	

WAR DIARY
or
INTELLIGENCE SUMMARY
(Erase heading not required.)

Army Form C. 2118.

Place	Date	Hour	Summary of Events and Information	Remarks and references to Appendices
WAILLY	25-3-18		Nos 1 and 2 Sections joined H.Q. and 3 & 4 Sections at Dunbar near BEAUFAINS – MERCATEL. H.Q. and Transport moved off from BEAUFAINS on MS3C at 7.30 a.m. and arrived WAILLY 9.30 a.m. Sections joined H.Q. from bivouacs in M28B. at 11.30 a.m. and arrived WAILLY at 10.30 a.m. Company bivouaced in huts at R.23.a.9.3. South of WAILLY.	War Diary Sept. II. Mart. C.
WAILLY	26-3-18		Company out working on PURPLE Defence Line.	
WAILLY	25-3-18		do	
do	26-3-18		do	
do	27-3-18		do Main refuge of SANDRIN Comp. for M.G. and Arty. at LAHERLIERE	
			2nd Lieut. H.F. MILLER joined Company. U.K. leave cancelled	
GROSVILLE	28-3-18		Company working on PURPLE Defence Line. Transport lines shelled at WAILLY 6 roads Ballast, 5 wounded. Move to R.23.s central (GROSVILLE) at 2.0 P.M. Company arrived billets near the Purple line along with remainder of Div. R.E. and Pioneers, north of pavilion at 2.0 P.M.	
			CASUALTIES: Killed No. 474499 Sapper BRIDGER. A; No. 247284 Sapper THOMPSON. W; No. 7056 Driver Wounded 474072 Driver ALLENBY, 474348 Driver WOODS. PARKER C.P.; No 474[?]581 Driver ROBINSON G.H.P. No 0474468 B & C. $QUIRE M.A. Concussion. No 478816 Driver BROCK. R. No 474518 Driver MARKHAM. E.	
Gouy-En-Artois	29-3-18		Company relieved in Purple Line by Canadians and moved back to GROSVILLE arriving 7-0 A.M. 6.15 P.M. Company moved to MENCHIET. route – BEAUMETZ – 10-0 P.M. Company moved to Gouy-En-Artois arriving 11-0 P.M.	
OPPY	30-3-18		3.30 P.M. Company moved to OPPY arriving 7.30 P.M. Route. FOSSEUX – BARLY – SOMERIN – BUS- -ST-LEGER – BEAUVOISCOURT.	
OPPY	31-3-18		Kit inspection and Church Parade. Bridging waggons went to LAHERLIERE to fetch Bridging equipments	

1/4/18
O.C. 529 Fd Co. R.E.

3rd Divisional Engineers

WAR DIARY

529th (~~WEST~~ EAST RIDING) FIELD COMPANY R.E.

APRIL 1918

529 4a Coy
Vol 21

War Diary.

For month ending 30th April 1918.

Unit   529 (East Riding) Field Co. R.E.

Army Form C. 2118.

WAR DIARY
or
~~INTELLIGENCE SUMMARY~~

Sheet No 1.

(Erase heading not required.)

Instructions regarding War Diaries and Intelligence Summaries are contained in F. S. Regs., Part II. and the Staff Manual respectively. Title pages will be prepared in manuscript.

Place	Date	Hour	Summary of Events and Information	Remarks and references to Appendices
DIÉVAL	1-4-18		Dismounted portion of Company moved off from OPPY at 6.0.A.M. marched to ESTRÉE-WAMIN, and entrained. They were preceded by lorries from DIÉVAL arriving 12 noon. Transport and cyclists moved off from OPPY at 2.10 P.M. and arrived MEZIL-ST-POL at 5.45 P.M. Route BEAUDRICOURT — ESTREE-WAMIN — HOUVIN — MONCHEAUX — BUNEVILLE. O. Lieut. R.V. TAYLOR left Company to report to C.R.E. II Corps Boryd. C.	MAP.REF. LENS 11. 1/40,000 BÉTHUNE 1/40,000 contoured sheet
	2-4-18		Company resting. Transport and cyclists left MESNIL-ST-POL at 9.15 A.M. and arrived DIÉVAL 1.30 P.M. Route TERNAS — LIGNY-ST-FLOCHEL — BAILLEUL-AUX-CORNAILLES — MONCHY -BRETON — LA THIEULOYE. C.	BÉTHUNE contoured sheet 1/40,000
DIÉVAL	3-4-18		Section drill + Arms Rifle exercise. Remounts — 9 mules. C.	
HERSIN	4-4-18		Company moved left DIÉVAL at 10.30 A.M. arrived HERSIN 3.30 P.M. Route: BURTON DIVION — HOUDAIN — MESNIL-LEZ-RUITZ — BARLIN. C.	
— do —	5-4-18		Company resting. C.	
— do —	6-4-18		Training. Section drill + Rifle exercises. C.	
AIX-NOULETTE	7-4-18		Company moved to huts in NOULETTE WOOD, have hire in AIX-NOULETTE. Company and 76th Inf. Brigade under orders of O.E. 1st Corps to work on MAISTRE Reserve line. C.	
— do —	8-4-18		2 Lieut. E.F.G. DUTTON joined Company. Company working on MAISTRE Defence Line. C.	
— do —	9-4-18		— do — C.	
— do —	10-4-18		— do — C.	
CHOCQUES AREA	11-4-18		Company moved to new area under orders along OBSERVES. Dismounted portion moved by lorries. Mounted portion marched, left AIX-NOULETTE at 5.30 P.M. Route: MONT-LES-MINES — BÉTHUNE-FOUQUEREUIL at 8.4.C. dismounted portion arrived at 11.4.C. Mounted portion arrived at Blue El. Sunday at 11.45 p.m. Two sections in W.19. a + c. Orders preparing bridges to demolition on LA BASSEE canal. C.	

A 5834 Wt.W.4973/M687 750,000 8/16 D.D.&L.Ltd. Forms/C.2118/13.

Army Form C. 2118.

WAR DIARY
or
INTELLIGENCE SUMMARY.   Sheet No 2
(Erase heading not required.)

Instructions regarding War Diaries and Intelligence Summaries are contained in F. S. Regs., Part II. and the Staff Manual respectively. Title pages will be prepared in manuscript.

Place	Date	Hour	Summary of Events and Information	Remarks and references to Appendices
CHOCQUES	12-4-18		Transport & H.R. moved to an orchard in CHOCQUES village. I/Lieut H.F. MILLER and 12 cyclists left for Merville, for duties on Brigade Front.	MAP REF: HAZEBROUCK 5-A. HECTOMETRIQUE BETHUNE-CONTOUR SHEET 1/40000
			LABARISE carried on 74th Brigade Front. Pte No 474595 Lpl KING S. wounded. M.	
—do—	13-4-18		I/Lieutenant E.R.H. DUTTON relieves I/Lieut H.F. MILLER on duties & cyclists sent forward to carry on around up the cinema. Enemy shelling town. C.	
LESGUEST	14-4-18		Coy HQ, Transport & H.R., I/Lieut E.R.H. DUTTON & men arrive 12.0 P.M. Nos 1,2, + 3 sections proceed to occupy new billets & all arrival at M.29.4.19.8. as Army billets. No 3 section took over duties for demolition of bridges & traps on Brigade front. Nos 1 + 2. Sections resting. C.	
—do—	15-4-18		Nos 1 + 2 section resting, ditto. C. 18 O.R. arrived as reinforcements. M.	
—do—	16-4-18		Ditto.	
—do—	17-4-18		No 1 Section working parties. No 2 section strengthening cellars for B. + R. and 12 H.H. H. R. C.	
BRAY PITS at D.24.b.3.9.	18-4-18		H. Qs, Transport & No 4 section shelling out of LESQUEST at 2. A.M. arrived BRAY PITT on TOURNEHEM-LASSEVVRIERE road at 8.30 A.M. Route ONNEQUES - LASSEVVRIERE. M.	
—do—	19-4-18		Nos 1 & 2 Sections - wiring RESERVE LINE. No 3 Section in charge of bridges & traps. H	
—do—	20-4-18		{ No 1 Section Dug Out for BATT. H.Q. W.23 c.8.5	
			{ No 2 Section finding shells BATT H.Q. W.24 b.2.9	
			and strengthening cellars p. 39-48 . Do	H
—do—	21-4-18		No 1 Section. Dug-out BATT. H.Q. W.23.c.8.5. No 2 section in charge of bridges & traps. No 4 section strengthening cellars & making alterations at BATT H.Q. W.24.b.2.9. M.	

No 542317 Spr. GARLAND A. ALEXANDER proceeds to England. Commuted to 5 months FR. No 1. No 12852 Spr. SCOTT J. B. awarded M.M. 3rd Div. R.O. No 119 dated 21 + 18.

A 5834   Wt. W4973/M687   750,000   8/16   D. D. & L. Ltd.   Forms/C.2118/13.

Army Form C. 2118.

WAR DIARY
— or —
INTELLIGENCE SUMMARY.

SHEET N° 3.

(Erase heading not required.)

Instructions regarding War Diaries and Intelligence Summaries are contained in F. S. Regs., Part II. and the Staff Manual respectively. Title pages will be prepared in manuscript.

Place	Date	Hour	Summary of Events and Information	Remarks and references to Appendices
Sand pits D24.d.30.75	22.4.18		Nos 1 & 4 Sections — dug outs for Batt HQ at W 23 c 8 3. N° 2 Section in charge of bridges & barges. HH	Map Ref HAZEBROUCK 5ᴬ
— do —	23.4.18		Nos 1 & 4 Sections — dug outs for Batt HQ's at W 23 c 8 3 and shells at W 24 b 1 2 9. N° 2 Section — do —	BETHUNE 1/20000 camp new sheet
			Lt B. on MRK attached for duty from 56ᵗʰ Co R.E. HH	36ᴀ 1/20000
— do —	24.4.18		Nos 1 & 4 Sections — dug outs for Batt HQ at W 23 c 8 3 and shells at W 24 b 2 9. N° 2 section — do — HH	
— do —	25.4.18		N° 1 Section maintenance of pontoon bridges. HH	
— do —	26.4.18		Sections resting. 26 o.r. arrived as reinforcements. HH	
— do —	27.4.18		N° 1 Section maintenance & supervision of Barnet Rd Bridge. N° 3 Section return to rest at LE VERTANNOY	
			N° 4 Section construction of shelters for Batt HQ at W 22 a 2 B. Capt BRANSWICK proceeded to Corps Offices Rest Station	
— do —	28.4.18		N° 1 Section maintenance & supervision of Barnet Rd Bridge. N° 3 Section — Shelters for Batt HQ W 5 605.95.	
			N° 4 Section — Batt H.Q. at W 22 a 2.B. and strengthening 890ᶻ H.Q. HH	
— do —	29.4.18		N° 2 Section maintenance & supervision of Barnet Peir Bridges. N° 3 & 4 same as 28ᵗʰ HH	
— do —	30.4.18		Nos 1, 3, & 4 sections same as 29ᵗʰ HH	
			H.Q. moved to D 24 a B 6.	

1ˢᵗ May 1918

N Nathwich Lt R.E 2/c
for O.C. 529 (F.2) Field Co R.E

529 Fd Coy.
Vol 22

ARMY FORM

War Diary.

For month ending 31st May 1918.

Unit 529 (East Riding) Field Co R.E.

Army Form C. 2118.

WAR DIARY
or
INTELLIGENCE SUMMARY.
(Erase heading not required.)

Instructions regarding War Diaries and Intelligence Summaries are contained in F. S. Regs., Part II. and the Staff Manual respectively. Title pages will be prepared in manuscript.

SHEET No. 1

Place	Date	Hour	Summary of Events and Information	Remarks and references to Appendices
SAND PITS D24a.B.6.	1.5.18.		No. 2 Section maintenance & repair of Barnel pont bridge. No. 3 Section constructing shelters for BATT H.Q. W22 a 2 B. No. 4 Section strengthening BRDE H.Q. No. 1 Section resting. HY.	MAP=BRUCK ST. 1/20000. BETHUNE 1/40000 SHEET 14/2000.
-do-	2.5.18.		Same as on 1st. HN	
-do-	3.5.18.		Same as on 2nd. 2/Lt. Capt. P. CRANSWICK reported for duty from 1st CORPS. Officers rest station HY.	
-do-	4.5.18.		No.s 2 and 4 Sections same as 3rd. No. 3 Section strengthening R.E. dump VENDIN. HN.	
-do-	5.5.18.		No.s 1 and 3 Sections constructing concrete M.G. emplacements N/U 22 and M/D G 23. No. 166246 Sjt. COOPER T. promoted 2/Lt.	
-do-	6.5.18.		No.s 1 and 3 Sections same as 5th. No.s 2 and 4 Sections erection of Heavy Bridge at EGLISE-A-ESSARS. No.166246 2/Lt. COOPER T. Resd, promoted. Capt. P. CRANSWICK admitted to hospital 6th. HN	
-do-	7.5.18.		No.s 1 and 3 same as 6th. No.s 2 and 4 Sections same as 6th. HN	
-do-	8.5.18.		No.s 2 and 4 Sections erection of Heavy Bridge at EGLISE-A-ESSARS. No. 3 Section demolition party for Bridges & Barges. No. 332651 Boy.4. ANDREWS W. self-injured wound admitted to Hospital. HN	
-do-	9.5.18.		No. 1 Section erection of shelters for Bgde. H.Q. N29 a 4.5. No. 4 Section strengthening R.E. dump VENDIN. No.s 2 and 3 Sections demolition parties for 3 bridges and Barges. No.147437 Sapper PETERSON= mattoe wounded Grd.M.	
-do-	10.5.18.		No. 1 Section erection of shelters for Bgde. H.Q. N29 a 4.3. No.s 2 & 3 sections same duty for Barges & Bridges. No. 4 Section refixing to road at V17.c. & strengthening R.E dump. HN	
-do-	11.5.18.		No.s 1, 2, 3 & 4 Sections work same do 10th. HN	

2353 Wt W2544/1454 700,000 5/15 D. D. & L. A.D.S.S./Forms/C.2118.

WAR DIARY
INTELLIGENCE SUMMARY
(Erase heading not required.)

Army Form C. 2118.

5427 N°2

Place	Date	Hour	Summary of Events and Information	Remarks and references to Appendices
SAND DIT'S QUARRIES	12.5.18		N°s 1,2,3 & 4 Sections. Construction of BGDE H.Q. N°s 2 & 3. Demolition party for Bargo + Bridge and erection of shelters for BATT. H.Q. N°s 23. & 95. S.D. I.O.R. issued as reinforcement	WS2 s. t. WS2 251 1000
			#74224 Kpl SMITH E. 26731 Cpl NELSON A. 474337 Cpl BINNS M. 542317 Cpl GARLAND A. 125452 Gdr MANNER J. and 51229 Pvt MONESS E. to wounded (GSW). Hospital. 404.95 Gdr BINNS DVY Wounded. Hospital. 118.	Sergeant Waron. Sergt Waron
-do-	13.5.18		N°s 1,2,3 & 4 sections work same as 12th + installation dug outs and fatigue party 1.8.6. 20 reinforced 56 to 85.	86 111
-do-	14.5.18		N°s 1,2,3 & 4 Sections work same as 13th. 1 O.R. reported as reinforcement. 88	
-do-	15.5.18		N°s 1,2,3 & 4 Sections work same as 14th 89.	
-do-	16.5.18		N°s 1,2,3 & 4 Sections work same as 15th 90.	
-do-	17.5.18		N°s 1 & 2 Sections Demolition party for CANAL. N°s 3 & 4 Sections resting 91.	
-do-	18.5.18		N°s 1 & 2 -do- -do-	92
-do-	19.5.18		N°s 1 & 2 -do- -do-	93
-do-	20.5.18		N°1 Section demolition party for bridges. Digging trench CANAL BANK W. №s 4.D. N°3 Section erecting shelter for BATT 118.	
-do-			N°s 4.3.7. and shelter for R.A.P. W.S2. 4.6. N°s 2 & 4 retng. 1. O.R. reported as reinforcement. 94.	
-do-	21.5.18		N°1 Section same as 20th. N°3 Section erecting shelter for R.A.P. W.S2. 4.5. N°4 erecting shelter for BATT. 1D. W.S2 3.7. N°2 resting 95.	
-do-	22.5.18		N°1 Section same as 21st. N°5 Section erecting shelter for R.A.P. W.S2. 4.5. 3. BATT H.Q. W.S2 3.7. N°4 working in M.G.E. W.D. c.6.5.D. N°2 Section resting 96.	
			1.O.R. Reported as reinforcement. N°2 Section resting 98.	

Army Form C. 2118.

WAR DIARY
or
INTELLIGENCE SUMMARY.

SHEET N°3

(Erase heading not required.)

Instructions regarding War Diaries and Intelligence Summaries are contained in F. S. Regs., Part II. and the Staff Manual respectively. Title pages will be prepared in manuscript.

Place	Date	Hour	Summary of Events and Information	Remarks and references to Appendices
SAND PITS Q24 a 8.6	25/5/18		N°1 Section demolition party for bridges. Laying north shell bank W10 4.0. N°3 Section erecting screens for N°1 R.P.	MAP REF
—do—	24/5/18		M/S at 5. O BATT HQ W6d 3.1. N°4 Section erecting for MGE W10 c 6.3. N°2 Section making BN.	1/40,000 GSGS 65th France
—do—	25/5/18		N°2 Section N GE W10 C 6.3. N°3 Section same as 25. N°4 Section demolition party for bridges. N°1 Section [illegible] for elevation to infantry HQ.	SHEET 14000
—do—	26/5/18		All sections same as 24th. 2 O.R. sentees as reinforcements. 474481 Cpl GODSAVE G. 2nd reinforcement infantry HQ.	
—do—	27/5/18		All sections same as 25th. M.	
—do—	28/5/18		All sections & one as 26.5. 2 o.r. proceed on reinforcements. M.	
—do—	29/5/18		All sections same as 27th. M.	
—do—	30/5/18		All sections same as 2 F.A. 474453 Spr HOLDASS G. wounded to hospital HQ.	
—do—	31/5/18		N°2 Section N GE W10 c.6.3. N°1 Section Advd Camp tanks N°4 section demolition party for bridges M. 4 T428 2nd Lt FLETCHER E.S. wounded	
—do—			N°1 Section tank camp BANK/section sellows to BATT HQ W5d 3.7. N°2 Section MGE W10 C 7.3.	
			N°4 Section demolition party for bridges. M.	
			During the month 3 o.r. proceed on leave to U.K. [illegible]	

1st June 1918.

WWilmot O R E14
for O.C. 529th Field Co. R.E.

5 29 Fd Coy RE
Vol 23

War Diary.

for month ending 30th June 1918

Unit 529th (East Riding) Fd. Co RE

Army Form C. 2118.

WAR DIARY
or
INTELLIGENCE SUMMARY.

(Erase heading not required.)

SHEET No 1

Instructions regarding War Diaries and Intelligence Summaries are contained in F. S. Regs., Part II. and the Staff Manual respectively. Title pages will be prepared in manuscript.

Place	Date	Hour	Summary of Events and Information	Remarks and references to Appendices
SAND PITS	1.6.18	6.1	Nos 1 & 2 Sections M.G.E. W10.C.7.3. No 4 Section demolition & maintenance party for bridges	Return to sand camp HAZEBROUCK MR REP HAZEBROUCK 5A No 000
D27a 8.6	2.6.18		Nos 1 + 2 Sections same as 1st. No 4 Section same as 1st HB	Bething comes
-do-	3.6.18		Nos 1 + 2 Sections same as 2nd. No 4 Section same as 2nd HB	
-do-	4.5.18		Nos 1 & 2 Sections same as 3rd. No 3 Section demolition & maintenance party for bridges. Return to sand camp canal bank	Sheet passed
			H.O.R. arrived No 18 reinforcements. HB	
-do-	5.6.18		No 2 & 3 Sections M.G.E. W10.C.7.3. Nos 1 & 4 Back billets HB	
-do-	6.6.18		Nos 2 + 3 Sections M.G.E. W10.C.7.3. Nos 1 + 4 -do-	Cpl. DIMBERLINE A.E. 474067 from No 3 Section to HB
-do-	7.6.18		No 2 Section M.G.E. W10.C.7.3. No 3 Section Batt. H.Q. W10.C.9. 10R reinforcements 32 reinforcement HB	
-do-	8.6.18		No 2 Section M.G.E. W10.C.7.3. Nos 1 & 3 Sections Batt. H.Q. W10.C.9. 10R reinforcements 14 reinforcement.	
			2/Lt DUTTON & 7 O.R. proceed to Engineer Camp at ZUTKERK - B.M.Y.CHAT. HB	
-do-	9.6.18		Nos 1 & 3 Sections Batt. H.Q. W10.C.9. No 2 Section M.G.E. W10.C.7.3. HB	
-do-	10.6.18		Nos 1 + 3 Sections same as 9th. No 4 Section 4 O.R. 430589 + 6 to Kinnard & wounded & returned at C.C.S.	
-do-	11.5.18		Nos 1 + 3 Sections same as 10th. No 2 Section inspectd 10 & carrying out Anew on canal	
-do-	12.6.18		Nos 1 & 3 Sections same as 11th. No 4 Section same as 11th HB	
-do-	13.6.18		No 1 + 2 Sections erecting bridges on canal. No 3 Section Batt. H.Q. W10.C.9. No 4 Demolition party for bridges HB	
-do-	14.6.18		Nos 1 & 2 same as 13th. No 3 same as 13th. No 4 same as 13th. HB	

Army Form C. 2118.

WAR DIARY
or
INTELLIGENCE SUMMARY.
(Erase heading not required.)

Instructions regarding War Diaries and Intelligence Summaries are contained in F. S. Regs., Part II. and the Staff Manual respectively. Title pages will be prepared in manuscript.

Place	Date	Hour	Summary of Events and Information	Remarks and references to Appendices
SAND PIT	15.6.18		Nos 1, 2, 3 & 4 Hunng N4.d.6.9 to N4.a.9.3	Map ref.
OLHA 26	16.6.18		No 2 Section demolition & maintenance party A bridge L10.c.7.2 & 9 OR wounded. XX	1/A7,500 CK SP 1/40,000 detail carried Sheet 36NW
	17.6.18		Nos 1 & 2 Sections wiring 11.7.a.7.4 & 10 H.a. Sgt No 3 Section demolition party for bridges X	
	18.6.18		No 1 Section demolition party for bridge 11.7.c.7.3. Section wiring No 3 Section concrete shelter N10.c.1.9 Sgt Farmer killed.	
	19.6.18		No 1 Section demn.coy party Pont d'Hinges No 2 & 3 Sections wiring No 4 Section concrete shelter N15.a.7.9 XX	
	20.6.18		No 1 Section demn.coy party Pont d'Hinges. No 2 concrete shelter N10.c.1.9. No 4 concrete shelter N15.a.7.9 XX	
	21.6.18		Nos 1, 2 & 4 Sections same as 20th XX	
	22.6.18		Nos 3, 2 & 4 platoons same as 21st XX	
	23.6.18		No 4 and 2 Sections same as 22.d. No 3 Section . Demolition party Pont d'Hinges & Gordon Line	
	24.6.18		Major P.d. M.Hall.M.C. A/C.R.E. 3rd Division Nos 1, 2 & 3 Sections same as 23rd	
	25.6.18		Nos 2, 3 & 4 Sections same as 24X. 60744. Dvt Preston S. (Wounded not duty).	
	26.6.18		Nos 2, 3 & 4 Sections same as 25X	
	27.6.18		No 4 Sect ad 26X, No 2 Section Concrete Shelter N10.c.1.9. No 3 Sect {Repairs a excav. line, Pont d'Hinges, 00 23rd. {Repairs to Winch Canal Bank	
	28.6.18		No 2 Sect. as 29X. No 3 Sect. Erecting Steel Shelter on Canal bank. Work on Gordon Line, Demolition party Parapet Hinges) LE-VERTANNOY. No 3 Sect. as 28X	
	29.6.18		Nos 2 Sectn as 28X. No 1 Sect preparing for Lewis Emplacement LE-VERTANNOY. No 3 Sect. as 28X	
	30.6.18		Nos 2, 3, & 4 Sect. ao 29X. 2nd Lieut Poolabank A. joined on Reinforcement. Lieut Roon M.R.K. gone on unit fur conference duty 2AX. 474013 Cpl S.M. Beam. D. awarded I.M.S.M. {during month {1811, 1 & 3 OR proceeded on leave to UK	

2353 Wt. W2544/1454 700,000 5/15 D. D. & L. Ltd. MSS/F. Gwr. CAME Date 17X.

for Off.Comdg. 529th Field Coy R.E.

Lieut R.E.
for Off.Comdg. 529th Field Coy R.E.

5299 Fd Coy. RE
WD 24

War Diary

for month ending 31st July 1918

529th (E. Riding) Fd. Co. RE.

Army Form C. 2118.

WAR DIARY
of
INTELLIGENCE SUMMARY.
(Erase heading not required.)

Instructions regarding War Diaries and Intelligence Summaries are contained in F.S. Regs., Part II. and the Staff Manual respectively. Title pages will be prepared in manuscript.

SHEET N° 1

Place	Date	Hour	Summary of Events and Information	Remarks and references to Appendices
Bois des Dames	1.7.18		N°1 Section making Block trench Redn. W.5, K.95. N°2 Section Trench Zonnebeke Redn. R.N.P. N°10 a.11. N°3 Nappes un con. Bund M.11.9.11.	WAR REFERENCE HAZEBROUCK R.5 A 1/100.000
D.21.6.3.5.	2.7.18.		Deepening & revetting GORDON LINE & CANAL BANK. N°2 & N°3 Wing G.O.1 Looked at revettments. W.11.7 Short to K.95 W.5.	SHEET 1/20000
-do-			N°1 Section same as 1st. N°2 Section, strengthening Bay Redn. N°3 Section same as 1st. N°4 Section resting as at 1st BETHUNE 0.36.20.50 R.A.P. N°10 a.11. W.O.P.
-do-	3.7.18.		All Sections same as 2nd. 1st.
-do-	4.7.18.		All Sections same as 3rd. 1st.
-do-	5.7.18.		All Sections same as 4th. 1st.
-do-	6.7.18.		N°1 & 5 Sections same as 5th. N°2 Section assisting in charging by Sect N°2 Section outside of demolition by R.A.P. N°10 a.W.o.P.
-do-	7.7.18		All Sections same as 6th. 1st.
-do-	8.7.18.		All Sections same as 7th. 1st.
-do-	9.7.18.		N°1.5 & 2 Sections same as 8th. N°2 Section took over MAJOR PDE H. HALL M.C. B Sector Rear N°3.S.
-do-	10.7.18.		N°s Section relief from Sunnyman M.T.E. M.S.S1 S.Q.S. N°3 S.14 same as 9th N°2 Section resting 1st.
-do-	11.7.18.		All Sections same as 10th 1st.
-do-	12.7.18.		All Sections same as 11th in addition section of M.G.A. Pill Box N° 1.2.0.50. 1st.
-do-	13.7.18.		All Sections same as 12th.	2st. N°3 Section & men R.R.S.O.
-do-	14.7.18		N°s 1.3 & 4 Sections same as 13th. N°2 Section demolition party Pont d'Haye 5th. Deepening & revetting FORDONLINE & CANAL BANK N°3 Section Jiton
-do-	15.7.18.		All Sections same as 14th. 1st.	Burham 3 MM Pl Bn 3 M9. a.0.50 Jiton

Army Form C. 2118.

WAR DIARY
INTELLIGENCE SUMMARY
(Erase heading not required.)

SHEET No 2.

Instructions regarding War Diaries and Intelligence Summaries are contained in F. S. Regs., Part II. and the Staff Manual respectively. Title pages will be prepared in manuscript.

Place	Date	Hour	Summary of Events and Information	Remarks and references to Appendices
Boisdoe Dame	16.7.18		No 1 Section section of truck barricade M.G.E. M.5.d.15.95. No 2 Section demolition poly Patted Hinges. Dummy trestling & noon line &	MAP REFERENCE HAZEBROUCK.51. 1/20,000
D22.6.3.5.			Canal Bank. No 4 Section erection of concrete shelter M.10.a.4 Section of Man Ru Box M.9.C.20.50. No 3 Section riding. 88	
-do-	17.7.18		No 1 Section carrying 184 No 2 Section. Demolition poly Patted Hinges. Gordon Line & Card Bank. No 4 same as 164 84	SHEET No 1
-do-	18.7.18		All sections same as 174 88	
-do-	19.7.18		No 1 Section same 184 No 2. Same as 184 and section of M.R. All Boxes at W.34.c.7 and 4.9.C. 15. N° 4 same as 184 84	
-do-	20.7.18		No 2 same as 194. No 3. Manoeuvre M.G.F. M.15. 6.15.95. N° 4. same as 194. N° 1 Section to Card field. 88	
-do-	21.7.18		All sections same as 204 88	
-do-	22.7.18		All sections same as 21st. Moir Pla. Box (N.4.E) at M.9.C.20.50. compass 88	
-do-	23.7.18		All sections same as 22nd 88	
-do-	24.7.18		All sections same as 23rd 88	
-do-	25.7.18		All sections same as 24th 84. 19th Section to Zeahoekes 88	
-do-	26.7.18		No 2 & 3 Sections same as 25th No 1 Section manoeuvre M.G.F. M.15.6.15.95. 8"	
-do-	27.7.18		All sections same as 26th 88	
-do-	28.7.18		All sections same as 27th. II Lieut L.A.W. D. joined unit as reinforcement	
-do-	29.7.18		All sections same as 28th	
-do-	30.7.18		Nos 1 & 3 Sections same as 27.7.18. C.6.4. Section same as N° 2. Sect on 17th No 2. Section to Gost Ballot	
-do-	31.7.18		All sections same as 30.4 + O.R's proceeded on leave to U.K. during month	

2253 Wt W.2341/1454 700,000 5/15 D. D. & L. A.D.S.S./Forms/C. 2118.

W.M. Russell Capt. C.E.(T)
For O E Major (5.E.2) 61st 6° R.E.

5-29 2nd Coy R.E.
96 25

War Diary.

for month ending 31st August 1918

5294 (E Hidens) 2d Co R.E.

Army Form C. 2118.

WAR DIARY
or
INTELLIGENCE SUMMARY.
(Erase heading not required.)

Instructions regarding War Diaries and Intelligence Summaries are contained in F. S. Regs., Part II. and the Staff Manual respectively. Title pages will be prepared in manuscript.

Place	Date	Hour	Summary of Events and Information	Remarks and references to Appendices
Hd Qrs & Waggon Line Bois du DAMES Sheet 44B D.22.c.30.40	1.8.18		3 Sections working in Line. 1 Section resting at Rear Billets, 2 sections were no time working in Rear M.G. Emplacement at W.2.C.67, also MOR OP at W.10.C.8.1. B ridge maintenance party at Pont de Hinges, constructing stile Blockhouse on Canal Bank. Lt/Capt. Heathcoate granted leave to U.K. 15/8.18. (Special Leave)	Major Pty BETHUNE Command Sheet 1/40000 TRS
Forward Billets VIEN DIN LES				
BETHUNE Sheet BETHUNE Central 36 A & E 36 36 B NG 38C E.3. a. 50.90.	2.8.18 3.8.18 4.8.18		Work same as for date 1.8.18 " " " 2.8.18 Work same as on 2.8.18 will the following additions aip unloads conveyed to special position Section 1 Section at Lapugnoy which in turn by motors from Rear billets, Ammunition boxes & tresch timber up to C.O. Bed O R. TRS	
	5.8.18		Work same as before. Captured T.J. O'SULLIVAN 36th own Company to remained from 466 co ey 46 Div. Artillery Ammunition Q.F. 55/3400 5th Army A/1/475 31/7/18. Captured gnr J.H Fdl Co.RE required to take over men Lolves TRS for Kampferfer Q.F. 55/3400 5th Army A/1/475.	
	6.8.18		Instruction begins up to 3pm. Taking one funded gnr J.K & FdL by arrival all traps transportation work to handed over to 94 Fd Coy. TRS	
	7.8.18		Company embused at LE BREBIS on REVEILLON-CHOQUES Rd for AMETTES at 5am. Transport returned at TRS 8am arrived AMETTES with by 8 First Billet granted 7 days leave to PARIS. Company No gr. 70 2049. R. TRS	
AMETTES Sheet 44B B.3.8.	8.8.18 9.8.18		General cleaning of equipment, waggons & first inspections etc TRS Company Parade Pay Parade. Started with of general cleaning TRS until Company at 1.30pm. Church Commander General Sir W.P. BRYUND?	

Major & OC 529 ? Tra Co R.E.

Army Form C. 2118.

WAR DIARY
or
INTELLIGENCE SUMMARY.
(Erase heading not required.)

Instructions regarding War Diaries and Intelligence Summaries are contained in F. S. Regs., Part II and the Staff Manual respectively. Title pages will be prepared in manuscript.

Place	Date	Hour	Summary of Events and Information	Remarks and references to Appendices
AMETTES South of Pa. 3.b.	10.8.16		General training of Company. Instruction as before from Brigade training Programme. Church Parade.	
	11.8.16		9.30am C.O. to England. R.E. school AMETTES church (A/NIVIN).	
	12.8.16		XII Corps School at FERFAY Company drew double Tent Cap 4 horses & artificer NCO. & Pioneer wagon 2 horse cart mounted NCO. & dis mtd NCO. all sent to Train.	
	13.8.16		General Training Transport moved from AMETTES to AUCHEL (LENS 1) N.E. of 5F13.6 at H/m under the Command of 2nd Lieut Miller.	
	14.8.16		Company marched to GEORGE'S (LENS 1) entrained at 1.45pm at 76 Brigade H.Q. (FERNES /A.30.c. detrained).	
	15.8.16		WAR 1016 Camp	
			Transport of Company ordered at 10.30am ..... Ryan of employ St.	
	16.8.16		General Training of Company Drew Bayonets & entire .... by Lieut Williams. & 2nd Lieut Campbell at O.C of ...... Lieut Miller at 9.30am. R.E. Service Officer Sth	
	17.8.16		Capt. J. HASTINGS ordered on Special leave to U.K Feb.	
	18.8.16			
	19.8.16		General Training of Company. ...... over to BERLES aux Bois & training of Platoon. ..... proceeded at SAL-ERVEAU Company left BERLES at 7.30 pm arrived BERLES at 4.45pm Working party Numbercan ... All HUMBER CAMP	
	20.8.16		Returned to BERLES all day. No 3 Section marched 2 Lieut NORMAN left 10 Jan 76 Inf Bde Bagade & arrived 14 MANCHY MILL South L.Lieut MILLER ordered 86 C.R.E J.W Day 15TH Bgd	

OC 529 + Sketches

Army Form C. 2118.

WAR DIARY
or
INTELLIGENCE SUMMARY.
(Erase heading not required.)

Instructions regarding War Diaries and Intelligence
Summaries are contained in F. S. Regs., Part II.
and the Staff Manual respectively. Title pages
will be prepared in manuscript.

Place	Date	Hour	Summary of Events and Information	Remarks and references to Appendices
BERLES AU BOIS	21.8.18		Company Stm 18-6-m (803 strong) moved to PONTRIE LING. SW. of ADINFER WOOD. Enjoying approach march to night opposite COURCELLES LE COMTE. Map Ry AYETTE A.14.a.v.6 and also another	
			Moved back to N.E. of Cross Roads	
HENIN	22.8.18		Company rested at Quarry. Line at night the above than	
AYETTE	23.8.18		Company moved up to AERODROME TRENCH A.14.a.15.20. Left at 7pm	
			Went to Ft. RONCOURT to obtain patrol of tanks we were going to protect. refused to go out — 2nd attacked.	
M.15.S.E SH.CW 5d.NE 57d.NW	24.8.18		Company (less 1 section) in Readerpen — Guarded at Railway A.14.b.4.42. One section spring here to RONCOURT	
			No 3 Section Had last position SE A.4.D.1.1 Lane 3E A.4.D.11 = 3.R.w.3.	
	25.8.18		Company moved at 6 pm to W.15.v.3. Laid dumps. 19-w.o.6/14 ng dumps at VAR T.20.	
	26.8.18		Company & events active. No. 1 & 2 sections ran Dumps as usual (No 3.4.7.& 8) 11 N.3.d.1.5 — 14 L.T.19.00	
	27.8.18		Company moved up to AYETTE & MORCHIES A.8.91.2 A.3.a.5.3	
	28.8.18		Company moved from B.A.L.M. to A.4.L.45.85	
	29.8.18		Company advanced on open from A.4.6.0.7. — 7.2.0.2.6.2. Afternoon reconnoiting forward	
			tanks and made tracks. From H. Stag. Dn.'s & var. Supply dumps E 10°44' + VRAUCOURT STN St.-MAIN	
	30.8.18		Company in Rd. upon Sr. LEGER de VRAUCOURT from front T.27.C.25 - B.19.c.5.1. Also making tanks & during my tracks. ANTI TANK MINES.	
	31.8.18		Company continued in advancing St. LEGER- VRAUCOURT road. 1. Officer & 3 prisoners went to	

OC 529 & 2dOGC
Major RE (?)

WAR DIARY or INTELLIGENCE SUMMARY

Army Form C. 2118.

Place: ERVILLERS

Date	Hour	Summary of Events and Information	Remarks and references to Appendices
April		Company in Camp at A.H.C.A.S (Kemper Section) x/04 attached to 76 Infantry Brigade thru Arras in Army. 9 NCO's & B 16 & O.R.S. One Officer attached to R.E. 2o/c. One Officer on leave to UK. Other officers employed in repairing the St LEGER - VRADCOURT Road.	
2.9.18		Company moved to SENSEE VALLEY at 7pm Mer Ref. R.20.d.15 Sheet 51A NW 7.P. 253.27. 10 R. in area of L.N. S.O.R.	
3.9.18		Company moved from SENSEE VALLEY to ST LEGER. Tp. Ref. T.35.b.27 Company (less Section) working on repairs to Ecoust - Mont Maison Road. 1 Section on night working tackle T.30. 4500	
4.9.18		Company moved from ST LEGER to MOYENVILLE Map Ref. A.4.d.6.7. Company moved from G.4 MOYENVILLE No 3 & SLEEPER B.C.G.1 Sections employed in ECOUST-VRAUCOURT Road, general repairs. 2.O.R. left for R.E.T. School Rouen (Bugle m 7.9./13). Pub	
5.9.18		Company supplied 2 Section Blount - Homme Mont Pt. 1 Section were Lieut McREVIL. LIEUT MILLER rejoined Coy to form C.R.S. 9pm R.C. Public magazine moved off to WARIN EGYPT to fetch up Pontoons &c.	
6.9.18		Company moved from S3 ST LEGER B.C.G.1. to Camp between BEALES & BIENVILLES Sheet 51.b.f W.27. a.30. Pontoons returned to coy. Company from Army Pontoon Park Tor.	

WAR DIARY
or
INTELLIGENCE SUMMARY.
(Erase heading not required.)

Army Form C. 2118.

Instructions regarding War Diaries and Intelligence Summaries are contained in F.S. Regs., Part II. and the Staff Manual respectively. Title pages will be prepared in manuscript.

Place	Date	Hour	Summary of Events and Information	Remarks and references to Appendices
Mob. Rd. Frame 57c 1/40000	7.9.16		Company employed in general cleaning of equipment etc. Training N.C.O.'s in reconnaissance for advance. 4th Div Area. 2 Officers & 2 Sergts. Reconnoitred by lorry to ROSSEL. Recce. a HOPKINS BRIDGE	
	8.9.16		construction trip	
	9.9.16		Company employed as above. 1 Section working on Hopkins Bridge at BUYELLES. Reconnaissance party continued from DOUCHY. Recce.	
			Company in general disposing on Trestle bridge & Timbers. 1 Section repairing track for R.E.A. at DOUCHY. 1 Officer & 7 O.R. proceeded by lorry to ROSEL for instruction in erection of Hopkins Bridge.	
	10.9.16		Some work and parade as to 9.9.16. 1 O.R. proceeded on leave to U.K.	
Mob. Rd. AYETTE (Sheet)	11.9.16		Company moved to Camp 6. at AYETTE F.16.a.7.3. 1 Officer (Lieut Chapman) rejoined Company off leave to U.K.	
	12.9.16		at MORT HOMME to ST LEGER - VRANCOURT Road	
	13.9.16		Company parade rifle inspection. Establish Dracks. Done Battery formation. Instruction in Platoon	
	14.9.16		Company employed as above.	
			Readying & line of trestles Trestles	
	15.9.16		8 men on Coy. 14.9.16. 1 O.R. proceeded on leave to U.K. (back 17.9.16)	
Mob. Rd. 57c N.E.	16.9.16		O.C. and 1 other Officer proceeded to the Canal Du Nord for reconnaissance north Company moved to S. of BEAUMETZ Mob Rd T.26.d.0.0	
	17.9.16		Company employed at an advancing post at Yorkshire Bank (K.22.a.4.4.) 1 Section repairing trestles	

This will dugy by R.E.F
OC. 529 Fld Coy R.E.

Army Form C. 2118.

WAR DIARY
or
INTELLIGENCE SUMMARY.
(Erase heading not required.)

Place	Date	Hour	Summary of Events and Information	Remarks and references to Appendices
Maple Redt S7.c.N.E. S4.r.7.C T.3.b.d.0.D	18.9.18		Company employed on 17.9.18. 2 O.R. Transfers reported. 2 Officers and party making camp table for 7 B. Staff Brigade. M5 who recently arrived during the afternoon	
	19.9.18		Company employed as per 18.9.18	
	20.9.18		Company employed as per 19.9.18	
	21.9.18		Do. on 20.9.18	
	22.9.18		Do. as 21.9.18. 1 O.R. arrived as reinforcement.	
	23.9.18		Company working on road - YORKSHIRE BANK K.32.a.44.69	
	24.9.18		Do. Do.	
	25.9.18		Do. Do.	
	26.9.18		Do. and track K.32.a.1.3.	
	27.9.18		Do. Do.	
	28.9.18		Do. Do.	
	29.9.18		Do. Do.	
	30.9.18	1.30pm	Company moved to SCREEN TRENCH K.24.a.6.3.	
			During the month 1 officer + 3 o.r. proceeded on leave to U.K.	

M.Whitworth Capt. R.E.
for O.B. 529 (F.D.) Field Co. R.E.

Army Form C. 2118.

WAR DIARY
or
INTELLIGENCE SUMMARY.
(Erase heading not required.)

529th Field Company R.E.

Vol. 27

Instructions regarding War Diaries and Intelligence Summaries are contained in F.S. Regs., Part II. and the Staff Manual respectively. Title pages will be prepared in manuscript.

Place	Date	Hour	Summary of Events and Information	Remarks and references to Appendices
Map Ref 57cNE	1.10.18		Company moved from K.27.a.6.3 to L.19.a.7.4. Company at work 10.R. from new Reigny Jan & by ???	
L.19.a.7.4.	2.10.18		Company deployed in search of items nothing through at G.26.a.6.8. (MASNIERES) and also at J.32.d.9.8. (MASNIERES) 10 officers and 10 O.R. attached to 76 Infty Regt (Lt. Ryant HLI) K.8.d.2.6.	
	3.10.18		Company employed on am 2.10.18 and in repair of Bridge (MASNIERES) ???	
			as for week to 2.10.18	
	4.10.18		" " 10.R. found to lear to ??? ???	
	5.10.18		" 1 officer & 10 OR against hut ??? 76 Inf Reg at 10R ??? ??? ??? SUNKEN ??? ??? to RESTE ???	
	6.10.18		1 officer at 10R. at 1.11 for ???	
	7.10.18		Company at rest (Sunday & no work)	
	8.10.18		All Section in repair of ??? ??? from ??? ??? via MX R.7 R.W. R.23.d. ???	
			Reconnoitring ??? ??? and MASNIERES. This	
	9.10.18		Company employed in repair to Bridge Tk Bg 57 c.m D.2.23.c.2.4. (MASNIERES) Pitts ??? ??? ??? ??? ??? ??? approach to L.32.a.6.7 Removement of ??? road on ??? ??? and approach to bridge opposite ??? ???	
	10.10.18		One Section employed round M. MASNIERES ??? ??? ??? repair of Bridges, Removing Craters	
	11.10.18		Casting attns 1 + 2. 20 ft span Trestle Bridges Sent 15 & 10 ORs to rate of proposed Ramlip at L.32 & L.22. Bridging had mark ??? ??? 242 c.5.4. / officers ??? & 6 Sappers ??? Tank Bridge L.24 c.5.4. / officer ??? in ???	
	12.10.18		Company building the (2 Ramlips at L.22. & 4.6. ???? ???? ??? at ??? ??? ??? ??? ??? ??? ??? ??? ??? ???	

Turned Out R.E.T
at 529 by R.E.T.

Army Form C. 2118.

WAR DIARY
or
INTELLIGENCE SUMMARY.

(Erase heading not required.)

Instructions regarding War Diaries and Intelligence Summaries are contained in F. S. Regs., Part II. and the Staff Manual respectively. Title pages will be prepared in manuscript.

Place	Date	Hour	Summary of Events and Information	Remarks and references to Appendices
Map Ref 57.C.N.E	13.10.18		Orders supplied to Infantry Tanks for an attack of Tanks at MARIN & LILBOIS	
L.19.a & 7.4			Regt assembled at 13:15 (our time) Rd Carol is the road that divides at Meusieres by former	
			Apparent Battle did not materialise This	
	14.10.18		Company continued to clean their forward vehicles, take Rd to found revival	
	15.10.18		Company supervised engineering Ramp to Bridge on above Rd after tanks to loops up	
			309 pmoded to Army Rest Camp This	
	16.10.18		Company making Swape to get through the sides of Bmedin as above. Lift/ same agent	
			Coldn C57 and 3.C.R. as unformed forme the bgy. This	
	17.10.18		Company supplied a working moterial (Read Mrsdch) Ramp of tn B. it go no above	
			Testing up Ram as marking maps. Branchy roads Troops at This	
	18.10.18		3 were on p. 10.18 This	
Map Ref 57 B.4.W →	19.12.18		Company went from RIBECORT to CATTENIERES under orders from 76 Bgds Report to OR arriving found by	
H.12 a 4.5 M.16 & 73/M9	20.15.18		Company moved from CATTENIERES to QUEVY 3.OR Reported on arrival to V.R.	
C.19.a	21.10.18		Company cleaning up their late arrival. Orders from 11R on cleane to V.B. (Spicer's dum)	Forwarded Major D.R.T H.529 by RST

A5831 Wt.W4973/M687 750,000 8/16 D. D. & L. Ltd. Forms/C.2118/13.

Army Form C. 2118.

WAR DIARY
or
INTELLIGENCE SUMMARY.
(Erase heading not required.)

Instructions regarding War Diaries and Intelligence Summaries are contained in F. S. Regs., Part II. and the Staff Manual respectively. Title pages will be prepared in manuscript.

Place	Date	Hour	Summary of Events and Information	Remarks and references to Appendices
AVIEVY. MARCYSTONS. 513A.41.	22·10·18		Company employed in reference to Abr Div Hdqrs Sr PYTHON, No 3 Section attached to 76 Infantry Brigade	
			moved up to SOLESMES. Constructing roadside footbridge near River HARRIES. A 47×16. Capts L.F. PETRIE	
			Bombarded Military Assist. 3O.R. proceed on leave to U.K. 7th	
	23·10·18		Company employed near Section Section's under Lieut H.F. Miller constructed on knight (Warden) Bridge	
			over the River HARRIES at Damage mode Kirangebach from Riverslip was provided for crew by 15 gross 7th	
			Sgt. 10·30 Riverslip Section 3 reported to 76 Infy Brigade expected 5 previous 18 M.G.R. and a	
			Machine Gun in ROMERIES, Bd	
	24·10·18		Company moved from AVIEVY to Solesmes (N.L.d.6.5.) No. 1 and 4 Sections relieved 16	
			438 Fd Coy in Billets at ROMERIES (M4 Ref. 51.N SE V 31.d.8.7) moved open for Troops	
			02·00 am. 25th Th	
	25·10·18		Company employed in Roads and several Bus. Section on above attached to 76 Infantry Brigade the	
	26·10·18		Companies employed on Roads where the Div Comd The	
	27·10·18			TL
	28·10·18			20

Two added maps REF
ex 529 Coy R.E.

Army Form C. 2118.

WAR DIARY
or
INTELLIGENCE SUMMARY.
(Erase heading not required.)

Instructions regarding War Diaries and Intelligence Summaries are contained in F. S. Regs., Part II. and the Staff Manual respectively. Title pages will be prepared in manuscript.

Place	Date	Hour	Summary of Events and Information	Remarks and references to Appendices
SALONICA	29.10.18		Company employed in various duties and Road Repair - 1 S. Trench Mort. Section as above attached to 76 & York & Lanc's. 1 O.R. to hospital.	
EPINE	30.10.18		On the 29.10.18 No 3 Section rejoined Company from 76 Infantry Brigade	
DOIRAN	31.10.18		Company returned to open the 5' Ruled on the 29.10.18. 2 O.R. joined in from R.E.B.	

A.5834. Wt. W.4973/M637 750,000 8/16 D. D. & L. Ltd. Forms/C.2118/13.

Army Form C. 2118.

WAR DIARY
or
INTELLIGENCE SUMMARY.
(Erase heading not required.)

Place	Date	Hour	Summary of Events and Information	Remarks and references to Appendices
Map Ref. 57 D NE 1/20000 D.6.d.65 Sa. ESNES	1.11.18		[illegible handwritten entries]	
	2.11.18			
	3.11.18			
	4.11.18			
Map Ref. 57A SE La CHALOUPERIE	5.11.18			
	6.11.18			
	7.11.18			
	8.11.18			
	9.11.18			
	10.11.18			

Army Form C. 2118.

WAR DIARY
or
INTELLIGENCE SUMMARY.
(Erase heading not required.)

Instructions regarding War Diaries and Intelligence Summaries are contained in F.S. Regs., Part II. and the Staff Manual respectively. Title pages will be prepared in manuscript.

Place	Date	Hour	Summary of Events and Information	Remarks and references to Appendices
LA LONGUEVILLE Shut 57/NW 36.A.7.6.c.	11.11.18		Company Paraded 07:00 hours for route march. 7.6 Infantry Brigade Band also was enrolled on all subsequent Route marches.	
	12.11.18		Company employed on roads at LA LONGUEVILLE.	
	13.11.18		Company employed in trains at TAISNIERE and on roads near T36.c.8.6. and LA LONGUEVILLE.	
			Moved in to J. 18.18.18 All Ranks of 76 Infantry Brigade were present on T33.o.4.9. at 14.00 hours to hear an address by the G.O.C.	
	14.11.18		R.E. Officers & Section arrived & have to move to TRITH 4.5 infantry.	
			Work done on 12.11.18.	
	15.11.18		Company employed on bringing transport from ground in all areas of.	
			Company moved with 76 Infantry Brigade from LA LONGUEVILLE to SOUS-LE BOIS SW. of MAUBEUGE.	
	17.11.18		Company on road repair organization etc.	
	18.11.18		Company moved to LOUVROIL.	
	19.11.18		Company and Pionier company employed clearing approach Rifle, hand grenades	
	20.11.18		Company moved with 76 Infantry Brigade from SOUS-LE BOIS to REGNILIES LAVOUE (Belgium)	
NAMUR Shut 6	21.11.18		Choising arrived at enemy Dumion at RYSEL and obtaining road bridge and river openings	
			Sections working parties to clear roads inside Area	Typed copy by PB to WD by Post

Army Form C. 2118.

WAR DIARY
or
INTELLIGENCE SUMMARY.
(Erase heading not required.)

Instructions regarding War Diaries and Intelligence Summaries are contained in F.S. Regs., Part II. and the Staff Manual respectively. Title pages will be prepared in manuscript.

Place	Date	Hour	Summary of Events and Information	Remarks and references to Appendices
NAMUR Sheet 8.				
L'ABBAYE BERSILLIES (Bodyam)	22/11/18		Instructions as per A1·11·18 (Read as army and Brigade Area)	
	23/11/18		— Do —	
	24/11/18		Company moved up 12 km from area 7/6 Infantry Brigade from to WALBES, 1½ miles N of THUIN	
	25/11/18	10.00	" Do " SOMZÉE	
	26/11/18	19.30	" " SERY N.W. of METTET	
			1st Company were Advance Guard and Brigade group Army Commander of Army &	
			Colin Cornwallis IV Corps inspected the Brigade on the March	
	27/11/18		Company st not no SCY.	
	28/11/18		Company moved with 7/6 Infantry Brigade to WARNANT	
	29/11/18		" " " from WARNANT to MIANZE (HQ. per own name) MARCHE SHEET	
	30/11/18		" " MIANOTES SCY MARCHE SHEET 10000	
			[signature] Lieut. Comdg. RE	
			OC 524 Coy RE T	

Army Form C. 2118.

WAR DIARY
or
INTELLIGENCE SUMMARY.
(Erase heading not required.)

Instructions regarding War Diaries and Intelligence Summaries are contained in F. S. Regs., Part II. and the Staff Manual respectively. Title pages will be prepared in manuscript.

WO 29

Place	Date	Hour	Summary of Events and Information	Remarks and references to Appendices
MARCHE SUR 'S SEY	1.12.16		Company employed clearing all equipment and transport from Baye Longuyan	
	2.12.16		C.R.E. Division in billets if the Company, all rations in for rations.	
	3.12.16		Snow severe employed 4½ what and rustic neutrilo stock and jumble trap 5½ x 4 x 1½ x 1	
	4.12.16		Company employed on Report Alpe Donnell	
	5.12.16		Company moved from SEY to MARESSEE (N.E. of HEURE) Mat. 76 Sqdn - Roy evalued Recomm. work.	
MARESSEE	5.12.16		" MARESSEE le Say "	Captain Hartmann injured entrained for Brigade Kozar
SEY	6.12.16		SEY to FANZEL. Coy of provided advance of S.A.W. He mowed E. of EREZEE, and also some farm houses and	
FANZEEL	7.12.16		Company moved with 76 Sqdn. Brigade to FRAITURE	
	8.12.16		" " FRAITURE to CIEREUX & QUELSALM	
	9.12.16		Company employed 1 Station allowing remains of ferrary leaving Gien if Mounds & others of much own BOVIGNY remains of Capy & clung camped etc.	
	10.12.16		Company office mobilised this Bernard & Quartermaster in the new of I. Transport	

Army Form C. 2118.

WAR DIARY
or
INTELLIGENCE SUMMARY.
(Erase heading not required.)

Instructions regarding War Diaries and Intelligence Summaries are contained in F. S. Regs., Part II. and the Staff Manual respectively. Title pages will be prepared in manuscript.

Place	Date	Hour	Summary of Events and Information	Remarks and references to Appendices
MARTZEN	11.12.18		Company marched from CIERREUX Belgium to the Home of (7th Infantry Brigade) Crossed the Belgium – German Frontier at BEHO – St VITH Road. Billeted at III Corps Coy area.	
BLUMENTHAL NEUNDORF	12.12.18		Route march 11.12–12.12 via 16.10 to NEUNDORF	
NEUNDORF ANDLER	13.12.18		Route march via 75.J Amis Ronaral from AGENDORF to ANDLER	
				ANDLER to FRAUENKRON
FRAUENKRON	14.12.18		"	FRAUENKRON to BLANKENHEIM
BLANKENHEIM MARL HOLZMÜLHEIM	15.11.18 16.12.18		"	BLANKENHEIM to HOLZMÜLHEIM 27 Comp. of 8th [?] Army [?]
MÜNSTEREIFEL	17.12.18		"	to MÜNSTEREIFEL From MÜNSTEREIFEL to KESSENICH
KESSENICH	18.12.18		"	mtd. K.R.R.C. (30th) relieved 6 R.B. at FRITZHEIM
FRITZHEIM	19.12.18 20.12.18		"	to DÜREN Billeted in Artillery Barracks
DÜREN	21.12.18 22.12.18		Completed Clearing ditches of equipment etc.	
			Wagon marked 15th B. with men available to Transport Ranges DÜREN	
				[illegible] were prevented in leave to [illegible]

Army Form C. 2118.

WAR DIARY
or
INTELLIGENCE SUMMARY.
(Erase heading not required.)

Instructions regarding War Diaries and Intelligence Summaries are contained in F. S. Regs., Part II. and the Staff Manual respectively. Title pages will be prepared in manuscript.

Place	Date	Hour	Summary of Events and Information	Remarks and references to Appendices
GERMANY SIVRY DUREN	23.12.18		Company marched subway from Abbey to Siend	
	24.12.18		Same as 23.12.18	
	25.12.18		Xmas Day Company at rest	
	26.12.18		Same as 23.12.18	
	27.12.18			
	28.12.18			
	29.12.18		Same as 23.12.18	
	30.12.18		2 N.C.Os about to U.K. for demob. one	
	31.12.18		Coys B & C drawing cap & Arm. 23.12.18. Strength of Coy B Officers to turn L Offers 16 " Horses 3	
				Total Strength Others 4

A 5834. Wt. W4973/M687. 750,000. 8/16. D. D. & L. Ltd. Forms/C.2118/13.

529th. 9th Coy. RE

Sheet 1.

WAR DIARY
or
INTELLIGENCE SUMMARY.
(Erase heading not required.)

Army Form C. 2118.

Instructions regarding War Diaries and Intelligence Summaries are contained in F.S. Regs., Part II and the Staff Manual respectively. Title pages will be prepared in manuscript.

Place	Date	Hour	Summary of Events and Information	Remarks and references to Appendices
DUREN Sheet 1. GERMANY	1.1.19		Company billeted in Barracks. Company Strength 8 Officers 198 O.R. (Officers 2 S.O.R. on leave in U.K.)	
			Company employed on ordinary trades of arm and taking over Barrack accom. from other troops.	
	2.1.19		Work same as for 1.1.19. No. 474245 Sergt. T. McNally awarded D.C.M. London Gazette 3 Jan 1919.	
			15 inhabitants known not to be their true identity Documents.	
	3.1.19		1 Officer and 60 O.R. proceed to 76 Brigade H.Q. for Pioneer work attached to 2/6 L.N.L.R.	
	4.1.19		2 O.R. to Reinforcement Camp for Demobilization.	
	5.1.19		Rifle Inspection	
	6.1.19		2 O.R. on leave to U.K.	
	7.1.19		Carpenters erecting work benches, abolition blackboards, tables etc. for Billets.	
	8.1.19		Company employed as for 7.1.19	
	9.1.19		" " "	
	10.1.19		" 7.1.19 2 O.R. proceeded on leave to U.K.	
	11.1.19		" 7.1.19 1 O.R. to Reinforcement Camp for Demobilization	
	12.1.19		Church Parade. Service at Garrison Church DUREN.	

T. Fowler Major
O.C. 529 9th R.E. P.N.

Army Form C.2118.
Sheet 2.

WAR DIARY
or
INTELLIGENCE SUMMARY. SHEET 2
(Erase heading not required.)

Instructions regarding War Diaries and Intelligence Summaries are contained in F.S. Regs., Part II. and the Staff Manual respectively. Title pages will be prepared in manuscript.

Place	Date	Hour	Summary of Events and Information	Remarks and references to Appendices
DUREN SHEET /L GERMANY	15.1.19		Company employed - work on huts	
	14.15		- do -	15.1.19. 1 Officer & 5 O.R. left Unit for demobilization 38
	16.6.18		- do -	18.1.19. 9. O.R. — do — 88
	19.1.19		Recreation	84
	20-22		Company employed - work on huts	22.1.19. 5 O.R. — do — 84
	23-26		- do -	89
	26.1.19		Recreation	
	27.1.19		Bn & I.R.T Company - work on huts	1. OFF & 2 O.R. Left Unit for demobilization 88
	28-31.		- do -	30.1.19. 9 O.R. — do —
				1 OFF & 1 O.R. demobilized whilst on leave 7.1.19 & 1.1.19.
				1 OFF & 2 O.R. struck off strength having taken up Comm: in other R.E.
				H Newburn Capt. R.E.
				66.534 (4R) Field Co R.E.

Army Form C.2118.

WAR DIARY
—or—
INTELLIGENCE SUMMARY.
(Erase heading not required.)

FEBRUARY 1919. 529 Fd Coy RE

Place	Date	Hour	Summary of Events and Information	Remarks and references to Appendices
DUREN.	1.	—	Company employed - close order drill & work in billets. HA	
	2.	—	Company parade - morning, afternoon - recreation. HA	
SHEET 14.	3&8	—	Mornings. Drill & P.T. Education & work in billets. Afternoons - recreation. HA	
GERMANY.	9	—	Company parade morning. Recreation afternoon. HA	
	10&15	—	Mornings - Drill, P.T. Education & work in BARRACKS. Afternoons recreation. 2/Lt COWAN evacuated to Hospital 13.2.19 HA	
	16	—	Company parade morning, afternoon recreation. 2/Lt CALDER and 6 O.R. attached to 76 Brigade for reconnaissance of Brigade area. HA	
	17-22.	—	Mornings: Drill, D.T. Education & work in Barracks. Afternoons recreation. 2/Lt CALDER returned to Unit HA	
	23.	—	Company parade morning. Recreation afternoon. HA	
	24-27	—	Mornings; drill, P.T. Education & work in BARRACKS. Afternoon recreation. 2nd Lt 2/Lt CALDER admitted to hospital. HA	
	28. 09.00		Company moved from DUREN to KERPEN. HA	
			6 O.R. proceeded during month to U.K.	
			2/Lt RICHARDS G.R. joined for duty from Base. 22.2.19	

HJAuthwaite Capt RE(s)
O.C. 529 (FB) Field Co RE

3 DIV / WO 32

CONFIDENTIAL

WAR DIARY

For Month Ending 31st March. 529th Field Coy RE.

Box 1110

Army Form C. 2118

WAR DIARY
- or -
INTELLIGENCE SUMMARY.
(Erase heading not required.)

MARCH 1919

Place	Date	Hour	Summary of Events and Information	Remarks and references to Appendices
COLOGNE	1.		Company arrived at COLOGNE from KEVEN. H.Q. established at 21 CHRISTIAN GAU STRASSE, BRAUNSFELD.	
"	2.		Company parade. Inspection by O.C.	
"	3,4.		Company parade. Military training.	
"	5-8		Company employed on work for R.E.A. de WEIDON.	
"	9.		Company parade morning. Recreation afternoon.	
"	10-15		Company employed on work for R.E.A. WEIDON.	
"	16.		Company parade morning. Rest of day afternoon.	
"	17-22		Company employed on work for R.E.A. WEIDON and RIEHL BARRACKS.	
"	23.		Company parade morning. Recreation afternoon.	
"	24-28		Company employed on erection of new AERODROME – MARSDORF.	
"	29.		Company parade. Military training.	
"	30.		Company parade. Inspection by G.O.C.	
"	31.		Company employed on erection of new AERODROME – MARSDORF. Lt A. BROOKBANK left Coy for demobilization 27.3.19. Lt H. C. ate Coy for demobilization 26.3.19.	

Army Form C. 2118.

WAR DIARY
or
INTELLIGENCE SUMMARY.

529TH (E. RIDING) FIELD COMPANY, R.E.
APRIL '19

(Erase heading not required.)

Place	Date	Hour	Summary of Events and Information	Remarks and references to Appendices
COLOGNE	1-4		Company employed on erection of new AERODROME - MARSDORF	
	5		Company parade - Military training	
	6		Company parade - Inspection by O.C. Reversion of Arms	
	7-11		Company employed on erection of new AERODROME - MARSDORF	
	12		Company parade - Military training	
	13		Company parade - Inspection by O.C. Reversion of Arms	
	14-18		Company employed on erection of new AERODROME - MARSDORF	
	19		Company parade - Military training	
	20		Company parade - Inspection by O.C. Reversion of afternoon	
	21-25		Company employed on erection of new AERODROME - MARSDORF	
	26		Company parade - Military training	
	27		Company Church Parade	
	28-30		Company employed on erection of new AERODROME - MARSDORF	
			During month 12. O.R. + 1 Offr. proceeded on leave to U.K. 1 Offr. leave in France	
			80. O.R. - Offrs & Offr demobilization	
			55 O.R. arrived as reinforcements	
			Lieut J.D. CHURCH joined 5-4-19	

Major R.E.
O.C. 529th Field Co. R.E.

M-2

Army Form C. 2118

WAR DIARY
or
INTELLIGENCE SUMMARY.
(Erase heading not required.)

May -19

Place	Date	Hour	Summary of Events and Information	Remarks and references to Appendices
COLOGNE	1-2		Company employed on Erection of new Aerodrome MARSDORF.	
	3		" Paraded for inspection by C.R.E	
	4		" Church	
	5		" with Division for inspection by A.O.C.	
	6-7		" Employed on Erection of new Aerodrome MARSDORF.	
	8		" Paraded with Division and were reviewed by H.R.H. Duke of Connaught.	
	9-10		" Employed on Erection of new Aerodrome marching.	
	11		" Parade for Church	
	12-16		" Company employed on Erection of new Aerodrome HARSDORF	
	17		" Parade for inspection by C.R.E.	
	18		" Church	
	19-23		" Employed on Erection of Aerodrome MARSDORF.	
	24		" Parade for inspection by O.C.; & Military training	
	25		" Church	
	26-30		" Employed on Erection of Aerodrome at MARSDORF.	
	31		" Paraded for inspection by O.C.	

Dennis Smith
Major Thorold joined for duty 14/5/19
29 O.R's. proceeded on leave to U.K.
30 O.R's. left coy. for demobilization.

Shuttock Capt. R.E.
for O.C. 529 Co R.E.

Army Form C. 2118.

WAR DIARY
INTELLIGENCE SUMMARY
(Erase heading not required.)

Instructions regarding War Diaries and Intelligence Summaries are contained in F. S. Regs., Part II. and the Staff Manual respectively. Title pages will be prepared in manuscript.

Place	Date	Hour	Summary of Events and Information	Remarks and references to Appendices
Cologne	1-2		Company employed on Riding School of C.R.E. N.D. & improving Coy. billets	
"	3		Holiday	
"	4		Company employed on Riding School for C.R.E. N.D.	
"	5		Training & Interior economy.	
"	6		Church Parades	
"	14-18		Company employed on erection of Soldiers' kin. Stables, compound, & Latrines etc.	
"	19		Holiday Parades	
"	20		Church Parades	
"	21-25		Company employed on erection of Soldiers' kin. Stables, compound, Latrines & dismantling Huts.	
"	26		Company employed on Interior economy	
"	27-31		Nos. 1,2,3 & 4 Sections employed on erection of Stables etc. at MERHEIM under orders of C.R.E. Southern Division.	
			During month	
			1 Off. & 37 O.R.s Proceeded to U.K. on leave	
			1 " & 5 " " " for dispersal	
			1 Lieut A Moody R.E. transferred to 438th Field Coy R.E.	

8/19

[Signature] Capt. R.E.
for O.C. 529th Field Coy R.E.

52nd
(E. RIDING)
FIELD COMPANY, R.E.

WAR DIARY
or
INTELLIGENCE SUMMARY.
(Erase heading not required.)

Army Form C. 2118.

AUGUST 1919.

Place	Date	Hour	Summary of Events and Information	Remarks and references to Appendices
Cologne	1st	-	Nos 1, 2, 3 & 4 Sections erecting stabling at Merheim under orders of C.R.E., Northern Division for Army Horse Show.	
	2nd		Company employed on interior economy.	
	3rd		Church parade and recreational training.	
	4th-8th		Company employed as on 1st	
	9th		Company inspected by O.C.	
	10th		Church parade and recreational training.	
	11th-15th		Company employed as on 1st	
	16th		Interior economy and practice review.	
	17th		Church parade and recreational training.	
	18th		Company participated in divisional review.	
	18th-19th		Army Horse Show.	
	20th		Company drill.	
	21st		Sections returned to H.Q. at Braunsfeld from Merheim.	
	22nd		Company transport moved to new waggon lines.	
	23rd			
	24th		Church parade and recreational training.	
	25th-28th		Erecting huts at Klettenberg and improving Company billets.	
	25th-29th		— do — — do — — do —	
	30th		Company concentrated in billets in Aachener Strasse.	
	31st		Church parade and recreational training.	

Stankuski
Captain R.E.
for O.C. 529 & Field Coy R.E.

Army Form C. 2118.

WAR DIARY
or
INTELLIGENCE SUMMARY.
(Erase heading not required.)

SEPTEMBER 1919

Instructions regarding War Diaries and Intelligence Summaries are contained in F. S. Regs., Part II. and the Staff Manual respectively. Title pages will be prepared in manuscript.

Place	Date	Hour	Summary of Events and Information	Remarks and references to Appendices
Cologne	1-6		Dismounted personnel employed on cleaning + Renovating billets	
"	7		Company "Church" parade	
"	8-13		Dismounted personnel employed on cleaning + Renovating billets	
"	14		Church parade + Recreational Training	
"	15-19		Dismounted personnel employed on cleaning + Renovating billets	
"	20		Company Parade full marching Order. O.C's inspection Bens etc.	
"	21		Church Parade. Recreational Training	
"	22-24		Dismounted personnel employed on cleaning + Renovating billets	
"	25-30		" " " " Erection of Jumps + marquees on VI Corps Show Grounds	

During Month

27 O.R.s were transferred to 231st Field Coy. R.E.
19 " " Joined from " " "
58 " " proceeded to U.K. for dispersal
25 " " " " " on leave.

J. Richards
1st Lieut R.E.
for O.C. 329th Field Coy R.E.

NORTHERN DIVISION
(LATE 3 DIV)

231 FIELD COY RE

1919 APRIL — 1919 OCT

From 40 DIV

CONFIDENTIAL

WAR DIARY

231 FIELD COY RE

APRIL 1919

WAR DIARY or INTELLIGENCE SUMMARY

Army Form C. 2118.

231st FIELD COMPANY, R.E.

Place	Date	Hour	Summary of Events and Information	Remarks and references to Appendices
COLOGNE (BRAUNSFIELD)	April 1st		9.30 hours Inspection by C.R.E. Northern Division, Army of Rhine. Work: Preparing Billets etc. 1 OR reported for duty from leave to U.K. Capt. C. J. M. Young took over command from Lt. C. E. Bent.	April
"	2nd		Work as above.	April
"	3rd		Took over huts from 56 Fd Coy R.E. Erection of Stables, Guard Room etc. for R.F.A. and other units in the Northern Division. 3 men detached with C7/s R.F.A. 1 officer C.R.E. 1 OR reported for Hospital.	April
"	4th		Work as above.	April
"	5th		Took over billets from 438th Field Coy R.E. in Braunsfeld Cologne. Effective Strength. 24 Infantry and 2 Sapper attached for Rations at Whitsit in R.E. Workshop. 7 Offrs. 115 ORs	April
"	6th		9.30 hours G.O.C's Inspection. Company Rest day.	April
"	7th		Work as above. 1 N.C.O & 7 men detached with C/75 R.F.A. 1 OR from Hospital 1 OR transferred to C.R.E. Rouen. 24 OR Reinforcement. 20 report to duty	April
"	8th		Work as above.	April
"	9th		Work as above. 2 OR report from leave.	April
"	10th		Work as above. ii Lt. Nottingham R.E. leave Coy for leave to U.K. 12/4/19 to 26/4/19	April
"	11th		Work as above. 1 OR reported from leave M.O's inspection.	April
"	12th		Work as above. 1 OR transferred to 207th Field Coy R.E. Effective Strength. 7 Offrs. 136 ORs. Gunnery Course taken over by MAJOR. L.E. VIELA M.C. He returned from leave.	April
"	13th		No work as above - R.Q.R. reported for duty	Bells Ref.
"	14th		Work as above.	
"	15th		Work as above 1 OR attached C.E. Y. Coys 1 OR duty - 1 OR attached in from transit -	Ref.
"	16		Work as above - 1 OR proceeded on leave to U.K.	Ref.

WAR DIARY
or
INTELLIGENCE SUMMARY.
(Erase heading not required.)

Army Form C. 2118.

231ST FIELD COMPANY, R.E.

Instructions regarding War Diaries and Intelligence Summaries are contained in F.S. Regs., Part II. and the Staff Manual respectively. Title pages will be prepared in manuscript.

Place	Date	Hour	Summary of Events and Information	Remarks and references to Appendices
COLOGNE (BRAUNS FELD)	17th April		Brauweiler Tulwis Suffices in Trenchis & Shuras Knilungah. 1 OR reported sick from leave.	Ap27
"	18th		Work as above. 6 ORs proceeded on leave 15.15	Ap28
"	19th		Modified training took place - 1/2 Coy at Hockey - 1 OR cleared for Schoof 2 Instruction Yr Schs. Effective Strength 7 Officers 137 ORs	Ap29
"	20th		Church Parade. No work done. 4 ORs proceeded on leave GCR	Ap30
"	21st		Work as above. 3 ORs proceeded on leave.	Ap31
"	22nd		Work as above. 29 ORs Infantry attached for duty to Company strength now 166	Ap32
"	23rd		Work as above. 3 ORs proceeded on leave	Ap33
"	24th		Work as above. 3 OR proceeded on leave. 1 OR demobilised	Ap34
"	25th		Work as above. 1 OR transferred to CRE Rotterdam. 1 OR O/R/RE ANTWERP	Ap35
"	26th		No work as above. Company strength in morning. Lecture on Cinema	Ap36
"	27th		No work. Church Parade. Rifle Inspection. 3 ORs on leave	Ap37
"	28th		Work as above. 1 OR proceeds to Duty from Hospital	Ap38 Ap39
"	29th		Work as above. 1 NCO (Honorary) GE35 - 2 Cpl more Arthur Brown	Ap40
"	30th		Work as above. 3 ORs proceeded on leave. Effective strength 8 Officers 12 & 172	Ap41

J. Jolly Major RE
O/C 231 St Fld Co
1/5/19

23/1 cr

WAR DIARY
or
INTELLIGENCE SUMMARY.
(Erase heading not required.)

Army Form C. 2118.

Instructions regarding War Diaries and Intelligence Summaries are contained in F.S. Regs., Part II. and the Staff Manual respectively. Title pages will be prepared in manuscript.

Place	Date	Hour	Summary of Events and Information	Remarks and references to Appendices
BERGISHFELD (COLOGNE)	1st May 1919		Company employed on Works. - STABLES HUTS etc - 3.ORs on leave - 2 ORs demobilised on Compassionate Grounds - 1.OR to Hospital	207
"	2nd "	"	Works as above - 4 ORs on leave - 1 OR returned from leave - Released for Perus by Works of Commanaught Return by SLR Northern Division	80
"	3rd "	"	Church Parade - 3 ORs on leave - 1 OR to Hospital	207
"	4 "	"		207
"	5 "	"	No work as above - 2/C SEN ARMSTRONG transferred to 132 A.T. Company as C.Q.M.S. - 4 ORs on Leave W/UK - 1 OR returned from leave - 1 OR to Hospital - Released for Perus by the Duke of Cornwaught later by G.O.C Northern Division.	207
"	6 "	"	Work as above - 3 OR returned from leave.	207
"	7 "	"	Work as above - Duke of Cornwaught Review postponed to the 8th May.	207
"	8 "	"	Company Paraded for Duke of Cornwaught - Review at EXERCIER PLATZ MERHEIM 3. OR on leave - 4 ORs return from leave to UK - 4 Reinforcements arrived from 2nd RJ.	207
"	9 "	"	Work as above - 1 OR from Hospital - 2 ORs to Hospital - 1 OR Reinforcement from 29th Inf Company	207
"	10 "	"	Company works charing up transport etc - Suspension of two Company transport by CRE Northern Division	207
"	11 "	"	Church Parade - 3 ORs leave to UK - 2 ORs leave from leave	207

Army Form C. 2118.

WAR DIARY
or
INTELLIGENCE SUMMARY.
(Erase heading not required.)

Instructions regarding War Diaries and Intelligence Summaries are contained in F. S. Regs., Part II. and the Staff Manual respectively. Title pages will be prepared in manuscript.

Place	Date	Hour	Summary of Events and Information	Remarks and references to Appendices
BRAUNSFELD (COLOGNE)	12"	am	Company employed on works Stolberg, Hüttig, SK; 3 ORs return from leave. 1 OR to hospital	
"	13"	"	Work as above. – 1 OR to hospital, 4 ORs return from leave – 3 ORs on leave.	
"	14"	"	Work as above – 3 Mn on leave to UK – 20th returns from leave	
"	15"	"	Work as above – 1 OR reinforcement from Base – 1 OR attached to hospital	
"	16"	"	Work as above – 1 OR reinforcement from Base	
"	17"	"	Company inspected by OC. 1 Northern Division – 2 ORs hospital to 436" DC 1 OR hospital to 5.29 a.E. – 4 ORs leave to UK. 1 OR returns from leave	
"	18"	"	Xmas. Capt Young MC RE returns from leave. Church Parade. Lt Burr proceeded on leave to UK	
"	19"	"	Work as above	
"	20"	"	do do 4 ORs proceeded on leave to UK	
"	21"	"	do do 1 OR returns from leave	
"	22"	"	do do warning order received of move in the event of emergency	
"	"	"	Operations in connection	
"	23"	"	Company/orders orders to move at short notice. Work as above. 3 ORs returns from leave to UK	

WAR DIARY
or
INTELLIGENCE SUMMARY.

Army Form C. 2118.

(Erase heading not required.)

Place	Date	Hour	Summary of Events and Information	Remarks and references to Appendices
BRAUNSFELD S.W. (COLOGNE)	25	am	No work as above - 3 ORs returned from leave - 3 ORs returned from leave.	
"	"		Church Parade - 1 OR returned from leave.	
"	26		Work on Cabling Sch: - 4 ORs returned from leave and 1 OR on leave GER.	
"	27		3 ORs reinforcements to the Company from 2rg" FC.	
"	27		Work as above - All leave suspended. Stopped until improved condition eth civilian.	
"	28		Work as above - 3 ORs returned from leave	
"	29		Company inspected by C.E. VII Corps Brig Gen STOCKLEY PS O PC - 1 PO. 6 hours 6 UK	
"	30		Work as above	
"	31		Company employed at discretion of O.C. Co. improvements E Company FO. (Bulck 56.)	

3/5/19

Noble Major Hk
O.C. 257 FC

― CONFIDENTIAL ―

231ˢᵗ FIELD COY. R.E.

WAR DIARY

JULY. 1919

Army Form C. 2118.

WAR DIARY
or
INTELLIGENCE SUMMARY.
(Erase heading not required.)

Instructions regarding War Diaries and Intelligence Summaries are contained in F. S. Regs., Part II. and the Staff Manual respectively. Title pages will be prepared in manuscript.

Place	Date	Hour	Summary of Events and Information	Remarks and references to Appendices
BRAUNSFELD	1st JULY		Company Employed on Camp Duties. - 2 ORs on leave	(Sd)
"	2nd	"	Advanced Regiment Proceeded to WHITE CITY DEUTZ on H.T. Corps Bridging School. Umpires footwear	(Sd)
" ↓ DEUTZ	3rd	"	Main body BRAUNSFELD - 1 OR returned - General Fence Holiday - 1 OR returned	(Sd)
" ↓	4th	"	Commencement of Course in Bridging - Pontooning - 30 ORs returned from leave - 1 OR hospital	(Sd)
"	"	"	L/C Postal Service	(Sd)
"	5th	"	Pontooning - 1 OR on leave - 1 OR admitted to hospital - 2/Lt BROWN reports for duty from Hosp.	(Sd)
"	"	"	do - 1 OR proceeded on leave - 1 OR returns from Hospital.	(Sd)
"	6th	"	Church Parade - Kit Inspection	(Sd)
"	7th	"	Pontooning - 1 OR on leave - 1 OR proceeded on leave - 1 OR Hospital	(Sd)
"	"	"	Pontooning - 3 ORs attached from Infantry - CSM proceeds to PARIS on leave	(Sd)
"	8th	"	Pontooning - 1 OR on leave - 1 OR rejoined from Infantry	(Sd)
"	9th	"	Pontooning - 1 OR proceeded on leave - 3 ORs to hospital	(Sd)
"	10	"	Pontooning - 2 ORs return from leave - 1 OR proceeded on leave - 2 ORs from Hospital	(Sd)
"	"	"	2 Officers Riders drawn from Collecting Camp	(Sd)
"	11	"	Pontooning 1 OR return from leave - 1 OR proceeded on leave - Lt. BONNER returns	(Sd)
"	"	"	from leave - 2 ORs to Hospital	(Sd)
"	12	"	Pontooning 1 OR from Hospital - 1 OR proceeded - 1 OR returns from leave	(Sd)
"	13	"	Church Parade - 1 OR on leave - 1 OR return from leave	(Sd)
"	14	"	Heavy Pontoon Bridging - 1 OR on leave - 1 OR Hospital - 1 OR struck off strength	(Sd)
"	"	"	Lt. CUNCLIFFE reports for duty on return from leave	(Sd)
"	15	"	Heavy Pontoon Bridging - Pontoon Spin handed over to 32D Corps Pontoon Division	(Sd)
"	16	"	Steel Girder Bridge Construction - Trestle Bridge Construction - 1 OR Re-Posted	(Sd)
"	17	"	Civilian 1 OR returns from attachment to MFC	(Sd)
"	"	"	Trestle Bridge Construction as Pt. " Corps School.	(Sd)

No. 231st FIELD COMPANY R.E.

Army Form C. 2118.

WAR DIARY
or
INTELLIGENCE SUMMARY.
(Erase heading not required.)

Instructions regarding War Diaries and Intelligence Summaries are contained in F. S. Regs., Part II. and the Staff Manual respectively. Title pages will be prepared in manuscript.

Place	Date	Hour	Summary of Events and Information	Remarks and references to Appendices
BRAUNSFELD & DEUTZ	18th July		Trestle Bridge Construction — 3 ORs from leave — 2 ORs proceeded for Educational holiday	
"	19th		A.S.C. Motor Boat Bridge Construction — 2 ORs from leave — General Peace Holiday — 2 ORs to hospital	
"	20th		Cement Parade — 1 OR transferred from 436 F.C. to 23 F.C.	
"	21st		Steel Trestle Construction at VI " Corps Bridging School	
"	22nd		do — 2 ORs from leave — 1 OR from hospital for transferred to 436 F.C.	
"	23rd		do	
"	24th		do — 1 OR from leave — 1 OR to hospital Lt. FITCH left the Company	
"	25th		Steel Girder Construction — 1 OR from leave	
"	26th		do — 1 OR from leave — 1 OR left unit for demobilization	
"	27th		1 OR returned from leave	
"	28th		Cement parade — 2 ORs proceeded on leave — 2 ORs returned from leave	
"	29th		Light Bridge Construction — 3 ORs on leave SOS — 1 OR from leave 2 ORs	
"	30th		attached to 157 F.C. Re 2 ORs to hospital — 1 OR from hospital	
"	1st		took on charge	
"	2nd		" 4 ORs on leave	
"	3rd		" 3 ORs on leave	
"	4th		Brownsfeld Personnel returned to BRAUNSFELD on completion of Tn_	
"	5th		Corps Bridging School Course — 3 ORs on leave	

1/8/19
O.C. 281st F.C.

FIELD COMPANY, R.E.

WAR DIARY or INTELLIGENCE SUMMARY

Army Form C. 2118.

(Erase heading not required.)

Instructions regarding War Diaries and Intelligence Summaries are contained in F. S. Regs., Part II. and the Staff Manual respectively. Title pages will be prepared in manuscript.

Place	Date	Hour	Summary of Events and Information	Remarks and references to Appendices
Bramshott Cologne	Aug 1/19		Company employed on Works Erection of Stalls, Cookhouses, Huts etc. 3 ORs proceed on leave U.K.	
"	2nd		Volunteer 30 ORs on leave U.K. 2 ORs from leave U.K., Cpl Acheson, Huts etc. 2 ORs to Hospital. 1 OR from Hosp. Sgt Strangth Off. 147 ORs	
"	3rd		Church Parade 9:30am 2 ORs on leave U.K. 1 OR from Hospital. Coy died diary	
"	4th		Work as above 3 ORs on leave U.K. 1 OR to Hosp. 2 ORs from Hospital	
"	5th		Do. 2 ORs on leave U.K. 1 OR from Hosp.	
"	6th		Do. 2 ORs on leave U.K. 1 OR from Hospital	
"	7th		Do. 1 OR admitted to Hospital 3 ORs on leave U.K. 1 OR to Hospital	
"	8th		Do. 3 ORs on leave U.K.	
"	9th		Do. 3 ORs on leave U.K. 1 OR from Hospital. Sgt Strength 6 Off. 146 OR	
"	10th		Church Parade 9:30 hours 30 ORs on Church U.K. 1 OR to Hospital Compulsory day	
"	11th		Works as above the Cleaning Coy Transport 5 ORs on leave 1 OR to Hospital	
"	12th		Do. 3 ORs on leave U.K. 1 OR to Hospital 1 OR returned from attachment to R.A.O.C Lieut	
"	13th		Do. 5 OR Capt 2 Hon. 1st Bn Lt. 1st Hospital Major Willi proceeded on leave U.K. 1 OR from Hospital	
"	14th		Do. Ref proceeding to Egypt and to Mitcham Camp	
"	15th		Do. 5 ORs on leave U.K. 2 ORs on leave U.K.	
"	16th		Hospital Report 40 K 11 Off. 3 Men leave 5 ORs from leave 5 ORs to Egypt	
"	17th		Do. from Hospital 3 ORs proceed on draft 1 OR from Hospital. Sgt Strength 5 Off. 193 OR.	
"	18th		Church Parade 9:30 hr 3 ORs from leave 1 OR from Hospital. Coy Rest day	
"	19th		L Corp Murray, Evans Cunliffe attached 4 ORs leave 2 ORs on leave U.K.	
"	20th		Work as above 2 OR from leave 1 OR from Hospital	
"	21st		Do. 1 OR on leave U.K. 2 ORs from leave 1 OR from Hospital	
"	22nd		Do. 2 ORs from leave	
"	23rd		Do. 1 Sgt from leave 2 ORs proceed on demobilization Sgt Strength 5 Off. 187 OR	
"	24th		Do. 2 ORs to Hospital 2 ORs on Leave U.K. 4 ORs from Leave 2 ORs to demobilization	
"	25th		Church Parade 9:30 hours 2 ORs from leave Coy Rest day	
"	26th		Work as above 5 ORs from leave 2 ORs on demobilization 10 OR to Hospital	
"	27th		Do. 3 ORs from leave 2 ORs on leave 2 ORs on demobilization	
"	28th		Do. 1 OR from Leave 1 OR to Hospital	
"	29th		Do. 4 ORs from leave 2 ORs to Hospital Lt. Cunliffe from Hospital Capt Evans left unit proceed to Egypt	
"	30th		Do. Major Willes from leave Others ORs continued from Hosp. 4 ORs from leave 2 OR on leave	
"	31st		Do. 3 OR from leave U.K. Others from leave 1 OR on leave Sgt Strength 4 Off. 181 OR	
			Church Parade 2 OR from leave 1 OR on leave U.K.	

1/9/19.

CONFIDENTIAL –

– WAR DIARY –
231 FIELD COY. R.E.

SEPTEMBER.
1919

WAR DIARY or INTELLIGENCE SUMMARY

Army Form C. 2118.

(Erase heading not required.)

Instructions regarding War Diaries and Intelligence Summaries are contained in F.S. Regs., Part II. and the Staff Manual respectively. Title pages will be prepared in manuscript.

Place	Date	Hour	Summary of Events and Information	Remarks and references to Appendices
ORAUNSFELD (COLOGNE)	1st Sept 1919		Company employed on Works for Artillery North Div. and on Company Transport & Equipment. 1 O.R. in Hospital. 1 O.R. returned from leave.	Q617
	2nd		Work as above. 1 O.R. returned from leave. 10 O.Rs. on leave.	Q617
	3rd		Work as above. 3 O.Rs. returned from leave. 1 O.R. proceeded on leave. 7 O.Rs. Reinforcements.	Q617
	4th		Work as above. 2 O.Rs. returned from leave. 2 O.Rs. proceeded on leave. 1 O.R. to U.K.	Q617
	5th		Work as above. 3 O.Rs. proceeded on leave. 1 O.R. to U.K.	Q617
	6th		Work as above. 3 O.Rs. proceeded on leave. C. of E.	Q617
	7th		Church Parade. R.C. & Presbyterian.	Q617
	8th		Work as above. 2 O.Rs. posted on transfer to H.Q.R. Transport from 231 Coy. 1 O.R. to Hosp. 1 O.R. to Eng. base depot.	Q617
	9th		Work as above. 3 O.Rs. proceeded on leave.	Q617
	10th		Work as above. 2 O.R. returned from leave. 3 O.R. proceeded on leave. 2 O.R. proceeded on leave. 26 O.R. transferred to 231 H.A.R.E	Q617
	11th		Work as above. 1 O.R. returned from leave. 2 O.R. proceeded on leave. 26 O.R. balance of 231. 2 O.R. returned from	Q617
	12th		Work as above. 1 O.R. proceeded on leave. 26 O.R. transferred from 231 Coy	Q617
	13th		Work as above. Baptistille (?) La Trinta(?) on Special leave. 1 O.R. transferred to U.K.	Q617
	14th		Work as above. 1 O.R. proceeded on leave. 1 O.R. transferred from 231 Coy.	Q617
	15th		Work as above. 2 O.R. proceeded on leave.	Q617
	16th		Work as above. 3 O.R. proceeded on leave. 1 O.R. returned from hospital.	Q617
	17th		Work as above. 3 O.R. proceeded on leave. 1 O.R. to hospital.	Q617
	18th		Work as above. 3 O.R. proceeded on leave. 1 O.R. returned from hospital. 1 O.R. from leave. 5 O.R. to U.K.	Q617
	19th		Work as above. 2 O.R. proceeded on leave. 2 O.R. returned from leave.	Q617
	20th		Work as above. 1 O.R. returned from leave.	Q617
	21st		Church parade. 1 O.R. returned from leave. 3 proceeded on leave.	Q617

WAR DIARY
or
INTELLIGENCE SUMMARY
(Erase heading not required.)

Army Form C. 2118.

Place	Date	Hour	Summary of Events and Information	Remarks and references to Appendices
BRAUNSFELD	22nd Sept.		ON. employed on work for HQrs. NORTH. DIV. 2 n.c.o. & 60 Egyptians of Transport. Coy returned from leave. 1 Off. & 1 O.R. admitted to hospital.	Qu.16
"	23rd "		Work as above. 6 m.d. returned from leave 1 O.R. proceeded on leave.	Qu.18.
"	24th "		Work as above.	Qu.16.
"	25th "		Work as above. 3. O.R. returned from leave.	
"	26th "		Work as above. Major J.E.Hill M.C. returned from leave to U.K. and took over Command from the Company from Lt: A.W. Cruickshank - All Reserve & Demolition Stopped on general P.W. improving Railway Sidings.	Qu.
"	27 "		Work as above	Qu.
"	28 "		Special work on construction of Jumps for Jumping Completion at KaLK.	Qu.
"	29 "		Work on Jumps.	Qu.
"	30 "		Work as above.	Qu.

1/11/19

[signature]
Major M.C.
O.C. 281 Fus Co.

231st Fd Co RE   Rhine Garrison

Army Form C. 2118.

WAR DIARY
or
INTELLIGENCE SUMMARY.
(Erase heading not required.)

OCTOBER 1919.

Place	Date	Hour	Summary of Events and Information	Remarks and references to Appendices
BRAUNSFELD (COLOGNE)	1st October		Company Employed on General T.O. Work. " All leave and Drafts Cancelled on account of Railway Strike in U.K.	
do	2nd		Work as above.	
do	3rd		Work as above.	
do	4th		Work as above.	
do	5th		Church Parade – Railway strike in U.K. ended 6.30 p.m.	
do	6th		Work as above.	
do	7th		Work as above.	
do	8th		Work as above.	
do	9th		Work as above.	
do	10th		Work as above – 11. ORs proceeded to Concentration Camp for Demobilisation	
do	11th		Work as above – 3 Recruits joined Coy unit into Area	
do	12th		Church Parade	
do	13th		Work as above	
do	14th		Work as above	
do	15th		Work as above	
do	16th		Work as above	
do	17th		do.	
do	18th			
do	19th			
do	20th			
do	21st			
do	22nd			
do	23rd			
do	24th Oct		Major J E Vile M.C. left the Coy on Demobilization Major B7Kilson arrived from Light Division to take over Coy.	
do	25th Oct		Work as usual	
do	26th Oct		No church parade on account of shortage of men – Check parade at 10.00	

Army Form C. 2118.

WAR DIARY
or
INTELLIGENCE SUMMARY.

(Erase heading not required.)

Instructions regarding War Diaries and Intelligence Summaries are contained in F. S. Regs., Part II. and the Staff Manual respectively. Title pages will be prepared in manuscript.

Place	Date	Hour	Summary of Events and Information	Remarks and references to Appendices
Braunsfeld Cologne	27th Oct.		Works Parade at 0800. AOR - Batt ADVS inspected arrivals at 1230 - Two rides - Two draught horses b/k returned to Collecting station.	
	28th Oct		Arrival of drafts from London Divisional R.E. - Practice of Civil Subsistence Scheme 9-11 C/AE visits OC. to see (1) White City Army + Workshop. - Lt Brent & Osborn (2.) Flour sorting Smarlans	
	29th Oct		Company organized in 4 sections and sent to medical inspection - C/AE visits OC. to see Eric and Coy Admin Garrison - On return from medical inspection ½ unit marched to all unemployed men	
	30th Oct		Parade 0800. Redistribution of men in billets according to sections - 1100 drill parade, inspection of rifles followed by section drill under section N.C.Os with Lt Boorman in charge of parade. 1430 Pay Parade - Lt Brent back from Oxford	
	31st Oct		Parade 0800. After inspection sections laid out kits for checking. Kits were deficiencies made section Nos. Lt Boorman - Cunliffe. At 1100 CO's inspection of billets with kits turnout arranged as they should be laid daily. 1400 Extra drill parade for 14 men late on kit parade - Bugle Lt C/AE CO Adjt visited MARIENBURG New horse trainer. Fri arranged for in the men's dining hall. Seemed suitable. Barracks with a view to staying behind billets of the company.	

xxxxx

Bottalion
Major
3/11/19.
OC 231 POCHE

www.ingramcontent.com/pod-product-compliance
Lightning Source LLC
Chambersburg PA
CBHW080819010526
44111CB00015B/2581